THE CZECH AND
SLOVAK REPUBLICS

NATIONS OF THE MODERN WORLD: EUROPE

edited by W. Rand Smith and Robin Remington

This series examines the nations of Europe as they adjust to the changing world order and move into the twenty-first century. Each volume is a detailed, analytical country case study of the political, economic, and social dynamics of a European state facing the challenges of the post–Cold War era. These challenges include changing values and rising expectations, the search for new political identities and avenues of participation, and growing opportunities for economic and political cooperation in the new Europe. Emerging policy issues such as the environment, immigration, refugees, and reordered national security priorities are evolving in contexts still strongly influenced by history, geography, and culture.

The former East European nations must cope with the legacies of communism as they attempt to make the transition to multiparty democracy and market economies amid intensifying national, ethnic, religious, and class divisions. West European nations confront the challenge of pursuing economic and political integration within the European Union while contending with problems of economic insecurity, budgetary stress, and voter alienation.

How European nations respond to these challenges individually and collectively will shape domestic and international politics in Europe for generations to come. By considering such common themes as political institutions, public policy, political movements, political economy, and domestic-foreign policy linkages, we believe the books in this series contribute to our understanding of the threads that bind this vital and rapidly evolving region.

THE CZECH
AND SLOVAK
REPUBLICS

Nation Versus State

CAROL SKALNIK LEFF

WestviewPress

A Division of HarperCollinsPublishers

Nations of the Modern World: Europe

Published in 1997 in the United States of America by Westview Press, 5500 Central Avenue, Boulder, Colorado 80301-2877, and in the United Kingdom by Westview Press, 12 Hid's Copse Road, Cumnor Hill, Oxford OX2 9JJ

Library of Congress Cataloging-in-Publication Data
Leff, Carol Skalnik.
  The Czech and Slovak republics: nation versus state / by Carol Skalnik Leff.
    p.   cm. — (Nations of the modern world. Europe)
  Includes bibliographical references and index.
  ISBN 0-8133-2921-3 — ISBN 0-8133-2922-1 (pbk.)
  1. Czechoslovakia—Politics and government—1945–1992.
2. Czech Republic—Politics and government. 3. Slovakia—Politics
and government. 4. Post-communism—Czech Republic. 5. Post-
communism—Slovakia. 6. Communism—Czechoslovakia. I. Title.
II. Series.
DB2238.7.L44   1997
320.9437—dc20   96-12080
                                                                        CIP

10   9   8   7   6   5   4   3   2   1

To Mark, Alison, and Ben

Contents

PART 1
THE HISTORICAL CONTEXT OF CZECHOSLOVAKIA'S POSTCOMMUNIST TRANSITION

PART 2
THE DOMESTIC POLITICS
OF THE TRIPLE TRANSITION

PART 3
THE INTERNATIONAL DIMENSIONS
OF DOMESTIC TRANSFORMATION

Tables and Maps

Acknowledgments

No one writes any book alone, however much colleagues, friends, and family may sometimes wish that could be the case. I owe thanks to my colleagues in the political science department and in the Arms Control, Disarmament, and International Security (ACDIS) program at the University of Illinois for their comments on the theoretical issues raised by the postcommunist democratization process, particularly Ed Kolodziej, Roger Kanet, Paul Quirk, and Gerardo Munck. Robin Remington deserves heartfelt appreciation for her scholarship, friendship, and insight in ways that go far beyond her editorship of this series. Special thanks to Andrew Green and John Lepingwell for the temporary diversion from their own research agendas to lend help with invaluable Internet resources; to James Krapfl for his close and intelligent reading of much of the manuscript; and above all to my family—Alison, Ben, and Mark—who allowed me to order them around like a drill sergeant during the final phases of the manuscript's preparation. I hope I've made it up to you. Finally, there are always people who richly deserve thanks for advice and support but who are unaccountably left unmentioned. You know who you are, and my appreciation is nonetheless sincere for the omission.

Carol Skalnik Leff

Chronology

1918 Establishment of the Czechoslovak state at the end of World War I

1938 Loss of Sudeten German territory of Czechoslovakia to Hitler's Germany under the Munich accords; Vienna Award gives Slovak territories to Hungary

1939 Czech lands become a German protectorate; Slovakia becomes a separate state under German sponsorship for the duration of World War II (1939–1945)

1944 Slovak National Uprising

1945 Czechoslovakia reunited; establishment of the Second Czechoslovak Republic (1945–1948)

1948 February. Seizure of power establishes communist regime in Czechoslovakia

1968 Prague Spring reform era, ended by the Soviet invasion; federation of the Czechoslovak Socialist Republic

1989 November. Velvet Revolution against communist rule

1993 January. Dissolution of Czechoslovakia into two states, Czech Republic and Slovakia

INTRODUCTION TO
A SMALL COUNTRY
AT THE CROSSROADS
OF EUROPE

The collapse of European communism has not only created a new post–cold war global order; it has also created a new Europe in which the cold war divisions are eroding under the impact of a series of modest but persistent experiments in democratization and marketization in the east. It is no longer possible to study Western Europe without paying serious attention to the transformations under way in Eastern Europe. This is true for several reasons, the most dramatic of which occupy the headlines in the form of violent regional instability in the former Yugoslavia and the former Soviet Union. Before 1989, Western Europe was insulated from such upheavals and their spillover effects by Soviet dominance in the region. The collapse of communism meant the end of this insulation—and the need to respond to conflicts with which existing institutions like NATO were not designed to deal. However, an equally important reason to pay attention to the east is the sustained effort of Central European countries to "return to Europe" by pursuing the unprecedented goal of converting communist economies into capitalist economies and redesigning moribund political institutions into functioning democratic mechanisms. In sometimes overly optimistic anticipation of success, these formerly communist countries are already lined up outside the doors of the North Atlantic Treaty Organization (NATO) and the European Union (EU), hoping for admission into a community of prosperity and security that none of these small and vulnerable countries can achieve alone.

Individually, none of these countries will have the international significance of a China or Russia. But their collective destinies will shape the future contours of European power as a whole, either adding to its political and economic weight or subtracting from it by deflecting attention and resources to regional conflict management. Czechoslovakia is not typical of all its postcommunist neighbors. There is no "typical" East European country, but if there were, Czechoslovakia would resent the label, since the Czechs in particular consider themselves simply

"European," without geographical adjectives.[1] However, Czechoslovakia's trek toward Europe bears the marks of the communist experience that the entire region shared, and its transformation effort is an excellent case study in the problems of major regime change on a shoestring budget. It is a case study of significant successes and spectacular failures, not the least of which was the dissolution of one of the region's more economically advanced, educated, and stable countries into two pieces in 1992.

On the eve of World War II, when the European great powers were about to carve up Czechoslovakia at Munich, the British prime minister, Neville Chamberlain, professed not to know exactly where it was and why it mattered; Czechoslovakia's plight, he said, was "a quarrel in a far-away country among people of whom we know nothing."[2] This chapter and the following one comprise an attempt to help to avoid Chamberlain's mistake. In these two companion chapters I will analyze the evolution of the Czechoslovak state from its inception in 1918 until the time of its break with communist rule in 1989. In subsequent chapters I will dissect the current transition period. In these introductory chapters, the emphasis will be on the legacies of the earlier experiences of political and social transformation and their relevance to the present.

The international media and the East European publics alike were euphoric at the sudden collapse of communism in 1989 and the promise of free elections soon to come. At that moment, the end of the old regime seemed tantamount to the arrival of democracy. As everyone has learned since then, a noncommunist government is not necessarily a democratic one. In the following discussion, I will frequently use the adjective "postcommunist" to describe the political and economic institutions in place throughout the region in the early 1990s. This is partly a simple description of fact; what we see is what exists after the collapse of the classic version of the communist system, with its dominant single party, administered economy, and lack of legitimate opposition.

The use of the term postcommunist is also, however, a reminder that what we see is not necessarily describable as democracy or capitalism simply because it is no longer communist. We know what these regimes are in transition *from*—from authoritarian communist regimes. We do not know what they are in transition *to*, and it is too soon to be sure that any or all of the efforts under way will turn out to culminate in economic and political regimes that resemble the ones we call capitalist and democratic elsewhere.[3] Some may succeed in replicating the Western European models sufficiently well to join the European Union and other Western institutions and to be studied comparatively as variants of European politics. Others may revert to authoritarian rule, but it will still be a *postcommunist* authoritarian rule, like that of Slobodan Milošević in Serbia, that builds on nationalism more than on socialism, and includes some features of competitive politics (an opposition press, for example, or electoral competition). Still others may find themselves suspended in limbo between the former authoritarian politics and the achievement of a stable, legitimate democracy. Scholars of democratization talk about "unconsolidated" democracies that lurch from free election to free election without ever achieving governments that can govern well or gain popular acceptance and legitimacy.[4] Many of the trappings of democracy are there, but the system does not work, and it stumbles from crisis to crisis, often reliant on emergency executive power instead of bargaining and compromise. Russia might turn out to be such a case. Or there are cases where the system achieves relative stability but is not fully democratized because certain political forces are barred from achieving any real power in the system, and others (the military or former communists, for example) exercise democratically unaccountable power behind the scenes. Romania or some of the states of the former Soviet Union might fall into this category.

"Postcommunist" may be the most responsible term to label all of these embryonic systems, acknowledging their possibilities without prejudging the eventual outcome. It also seems valid to refer to them as "transitional" regimes, as long as it is not implied that the transition will automatically end in successful democratization. However, the label "postcommunist" has an additional usefulness. Scholars are still debating whether these cases can be incorporated into the larger universe of cases of attempted democratization that have appeared globally since the 1970s, amounting to what Samuel Huntington has called a "third wave" of global democratization.[5] The doubters are those who see the postcommunist regime changes as especially complex; Latin American and most South European countries that have undergone recent democratizing transitions, they argue, only need to concentrate on one kind of transformation—a political one to resurrect or create democratic institutions. They already have capitalist economies and are, with the exception of Spain, culturally and ethnically homogeneous enough to avoid the pain of simultaneous negotiations to resolve long-standing nationalist tensions.

This is not so in the postcommunist countries. Because of their socialist economic system and their multinational complexity, they must undergo what Claus Offe calls a "triple transition" if they are to reconstruct the old order: the political transition common to the other cases, plus an economic transition to establish markets and private enterprise, plus an identity-security transition to negotiate internal differences among national groupings and determine the state's territorial boundaries.[6] As we will see, these simultaneous transitions interact with one another, often in ways that delay and complicate the individual tasks. Offe himself poses several variants of this "dilemma of simultaneity," raising the question of whether it is really possible to graft a democratic political system onto a communist society before the economic transition has produced a new class structure with a stake in the new political system. And yet, how to pursue an often painful economic transition without democracy to give legitimacy to the effort? Labeling Czechoslovakia and the other current regimes of the former Soviet bloc "postcommunist," therefore, is a reminder of the special problems that these countries face. The framework of a postcommunist triple transition effort is a useful one for thinking about the tasks the Czech and Slovak governments have faced since 1989 and the way in which their approaches have differed from each other's and from those of other states in the region.

At the same time, the special problems of rebuilding after communism do not make these states completely incomparable to other transitional regimes in other times and places. In fact, in reviewing the antecedents of the current period of transformation, it is clear that Czechoslovakia's earlier history contains several periods of multiple transformation, all of which have shaped the chances for a successful consolidation of a prosperous, stable regime in the present.

At the time of its demise in 1992, Czechoslovakia was still a rather young European state, emerging from the drawing boards of the Versailles Peace Conference after World War I as part of a larger experiment in replacing the collapsed empires of East Central Europe with smaller successor states that might stabilize the region and facilitate workable parliamentary democracy on the basis of national self-determination. The experiment involved the attempt to make a rough fit between state boundaries and national groupings, in order to avert the repetition of the kind of internal ethnonational conflict that had afflicted the former empires and plunged Europe into war in 1914. The effort was hardly an unqualified success, not least because it was nearly an impossible task to divide the complex and intermixed national groupings of the region along neatly demarcated territorial lines; the interwar states in East Central Europe remained multinational and further inflamed matters in most cases by behaving as if they were not. This was the first attempted transition to democracy in modern Eastern Europe, and it ended in failure both domestically and internationally. The author of one textbook on East European politics entitled his chapter on this period "Flunking Democracy."[7] The democratic features of these states broke down under the pressures of governance, internal divisions, and external threats; by 1938, Czechoslovakia was the only functioning parliamentary democracy in the region. Internationally, the region remained a zone of instability and conflicting great power interests; it ultimately fell to Hitler in his quest to construct a thousand-year Third Reich.

East Central Europe's second chance at democratic transition was briefer still. The reconstruction of the regimes following the Allied victory over Nazi Germany soon succumbed to the authoritarian model imposed on the region by Stalin and his "liberating" Red Army. The regional democratization experiments that followed the collapse of communism in 1989, therefore, are the third set of such efforts since the reorganization of the European state system in 1918, and the legacies of the previous regimes are highly relevant to the chances for successful transformation in the present.

Czechoslovakia's experience of political and economic change in this twentieth-century period shares many commonalities with its eastern neighbors that make it a valuable case study in the general patterns of postcommunist regime transformation. Like its neighbors, it was constructed on the ruins of one of the four imperial powers that had governed the region before the twentieth century, all of which failed to survive World War I in their previous form. Czechoslovakia was formed from adjoining territories of the Austro-Hungarian empire: the Czech lands of Bohemia and Moravia, administered from the imperial capital of Vienna by the Austrian half of the dual monarchy; parts of Austrian Silesia; and Slovakia, an integral part of the Hungarian half of the dual monarchy. Like its neighbors, the newly constructed state would lose its sovereignty to Hitler in World War II. The Nazi pattern of dominance varied from state to state. In the case of Czechoslovakia, the Czech lands were directly ruled by Berlin as a protectorate, and Slovakia was permitted nominal independence under the umbrella of German foreign policy goals. After the war, Czechoslovakia also met the regional fate of subordination to Soviet hegemony; following the events of 1948, variously described as a communist coup or the "Glorious February Revolution," depending on the viewer's ideological standpoint, Czechoslovakia became the last of the East Central European states to fall under Soviet domination and to undergo political and economic communization. And finally, Czechoslovakia broke with the Soviet model in 1989 as the bloc as a whole disintegrated. Like the rest of the region, then, Czechoslovakia had been an often unwilling experimental laboratory for all the major Western political experiments of the twentieth century—democracy, communism, and fascism.

These general parallels do not mean that Czechoslovakia's experience was "typical" in every important respect. All of the region's states were in some sense multinational, but each configuration was different and changed differentially over time. Levels of economic development varied considerably from north to south in Eastern Europe; Czechoslovakia inherited one of the more favorable economic bases. All the countries had to cope with the reality of being wedged between two large and potentially threatening neighbors, Germany and the Soviet Union; in fact, they were created in order to provide a buffer zone, or, perhaps more appropriately, a shatter zone, between east and west. But the mix of threat and hostility from these larger powers varied from country to country. In Czechoslovakia before 1945, the overwhelming concern was with Germany, whereas Poland, having been both invaded and territorially partitioned by both big powers in its modern experience, was hard pressed to decide which of its large neighbors was the more dangerous. In the following chapters, these and other distinctions will be part of the larger picture of common experience that places into perspective the individual Czechoslovak transition and the uniquely peaceful disintegration of the state.

In the present chapter, however, the main purpose is to introduce students in North American universities to the citizens of the Czech and Slovak states—citizens who shared a joint state between 1918 and 1939, and again between 1945 and 1993. Joint statehood was in part an experiment in coping with the problem, already very obvious, of being a small state in Central Europe, since the conjoining of two smaller nations into a somewhat larger one was an exercise in self-defense against predatory neighbors. This certainly was not a sufficient deterrent to Nazi or Soviet expansion. Ultimately, Czechs and Slovaks would seek their security in a broader European framework after the collapse of the communist regime in the peaceful "Velvet Revolution" of 1989. But by that time, the original rationale for a common state had eroded so badly that two new Czech and Slovak Republics sought their security separately after the final decision to divide the state in 1992. This oddly peaceful disintegration of a functioning country has been tagged the "Velvet Divorce" by those who want to contrast it with the more violent and tragic events in Yugoslavia.

The Constituent Nations of Czechoslovakia

The failed political marriage of Czechs and Slovaks makes it especially important to define who they are. What commonalities caused them to consider a common state in the first place, and what differences ultimately caused them to abandon the joint project after a seventy-five-year trial marriage? These questions will take a whole book to answer, but certain basic facts are important as building blocks for later discussion. Czechs and Slovaks are both Slavic peoples, descendants of tribes that settled the central European basin in the fifth century. The languages they speak, codified during the nineteenth-century national revival period, are closely related. (See Box A).

Unlike the larger eastern Slavic populations, however, the Czechs and Slovaks were never part of the Russian empire. Their languages were printed in the Latin alphabet, rather than in the Cyrillic alphabet of the Russians, and their Christianity was Catholic and Protestant rather than Orthodox. Too small to avoid being engulfed by stronger neighbors, Czechs and Slovaks remained closer to European

---

BOX A
A Few Simple Tips on Pronunciation

Czechs and Slovaks use the same Latin alphabet that we do in English. But there are some special accent marks. The most distinctive is the "haček" that appears as a check mark over the letters *č, š, ž,* and *ř* in many words. If you see a haček over the consonant *s* or *z*, mentally add an "h" and pronounce it as you would pronounce "ch" or "sh" in English. A *ž* would be like a "zh" if we had such a thing in English; since we do not, think of the way we pronounce "measure." Pronouncing the *ř* is the hardest thing for foreigners (only the Czechs use it); we have no such sound in English. It is—approximately—a rolled "r" closely followed by a "zh" sound. Don't try this at home. In Czech and Slovak the unaccented *c* is pronounced "ts," and the *a* is an "ah," so if you have to mention Václav Havel, pronounce his first name "Vahtsclahv" (or cheat a bit and say "Vahslahv").

---

history and culture than the more easterly Slavs because their stronger neighbors, and eventual rulers, came from the Austrian Habsburg dynasty.

These common bonds, however, brought them close enough in background to consider a common state without bringing them close enough to share a common identity. It is misleading to describe them as sharing their sojourn in the Habsburg empire, because of the divisions within it that left the Czech lands and Slovakia in different parts of the dual monarchy. The Czech lands of Bohemia and Moravia were incorporated into the Austrian half of the empire after the defeat of the independent Czech kingdom in the seventeenth century. Around the year 1000, King Steven of Hungary had incorporated neighboring Slovakia into his kingdom, and there it remained, sharing the Hungarian historical experience, for more than 900 years. Despite Czech and Slovak coexistence in the Habsburg empire, therefore, Slovaks historically defined their identity in terms of the Hungarian overlord, just as in a rather more favorable context, Czechs defined their historical understanding of themselves in relation to the Germans. Historians who wished to find a truly common political frame of reference had to go back to the Great Moravian empire of the ninth century, which was a small, pre-national dynasty rather than a nation-state, and too historically distant even for the tenacious memories of Europeans to build a shared identity around.

Later chapters will explore the consequences of these long-separate historical experiences more fully. But it is important at the outset to recognize that the historical separation existed and to define how the Czechs and Slovaks differed from each other as a result of it. By accident of geographical location, the Czech lands fell to the more economically developed and nationally tolerant Austrian part of the dual monarchy. The result of independence in 1918 was that Czechs ranked higher on almost all development indexes than Slovaks: literacy, political and professional advancement, industrialization, diversity of class structure, and national income. Even the Czech agricultural sector was heavily commercialized and tied into the larger continental economy. Slovak agriculture remained primarily a peasant-based subsistence sector. The central city of the Czech lands, Prague, had been a major center of culture and trade since the fifteenth century, whereas Slovakia's main city, Bratislava, had never laid claim to that distinction, despite its location on the important Danube River commercial artery.[8] Czechs were able to build on a stronger middle class and a less constrained political environment to generate a more vibrant and self-confident national revival movement in the nineteenth century. Despite a promising start, this became impossible in Slovakia during the same period because Slovaks were increasingly subject to the pressures of a government *magyarization* (Hungarianization) policy that closed Slovak schools and limited career advancement for all Slovaks who failed to assimilate. These advantages not only gave the Czechs a head start in the new state, but also sustained their developmental lead thereafter. This in itself would become a source of tension.[9]

In part because of the higher levels of economic development, and in part because of the earlier influence of a strong Hussite reformation movement in the
Czech lands,[10] Czechs were also more secular than Slovaks. In percentage, the
people of the Czech lands remained nominally more Catholic than the Slovaks,
who possessed a sizable Protestant minority, but it was the Slovaks for whom religion was most clearly an integral part of national identity. Tension over religion
was a distancing factor between Czechs and Slovaks even before the joint state;
Slovak nationalists of the nineteenth and early twentieth centuries worried that
making common cause with the Czechs would secularize the next Slovak generation, whereas a number of Czech national leaders regarded their Slovak counterparts as benighted and "priest-ridden."

The difference in attitude and context showed up in the backgrounds of national leaders as well. In Slovakia, well into the First Czechoslovak Republic,
priests were important political figures. The leader of the Slovak nationalist party,
Andrej Hlinka, was a priest, as was Jozef Tiso, president of the Slovak state in
World War II. In the interwar parliament, only 1 percent of the Czech deputies
and 16 percent of the Slovak deputies (and almost a third of the Slovak Populists)
were religious figures.[11] This difference was understandable. Because there were
fewer educated Slovaks, and because the path to education often led through conversion to Hungarian language and values, the priest was often the most educated
and nationally conscious person in the village—a teacher and spokesman as well
as a priest. In the Czech lands, a more developed and diversified economy produced a broader leadership base.

Nevertheless, the difference in outlook was very pronounced. The religiously
based Slovak Populist Party tried to defend Catholic values as part of the national
birthright of Slovaks, clashing with Czechs over religious education and relations
with the Vatican as well as over broader social values. Many Czechs in turn regarded the Slovak orientation with impatience and even condescension, earning
a reputation for insensitivity to the religious differences that many scholars have
noted. The higher levels of Slovak religious identification, particularly with
Catholicism, remained very evident even through general erosion of religious belief in the communist period, despite the efforts of the party and state to restrain
it. Difference in religious outlook was embedded in the difference in national
identity and raised a powerful barrier to communication between Czechs and
Slovaks.

The two nations did historically share a common context of living in a multi-
ethnic environment, however. The sizable German minority in the Czech lands
and the sizable Hungarian minority in Slovakia gave the two Slavic nations cause
to see one another as protection against internal as well as external threats. The
original state of Czechoslovakia also included a Jewish minority, a sizable Polish
minority in Silesia, and an even larger Rusyn population in the eastern province
of Subcarpathian Ruthenia and in eastern Slovakia. From its inception in 1918,

Czechoslovakia was more ethnically diverse than any East European state except Yugoslavia.

Time and historical experience have streamlined the former complexity. The Czech lands were only about two-thirds Czech in 1938, and Slovakia only two-thirds Slovak. By 1989, the year the communist regime collapsed, Czechs made up 94 percent of the Czech Republic's population, and Slovaks constituted 87 percent of Slovakia's.[12] World War II was a watershed in this evolution. First, the state as a whole lost three-quarters of its Jewish population to the Holocaust. Jews had accounted for only about 2 percent of the interwar population, but the Jewish community had played a disproportionately important historical role in culture and the economy. Nazi rule was also indirectly responsible for the other major war-induced population movement: The postwar Czechoslovak government undertook to deport all but a few hundred thousand of its 3 million German citizens in retaliation for their alleged complicity in Hitler's designs. Slovakia, less successful in attempts to deport its Hungarian minority, remained substantially more heterogeneous. In 1989, there were nearly 600,000 Hungarian citizens in the Slovak Republic, 11 percent of the population. Hungarian settlements are concentrated on Slovakia's southern border with Hungary itself.

The population balance between Czechs and Slovaks also shifted over time. In 1918, Slovakia made up about a quarter of the new state's population. Seventy-years later, the Slovak Republic had grown to one-third of the Czechoslovak population; the higher Slovak birthrate was attributed even by communist-era scholars to the impact of Slovak Catholicism. A substantial size differential remained between the two nations, however, and reinforced the developmental gap that put Slovakia in a politically and numerically subordinate position as well as an economically weaker one.

However, a demographic statistic that is nearly as important as ethnic diversity is the country's relatively modest population size. With a population of 15 million, the state of Czechoslovakia was smaller than any East European country except Hungary and Albania. After the country's division into two states in 1993, the Czech Republic registered only 10 million citizens (about the size of Hungary), and Slovakia's numbers fell well below Hungary's to rank it next-to-last place in Eastern Europe with a population of 5 million. For Americans accustomed to national size and strength the implications of living in a country less than one-twentieth the size of the United States may be difficult to imagine. Small countries cannot sustain economic growth through reliance on their own domestic markets alone, which are too limited in size to support efficient production and to permit taking advantage of economies of scale. They must become trading states. Small countries are also unlikely to be able to defend themselves. Neutral Switzerland is a rare exception to the painful and often futile quest of the small state to gain security through negotiation with external powers. This quest often fails, as it did so frequently for Czechoslovakia.

The Geopolitical and Physical Setting

It was once fashionable to call Czechoslovakia a small state at the crossroads of Europe. Living at a crossroads makes one vulnerable to being crushed by the traffic of great powers moving through. And this central location certainly made Czechoslovakia as liable to conquest in the twentieth century as it had been in earlier periods.

A central location can, of course, be advantageous. It historically placed Czechs and Slovaks in a context that promoted greater economic development than occurred in the southeast. In times of relative stability, central location can enhance trade through cheaper transport costs and cross-border economic contacts. The Czech Republic in the 1990s sits next to the valuable Austrian and German markets and benefits substantially from that location. Slovakia to the east aspires to form a bridge between Western Europe and the countries of the former Soviet Union. Despite the uncertainties of the current attempts to transform communist political and economic systems, the immediate international context of that effort is more favorable to East European development than it has been at any time since Czechoslovakia became an independent state in 1918. At that time, Czechoslovakia saw itself as Central European in all senses. It would become truly East European, in a political sense, after the communist seizure of power in the region gave Eastern countries a common regime as well as eventual common communist legacies to unravel. Once the bloc dissolved, Czechoslovakia, and the rest of the politically Eastern European countries, made a concerted effort to "return to Europe," and to Central Europe in particular. That is where Czechoslovakia started in its first effort to build a viable and prosperous state after World War I; that attempt is the subject of Chapter 1.

Maps defining the changing boundaries of the Czech lands and Slovakia are dispersed at appropriate points throughout the book; they are a visual record of the concrete shifts in the Central European balance of power and Czechoslovakia's place in it.[13] Borders matter. The maps underline Czech proximity to the West. Prague is considerably further west than Vienna, for example, and communist Czechoslovakia bordered *both* East and West Germany. The postcommunist Czech Republic borders only two former communist countries, Slovakia and Poland. Slovakia, in contrast, is almost completely surrounded by former communist countries, the exception being Austria. The differing Czech and Slovak geographical distances from the West are, as we will see, also reflected in differing socioeconomic distances from the West.

The maps also trace the pattern of Czechoslovakia's relations with its more powerful neighbors. The interwar history of tensions with Germany is written in the map of a shrunken and divided Czechoslovakia after the Munich Conference. (This map also shows how smaller neighbors participated in the division of the country.) The changing importance of Soviet power in Czechoslovakia also shows up on the map. Interwar Czechoslovakia had no common border with the

USSR; the Soviet landgrabs after World War II produced a common Soviet-Czechoslovak border. In 1938, the Soviet Union argued that the absence of a common border prevented it from coming to Czechoslovakia's assistance against Hitler. In 1968, the common border was useful in coming to Czechoslovakia's "assistance" in defense of Soviet-style socialism. Geography is not destiny, of course, but it does much to shape that destiny.

Economic and Social Structure

Industrial societies are not all alike, and the contemporary Central European societies that went through a common pattern of development under imperial rule, brief interwar independence, and communist reconstruction all bear the marks of that distinctive experience. As we will see, pre-communist Czechoslovakia was an amalgam of unevenly developed industrial regions that from its founding made the country one of the world's largest industrial producers. Socialism did not enhance that industrial structure, but it did reshape it. As in other communist economies, its service sector was stunted. In the West, this mixed sector, embracing sales clerks as well as computer technicians, employs almost two-thirds of the population; the service sector was only a little more than half of that size in the East. Czechoslovakia's heavy industrial sector was as much as 25 percent larger than in a capitalist economy of equivalent size, with thousands of workers concentrated in large factory complexes. Soviet leader Nikita Khrushchev referred to the economic overlords of socialism as "steel-eaters" because of the system's emphasis on the big machinery plants, iron foundries, and other factory enterprises geared toward nonconsumer production. This same pattern prevailed in Czechoslovakia and the Soviet-type economies of Eastern Europe. The difference in Czechoslovakia lay in the long working-class tradition that had preceded communism, a tradition that initially gave the Communist Party a popular base, as we will see.

Czechoslovakia, as did many of its neighbors, underwent successive phases of urbanization in the twentieth century. The interwar urban pattern tended to focus on the major existing cities, scattering a few metropolitan islands in a sea of rural villages. The rapid urbanization of the communist period was more diffuse; a number of smaller towns exploded in population growth as new industrial facilities were built according to economic plan.[14] In time these new centers acquired additional urban resources, such as the new technical universities of Slovakia, geared to meet the new industrial emphasis (young Slovaks had demanded but never received a technical university in the interwar Republic).

As in many European urban environments, especially those in the socialist zone, living patterns were very different from those in the United States. Most citizens lived in crowded apartments (now going condo). There was no real equivalent of the postwar American middle-class suburb; the middle class lived in the city, and the working class lived in the dreary suburban housing developments, monuments to the Stalin period of construction Their façades resembled some of the larger American ghetto "projects" far more closely than the American image of the suburb. Only in the postcommunist 1990s did tracts of detached suburban houses begin to appear around Moscow or Prague—and these developments were for the elite; the first suburban houses built near Prague carried price tags of more than $200,000.

Czechoslovakia's urbanization differed from that of its neighbors in two respects. First, it had started the communist period as the second most urbanized country, next to East Germany, and it retained that initial lead through the 1980s. Second, because the country had been spared the physical devastation of World War II, much more of the historical architecture and city layout has been retained. Bombing raids and the Warsaw uprisings destroyed 85 percent of Poland's capital city and virtually all of its oldest sections. It was rebuilt, largely in drab Stalinist housing blocks and office buildings, in the communist period. Only the central historical core was restored from the ruins.

Prague, however, was basically untouched. The Germans needed its intact economy for the war effort, and the Allies spared it from bombing. So the present-day visitor to Prague can visit eleventh-century Vyšehrad, the royal residence of the Přemyslid dynasty, or St. Vitus Cathedral, started in the fourteenth century. Prague's "New Town" dates from the fourteenth century! The Castle (Hrad) that serves as the presidential residence of Václav Havel is more than 1,100 years old. All that was preserved from wartime destruction as a result of geopolitical good fortune survived further, it is often said, because of the economic stagnation of the communist period. Communist Prime Minister L'ubomir Štrougal liked to joke with foreign visitors that there was a sign on the country's border reading "Welcome to the Museum of the Industrial Revolution."[15] But this stagnant growth saved many a historical façade from urban redevelopment. In general, the country's antiquity is now one of the new postcommunist state's most useful assets, since it has become the leading tourist magnet of the Eastern Europe of the 1990s, attracting nearly as many foreign visitors annually as the country's population. Urban developers have already begun to battle with the historical preservationists over the physical landscape of the cities. In Prague itself, the medieval central section of the city became a historical reservation in 1971, but there has been considerable controversy over the issuing of permits for building reconstruction in the boom period that followed the Velvet Revolution.

Despite its charm, however, Prague bears the physical evidence of another, less enviable, legacy. It is the third most polluted area in the Czech and Slovak Republics, following on the heels of the environmentally devastated mining and industrial regions of northern Bohemia and northern Moravia—regions that have been described as "lunar landscapes" because they are devoid of vegetation. The Hron Valley in Slovakia is also heavily polluted. The primary culprit in all of these cases is air pollution generated by the use of brown coal for industrial production and heating; this high-sulfur coal releases noxious sulfurous gases that destroy building façades, large tracts of forest land, and human health. The environmental destruction that has been a by-product of socialist development strategies will be discussed later. But the fact that highly pollutant coal is the country's sole abundant energy resource is a reflection of the limited resource base of a small country, a problem that the Czech and Slovak Republics share with the rest of Central Europe.

The urban pollution problems of Czechoslovakia on the eve of the Velvet Revolution were particularly troublesome because still largely missing from the equation was the primary atmospheric polluter of Western industrial society—the automobile. Cars produced in the communist bloc were an environmental hazard; they ran on leaded gasoline and were notoriously inefficient environmentally. Their major virtue was their relative scarcity. Most East Europeans traveled by bus, train, or tram; Prague has a cheap and efficient subway system. A striking symbol of postcommunist society is the proliferation of secondhand cars, whenever possible Western models instead of the Czechoslovak Skoda. The new explosion of automobile use clogs arteries of cities that developed in a pre-automotive age, with narrow, winding streets. The more consumer-oriented society raises the specter of further pollution as the availability of private cars continues to grow.

Rural Czechoslovakia remained a relatively productive agricultural economy, by socialist standards at least, even under the collectivization programs that absorbed private agriculture in the 1950s. The proportion of the population employed in agriculture was distinctly lower than in other socialist countries—more comparable to Western countries—and production from the private plots permitted under communism was also smaller.[16] The countryside is still a broad vista of cultivated land punctuated by tiny villages consisting of a sign and a cluster of houses.

Perhaps surprisingly, the Czech and Slovak farmers have not shown marked enthusiasm for privatizing the collective holdings; even now, there has been nothing akin to the burst of rural entrepreneurial energy that sparked the surge of economic growth in socialist China in the late 1970s. There are many possible cultural and demographic reasons for this difference. However, one obvious explanation is structural and technological. Chinese agriculture is labor-intensive and based on rice, a labor-intensive crop. The large mechanized collective farms of the USSR or Czechoslovakia are not readily broken up into smaller private units that can easily be farmed by a family group. Who gets the tractor or the reaper from the collective's shared machinery stock? Polls reveal a deep sense of caution in the rural areas of the Czech and Slovak Republics about the adjustments necessary to live under capitalism.

The physical face of the Czech and Slovak Republics and the living standards and social structure of its populations are in the process of radical change. Privatization, democratization, and marketization do more than reconfigure institutions; they change class structure, living standards, and attitudes. However, adjusting to radical change has been an all-too-frequent phenomenon in twentieth-century Central Europe. In the following chapters, we will see how the layered legacies of past transformations have been absorbed in the present one. Organizing this kind of inquiry presents certain complications in the case of Czechoslovakia, because we are trying to understand a transformation process that bifurcated midway through the transition process into separate Czech and Slovak states—in fact as a *result* of that process. Is this a study of one case or two cases? Should we follow the Czech and Slovak experiences side by side or separately? This is an awkward problem because both approaches are useful. The two units shared a substantial history of common statehood, yet even their historical experiences in that common state are different, and they diverged even more clearly after 1992 in separate states that still shared common formative experiences. I have tried to compromise between separate and integrated discussions of these experiences in order to avoid unnecessary repetition. In Part One I trace the joint Czech-Slovak historical odyssey from interwar parliamentary republic to communist state. In each period, I have tried to lay the groundwork for the analysis of the postcommunist triple transition in politics, economics, and national identity, with particular attention to the historically conditioned differences between the Czech and Slovak approaches. In Part II, centered on the domestic politics of the triple transition, the Czech and Slovak paths are seen to diverge in the course of the initial efforts to transform politics after the Velvet Revolution, which are discussed in Chapter 3. In Chapter 4 I examine the culmination of Czech and Slovak differences in the Velvet Divorce that emerged after efforts to preserve the joint state had ended in deadlock, and in Chapter 5 I trace their separate political paths after independence. In Chapter 6 I compare the divergent Czech and Slovak approaches to economic reform before and after independence. Part III is an analysis of the international dimensions of the triple transition and the search for a security broader than mere military guarantees could provide, a search that led the Czech and Slovak Republics to seek integration into the whole range of West European institutions. In Chapter 7 the focus is on national security as traditionally defined in terms of military power and alliances, and in Chapter 8 I place the search for security into the context of the triple transition, focusing particularly on the postcommunist foreign economic policy, the pursuit of European Union membership, and national identity politics.

Notes

1. The label "Eastern Europe" has often, and justifiably, been condemned for implying a uniformity of historical experience among the states so labeled. It is generally better to differentiate between, for example, the "Central European states" of Poland, Hungary, or Czechoslovakia, and the "Balkan" states to the south, with their distinguishing history of Ottoman rule. The U.S. State Department has dropped the term "Eastern Europe," and

official documents now refer to "North Central" and "South Central" Europe. However, all these states share a common communist experience; to the extent that Eastern Europe describes a political legacy rather than a geographic or cultural identity, it makes sense to retain the term East Europe when describing, as I do here, the commonalities and differences among states in transition from communism. Although this analysis sometimes invokes parallels with the Soviet and post-Soviet experience, the term East Europe does not extend to include these states, even if a valid argument can be made that the Baltic states of the former Soviet Union (because of their interwar independence) ought to be considered in the same class with the countries labeled here as East European. However, their experience of separation from the USSR after 1991 is a distinctive one.

2. Cited in Winston Churchill, *The Second World War: The Gathering Storm* (Boston: Houghton Mifflin, 1948), p. 315.

3. When will we know that a transitional period is over and it is appropriate to talk about an established or "consolidating" regime? This is both a resolvable definitional question and a more complex conceptual one. The democratization theorists have tended to regard the transition, in delimited terms, as completed when a new government is installed by competitive elections and a new constitution is approved. Thereafter, the new regime is viewed as attempting to consolidate itself. There are some problems with this definition: Which of these two events is the definitive marker of the end of the transition period? In Eastern Europe, there may be a substantial passage of time between the installment of a new government following competitive elections and the approval of a constitution. In Poland, for example, three parliamentary elections into the transition from communist rule, there is still no constitution. More broadly, the conceptual problem with defining the idea of transition is that any given terminal point for transition may be quite arbitrary. There may be no definitive closure in a process that continues indefinitely to be partially open-ended. Nevertheless, there seems to be considerable logic, whatever one's terminology, to the idea that a point is reached at which the old regime is so fundamentally revised that the subsequent processes of change focus on the dynamics of the new system, and not on extrication from the old one. That seems to be the sense behind giving the idea of "transition" a specific end point.

4. See Philippe C. Schmitter and Terry Lynn Karl, "What Kind of Democracies Are Emerging in South America, Central America, Southern Europe, and Eastern Europe?" (paper presented at the international colloquium, "Transitions to Democracy in Europe and Latin America," University of Guadalajara, Mexico, January 1991); and Scott Mainwaring, "Transitions to Democracy and Democratic Consolidation: Theoretical and Comparative Issues," in Mainwaring et al., eds., *Issues in Democratic Consolidation* (South Bend, Ind.: University of Notre Dame Press, 1992), pp. 294–342.

5. Samuel P. Huntington, *The Third Wave: Democratization in the Late Twentieth Century* (Norman: University of Oklahoma Press, 1991).

6. Claus Offe, "Capitalism by Democratic Design? Democratic Theory Facing the Triple Transition in East Central Europe," *Social Research* 58:4 (Winter 1991):865–892.

7. Michael Roskin, *The Rebirth of Eastern Europe* (Englewood Cliffs, N.J.: Prentice Hall, 1994).

8. Bratislava had, however, been the capital of Hungary between 1535 and 1784, during the period of Ottoman pressure on the region.

9. See the historical survey of the interwar Republic by Victor Mamatey and Radomír Luža, eds., *A History of the Czechoslovak Republic, 1918–1948* (Princeton: Princeton University Press, 1973); the summary historical surveys in Sharon Wolchik, *Czechoslovakia in Transition: Politics, Economics, and Society* (London: Pinter, 1991), pp. 1–59; and Carol Skalnik Leff, *National Conflict in Czechoslovakia: The Making and Remaking of a State, 1918–1987* (Princeton: Princeton University Press, 1988), pp. 11–42.

10. Jan Hus, a Bohemian priest and rector of Prague University in the early fifteenth century, had been burned at the stake for renouncing the authority of the pope. The subsequent Hussite revolt launched a century of strife that ended with the defeat of the Bohemian nobility at White Mountain in 1620, which ended the independence of the Bohemian state. Although Hus was a religious reformer, key figures of the nineteenth-century Czech national revival, who saw Catholicism as a pillar of Habsburg rule, put central emphasis on the Hussite movement as a defining moment not only for Protestantism, but also for the formation of Czech national identity. Hus himself was understood as a martyr to the Czech national cause. See, for example, Hugh LeCaine Agnew, *Origins of the Czech National Renascence* (Pittsburgh: University of Pittsburgh Press, 1993).

11. Leff, *National Conflict*, p. 189. Priests were also the largest single occupational group represented on local councils in Slovakia.

12. "Cesko-Slovenské vztahy ve svetle demografickych udeju," *Hospodárské noviny*, 25 October 1991, p. 4.

13. Maps even reflect the quest for Czech national identity in indirect form. Whereas there was no question that mapmakers should label the new Slovak Republic as "Slovakia" on the new European map after the dissolution of the state, there was heated controversy over how to label the Czech Republic. Historically, this territory had defined boundaries, and was known as the Czech lands. Yet the new state was variously styled by its formal designation "Czech Republic," and shorthand alternatives such as "Czechia" or "Czech" did not trip naturally off the tongue and were contested by cartographers.

14. David Turnock, *The Human Geography of Eastern Europe* (London: Routledge, 1989), pp. 151–190.

15. Andrew Nagorski, *The Birth of Freedom: Shaping Lives and Societies in the New Eastern Europe* (New York: Simon & Schuster, 1993), p. 29.

16. Daniel Fogel, ed., *Managing Emerging Market Economies: Cases from the Czech and Slovak Republics* (Boulder: Westview Press, 1992), p. 7; and Wolchik, *Czechoslovakia in Transition*, p. 169.

PART 1

THE HISTORICAL CONTEXT OF CZECHOSLOVAKIA'S POSTCOMMUNIST TRANSITION

1

CZECHOSLOVAKIA'S FIRST EXPERIMENT WITH DEMOCRACY: THE INTERWAR REPUBLIC, 1918–1938

Czechoslovakia did not exist until 1918. It formally came into being at the sufferance of the Allied victors of World War I, and its fate has been dependent on the interests of the European great powers ever since. Before the war, Czech and Slovak politicians had seen no serious possibility of independence and had concentrated their efforts on gaining a more equitable position within the Habsburg empire. Many key figures in the nineteenth-century Czech national revival argued for the federalization of the empire in order to accord more autonomy to its many national groups.

The war changed everything, particularly the defeat of the Central alliance that included both Germany and Austria-Hungary and left the future of the losers to France, Britain, and the United States. During the war, politicians at home faced serious restrictions on what they could do about a more independent political future; discussion of independence was treason until fairly late in the war. In fact, two of Czechoslovakia's future cabinet ministers were in Habsburg jails awaiting execution for treason until amnestied in 1917. However, exiled and expatriate politicians, particularly Tomáš Masaryk, Edvard Beneš, and Milan Štefánik, were in a position to lobby the West for *national self-determination*, a right that U.S.

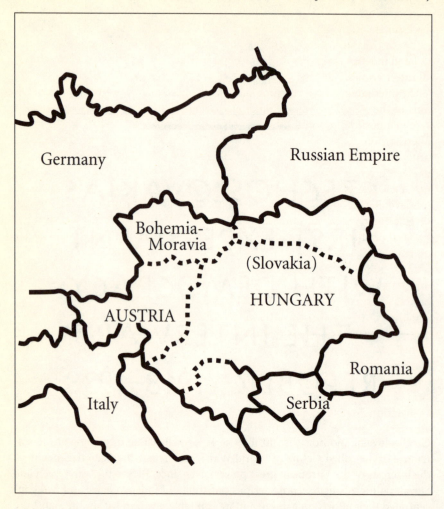

MAP 1.1   Czech lands and Slovakia in the Austro-Hungarian empire

President Woodrow Wilson championed in general terms as a necessary part of a just peace. The Czech, Slovak, and Ruthenian or Rusyn immigrant communities in North America also mobilized in favor of an independent Czechoslovakia, with rights guaranteed in particular for the smaller Slovak and Rusyn nations.[1]

The independence effort from abroad, launched just months after the outbreak of the war, came to fruition with Allied recognition of the Paris-based Czechoslovak National Council in the fall of 1918. In the chaos of the last weeks of the war, in late October and early November 1918—after the failure to stabilize the empire with a federalization plan—the Habsburg monarchy simply crumbled. The emperor abdicated, recognizing national councils to speak for the successor states; the Hungarians seceded; the German Austrians (including those in the Czech lands) opted for union with Germany; and the Czechs and Slovaks declared independence, moving to occupy their future territory with improvised volunteer armies.

The international legal resolution of these tangled affairs awaited the deliberations of the Versailles Peace Conference, where the U.S. and European victors were in a position to fulfill the promises they had made to Czechs, Slovaks, and other East Europeans.[2] They faced a set of new geopolitical realities that significantly shaped their decisions. Ottoman Turkey had been crumbling since the nineteenth century.[3] Austria-Hungary and Germany were defeated powers, and Russia had lost vast stretches of territory in its withdrawal from the war after the Bolshevik Revolution of 1917; an international pariah on the brink of its own civil war, the emerging Soviet state was in a weak position to retrieve lost territory except at the sufferance of the peace conference. Thus, part of the Versailles peace settlement was, and had to be, a program of new state creation. The principle was national self-determination, but the underlying goal was a more durable European order that would not fall prey to instability in the East. One of the central weaknesses of the previous order, the peacemakers agreed, was the explosive containment of dissatisfied national groupings within the now dissolving empires—a "powder keg" ready to blow up when the fuse was lit. The establishment of smaller, independent successor states in the region might resolve nationalist grievances and offer hope for a durable peace.

Historians have criticized this experiment in state creation from several angles, above all for its failure to avert a second and even more destructive European war a generation later. The successor states created at Versailles and other postwar settlements have been deemed too weak, and too divided among themselves, to have served as a bulwark against great-power ambitions. The architects of Versailles have been castigated especially for the imperfections of their implementation of national self-determination. The Wilsonian formula of building states along "historically established lines of allegiance and nationality" was not as clear-cut as he may have thought. The new countries remained multinational—large numbers of minorities were trapped in the "wrong" state, with Poles or Germans or Hungarians separated from ethnic kin next door serving as a standing invitation to external intervention.

To some extent, these critics miss the point. Even the most conscientious peacemaker could not have drawn borders that neatly separated one group from another; the populations of Eastern Europe were hopelessly intertwined. Taking into account certain natural boundaries and the logic of economic viability in drawing boundaries hardly seemed irrational either. The real problem was larger. Eastern Europe could only be as stable as the larger continental balance of power outside its immediate boundaries. If the larger powers persisted in using East Europe as an arena in which to play out their conflicts, it would never be stable; the East European chances for stability rested then and rest now on the ability of larger powers like Britain, France, Germany, and Russia to find grounds for cooperation.

The search for stability among great-power interests would occupy the generations to come. In the meantime, the Versailles conference had a practical task to accomplish. The peacemakers confronted the fact that recognizing the right to independence of states like Czechoslovakia or Poland did not establish territorial boundaries. In many cases, the lines of allegiance were in fact heavily disputed, and the Versailles conference had to arbitrate boundary disputes as part of the postwar settlement. Hence after gaining independence for something called Czechoslovakia, it was necessary to decide what Czechoslovakia was, what territories and population it would include.

The postwar settlement of Versailles was especially generous to the new state of Czechoslovakia; the Versailles peacemakers honored nearly all of its territorial claims. Because none of the Allies had any intention of letting Germany acquire new territory as a result of the war, Czechoslovakia's case for retaining Sudeten German regions—included within the historical boundaries of the Czech lands—was very secure. The German remnant of Austria was not permitted to join Germany either. In the end, all of the traditional and well-defined territory of the Czech lands went to the new state, in addition to disputed territory in Silesia that contained a considerable Polish population. There was no historically recognized boundary between Hungary and Slovakia; because Hungary had been an enemy state in the war, however, the Allies were generous in drawing the boundary in Slovakia's favor (a settlement ratified in the separate Treaty of Trianon with Hungary), leaving it with a large Hungarian minority in the south. To the east, Czechoslovakia claimed and received Subcarpathian Ruthenia from Hungary. There is an old proverbial warning: Be careful what you wish for, because you might get it. This warning certainly could have applied to Czechoslovakia, a state that "won" its territorial maximum and thus inherited large minority populations into the bargain. We will see that this later proved to be an equivocal victory.

At its christening, therefore, the new state of Czechoslovakia that made its modern debut from the ruins of the Austro-Hungarian empire was visited both by the proverbial good fairy, who endowed it with territorial, human, and economic resources, and her evil twin, who bestowed ethnic complexity and international insecurity on the fledgling country. What a "small nation at the crossroads of Europe" would do with these advantages and liabilities is worth examining for two reasons. First, the legacies of the First Czechoslovak Republic—its successes and its unresolved problems—marked the state for the rest of its existence. Second, Czechoslovakia's experience is a reminder that the postcommunist attempts of the current era to weather the transition from authoritarian rule to democracy and economic development are not unique. They are merely a distinctive subset of twentieth-century efforts that transcend time and region.

It is quite possible to describe interwar Czechoslovakia as undergoing a triple transition of its own. First, it was attempting to develop the stable parliamentary democratic institutions of a political transition from Habsburg rule to independent statehood. Second, it was attempting to build a new independent economy, to extricate itself from the imperial economy, and to integrate separate Czech and

MAP 1.2   The boundaries of Czechoslovakia in 1918

Slovak economic experiences in the Austrian and Hungarian parts of the former dual monarchy. This economic transition differed from the current attempted transition to capitalism but represented nonetheless a major task of economic reorientation. Finally, the new state needed to find a viable national bargain, or contract, to accommodate not only the Czechs and the Slovaks, but also substantial numbers of German, Hungarian, Polish, Jewish, Rusyn, and other minorities. All of these agendas overlapped, and all of them were critical to the survival and success of the new state.

The Problem of National Identity

The name "Czechoslovakia" represented a hope and aspiration rather than a reality. It is important both for what it said and did not say. In the first place, the name blended two different Slavic peoples with different languages and historical experiences. There was no such thing as an ethnic Czechoslovak, no such language as Czechoslovak. However, many Czechs and even some Slovaks hoped that a common Czechoslovak identity would evolve over time—not an ethnic merger perhaps, but at least a sense of shared destiny and values that would give some cohesion to the state. This hope, however, and the ideology of "Czechoslovakism" that lay behind it, was the source of endless conflict between Czechs and Slovaks from the very inception of the state. Nationally assertive Slovaks wanted no part of a merged identity; they wanted to see a hyphen in the state's name—"Czecho-Slovakia"—as an acknowledgment that Czechs and Slovaks were two different nations. The "hyphen controversy" would reappear periodically whenever debates over the definition of the state re-erupted—particularly in the late 1930s and the early 1990s[4]; it was never a simple question of punctuation but rather symbolic of basic identity conflict. Throughout the First Republic, proponents of "Czechoslovakism" continued to insist that Czechs and Slovaks were two branches of a single nation, and Slovak nationalists would vehemently challenge them. The unifying "Czechoslovak" concept was reflected in the interwar constitution, above all in the fact that this multinational state was also a highly centralized one. Neither the Slovaks nor the state's minorities (except for the Rusyns to the east) were acknowledged to have a right to any form of regional self-government; the National Assembly in Prague made all key policy decisions.

To many political leaders, certainly to the Czechs and even to many Slovaks, this centralism was unavoidable. The reason that "Czechoslovakism" and a unitary state seemed essential to them points to the other omission of the country's name; since Czechs and Slovaks share the honors of nomenclature, it might be supposed that they were the only significant national groupings in the state. This was not the case. There was a very substantial Hungarian minority of some three-quarters of a million in Slovakia, and there were also some 3 million Germans in the state—as many Germans as there were Slovaks, in fact.

Apart from the cumbersome problem of inventing an inclusive name (Yugoslavia, after all, was then known as the Kingdom of Serbs, Croats, and Slovenes), the focus on the two major Slavic groups was quite deliberate—the Czechs and the Slovaks were *státotvorné* peoples (the official constituent nationalities of the state); others were minorities. To a significant extent, the name Czechoslovakia reflected the fact that Czechs and Slovaks had agreed to a common state in the first place to shore each other up and provide a counterweight to these large German and Hungarian minority groups; in the words of Czechoslovakia's first president, Tomáš Masaryk, "Together, [a Czech-Slovak alliance] would raise the Slav majority of the population to almost 9 million, and be so much the stronger vis-à-vis the minority."[5] The German and Hungarian minorities in the new state were all the more threatening to Czech and Slovak identity because they had been the former masters during the Habsburg empire. The larger Czech nation did not fear an identity challenge from the smaller and less developed Slovak nation; however, after more than a half century of struggle to gain an equal footing with Germans in the Czech lands, they did fear the German economic and political power, at home as well as in neighboring Germany and Austria. And Czechs also feared that allowing Slovaks special status—regional autonomy, for example—would only whet the appetites of the minorities for their own institutions or even for secession. The name Czechoslovakia, therefore, both reflects and disguises a very serious identity problem in the multinational state.

During the two decades of the First Republic, it became apparent that nearly everyone was dissatisfied with a unitary state of two constituent nations and minorities—except the Czechs. The sense of separate national interests was reflected indirectly in the party system, where the proportional representation schema of the electoral system gave free rein to individual choice and permitted the multiplication of smaller, national, class-based parties. In this institutional setting, most Germans voted for German parties, most Hungarians for Hungarian parties, and so on. An ardent working-class German voted for the German Social Democrats, not the statewide Czechoslovak Social Democratic Party, and a German farmer for the German Agrarians. Even Slovaks, who did vote for some of the statewide parties, also threw substantial support to regionally based parties. Ironically, the party with the broadest electoral appeal across national lines was the Communists; there was only one communist party rather than separate nationally based parties.

If the segmentation of the party system along national lines is a clue that individual national groups did not consider the state a unified whole, any ambiguity was resolved by what these parties' politicians said in the political debates of the period. The Slovak delegation to the founding constituent assembly of the republic had accepted centralism, in some cases only provisionally, in recognition of Slovak political inexperience and the traumatic impact of the 1919 invasion by Béla Kun's short-lived Hungarian Communist revolutionary regime.

In subsequent years, as Slovakia stabilized, many of its political leaders began to reconsider this constitutional choice. The nationalist parties of Slovakia were the most persistent and vociferous in pressing for greater autonomy, but even some Slovak politicians associated with the statewide parties gave consideration to alternative distributions of power. The Slovak wing of the ruling Agrarian Party, for example, tried in vain to press for greater recognition of regional interests.[6] Minority representatives also claimed the need for greater policy input and criticized government policy as beneficial largely to the Czechs and Slovaks. The different national groupings were too divided among themselves to present a united front. Nationally assertive Slovaks, for example, were at odds with the Hungarians and could cooperate with German nationalists only at the risk of triggering roars of outrage and retaliation from the Czechs.[7]

A more flexible political system might at least have done more to accommodate the grievances of the Slovak "junior partner," but the complex and easily deadlocked system, coupled with fears of state disintegration, resulted in a continued postponement of a mutually satisfactory resolution of the "Slovak question." In October 1938, on the heels of the Munich crisis, the central government did grant Slovakia a significant measure of autonomy under the Žilina Accords, but this crisis concession was submerged in the partition of the state by the Nazis five months later. In the end, it was left for later governments to confront the national problem—and to fail.

An additional impediment to resolving the Slovak question was the fact that Prague politicians thought that they did have a painless formula for doing so, a formula that avoided sensitive institutional changes. This was essentially a cultural solution that relied on what turned out to be a misguided piece of sociological reasoning (a good politician, after all, is a practicing social scientist). President Masaryk, the erstwhile sociologist, was convinced that educating the next generation in Slovakia to Czechoslovak values was the long-term solution to Czech-Slovak differences. In 1921, Masaryk told a French journalist: "There is no Slovak nation. . . . The Czechs and Slovaks are brothers. Only cultural level separates them—the Czechs are more developed than the Slovaks, for the Magyars [Hungarians] held them in systematic unawareness. We are founding Slovak schools. We must await the results; in one generation there will be no difference between the two branches of our national family."[8]

Education would spur development, but even more important, civic education would create a common Czechoslovak identity (an identity that, to be sure, carried strong overtones of the idea that Slovaks would become more Czech) that would bring the country's name from the realm of aspiration to reality. And then the national tensions would subside.

Like many subsequent analysts, the leaders of the interwar Republic thought of nationalism as a "childhood disease" that would yield to maturity and modernization. On this issue, Masaryk may have been a better president than he was a sociologist, because he was quite wrong—the next generation of Slovaks that emerged in the 1930s was more radical in its nationalism than its elders, who could better remember the previous subordination to Hungary. Moreover, the depression-bred younger generation of Slovaks was angry that the central government put insufficient emphasis on Slovakia's economic development; they tended to see the educational effort—and "Czechoslovakism" itself—as carrying out a thinly disguised project of assimilation or Czech colonization (if so, it was quite unsuccessful).

This viewpoint was matched by a very different Czech perspective. Czechs and some Slovak leaders tended to see these complaints as gross ingratitude for Slovakia's rescue from Hungary and for the Czech "subsidization" of the weaker Slovak partner. Czech National Democrats leader Karel Kramář chided the Slovaks: "If it were possible to experiment in the constitutional order without fear of the future, I would give you full freedom so that you could know how we subsidize you. I am strongly convinced, that in a half year you would beg on your knees for us to take you back."[9]

Was this struggle over national identity the plaything of politicians or the expression of deeply rooted popular concerns? Exasperated Czech politicians certainly embraced the first of these suppositions and tended to view the politics of Slovak nationalism as an exercise in blatant political demagoguery.[10] President Masaryk himself originally rejected the idea of a plebiscite or referendum to determine the status of Slovakia with the argument that the general Slovak public had been too oppressed under Hungarian rule to decide their own fate.[11] Slovak nationalists, of course, bristled at this characterization of the Slovak people and claimed to be the embodiment of their genuine national aspirations. It is impossible to shed light on this question with public opinion surveys (such polling did not reach Czechoslovakia until 1946 and was shortly thereafter curtailed by the communist rise to power). We do know, however, that nearly half of the electorate of Slovakia (some of them Hungarian, of course) persistently voted for regionally based, nationally oriented parties, despite the superior benefits of patronage that accrued to voters for the governing statewide parties. Yet this in itself does not tell us whether political leaders were responding to nationalist sentiment or creating it by defining the transitional problems facing Slovakia in readily comprehensible terms of the national question. In the context of interwar Slovakia, it may be impossible to unravel the connections between elite and mass commitment to the nationalist cause. The first Czechoslovak census, in 1919, showed that national identity had been a slightly confusing concept for the new Slovak citizenry, some of whom continued to define themselves in religious or local terms, and others by odd national hybrids such as "Hungarian-Slovak."[12] Yet by 1925, Andrej Hlinka's nationalist party had won what proved to be a substantial and fairly stable core of the electorate, and there is little doubt that the preservation and development of Slovak identity was much more broadly rooted and resonant than the narrow partisan base of a single movement. Hungarianizing (magyarizing) restraints on national identity had disappeared with a striking rapidity, suggesting that magyarization had been more shallowly rooted than had been supposed,[13] paving the way for the emergence of a durable identity politics that became more firmly rooted with each passing decade. The 1920s, then, were a critical period of elite-mass interaction on the national issue, and by the 1930s the leaders and the led almost certainly shared a mutually reinforcing set of convictions about the distinctiveness of being Slovak.

The concept of "Czechoslovakism" therefore turned out to be a cause of division and controversy rather than the unifying factor it was formulated to be. Czechs and Slovaks not only lacked a common history before 1918; they even seemed to be living in separate histories in the present, since they viewed that present in such a different light. Years later, during the 1968 reform period, public opinion polls would show that Czechs regarded the First Republic as their primary historical "golden age." For Slovaks, it came in a poor fourth.[14] Historically, and in comparative terms, what may be equally important is that this conflict largely played itself out within available institutional channels, domestic and international. "Street politics" remained a subordinate element in the equation, and there was no secessionist revolutionary movement that would have bequeathed a higher level of threat and a bloodied national history to later generations.

One puzzle of the national identity question in twentieth-century Czechoslovakia was that there appeared to be no purely Czech nationalism apart from the "Czechoslovak" paradigm. If the concept of "us" requires a "them," then certainly it also requires an "us," a sense of national self. It is in this respect that the Czechs had presented something of a conundrum to specialists on the region as well as to the Czechs themselves. It was frequently questioned in dissident publications before 1989, and in the public press thereafter, whether the Czechs had in fact attained a clear sense of their own, distinct identity within the Czechoslovak state. The scholar Olga Šmidová surveyed public opinion on the issue of national identity in January 1991 and found that 37 percent of Czechs thought that there was no such thing as Czech national character, although they were much more willing to define the character traits of other, neighboring nations. Moreover, those traits that Czechs *did* see in themselves, Šmidová argues, were neither heroic nor "overly flattering"—envy and submissiveness, for example.[15] The anti-hero of the well-known Czech novel *Good Soldier Svejk* is often described as a quintessentially Czech character; he foils his adversaries (superior officers) not by direct confrontation or defiance, but by the more sly expedient of overelaborate compliance. The Czech is no hero who sacrifices nobly for the cause, but rather a canny realist more accomplished in political and diplomatic judo than swordplay, constantly confronting superior German or Russian power, and trying to survive. However valid this image might otherwise be, it was reinforced by two major twentieth-century crises that evoked much soul-searching among the Czech intellectual community. Czechs were sensible and pragmatic at Munich in 1938 and during the Soviet invasion of 1968; they bowed to superior force and minimized the loss of life that heroic resistance, in the style of the Hungarian Revolution of 1956 or in the manner of their own heroic defeat by the Habsburgs at White Mountain in 1620, would have caused.[16]

Moreover, Czechs had tended, from the inception of the state in 1918, to fuse their national identity with the larger identity of the state itself—Czechoslovakia. While this identification with the state might be perceived by Slovaks as the arrogance of the larger nation equating its own interests with *raison d'état*, it is nevertheless true that it is hard to find a pattern of Czech national self-assertion comparable to that of the Slovaks: no Czech demands for a separate Czech Republic, and little sense that *both* Czechs and Slovaks would benefit from devolving additional power to two individual republics so as to give freer expression to national identity and interest. In the 1920s and 1930s, no Czech autonomy movement paralleled the one in Slovakia; as we have seen, the Czechs were more inclined to approve of the eventual emergence of a Czechoslovak unity—largely Czech in content, of course, because the Czechs were the larger and more developed of the two branches and could be assured of a decisive say in any joint definition.

There had a been a strong Czech national movement in the nineteenth century. What had happened to it? A simple answer is that the Czechs were the largest national group in the state. Moreover, the earlier Czech national movement had defined itself in terms of a German threat to identity within German Austria. After independence, the German threat changed character. The Czechs now incorporated a Czechoslovak ethos into their self-definition as a counterweight to the German minority; they could live with a broader identity where they outnumbered the weaker Slovak partner, and they did not want to abandon the identity if it meant unleashing centrifugal forces. This is a very rational explanation; it is certainly incomplete, but it does suggest that the way national self-assertion is expressed can depend significantly on the context.

The missing, or disguised, Czech nationalism of the interwar period is not just a historical curiosity. It is a long-term pattern. The restoration of Czechoslovakia after World War II did not inspire Czech support for their own Czech republic in a federal state, even after their own German minority had been deported and the Czech lands had become overwhelmingly Czech in ethnicity; it was the Slovaks who pushed for a federal state in order to reflect differing national interests during the Prague Spring reform period of 1968. And after 1989, it was again the Slovaks rather than the Czechs who were interested in greater decentralization to protect national identity. Even independence does not seem to have inspired a full-blown Czech nationalism, as the Czech Republic remains focused on the larger prospect of integration into Europe. As will be apparent later, however, the "German question" has not evaporated but rather taken on a more complex form, because the problem of the deported Sudeten Germans has continued to inspire controversy and because Germany's economic clout continues to raise the question for all of Germany's neighbors of whether there will indeed be a "Europeanized Germany" rather than a "Germanized Europe."

Domestic Politics

Every other East European state created in the aftermath of World War I lapsed into some form of authoritarian government by the time that Hitler launched his expansionist drive. Czechoslovakia remained a functioning parliamentary democracy. Free competitive elections were held in Czechoslovakia at approximately five-year intervals, and a wide array of parties were permitted to compete, including the only legal communist party in the region. From independence to 1935, the "President-Liberator," Tomáš G. Masaryk, put his humanist stamp on Czechoslovak democracy. Although minorities remained vocal about their grievances, the state nonetheless made efforts to integrate them into the political system. The Germans, in particular, were not only permitted to organize their own parties but were also, after 1926, always included in governing coalitions as junior partners. This interlude, although scornfully dismissed as "bourgeois-democratic" by the communists and subjected to heavy official criticism during the communist era, remained a source of inspiration to later democratizing efforts, a reference point for the invocation of a democratic tradition after the Velvet Revolution.

The symbolic anchor of the system was Masaryk. As Czechoslovakia's first president, he was a dignified, white-haired figure who on ceremonial occasions rode horseback. His value to the country was not merely ceremonial, however. A sociologist and moral philosopher at Charles University during the period of Habsburg rule, he was a promulgator of the "Czech question" in counterpoise to German predominance, an instigator of Czech ties with Slovakia, and a political activist who was representative of the engagement of the East European intellectual in politics from at least the nineteenth century onwards. During World War I, he went into exile to promote the cause of Czechoslovak statehood with the eventually victorious Western Allies, risking treason charges at home, where Austria-Hungary was allied against the West with Germany. With his disciple, Edvard Beneš, who would serve as foreign minister in the new state, and expatriate Milan Štefánik, who before his untimely death in a plane crash complemented the triumvirate with his technical skills and Slovak ethnicity, Masaryk won allied assent to his cause. His international recognition and prior service to the cause made him a natural choice for the Czechoslovak presidency, an office he held until retirement at age eighty-five in 1935. Even in the communist period, when Masaryk was officially vilified, he remained the unrivaled Czech national hero, and student demonstrators chanted his name in the streets of Prague during the Velvet Revolution of 1989.

Masaryk's prominent presidential service to the republic however, should not obscure the significant differences between Czechoslovakia's parliamentary system and the U.S. congressional-presidential system. A student accustomed to the workings of American politics must be prepared for an adjustment: The two-party system with winner-take-all district races and the bicameral legislature sharing power with a president are not at all the components of the Czechoslovak model. Nor, in fact, is the U.S. approach replicated in any of the other stable Western democracies. In its pedigree, the Czechoslovak system was a European parliamentary democracy, owing its distinguishing electoral and institutional features both to the previous Austrian system and, more generally, to West European rather than U.S. templates.[17] The essence of this kind of parliamentary system is the fusion of legislative-executive power. The elected assembly draws generally from its own membership a party or coalition of parties with a governing majority of seats, and this political constellation negotiates the allocation of cabinet posts. The cabinet and its prime minister then govern—references to "the government" in East Europe mean this core cabinet group—but they are ultimately responsible to the legislature from which their authority derives, and they may not stay in power if parliamentary support is withdrawn through a vote of no confidence. In such systems, a presidency may exist, but it tends to be weak

or ceremonial, even if directly elected. Czechoslovakia's president was more powerful than most, but not nearly as powerful as the U.S. presidency. Masaryk could
appoint the members of the governing cabinet, but he had to choose from among
the members of the leading parties of the National Assembly who had agreed to
form a government; if that government lost its majority, it had to be reorganized
on the basis of a more workable parliamentary coalition. Moreover, Masaryk was
not elected by the public, but rather by the National Assembly itself. From 1918
to 1938 the interwar Republic was therefore essentially a parliamentary system.

Czechoslovakia and many other parliamentary systems also differ from the
U.S. model in being multiparty systems. Why? One answer to this question focuses on the choice of electoral system. It is usually argued that the U.S. electoral
design is tilted in favor of a two-party system because of its winner-take-all
arrangement. One and only one congressional representative is elected from each
district. The losers get nothing, so there is not much incentive to vote for a
smaller party—and thereby waste one's vote. The result is that the two largest
parties usually fight it out. Most parliamentary systems are based on some form
of *proportional representation*, in which parties are represented in the parliament
in rough proportion to the number of votes received. The voter can feel free to
cast a ballot for a party that can only hope to get 7 percent of the vote, because
even that low a percentage can get one's party into the legislature, and maybe
even into a multiparty government. Czechoslovakia's interwar parliamentary system, like the postcommunist electoral system of the 1990s, was based on a form
of proportional representation. The field was open for class-based parties (such
as the Social Democrats, the Small Tradesmen, and the Agrarians), religiously
based parties (the Catholic People's parties), and ethnically based parties.

However, it is likely that the First Czechoslovak Republic would have been a
multiparty system even under U.S. rules because of its complicated national divisions. In any given district, the voting majority was Czech, Slovak, Polish,
German, Rusyn, or Hungarian. Each of these national groupings was anxious to
protect its national interests, and each of them could have voted for a different
nationally based party without wasting votes in districts in which they were in a
majority. Multiparty systems can emerge even without proportional representation, therefore, wherever there are politically important, territorially based divisions in a country. Since interwar Czechoslovakia had both proportional representation and significant social and ethnic divisions, it had a very complicated
party system representing most of the permutations and combinations of the
electorate: a German Agrarian Party, for example, or a Slovak Catholic nationalist party (the Hlinka Slovak People's Party). Any American voter who is fed up
with the two existing parties might be envious of the wide range of choices in the
Czechoslovak system—a party for every political view, and one of them probably
pretty close to yours.

However, despite the durability and representativeness of its politics,
Czechoslovakia was hardly a model democracy. The very complexity of its multiparty system produced very fractionalized parliaments in which as many as fif-

teen parties won seats in each election. When the largest party usually won only 15 percent of the vote—nowhere near a majority—elections did not by themselves determine who would govern. That depended on which parties could negotiate a cooperative working relationship, and those options turned out to be severely limited in practice. Tortuous negotiations followed every election, with the "usual suspects" maneuvering for a redivision of the electoral spoils. New governments were also formed between elections, totaling fifteen cabinets between 1918 and 1938, each lasting an average of a little over a year.

The typical interwar government coalition contained five or six parties, four of them more or less perpetual governing parties. Therefore, new elections at best caused a shift in the balance of governing parties; regardless of electoral outcome, the Agrarian Party, for example, served in every interwar coalition and usually provided the prime minister. One man, Edvard Beneš, guided foreign policy from the inception of the Republic to his ascension to the presidency in 1935. Certain cabinet ministries became the province of specific parties—and accordingly a base for party patronage and preferential treatment for party members. The complexity of the system, in other words, tended to concentrate leadership attention on assuring stability. This in turn made it rather rigid and inflexible, with a core of experienced and increasingly aging cabinet ministers dominating policymaking despite frequent cabinet reshufflings and interim governments.

If this situation sounds like a political nightmare, bear in mind that it is also not unusual. Any multiparty system based on proportional representation has some of these problems. Philip Longworth points out that, between the two world wars, Yugoslavia had twenty-four governments in ten years, and Poland fourteen in seven years;[18] the postcommunist regimes in Czechoslovakia and elsewhere in the region would face such instabilities again after 1989. What is unusual is that interwar Czechoslovakia regulated the problems well enough to avoid chaos and breakdown into authoritarianism. But the price was that the system was not as responsive to changing political currents as the proliferation of parties might have suggested. Theorists often include the rotation of power between opposition and government as a very important feature of democracy; what good are elections if the voters cannot periodically "throw the rascals out" and give new leadership a chance? This really did not happen in interwar Czechoslovakia.

Moreover, the system was not as open to rival views as the multiparty electoral competition might suggest. It is true that Czechoslovakia was the only East European state in which the communist party was permitted to function legally, to win parliamentary seats, and engage in political debate. However, freedom of expression was hardly absolute. Public political gatherings were closely monitored by the police, and rhetoric (left-wing or nationalist rhetoric in particular) deemed too inflammatory was not infrequently punished through prosecution for libel and slander or for violating the law on the protection of the republic. One of the busiest parliamentary committees in interwar Czechoslovakia was the one that investigated the public remarks of its own deputies to see whether they had transgressed the boundaries of parliamentary immunity from prosecution. It was not unusual for opposition periodicals to appear with glaring blank spaces marking where government action had killed an inflammatory story.

This system had decidedly mixed blessings. On the one hand, it provided institutional stability for a new country and continuity in areas such as international relations, where Czechoslovakia's security problems were always very substantial. On the other hand, it was hard to make a policy breakthrough, and certain pressing issues tended to be postponed by a closely held political corporation with limited vision; the most significant of these postponements may have been the problem of Slovak political participation in the system. (See Box 1.1.)

However, one cannot mark the limits of Czechoslovak democracy without also trying to understand why such limits were imposed. As we will see, a crucial piece of the puzzle was the ominous international context of the new state, and the security threats it faced. A Czechoslovakia that lacked a true commonality of interest with often hostile neighbors, too small to protect itself against the violent forces unleashed on the continent during the 1930s, felt that it had no option but to attempt to increase its survival chances by constraining the forces—particularly the potentially explosive national forces—that might pull it apart if left unfettered.

To focus on Czechoslovakia's limits and liabilities should not come at the price of ignoring its strengths. Czechoslovakia's relatively open educational system and high literacy rates meant that the political system was bolstered with a relatively sophisticated electorate. The Habsburg empire had also been a more valuable political training ground than that of Ottoman Turkey and tsarist Russia. This was true for the Czechs at least. There had been Czech parties in legislative forums since the 1870s, and, especially after the enactment of universal male suffrage in 1907, there was the breeding ground for a broad-based Czech party system by 1918. The imperial bureaucracy was also comparatively efficient and uncorrupt, with strong Czech participation; the new state would not have to train new bureaucrats from scratch, although the inherited bureaucratic mentality was somewhat officious and rank-conscious. Slovakia inherited fewer political assets. Corruption, magyarization, and limited suffrage had combined to restrict Slovak electoral representation to a peak of five deputies, barely enough for a single party, let alone a party system. And this narrow base was only the most obvious example of the systematic political limitations placed on Slovaks, particularly the tiny nationally conscious Slovak elite, before independence. It is not surprising, therefore, that Czechs colonized both the post-independence Slovak bureaucracy and its party system to a significant extent, in somewhat the same way that the larger and more developed West German political system absorbed East Germany's after unification in 1990. Slovaks did resent this, but even they quarreled less with the initial Czech intercession, which helped to launch the state, than with the continued Czech presence in Slovakia after the founding crisis had passed.

BOX 1.1
The Institutionalization of a New State

However difficult it may be to gain independence for a new state, that effort usually turns out to be the easy part. The hard part is to develop workable political institutions that are capable of responding to public needs for welfare, security, and order on a reliable basis. Czechoslovakia inherited and adapted many of its political institutions from the Austro-Hungarian empire; more accurately, the Czech lands inherited a political system from the Austrian half of the empire and adapted it in two major ways: fuller democratization, and the incorporation of Slovakia into the existing framework. This inheritance included the structure of the imperial bureaucracy and the basic outlines of the parliamentary system. The new state leadership extended the democratic features of the former Habsburg system by expanding Austria's universal male suffrage (granted in 1907) to include women; by establishing the parliamentary government as the primary legitimate authority (the Austrian parliament had been subordinate to the emperor); and, of course, by extending the more open representative system to Slovakia, where a more restrictive and corrupt electoral system had existed under Hungarian rule. Reorganizing the bureaucracy was a more protracted, evolutionary process. For some time, the government left in place two somewhat different administrative systems in the Czech lands and Slovakia; it was not until the mid-1920s that the country was finally administratively reorganized in a more uniform fashion. Adapting the educational system and the mechanisms of economic regulation took even longer. Moreover, it was not only the formal government structures enshrined in the constitution and law that required institutional stabilization. The same was true of the informal structures such as the parties and interest groups that mediate between the government and the public. Czechoslovakia's multiparty system gained a bit of stability from the pre-independence experience of more limited parliamentary government. Many of the "new" parties were carryovers from the Habsburg period. By the same token, new forces broke into the inherited system and necessitated constant, but not always successful, reequilibration; an obvious example of a new force was the emergence of the Communist Party as an offshoot of the Social Democrats in 1921. By and large, although the results were somewhat rigid and the need for further reform continued, the Czechoslovak political system did succeed in political institutionalization during its two decades of existence. Perhaps the most important point about this process of democratic state-building in the 1920s and 1930s is that the First Republic in some respects actually had a more promising starting point than the democratizers would have after the Velvet Revolution in 1989. It is true that the interwar democratic experiment had to confront the daunting task of bringing together the separate units of the Czech lands and Slovakia for the first time. However, the postcommunist institution-builders had less to build on in many other respects: no recent experience of electoral competition on which to base the new party organizations; no politicians seasoned in parliamentary politics; and a long interlude in which the rule of law had been subordinate to the policy direction of the Communist Party. Each new state faces the challenge of political institutionalization, but the obstacles and advantages differ from case to case.

Economic Transformation in Interwar Czechoslovakia

The economics of the First Republic are worth examining for two reasons. First, the economic legacies of this period, both positive and negative, have been of critical importance for the country's subsequent evolution. Second, the way in which economic, national, and political agendas interacted in interwar Czechoslovakia bears a very striking resemblance to the interactions of the later postcommunist period.

The most important legacy of the interwar period was the maintenance of economic advantages inherited from Austria-Hungary at independence. Czechoslovakia's literacy and urbanization rates were higher than elsewhere in Eastern Europe. Not only were the Czech lands the most economically developed part of imperial Austria, but even less-developed Slovakia was still the most industrialized part of Hungary; together, they siphoned off only one-fourth of the population of the former empire, but over two-thirds of its industrial base.[19] At birth, so to speak, Czechoslovakia was Europe's fourth largest steel producer and third largest coal producer, and economic production grew by approximately two-thirds over the next eighteen years. Although the global depression of the 1930s hit the country hard, Czechoslovakia's industrial base had almost recovered to its pre-depression levels by 1937 and so it was still a leading international industrial power at the time of the Nazi intervention in 1938.[20]

This level of economic development gave Czechoslovakia an economic class structure similar to those of the economically advanced West European states and different from those of its East European neighbors, at least in the Czech lands: a strong, organized, working class, fairly vigorous entrepreneurial and commercial classes, a commercialized agricultural sector, and so on. In turn, the political system incorporated economic interests in ways that would be recognizable in the West: worker-based Social Democratic parties, parties that represented industrial and agricultural interests—all major economic interests typical of industrialized society. It is understandable that the Czechs did not think of themselves as "East" Europeans (maybe those less-developed Slovaks were, they thought); Czechs saw themselves as Europeans, without the qualifying regional adjective, a competitive part of the continental and global economy as well as a contributor to European culture. Hadn't Kafka been from Prague? Hadn't Mozart loved Prague? Wasn't Prague's Charles University among the oldest seats of learning on the continent?

Political scientists would see a strong link between this socioeconomic setting and Czechoslovakia's relative success in sustaining interwar democracy. In his survey of the new wave of global democratization in recent decades, Samuel Huntington reminded readers of the findings of earlier researchers who had looked for the "prerequisites" of democracy—the factors associated with establishing and maintaining a democratic regime. The most striking association was the apparent correlation between democracy and higher levels of wealth and economic development. As Huntington put it, "most wealthy countries are democratic, and most democratic countries—India is the most dramatic exception—are wealthy."[21] This is hardly an iron law; rich oil-exporting countries do not fit the profile, and the middle-income countries present a very mixed picture. But economic development clearly helps. Why? A common answer is that industrialization produces a differentiated class structure, and that these classes help to democratize the system by demanding political participation. Looking at the early European and U.S. "success stories," a number of theorists see the engine of democratization as the rising industrial middle class; as Barrington Moore summed it up: "no bourgeoisie, no democracy."[22] Not all agree with the assignment of the heroic role to the middle class; other analysts assign greater weight to the political impact of the increasingly organized working class. In either case, industrial development creates both wealth and the economic interests that push for a more open political system. A more developed economy may also have more resources with which to respond to popular demands for services and social welfare, whereas an impoverished democracy might collapse under the pressure of demands it cannot hope to satisfy with such a small economic pie to divide. Anyone looking for a confirmation of this hypothesis in interwar East Central Europe would have selected Czechoslovakia, with its relatively sophisticated industrial economy, as the candidate most likely to achieve a functioning democratic system. And that prediction holds. In addition to its political resources, therefore, Czechoslovakia also had economic advantages over its neighbors, advantages that would persist even after the economic dislocations and stagnation of the communist period. On the threshold of the 1989 transition, Czechoslovakia retained one of the highest GNPs in the Soviet bloc.

This is not to deny that the creation of the new economic order after World War I encountered considerable difficulty. Dividing an empire into subunits is no assurance that new borders will follow the borders of economic activity. Suppliers were separated from their customers, migrant laborers from their hirers. Transportation systems linked cities in different countries, but not necessarily to neighboring cities within the new borders. In the beginning, for example, there was no northern railroad line linking the Czech lands with Slovakia until Polish Silesian territory was added to the settlement. The old rail network had run north-south, from the Czech lands to the Austrian center, and from Slovakia to the Hungarian. Prague and Bratislava had closer ties to Vienna and Budapest than to each other. Trade in the region of the former imperial market was considerably hampered by the fact that the old Austria-Hungary was now seven different successor states, each with its own economic regulations and tariff barriers.

Moreover, the relative economic prosperity of the interwar state was still further strained by the stresses of both politics and national divisions. The complicated, delicately balanced political system did not adapt creatively to the depression crisis of the 1930s, for example, with the result that the depression lingered longer there than in some other countries.

Divisions between national groups created even greater stresses on the economy. Any U.S. citizen is quite accustomed to the differential impact of public policy on different economic groups, leading to complaints that a given tax or health-care policy "hurts the middle class" or "deprives the rich of incentives." No public policy benefits or hurts all groups equally. Economic policy is never neutral toward national groups either, a fact of life that creates endless political controversy in multinational states. Splicing together the Czech and Slovak economies after 1918 was complicated enough as an economic transition, but what worsened it was that the German minority felt that it was being dispossessed of its resources by the new national state. When the depression hit, the Germans were hardest hit of all because they were still disproportionately in control of the industrial export industries that were particularly vulnerable to the collapse of world trade. They became convinced that the state favored Czechs in its response to the depression. Slovaks, too, were exposed to economic dislocations that could all too easily be blamed on Prague. Slovakia's industrial base had been carefully protected in Hungary by tariff walls and other government protectionist policies and subsidies. When this infant industrial complex was grafted onto the more powerful Czech industrial base after 1918, the shock was considerable. Slovakia may even have "deindustrialized" somewhat in the 1920s as a result of unprotected competition from the Czech lands.[23] What may look to outsiders (and to the Czechs) like the normal operations of the market—the more efficient and profitable enterprises driving out the less well equipped—looked to a number of disillusioned Slovak leaders as a deliberate policy of colonization from Prague, or at best as a natural market effect that Prague should have anticipated and corrected for. This is not to say that economic grievances had a simple and direct causative effect on democratic viability but rather that the interaction of economic and nationalist issues made them more burdensome in combination than they were individually. This was true in Czechoslovakia seventy years ago, and it remained true after 1989.

Note that it does not necessarily matter whether these German and Slovak perceptions of discrimination were "true." Members of a nationally conscious group tend to measure personal well-being partly as a function of the well-being of their own group; there is an absence of what J. S. Furnivall calls "common social demand," with each subgroup responding to economic and political changes through the prism of the way it affects the subgroup rather than the country as a whole.[24] In good times, the tensions that arise from this divergence of perspectives may not be unmanageable; an expanding economic pie will allow everyone a bit more. Everyone will grumble about being shortchanged, but the controversy will not escalate to a crisis. In times of acute dislocation, however, the differential impact of economic and political decisions may be impossible to compensate for; at that point, national divisions can add one more explosive problem to an already overburdened agenda. This was the case in Czechoslovakia, where the impact of the global depression followed on the heels of the tensions produced by the post-imperial economic adjustment.

One solution to the problem might have been to decentralize power, so as to accord the affected groups more policy input and more share in responsibility. Given the vulnerable international situation of interwar Czechoslovakia, however, the predominantly Czech leadership thought that it could not risk decentralization, because it might have started a chain reaction capable of destroying the state.

The International Environment

Czechoslovakia was one of the winning states in the Versailles settlement. The satisfaction of almost every Czechoslovak territorial claim was an enviable position in the short run but a perilous one in the longer term, because Czechoslovakia was almost completely surrounded by dissatisfied neighbors—the losers in the territorial settlement who harbored irredentist claims on Czechoslovak territory. What made these foreign policy disputes particularly volatile and explosive was the fact that most of them rested on claims and counterclaims about the ethnonational identity of the disputed territory. Poland resented the loss of Silesian territory with a large Polish minority. Even more threatening were the Hungarian and German irredentas. Hungary was the biggest loser in the postwar territorial settlement. Shrunk to one-third of its former size by the Treaty of Trianon of 1920 (the mere mention of which was a source of national trauma), Hungary looked across its own borders to substantial Hungarian minorities in Romania, Serbia, and, most important for our purposes, Slovakia, where almost three-quarters of a million Hungarians lived. The Hungarian battle cry "No, no, never!" was a reminder never to accept the mutilation of the Hungarian state, and its neighbors were constantly sensitive to the possibility of renewed Hungarian claims.

Though historians may dispute how central Hungary's irredentism was to its practical day-to-day foreign policy objectives, it is perhaps understandable that neighbors would take no chances. At the very least, Czechoslovakia was faced with periodic Hungarian campaigns to dramatize the mistreatment of the Hungarian minority in Slovakia, campaigns that won considerable sympathy in Western Europe. These campaigns prefigured a more sophisticated pursuit of protection for minority rights in postcommunist Europe.[25] At most, the state was on guard against internal provocations, and there is evidence of Hungarian governmental subsidies to opposition groups, both Slovak and Hungarian, who might be counted upon to criticize Czechoslovak policy. In this context, Czechs and those Slovaks who shared a "Czechoslovak" perspective were ever vigilant to detect signs that opposition criticism was backed by foreign intrigue to encourage secession, and there were several highly publicized treason trials, notably that of Béla Tuka, that highlighted a supposed link between domestic opposition and Hungarian interests in weakening the state. This era intensified the tensions generated by the previous period of Hungarian rule to bequeath to postcommunist Slovakia a legacy of troubled relations with its Hungarian minority.

The most sensitive of the territorial claims, however, was the German. The historical pattern of settlement by ethnic groups left the Czech territories of Bohemia and Moravia ringed by German population concentrations. These German populations became a tempting target for Hitler's propaganda in the 1930s. Germans who had made their peace with the new Czechoslovak state in the 1920s were increasingly called to national assertiveness under the aegis of their powerful co-ethnic Nazi neighbor (the irony that these Germans had never been part of Germany, but rather of German Austria, was blurred once Germany absorbed Austria in the *Anschluss* of April 1938). Hence after Hitler's rise to power, the German state championed the cause of neighboring German minorities, providing encouragement and funding for political activism and undermining Czechoslovakia's standing in Western Europe. At home, the so-called Sudeten Germans of Czechoslovakia voted in increasing numbers for the shrilly nationalist Sudeten German Party, raising Czech doubts as to their ultimate loyalty to the state.[26]

The local minorities were therefore persistently perceived as stalking horses for foreign powers. This international context affected even the claims of Slovaks for greater political autonomy. Although Slovaks had no foreign protector across the border, the central government came to perceive any devolution of power from the center as a slippery slope into disintegration. In 1932, Foreign Minister Beneš insisted that decentralization of power to Slovakia would "mean for this state the slogan Slovakia to the Slovaks, German regions to the Germans, Magyar regions to the Magyars."[27] A unitary state was seen as a defense against possible foreign intervention, a linkage that bedeviled any attempt to satisfy Slovak nationalist aspirations.

These perceived threats to Czechoslovakia's territorial integrity, in short, tended to tighten the arena of domestic politics and limited the boundaries of free expression. It was all too easy to read opposition strategy as a threat to security in a genuinely insecure environment. Ultimately, the worst fears would be realized: Between 1938 and 1940, Hungary would join in with German territorial demands on Czech lands to reclaim significant chunks of Slovak territory. Poland, too, "cried and took her share."

More broadly, Czechoslovakia was a victim of the insecurities of geopolitical position. Poised between the new Soviet Union to the east and Germany to the west, its foreign policy makers could only try to balance interests in a larger and unstable power alignment in Europe, its diplomatic interests inevitably subordinate to those of the larger powers—who themselves were incapable of warding off the approaching second world war.

Ultimately, Czechoslovakia's unenviable position reached its low point at Munich in October 1938, where the larger western powers agreed to the territorial division of Czechoslovakia, at Hitler's demand, in the interests of what they hoped would be "peace in our time." Czechoslovakia was not invited to the negotiation of its own dismemberment; it was only asked to accept the consequences. The democratic experiment essentially ended at Munich. The old party system was dismantled, and Slovakia gained autonomy and eventually a short-lived wartime independence at German hands. No one intervened or even consulted the Czechoslovak government as Hungary regained Slovak territory by the Vienna Award of November 1938, Poland (temporarily) Silesia, and Germany first the country's concentrated German border settlements and eventually (in March 1939) the entire territory of the Czech lands as a protectorate.

The influence of the international setting on internal politics is worth emphasizing for several reasons. In the first place, it is a reminder of the general importance of external context for internal political development. An insecure international environment can impinge on democratic rights even in a fairly stable democratic state; the U.S. internment of Japanese Americans during World War II and the investigations of the McCarthy era during the cold war are clear examples. The international context is likely to be still more threatening and influential to countries that lack the size, wealth, and relative geographical insulation of the United States. In the second place, and more specifically, we will see a much more supportive international context playing a role in the postcommunist democratization efforts, and the contrast should be instructive. Finally, the specific constellation of geographical forces around Czechoslovakia presented problems that did not expire with the demise of the First Republic and that continue to shape the contours of Czech and Slovak domestic politics in the 1990s.

Interregnum: From the First Czechoslovak Republic to the End of World War II

The state of Czechoslovakia temporarily disappeared from the European map by the spring of 1939 for the duration of World War II. But it is worth considering its immediate legacies, legacies that made it impossible to pick up in 1945 where German conquest had interrupted things six years earlier.

The trauma of Munich and its aftermath left many scars. To begin with, the country's leadership was tainted domestically for having given up on Czechoslovakia's integrity and sovereignty without a fight. Moreover, the democratic West had abandoned Czechoslovakia to its fate. In the process, the Soviet Union gained considerable mileage with Czechs and Slovaks because of the perception that its willingness to help was stymied by Western inaction: Soviet treaty commitments to support Czechoslovakia's sovereignty were to be triggered in the event of a French intervention, which never came. Since the USSR did not border Czechoslovakia directly until after World War II, it could claim that it was not positioned to intervene directly and unilaterally. Thus the USSR was in the felicitous situation of garnering credibility without needing to do anything to earn it.

A second trauma was the perceived defection of Slovaks and Germans from their commitment to the Czechoslovak state. German voters in Czechoslovakia

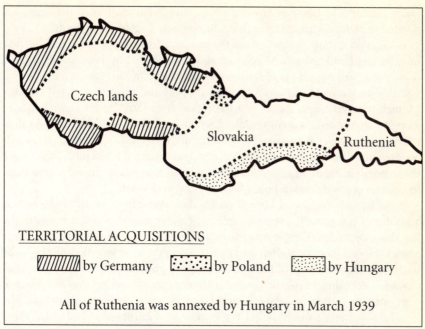

TERRITORIAL ACQUISITIONS

⬛ by Germany ⬛ by Poland ⬛ by Hungary

All of Ruthenia was annexed by Hungary in March 1939

MAP 1.3 *Czechoslovakia's partition after the Munich Conference*

had given their votes to the stridently nationalist Sudeten German Party in the last free election, in 1935, and Czechs saw them as complicit with Hitler in dismembering the state. They also saw the Slovak defection to form a Slovak state under Hitler's tutelage as a treasonous betrayal of the republic in its hour of need. Germans and Slovaks saw things differently; they thought the Czechs were ignoring the fact that they were as subject to Hitler's whims and his coercive power as the Czechs were. The Germans pointed out that Hitler's pretense of concern for the Sudeten Germans was more of an excuse for territorial acquisition than a genuine response to their needs. And Slovaks reminded everyone that their leaders had been summoned to Hitler with an ultimatum: accept a separate state willing to coordinate military and foreign policy with the Germans, or else. During the war, exiled Slovak leader Štefan Osuský rebuked President-in-exile Beneš: "That the Slovaks are forced to do the things that help the Germans, that is proclaimed as treason, but that tens of thousands of Czech workers are forced to labor in factories [for the German war effort], that is rightfully proclaimed as Nazi slavery."[28] In other words, the other national groups saw the Czechs as applying a double standard that excused their own subordination to Berlin and vilified Hitler's other victims as collaborators. As in the conflict over economic discrimination in the interwar Republic, it may be that what is politically important is not the truth or falsity of any one perspective; what matters is that nationally divided societies are prone to such conflicting interpretations of events.

What is even more important are the lessons Beneš drew from Munich. Once in exile, the London-based Czechoslovak leadership led by President Beneš did some hard thinking, and made two critical choices. The first conclusion was that Czechoslovakia had been too reliant on the will and interest of the West—the Munich betrayal taught Beneš that the future state must have a more balanced foreign policy, one that accommodated Soviet interests as well, and that would in return gain additional guarantees of protection from the East. A small state on its own was helpless. Having reached this conclusion, Beneš acted on it even before the war ended, pursuing an accord with the USSR that was the initial step in plans to balance postwar foreign policy between East and West.

Beneš had always prided himself on his diplomatic magicianship, and he was a master of the game.[29] Even so, diplomatic gamesmanship could not alter the fact that Czechoslovakia was never strong enough to chart its own fate or to forge a workable alliance with often antagonistic neighbors. It would continue to be hostage to the intentions of the major European powers, and the only true security for Czechoslovakia would come not from clever alliance politics and bilateral treaty-making, but from the stability and security of the continent as a whole. The Beneš balancing act would only have worked in a Europe that had not divided into irreconcilable blocs. Once the cold war division of Europe developed momentum, Czechoslovakia proved unable to sit on the fence between East and West—and indeed, a number of politicians were critical of Beneš for attempting it. The balancing act ended with the communist takeover in 1948. The country's next opportunity to find an international balance that would assure its sovereignty had to await the events of 1989.

The second momentous choice Beneš faced after Munich concerned the German minority. The German minority had been the entering wedge of Hitler's dismantling of Czechoslovakia, and Beneš now concluded that the Germans would also be a Trojan horse in any subsequent reconstruction of the state. His draconian solution was to deprive Germany of external leverage in Czechoslovakia by means of the wholesale expulsion of the German population from the Czech lands, and to that end he had secured Allied acquiescence to German deportation after the war. The expulsion of some 3 million Germans in the postwar period was justified as a result of collective German guilt in furthering Hitler's war aims; only those Germans who could prove a record of sustained antifascist activity were spared deportation.[30]

Later, critics would term this an application of the principle "guilty until proven innocent"—a reversal of the emerging international human rights norms, even a legalized form of "ethnic cleansing." At the time, however, and in fact all the way to the present, the deportation remained very popular with the Czechs, who considered the punishment commensurate with the crimes of the occupation period. Beneš was not entirely correct, however, in thinking that he had finally resolved the German question that had haunted Czechs since the nineteenth century. The issue would resurface dramatically in the postcommunist period, as deported Germans and their descendants mobilized to challenge the justice of the decisions of the 1940s.

The wartime stresses on the Czech-Slovak relationship further extended the previous pattern of tension. The two separated nations reunited in 1945 in recognition of the practical benefits of reunion but with new grievances generated by the war period as well. Beneš wanted the consequences of Munich declared null and void, and that of course extended to the restoration of all former territory. Slovaks had revolted against their Nazi-dominated state in the Slovak National Uprising of 1944; the tarnished international image of the wartime Slovak state was certainly not a basis on which to ask for the continuation of Slovak independence even if the citizens had wanted that. Slovakia returned to the joint state under the promise of a new deal—a state based on the principle of "equal with equal" in Czech-Slovak relations. What they got in concrete terms was neither a unitary state nor a federation, but a compromise that was later referred to as political "asymmetry"—Slovakia got its own Slovak National Council (SNR) and its own regional government, but symmetry was violated by the absence of any Czech national council. By now, it should be predictable that the Czechs saw this setup as subsidizing special privileges to the Slovaks, and the Slovaks saw it as a halfway measure that gave Czechs control of the statewide government, with a narrow spectrum of leftover power to the SNR and its leadership.

Conclusion

The political and economic experience of interwar Czechoslovakia was by no means a storybook case of uninterrupted success. Among the most important negative legacies were a poisonous distrust and sense of betrayal among ethnonational groups. Czechs and Slovaks had failed to reach consensus on the proper relationship between them. The continued deadlock on this issue contributed to the gradual accumulation of additional grievances, and many of the unresolved national problems of that period would later resurface to bedevil future governments. However, the legacy of the First Republic compares rather favorably with those of its Central and East European neighbors and even with the political strife and economic and social crises of some West European countries of the period. The Munich and post-Munich events that destroyed and dismembered the First Republic had a basis in internal ethnonational divisions, but it is still possible to argue that the republic would have survived in a less threatening international environment, a Europe in which Hitler had been accepted to the Viennese architectural school that had rejected him before World War I, and other, less militarily adventurous and less territorially acquisitive German nationalist leaders had pursued German grievances.

Another important lesson to draw from the experience of the First Republic is the way in which three clusters of issues discussed in this chapter—economic, political, and national—interacted. Some of this interaction may have had positive effects. For example, Czechoslovakia's advanced economic base may have bolstered democratic governance. However, other interactions acted as complicating factors. National divisions created economic tensions and unresolved political grievances, a combination that contributed to the breakup of the state by Germany. The interaction of these issues was not identical after 1989, but we can expect to see a very similar general pattern in which national divisions deadlock politics and complicate the process of marketizing and privatizing the socialist economy. In Chapter 2, we will examine the legacies of a more enduring system, the communist regime that governed Czechoslovakia from 1948 to 1989.

Notes

1. To reinforce their case, the exile politicians helped to support a Czechoslovak Legion, composed of volunteers from the Czech, Slovak, and Rusyn communities in the Russian empire and of deserters from the Austro-Hungarian army who fought on the Russian front against Germany and Austria-Hungary until the Russian Revolution.

2. An overview of the wartime movement for Czechoslovak independence is available in Victor Mamatey, "The Establishment of the Republic," in Victor Mamatey and Radomír Luža, eds., *A History of the Czechoslovak Republic* (Princeton: Princeton University Press, 1973), pp. 3–38.

3. Romania, Serbia, and Bulgaria had all gained independence in the 1870s.

4. See Chapter 4.

5. T. G. Masaryk, cited in Karel Pichlík, *Zahraniční odboj 1914–1918 bez legend* (Prague: Svoboda, 1968), p. 214.

6. See for example, Susan Mikula, "The Politics of Frustration: The Slovak Political Experience, 1918–1938," in Stanislav J. Kirschbaum and Anne C. R. Roman, eds., *Reflections on Slovak History* (Toronto: Slovak World Congress, 1987).

7. This dilemma is explored in James Felak, *"At the Price of the Republic": Hlinka's Slovak People's Party, 1929–1938* (Pittsburgh: University of Pittsburgh Press, 1994).

8. T. G. Masaryk, *Spisy*, vol. 2 (Prague: n.p., 1934), p. 78.

9. Cited in *Slovenská politika na pôde pražkého snemu (1918–1938)*, vol. 1 (Bratislava: Andreja, 1943), p. 274.

10. See Carol Skalnik Leff, *National Conflict in Czechoslovakia: The Making and Remaking of a State, 1918–1987* (Princeton: Princeton University Press, 1988), pp. 194–207.

11. T. G. Masaryk, *Spisy*, vol. 3: *1918–1920* (Prague: n.p., 1933), p. 69.

12. Josef Mráz, "O předběžném sčítání lidu na Slovensku roku 1919" (Part 2), *Československý statistický věstník* 2:3 (February 1921):135–136.

13. David Warren Paul and Owen V. Johnson make convincing cases for the vitality of Slovak national awareness before 1918. See Owen V. Johnson, *Slovakia, 1918–1938: Education and the Making of a Nation* (New York: Columbia University Press, 1985), pp. 15–49; and David Warren Paul, "Slovak Nationalism and the Hungarian State,

1870–1910," in Paul Brass, ed., *Ethnic Groups and the State* (London: Croom Helm, 1985), pp. 115–159.

14. See Archie Brown and Gordon Wightman, "Czechoslovak Revival and Retreat," in Archie Brown and Jack Gray, eds., *Political Culture and Political Change in Communist States* (New York: Holmes & Meier, 1977), pp. 159–196.

15. Findings of the January 1991 survey conducted by the Prague Institute of Social and Political Sciences, cited in "Svejk after Slovakia: Czech National Identity Now," *East European Reporter* 5:5 (September-October 1992):14.

16. There are some interesting discussions of this issue in Norman Stone and Eduard Strouhal, eds., *Czechoslovakia: Crossroads and Crises, 1918–1988* (New York: St. Martin's Press, 1989).

17. See Arend Lijphart, *Democracies: Patterns of Majoritarian and Consensus Government in Twenty-one Countries* (New Haven: Yale University Press, 1984).

18. Philip Longworth, *The Making of Eastern Europe* (New York: St. Martin's Press, 1994), p. 73.

19. Joseph Rothschild, *East Central Europe Between the Two World Wars* (Seattle: University of Washington Press, 1974), pp. 86–87. See also Zora B. Pryor, "Czechoslovak Economic Development in the Interwar Period," in Mamatey and Luža, eds., *A History of the Czechoslovak Republic*, pp. 188–215.

20. Comparative economic indicators are from B. R. Mitchell, ed., *European Historical Statistics, 1750–1970* (New York: Columbia University Press, 1978), p. 180.

21. Samuel P. Huntington, *The Third Wave: Democratization in the Late Twentieth Century* (Norman: University of Oklahoma Press, 1991), pp. 59–60.

22. Barrington Moore, Jr., *Social Origins of Dictatorship and Democracy* (Boston: Beacon Press, 1968).

23. Zora B. Pryor, "Czechoslovak Economic Development in the Interwar Period," in Mamatey and Luža, eds., *A History of the Czechoslovak Republic*, p. 213.

24. See Leff, *National Conflict in Czechoslovakia*, pp. 278–279.

25. While minority status was protected by international treaty in some of the East European successor states, the Czechoslovak government was internationally responsible only for its tiny Rusyn minority in eastern Slovakia and Subcarpathian Ruthenia. In any case, the international legal constraints on the treatment of minorities were widely ignored by the contracting states in the interwar period, on the grounds that they represented an infringement of sovereignty.

26. Discussion of the relations between Nazi Germany and the Sudeten Germans may be found in J. W. Bruegel, "The Germans in Pre-War Czechoslovakia," in Mamatey and Luža, *A History of the Czechoslovak Republic*, pp. 167–187.

27. Cited in František Janáček, "Poznámky k hodnocená Čechoslovakismu v odboji," in Jaroslav Cesar and Zdenek Snitil, eds., *Československá revoluce 1944–1948* (Prague: Academia, 1979), p. 78.

28. Štefan Osuský, *Beneš and Slovakia* (Middletown, Pa.: Jednota Press, 1943), p. 296.

29. See Piotr Wandycz, *The Twilight of France's Eastern Alliances, 1926–1936* (Princeton: Princeton University Press, 1988); and Piotr Wandycz, "Foreign Policy of Edvard Beneš," in Mamatey and Luža, *A History of the Czechoslovak Republic*, pp. 216–238.

30. See Radomír Luža, *The Transfer of the Sudeten Germans: A Study of Czech-German Relations, 1933–1962* (New York: New York University Press, 1964).

2

CZECHOSLOVAKIA UNDER COMMUNISM

The Czechoslovakia that succumbed to communist rule in 1948 was not the Czechoslovakia of 1938. It was ethnically more homogeneous, with Czechs and Slovaks making up over 90 percent of the population. And it was, for the first time, organized in a way that gave partial recognition to Slovak national distinctiveness. The ban on collaborationist political parties extended to the previously dominant Agrarians, so that politics was something of a clean slate as well. Since this second attempt to establish a democratic system lasted only three years, from 1945 to 1948, it is too brief to be intensively analyzed here. Our focus will be on the ways in which the postwar period paved the way to the communist seizure of power and the consequences of that "revolution."

While the single most important element of Soviet dominance of Eastern Europe was its initial military occupation and the continuing threat of intervention, it would be highly misleading to limit explanation of the communist seizure of power in the region merely to its coercive aspects. This is particularly true of Czechoslovakia. In most of the region, communist parties were illegal, underground organizations during the interwar period; the Czechoslovak Communist Party (KSČ), although closely monitored and constrained, never lost legal standing to mobilize and contest parliamentary elections. Indeed, the party consistently won over 10 percent of the vote and seated a sizable parliamentary delegation all the way through the Munich crisis of 1938; the party went underground only as a consequence of German occupation. Despite the repeated decapitation of its leadership through execution and imprisonment during the Nazi period, the KSČ was therefore an existing force in the political landscape even before gaining the advantages of Soviet "liberation" of the region.

MAP 2.1   The boundaries of Czechoslovakia after World War II

It is often said that communists have never won a free election. That depends on how strict one's standards are. In the free elections of 1946, the Czechoslovak Communist Party was the single largest winner in a multiparty field, garnering 43 percent of the votes in Bohemia, 35 percent in Moravia, and 30 percent in Slovakia,[1] a much larger share of the vote than any interwar party had attained after 1920. This strong showing won them the right to major cabinet positions— and the prime ministership for KSČ leader Klement Gottwald. In no other country in the region did the communists fare this well, often even in rigged elections.

Two things contributed to the communist appeal. One was the willingness of the so-called bourgeois parties to recognize the legitimacy of Soviet interests in the region. Remember that for Czechoslovakia in particular, the lesson of Munich had been a Western sellout of its interests; the moral seemed to be that the Western powers would never make Central Europe a sufficient priority to protect small countries against German expansion. President Beneš's conviction that a good working relationship with the USSR was essential to Czechoslovak security persisted into the postwar period, despite the uncomfortable evidence of growing communist dominance in neighboring countries. Accordingly, communism as such was not fully demonized even by those who hardly wished to see its Soviet variant implanted domestically.

Moreover, it was not only Western intentions that were discredited at Munich. Retrospectively, Czechoslovakia's entire interwar democracy was tainted by what many saw as a failure of will and vision, a failure to achieve social cohesion and economic justice, and a rigidity and complexity of structure that was not truly democratic. As Jon Bloomfield noted, the wartime "resistance movement was not just concerned with the defeat of the Nazis. They were also fighting for a new social order after the war had been won."[2] To a significant extent, communists all over the continent benefited from communist participation in the antifascist resistance and from the popular search for a society and polity that would behave more justly to ordinary people than the interwar governments had; even in France and Italy, the communist parties registered strong postwar electoral gains. In Czechoslovakia, that sentiment was reinforced by the existence of a strong industrial base, and therefore a strong working-class base for communist efforts to articulate an alternative vision of what democracy could mean. The interwar Communist Party, after all, had been both legal and not particularly militant; the Communist International had to push it into a more orthodox stance more than once. The visionary hopes of a Marxist "people's democracy" were never shared by the whole electorate and would be cruelly disappointed in any case by the eventual workings of Czechoslovak communism on the Soviet model, but all the same, the communist seizure of power in Czechoslovakia was more than a coup.

It is often debated whether Stalin had a clear agenda of full conquest and control in Eastern Europe, whether he had envisioned from the outset that "friendly" governments in the region would ultimately have to conform to the Soviet model domestically.[3] The Soviet Union had been a Western ally against Hitler in World War II; Western participants at the Yalta summit of February 1945 were disinclined and unable to challenge the agenda of a powerful Soviet state that was still needed in the final assault on Hitler's Germany. They effectively relegated East Europe to the Soviet sphere of influence, settling for nebulous Soviet pledges to respect East European sovereignty and democratic institutions in what later became notorious as a Western sellout. It is unclear, however, that searching questions and stricter constraints would have affected Stalin's policy in any case. The Yalta accords were pieces of paper. At the time of Yalta, the Red Army already occupied most of Eastern Europe as it forged on to Berlin. A British diplomat at Yalta later argued, "[t]he suggestion that East Europe was carved up at Yalta is an illusion; it was carved up by the advance of Soviet armies into East Europe."[4]

The loose Soviet interpretation of its East European mandate—the steady communist inroads into the domestic politics of the region—soon outraged and alarmed Western observers. By March 1946, wartime British Prime Minister Winston Churchill made public his earlier warning of an "iron curtain" dividing Europe; President Harry S Truman's desire to deter any further expansion of the Soviet sphere of influence led to a multipronged initiative. The 1947 Truman Doctrine pledged open-ended U.S. support to "free peoples who are resisting subjugation by armed minorities or by outside pressures," and the Marshall Plan was implemented in support of European economic recovery, contributing to both the political and the economic stabilization of Europe—not incidentally bolstering the participating countries against communist influence. The pattern of Western and Soviet response and counterresponse makes it more difficult to differentiate Stalin's initial program for East Europe from his subsequent actions. The heavily debated question of his intentions therefore cannot be resolved here, but what is important is that there was a period of transitional ambiguity in the politics of many of the eventual Soviet satellites (the coalitions of communist and noncommunist parties, for example) that for a time left Czechoslovakia's ultimate fate uncertain. The pressure of Soviet influence on internal Czechoslovak politics was already substantial in the mid-1940s, but only in 1948 would the crisis occur that pulled the country definitively into the Soviet bloc, the last East European country to be subordinated.

By early 1948, the noncommunist parties in Czechoslovakia had grown increasingly sensitive to the behavior of their communist coalition partners. Elections loomed in the early summer, and no one was certain what the outcome might be, although the communists stood to lose substantial ground. It was the noncommunists who moved to force a showdown, with a lack of cohesion that goes a long way toward explaining the eventual outcome. The noncommunists resolved to bring down the government and force new elections by the time-honored expedient of threatening collective resignation from the coalition cabinet unless communists agreed to desist from abuse of police and security forces. It was expected that the communists would be unable to govern alone as a minority. President Beneš had agreed to back up the challenge. However, disastrous confusion ensued. When Gottwald failed to respond, the cabinet ministers resigned. No one had secured the agreement of the left-wing Social Democrats or the nonparty ministers to this tactic; a parliamentary majority remained in place.

With a legal majority behind it, the KSČ issued a call for the continued pursuit of the government program, including land reform and tax relief for farmers, a new national insurance law, and other popular reforms. The noncommunist parties now faced a legal government pressing for further socioeconomic change, and mass mobilization as well. Scheduled agricultural and workers' council congresses were held early, supporting the communist-led government; massive public rallies did the same. The right had no comparable mobilizational resources, despite its own popular base. The government organized and armed worker militia groups, whereas the opposition had no capacity to resort to force. Helplessly, the president acquiesced in Gottwald's ultimatum, accepted the resignations of the noncommunist ministers, and left the communists in control of the government.

This scenario is worth attention because it was not merely a coup; the street rallies and worker/farmer resolutions in support of the government, whether they represented a majority of the population or not, did demonstrate a core of popular support for the communists. The crisis would hereafter be officially referred to as the "Glorious February Revolution," not a coup d'état.[5] Even as late as 1989, public opinion polls showed that there was a significant minority of the population who rejected communist rule as it developed in practice but who continued to feel that the aims of the February revolution were worthy and refused to disown it.

Even after massive purges had disillusioned many of the original true believers, therefore, the communist regime continued to draw support from some of the population and nonresistance from much of it. Part of this response was a legacy of the earlier period, part came from a lack of alternatives, and—importantly—part came from the fact than any established regime creates its own clientele. Even before 1948, German property seized after the deportations could be parceled out to the faithful: The Ministry of Agriculture was in communist hands. In all socialist states after the communist seizure of power, the party's following was bolstered by the initial opening of the opportunity structure to people who had never before had a chance for social mobility. Peasants' sons could become generals in the Czechoslovak army; workers' sons could get an education in party schools and rise to political prominence. The revolution needed new expertise and was ideologically and politically prepared to capitalize on the loyalties of those it could elevate to unexpectedly high status. The payoff was not always effective leadership; by the 1960s, Czechoslovaks thought themselves governed by a "conspiracy of the below average." But an authoritarian state with a public sector much larger than those of the West has rewards as well as punishments to dole out and consequently could assure that a core group of the public would be dependent on the regime for advancement they could not otherwise have achieved. Many others, of course, lost their property and even their freedom or were forced into exile. But there were winners as well as losers in the communist takeover.

As in Yugoslavia, then, the Czechoslovak communists had a certain amount of autonomous support at the outset. The comparison ends there, however, for the newly minted Czechoslovak People's Republic mounted no dramatic challenge to conformity with Soviet expectations. Even the reform experiment of 1968, when it came, was a cautious and carefully justified attempt both to please the public and to avoid panicking the Soviet Union. It was in any case the exception to a long record of leadership subservience to the Soviet model.

Through political and economic inflexibility, the KSČ proceeded to squander the advantages that its initial popular base might have given it. Almost immediately after the February takeover, the leadership began to imprison its "bourgeois" foes by the thousands; by 1950, top party leaders themselves were on trial in an incomprehensibly cannibalistic purge of the party itself.[6] Particular targets were communists who had spent the war in the West, Jews in the party's leadership, and Slovak "bourgeois nationalists." This latter group, which included future party leader Gustav Husák, is particularly worth noticing. The Slovak victims of the purges had led the home front communist resistance during the war; the central party leadership saw them as too independent in their pursuit of Slovak interests. They were accused of isolating themselves from Czech culture. Understandably, these trials appeared to the Slovaks as a betrayal of the promises of equality given in 1945, and they contributed greatly to the Slovak sense that Czech communists were just as bad as Czech democrats when it came to the Slovak question.[7]

More generally, the purges eliminated anyone suspected of insufficient subservience to the Soviet model. Not until the late 1960s did the leadership attempt political renewal, and then only after Antonín Novotný, Gottwald's successor, was ousted. In the meantime, the party established a rigid political control of state and economic institutions on the Soviet model. The economic record of the regime, which humbled one of the world's most advanced industrial economies, is the subject of the following section.

Communist Economics:
The Inappropriateness of the Soviet Model

The irony of Soviet hegemony in Eastern Europe and the imposition of the Soviet model there was that the dominant Soviet power was actually less economically developed and advanced than many of its satellites, East Germany and Czechoslovakia in particular. Although the USSR may not have been a "Third World country with rockets," as it was often described, its control of Eastern Europe was based primarily on size and military strength rather than technological superiority. This was very clear in trade relations, where its client states provided the USSR with manufactured goods and the Soviet Union reciprocated with raw materials (especially oil and natural gas). This is just the opposite of what might be expected from an imperial power and its tributaries.

It has frequently been noted that the imposition of the Soviet economic model on Eastern Europe was particularly unfortunate for the more developed states.[8] Czechoslovakia's first Five-Year Plan has been described as a slavish imitation of the Soviet plan, right down to the provision of production targets for oceangoing ships (a dubious asset for a landlocked country). Regardless of the individual details, the larger truth is indisputable—the advanced industrial economy of Czechoslovakia was indeed forced into conformity with the Soviet blueprint for overcoming an economic backwardness that did not exist in the case of Czechoslovakia. Scholars of the region can credibly argue that the Soviet emphasis on heavy industry may indeed have stimulated economic growth in a peasant economy such as that of Bulgaria (although even in such cases, it may well be that alternative capitalist models might have produced the same or better results). But for Czechoslovakia, the Soviet model was a significant impediment. In time, it became a source of national humiliation for a formerly world-class economy.

Moreover, the communist economy of Czechoslovakia, of course, shared the general shortcomings of the Stalinist model. These systems were, as the economists put it, "deficit economies" plagued by chronic shortages that persisted, in spite of regime efforts, in the absence of a market mechanism or profit incentives. Even though a communist enterprise might be organized for production in a manner similar to a capitalist one, it does not act like a capitalist enterprise in other respects. Periodically, a communist regime would invest in the full production machinery of a Western enterprise, calling in a Western firm to build a so-called "turnkey" plant from the ground up to produce goods according to Western technology. But these technology transplants did not operate in the East as they did in the West. Productivity would be one-third to one-half lower; this was inevitable because worker discipline was lax ("We pretend to work and they pretend to pay us," went the saying) and maintenance and quality control poor. The basic measure of success in the administered economy was meeting quantitative output targets. As long as you made the number of blouses, nails, or machinery required by the plan, quality was secondary. The recipient had no choice but to accept the product because there were no competitors in this monopoly environment. And if a firm went into red ink meeting the plan, the state carried the losses by subsidizing it. No firm went bankrupt; the banking system was little more than a conduit for channeling funds. The whole economy operated, as the celebrated Hungarian economist Janos Kornai said, under "soft budget constraints."[9]

Staggering under the weight of the planning bureaucracy, the Czechoslovak economy actually ground to a halt by the early 1960s, registering zero growth in 1962. Efforts to energize sagging economic growth through reform were an important part of the Prague Spring of 1968, but the Soviet invasion curtailed the continuation of any major economic experiments. The heroic rhetoric of storming the industrial heights gave way to a more sober discussion of "actually existing socialism," a phrase that consigned utopian goals—and healthy economic growth—further and further into the future. Though basic wants were satisfied—and the people of Czechoslovakia certainly had a higher per capita income than any other bloc country save East Germany—the country's economic base began to corrode through underinvestment in all the important long-term areas: education, health, infrastructure, and capital plant.

The economy was basically still operating according to the logic of the original nineteenth-century industrial revolution, with a base in the so-called "smoke stack" heavy industries. Compared to capitalist economies at a similar level of economic development, Czechoslovakia and other socialist states had proportionately more blue-collar workers employed in factories, and proportionately fewer white-collar workers in service industries. This was symptomatic of the fact that the postindustrial scientific and technological revolution, which had such a profound impact on the West after World War II, was leaving the socialist states behind. In modern capitalist industrial states, the service sectors expanded rapidly, not only to meet consumer demand but also in response to the growing role of technical knowledge as a marketable commodity.

What was particularly absent in socialist states like Czechoslovakia was an expanding white-collar sector based on computer technology. The information revolution was doubly inhibited in communist countries. First, it was ideologically suspect; widespread dissemination of new electronic information systems threatened to undermine the regime's monopoly on information. Knowledge truly is power. The idea of a new informational environment in which ordinary citizens could photocopy freely upset every party bureaucrat; photocopying machines were not widely available, and access to those in use was carefully guarded. Personal computers were an even worse nightmare for the bureaucrats.[10] The second obstacle to the extensive utilization of computer-based economic advancement was the general socialist weakness in technological innovation. Computer technology was not only highly sophisticated but also rapidly changing. The older industrial technologies often had decades of utility before obsolescence; this was a timescale that even a weakly innovative economy could cope with. Computer technologies, however, can become outdated in a few years. In short, the scientific and technological revolution accelerated the pace of change beyond the capacity of the socialist economy to adapt and threatened to perpetuate an ever widening gap between East and West. The whole communist bloc made serious efforts to confront this problem, all of them largely unavailing.

As elsewhere in the region, an additional obstacle to economic performance was the growing corruption that surrounded the dealings of daily economic life. Graft permeated the system from top to bottom in a network of personal favors and bribery. A low-salaried sales clerk withheld the store's goods to exchange for something else that was useful. A mechanic used the state's automotive parts to do repairs on the side. This behavior was so systematic that it became known as the "second" or "gray" economy; it was regarded as necessary to compensate for the rigidities of the official economic system. The watchword was "He who does not steal from the state steals from his family"; the pilfering of state property was regarded as stealing from no one in particular, and in consequence the supply shortages were only intensified. The guilt of ordinary people was assuaged because the corruption and special privileges of the leaders were even greater. As former dissident Miroslav Kusý said, "Where leading members of the nomenklatura stole from the nation wholesale, many ordinary citizens stole retail."[11]

Why did the public put up with this system for so long? Part of the answer, of course, is that they had no choice: Soviet intervention could, and did, follow swiftly in response to any attempted jailbreak. But it is also important to recognize that the regime had struck a tacit bargain with its population, a bargain that in some communist countries has been called a "social contract" or even "goulash communism." The regime in effect offered concessions to consumer needs and economic security in exchange for political peace and quiet. Ordinary people were encouraged to accumulate a modest supply of consumer goods and live their own lives, provided they did not challenge the political status quo.

The symbol of the regime bargain, and of the public's "inner emigration," was the country cottage. These were not the luxury dachas of the Soviet elite but rather small wooden structures into which three generations of family members could be crammed during the weekends, sleeping on beds and couches and floors. By the late 1980s, Czechoslovakia ranked second in the world in the number of summer cottages per capita; as much as 80 percent of the population had access to a cottage through their extended families. The usually modest dwelling represented a retreat from the negatives of communist life, away from urban pollution—a small personal island. Building and improving, gardening, beekeeping—all this was as important as relaxation there; it was a place to invest personal energy and feel a sense of accomplishment. As the saying went, a Czech's first job is his cottage, and his second one is the job where he makes the salary to pay for the cottage. And so the regime permitted millions of citizens to skip out on that "second job" on Thursdays to spend long weekends in their "real" homes. Allowing the country cottage was a regime concession to popular needs, a concession that had the political virtue of channeling alienation in a "constructive" and *nonpolitical* direction.

The rest of the bargain was economic security. Prices were held constant, and the most sensitive costs of living, such as rent, food, and energy, were heavily subsidized. Employment was guaranteed, indeed even mandatory;[12] even a modest income is more valuable when it comes with virtually total job security. An enterprise that was eternally safe from bankruptcy could afford to bargain for a large, even an unnecessarily large, workforce. The system could therefore deliver full employment year after year; no traditional communist economy had an unemployment compensation system in place, because it simply was not needed. Many workers were certainly underemployed, but this was not a real hardship. There were few incentives to work hard except when a plant deadline loomed, and no incentive at all to work efficiently. Workers could take long breaks to go shopping and absenteeism was rife, and yet at the end of the pay period, the check would be there.

The Czechoslovak constitution formally recognized this guarantee of full employment. In addition to the standard U.S. guarantees of civil or political rights that it included (but frequently ignored), the document incorporated a whole range of economic rights—to a job, to free health care, to extensive maternity leave, and so forth. The job might be bad, and the health care worse, but the safety net was there. A study of communist welfare state benefits concluded that, compared to states at a similar level of economic development, socialist systems delivered higher benefits, at lower direct costs, to workers.[13] This does not at all mean that ordinary people were better off under communism than under possible alternatives. Judging from its pre-communist performance, Czechoslovakia would almost certainly have been far more economically advanced had it retained its interwar capitalist market economy. Still, there was a cushion against the kind of desperation that might have inspired revolt. Blue-collar workers were treated very carefully in Czechoslovakia; one sign of this was the relatively small differential between working-class wages and those of professionally educated employees (that gap widened considerably after communism ended). Even after the collapse of the regime, the scope and solidity of economic guarantees under the old system remained very popular.

One significant feature of the communist economic policy remained fairly constant from the outset. Whereas the interwar Republic had not emphasized economic investment in Slovakia as a strategy of equalization with the Czech lands, the communist government saw this omission as a primary cause of previous national tension. Party ideologists criticized the interwar approach because its "theoretical starting point for the resolution of the national question was that national relations were purely political, cultural or religious."[14] The party sought to rectify that perceived mistake with a remedial program of investment in Slovakia. To blame national tensions on economic exploitation was quite orthodox Marxist analysis, which the communist leaders seemed to take seriously. While Slovak *political* power was curbed, Slovakia's *economy* was bolstered. Czech economists later estimated that about 10 percent more investment was directed to Slovakia than to the Czech lands per unit increase of output during the communist period, and differentials in educational, health, and culture spending were possibly even greater.[15] Western scholars concurred that the communist state had made progress in closing the developmental gap.[16] According to official statistics, Slovak per capita income had grown from 68 percent of the Czech level in 1953 to 92 percent in 1990 (the communist government had announced the gap largely closed several years before).[17]

After 1989, Czechs and Slovaks expressed contradictory views of the equity and results of this sustained investment effort. Echoing the complaints of the interwar Republic, many Czechs argued that "the Czech republic has 'lost out' through the common state" because of the state's tilted investment flows and budgetary patterns.[18] Slovaks saw themselves as the losers, through an inappropriate development policy designed more to suit the needs of the bloc than the needs of the Slovaks, and controlled from Prague into the bargain. In the lone reform period of 1968, Slovak politicians tried to gain some independent economic policymaking authority, but this effort was crushed and could only be revived after the Velvet Revolution.[19] In any case, the Slovak critique was prophetic. Whatever its interim results, this policy was booby-trapped in certain important respects. Slovak development patterns, and in particular its dependence on bloc trade, would later make Slovakia extremely vulnerable to the trade collapse that followed communist regime collapse after 1989. Both Slovakia's economic vulnerability and the general economic stagnation were troublesome legacies in the postcommunist period.

Communist Politics

The communist constitution was, as written, a fairly exemplary democratic document promising a broad range of rights and providing for elected legislatures and parliamentary government. Czechoslovakia was described as a "people's democracy" until 1960, when the party leadership was sufficiently confident of its consolidated position to be the first in the bloc to announce that the country qualified as a socialist state. It would thereafter be known as the Czechoslovak Socialist Republic (ČSSR). The primary constitutional clue that this was a very circumscribed definition of democracy was encoded in Article 4, which granted the Communist Party a "leading role" in politics. In practice this clause, a variant of which appeared in every communist constitution, meant that the important political decisions were made by the top organs of the KSČ rather than by formal government structures. Control was maintained through a network of party organizations in every major government bureaucracy and economic enterprise and through the staffing of all key politically sensitive positions with party members. This staffing policy was known as the nomenklatura system; references to the nomenklatura were references to the ruling class.

To get ahead in this system, political reliability and the right "class" credentials were at least as important as competence. One of the most famous movies of the liberalization period of the 1960s was a satire entitled *The Firemen's Ball*, directed by Miloš Forman, who later made a successful career in the West. The story line followed a day in the life of a local fire brigade during its incompetent efforts to honor the emeritus fire chief. The event was a fiasco; the invited guests stole all the lottery prizes when the lights went out (a thinly veiled commentary on the socialist economy?), the attempt to organize a beauty contest degenerated into farce as the reluctant contestants fled (a commentary on popular enthusiasm for socialism?), and the affair finally broke up when a real fire broke out. The brigade could only watch helplessly as fire consumed the dwelling of an elderly retiree. "Turn around and don't look," was the best advice they could offer to the bereaved gentleman. The guests at the celebration responded to the old man's plight by taking up a collection—he is then presented with a hatful of now-worthless lottery tickets! As symbolized by the fire brigade, Czechoslovakia's communists could deliver neither security nor prosperity. In Western distribution, the film is introduced by Forman himself, who solemnly assures us that this is just what it seems—a film about firemen. But he is metaphorically winking at the audience when he says this. Undoubtedly, domestic Czech audiences would understand the political allegory. This film is interesting above all for its view of the communist political leadership. The members of the fire brigade are not particularly evil or menacing; rather, they are bumbling incompetents who have no control over events and are unable either to deliver the prizes or convince the public to participate in the evening's events as planned. This is what the socialist experiment seemed to have come to by the mid-1960s.

The Prague Spring

Throughout the life of the communist regime, only one serious and sustained effort was made to come to terms with the country's economic and political problems. This reform era, known as the Prague Spring, lasted about eight months, from January 1968 to August 21, 1968, starting with the ouster of longtime party leader Antonín Novotný and ending with the Warsaw Pact invasion of Czechoslovakia by its socialist "allies."[20]

The reform effort had a long gestation period, as discontent mounted even inside the party against the "conspiracy of the below average." While experts debated what to do behind closed doors, the cultural elite became increasingly restless and willing to challenge government restrictions. Novotný's efforts to bolster his position with a show of Soviet support fell flat (Soviet leader Leonid I. Brezhnev reportedly ended an emergency visit to Czechoslovakia in December 1967 by washing his hands of the succession crisis), and Novotný was succeeded as party first secretary by the younger Slovak Communist Party (KSS) leader Alexander Dubček.

Nothing in Dubček's biography indicated that he would become a crusader for reform, the embodiment of "socialism with a human face." On the contrary, his childhood in the Soviet Union and a bureaucratic career in the party apparatus sound like a formula for conformity to the communist system. Dubček was, however, more flexible than his résumé, and he had behind him not insubstantial support from important elements of the party who had given years of thought to how to revitalize politics and economics when the opportunity arose.[21] Some criticized him for indecisiveness, but he was above all a consensus-maker, flexible enough to be willing to spearhead change and to mediate among the members of a politburo divided among reformers, moderates, and dogmatists. His credentials probably made him acceptable to the Soviet leadership; among other things, he spoke Russian well without a translator. It was too soon for anyone to realize that some of the goals of the Prague Spring did not translate into Russian at all!

The goals of the 1960s were not those of the later Velvet Revolution; these reform communists are better compared to Mikhail Gorbachev and other Soviet reform Communists a generation later (see Box 2.1). Dubček and the reform wing of the KSČ envisaged a renewed system in which the Communist Party would retain its leading role, but this time by *earning* it in responding to popular needs and demands.

The key elements of the reform were promulgated in April 1968 in the party's new Action Program.[22] This document pledged economic decentralization and reform to revitalize growth, a federal solution to Slovak dissatisfaction with centralized government, and much greater openness of public discussion, so that needs could be identified and corrective measures taken. Underlying these programmatic elements was the attempt to institutionalize the capacity for adaptive response to pending problems, above all by transforming the tightly controlled Leninist party model into a more flexible forum for responding to societal interests and demands. There was, however, no mention of competitive multiparty elections or privatization of enterprise, pledges that were central to the events of 1989. The party of 1968 that made even the more limited pledges, however, was still divided and in need of reconstruction to phase out unrepentant hard-liners.

BOX 2.1
The Prague Spring and Perestroika

During the Soviet heyday of perestroika and glasnost, Gorbachev's attempts to revitalize socialism were frequently compared with the Prague Spring. Some Soviet leaders even acknowledged the similarity. The comparison is close, but not exact. Gorbachev's *glasnost*—the greater freedom to discuss societal problems—was for some years limited to those problems the government wished to address. By contrast, the first important step of the Prague Spring was a virtually complete abolition of censorship; the only major topic that remained taboo was the relationship with the Soviet Union, a subject that was too dangerously sensitive to risk incurring Soviet wrath. *Politically,* the Czechoslovak reformers were not planning to permit competitive multiparty elections; this was not an element of the original perestroika plan, either. Gorbachev only resorted to the opening of the Soviet political system more than three and a half years after he had gained power; by then, he had abandoned the hope of gaining his economic reforms without using more open political competition to put pressure on the conservative holdouts against reform in the Soviet party and government bureaucracy. The Prague Spring *economic program* was similar to Soviet perestroika in its aim for a "socialist market," a system in which decisionmaking authority would be decentralized to individual firms that could make their own decisions about production, investment, and supply. Reformers hoped that these firms, once released from the constraints of a central plan, would be more efficient and profitable and more responsive to public needs. This system was still "socialist" because the individual firms would remain under state ownership, but they would behave in response to supply and demand more in the ways that capitalist markets do. To the end, Gorbachev did not see full-scale privatization as a desirable option for the USSR. The comparison between the Soviet reforms of the 1980s and the Prague Spring is therefore not perfect, but the family resemblance is very strong. That raises an interesting question. In Gorbachev's USSR, the liberalization experiments eventually spun out of control, destroying the party's monopoly of power and pushing the system toward more radical experiments in democratization and capitalism. Many later scholars of the Prague Spring have suggested that Dubček's reforms might have met the same fate if the invasion had not halted the Czechoslovak domestic experiments. In that sense, the biggest difference between perestroika and the Prague Spring may have been the identity of the reformers. Soviet reformers faced no large external power to halt reform experiments, as Czechoslovakia did. The logic—or partial logic—of Soviet perestroika was allowed to play itself out.

That revitalization process was planned to occur at the Fourteenth Party Congress scheduled for September 1968. But in the interim, popular pressure for reform was unleashed with the abolition of media censorship in March 1968, and the party gave tacit permission for the formation of unofficial groups to express citizen demands. Through it all, the reform leadership gave repeated assurances to Moscow that socialism was alive and well, and that Prague would remain loyal to the international socialist community and to Soviet-Czechoslovak friendship.

What the Prague Spring might have accomplished if it had run its course is difficult to project, because mounting Soviet concern over this unorthodox experiment eventually culminated in an intervention by the neighboring bloc countries. What threat did the Soviet Union see in this effort to promote "socialism with a human face" that necessitated its suppression by force? For one thing, the Prague Spring was a destabilizing example to citizens in neighboring communist countries, a virus that might spread and undermine control. East German leaders were particularly nervous about this "infection of liberalism," and neighboring Poland was undergoing one of its own periodic crises in 1968, a confrontation between the regime and a generation of university students who would later contribute intellectual force to the Solidarity movement. Worst of all, the response of some Russian and Ukrainian intellectuals to the ideas of the Prague Spring suggested that the reform effort might even contaminate the Soviet Union itself.[23]

Then, too, there was the question of where the Czechoslovak reform experiment would end. The abolition of censorship had unleashed the voices of noncommunists and anticommunists, voices that were dissatisfied with the carefully circumscribed limits of the reform program. The open climate spawned a host of informal noncommunist groups such as the Club of Engaged Non-Partisans (KAN) that might subsequently have challenged communist power. The young Writers Union activist, playwright, and future Czechoslovak president Václav Havel, even published an article contemplating the establishment of an opposition party.[24]

The Soviet leadership was especially horrified by a document published in June 1968, entitled "Two Thousand Words."[25] Its authors characterized the reform to date as "not contributing any very new things" and called for grassroots efforts to push the revitalization further. Although the signatories of this appeal urged support for the communist reformers as the only viable option under the circumstances, the Soviet media response branded the document as "counterrevolutionary" and "an overt attack on the socialist system." The Soviet media drew ominous parallels between contemporary Czechoslovakia and Hungary in 1956, where the Soviet Union had previously intervened.[26] Clearly, these commentaries were a warning that the Soviet leadership saw the Prague Spring as spinning out of control, a warning to the reform communists to watch their step. Actually, Soviet fears may not have been paranoid. Whatever Dubček's intentions, political scientists who study transitions to democracy see them as frequently triggered by a liberalization effort that got out of hand and developed its own momentum.[27] Since this was a completely unacceptable outcome for Czechoslovakia's communist neighbors, the decision to crush "socialism with a human face" may not have been as senseless as it might appear. On the other hand, the invasion did crush any possibility of generating a successful response to the regionwide problem of reengineering the existing communist framework into one with the institutional capacity to meet its political and economic challenges.

Repeated summits with bloc leaders gave further warning that intervention might halt the reform experiment. Still, Dubček apparently refused to believe that his own socialist credentials and convictions, and the stated revitalization goals of the movement, would be so flagrantly disregarded. When the news of the invasion reached him on the night of August 20, 1968, he found it incredible that something so "contrary to my deepest idea of the value system I thought governed the relationships between socialist countries" could have occurred. In his memoirs, Dubček admits that his estimate of Soviet intentions had been proven wrong and that his reasoning had been naive. All that remained was the effort to limit damage. Dubček ordered the army not to resist—"military resistance was impossible anyway, because our defenses were directed toward the western border." The whole leadership was flown to Moscow, where they mounted a futile effort to negotiate with superior Soviet power.[28]

Because the invasion was so unpopular, even the hard-liners who had schemed to restore the previous order did not dare associate their names with the invaders. Moscow was forced to reinstall most of the reform leadership, but this was an empty victory that amounted to forcing the architects of the Prague Spring to preside over the gradual destruction of virtually all important elements of the reform program. The most significant exception, the federalization of the state in accordance with the KSČ Action Program, was a divisive one, as we will see, since it was regarded as a Slovak rather than a statewide priority.

In six months, the initial phase of what became known as "normalization" was essentially complete. The Soviet leadership seized on the excessive "anti-Soviet" celebrations that followed Czechoslovakia's victory over the Soviet Union in the world ice hockey championships in March 1969 as an excuse to force Dubček's resignation (Dubček himself even speculated about the possibility that the Soviet hockey team was "advised" to lose in order to generate the provocative victory celebration). By then, any excuse would suffice. Dubček was replaced by another Slovak, Gustav Husák, who the Soviet leadership may have felt would be accepted by Slovaks as a compatriot and by Czechs because he had been victimized in the purges of the 1950s. Reform communists had worked hard to rehabilitate him and the other purge victims and might trust him. Dissidents would later ruefully comment that they had suffered first "for Husák" and then "under Husák," since his rehabilitation had given him a springboard to exercise repressive power over Czechoslovakia for more than twenty years after the Prague Spring.

The Prague Spring and its brutal suppression delivered several messages, both to Czechs and Slovaks, and to citizens of the bloc as a whole. The architects of reform, who had tried so hard to construct an "intervention-proof" program—one that would not arouse Soviet alarm—by maintenance of the party's leading role and adherence to bloc foreign policy, could now only conclude that no reform effort serious enough to be effective would be tolerated by the Soviet Union. If reform within a socialist framework was therefore impossible, if there could be no such thing as "socialism with a human face," East European dissidents would subsequently reason, then there was no value in limiting one's intellectual imagination to socialist alternatives. In fact, before 1968, even some, like future dissident and post-1989 foreign minister Jiří Dienstbier, who hoped for a multiparty, democratic Czechoslovakia, had joined the KSČ as the only possible channel of national revitalization. August 21, 1968, he reported later, was "the definitive endpoint to all illusion."[29]

Increasingly, the dissidents of the region would investigate broader horizons beyond the party; in the 1970s and 1980s, interest in European and Central European ideas burgeoned in a renewed insistence that, although "kidnapped, displaced and brainwashed" by the Soviet Union, East Europe was still fundamentally a tragically separated part of Western culture and identity.[30] From this logic it followed that the Stalinist model, and even the variants of post-Stalinist socialism, could never be an appropriate expression of regional needs and values.

The opposition movements of the region increasingly reflected this understanding. There was stunned and demoralized political silence in Czechoslovakia in the years immediately following the invasion and normalization. However, the mid-1970s saw a regrouping of dissident efforts. An opposition that had originally been comprised largely of Prague Spring socialist reformers, now expelled or resigned from the party, took on a broader perspective with the emergence of Charter 77. This loosely organized and heterogeneous movement embraced ex-communists and anticommunists, Christian dissidents and secular humanists. Its credo was the insistence that Czechoslovakia adhere to the human rights commitments that the communist government had rather cynically signed when it approved the Helsinki Accord of 1975. The revived opposition, then, shifted its focus from the reform of socialism to "dreaming about Europe," as Dienstbier put it. As quixotic and hopeless as this seemed, it did mark an active intellectual engagement with the democratic ideas and purposes that would be central to the revolution of 1989, when the dissidents of the 1970s and 1980s would provide leadership for the Velvet Revolution.

The dissidents were hardly universal popular heroes, however. They were a fairly narrowly based group of urban intellectuals, largely from the major cities of Prague, Brno, and Bratislava. The public only knew the most prominent of them, and even they were frequently seen as rocking the boat in a hopeless cause or as egoists who had their heads turned by the adulation of the West. Philosopher and Charter activist Ladislav Hejdánek summarized the atmosphere this way: "After forty years of a regime, it is not possible to deny the truth of the public's massive collaboration with the regime. . . . Most people here have a bad conscience. . . . They all knew that what we [the dissidents] said was correct, but they thought we were silly to say it so loudly."[31]

The regime made sure that the public knew which of the dissidents, for example, had nice cars because of their royalties from Western publications; official press coverage oscillated between vilification and silence on their activities; Rudolf Převratil of the International Journalism Institute in Prague argued that "propaganda campaigns in the official media helped substantially to isolate the dissidents from society and to create an atmosphere of fear and hostility toward them."[32] The government made equally sure that it would be very difficult to circulate their messages to a broader audience. The personal networks of the dissident community therefore remained isolated from the public in *samizdat*—an underground distribution network—substantially smaller than those in Poland and Hungary; dissidents were also, to a certain extent, geographically isolated from one another, since the state was particularly alert to discourage contacts between the largely Czech Charter 77 movement and the cluster of intellectual, environmental, and religious dissidents in Slovakia.[33]

The dissident community that coalesced around Charter 77 and other such initiatives was not under the illusion that their actions would prove immediately, or even eventually, effective in changing regime policies. At bottom, dissidence was an individual choice made for the survival of personal integrity, regardless of its efficacy. The dissident saw passive acceptance of the regime as complicity with those in power; each had come to a personal crisis of what was to be tolerated.[34]

Havel would later argue that under communism, no one was innocent. The regime could not have survived without the passive acceptance of the public. Yet dissidents did not expect that many would or could follow their lead; the costs were high, and they extended to one's whole family. Jan Urban, a Charter 77 activist and Civic Forum leader, is a case in point. As a sympathizer of the Prague Spring, he had lost his teaching job and spent years thereafter working variously as a stable hand, a general laborer, and a forklift driver. He was disgraced, but not beyond the pale, and by 1977 he was again teaching high school history and civics in Prague. Then came the circulation of Charter 77, and the Husák government, anxious to crush it, mobilized a countereffort; state employees were asked to sign a petition condemning the Charter (sight unseen—the text had not, of course, been published in the official media). Urban was among those called in to add his name to the signatories who chastised the Chartists as "plague disseminators" and "those who poisoned the wells." His own account of this personal crisis is representative of the way many felt "forced" to become dissidents; he refused to sign the petition.

> I defended myself by saying that it was immoral to protest against an unknown text. I was afraid to say that I knew some of the Charter people. Ten days after my refusal, . . . I was summoned to the Director's office where I was handed a piece of paper which informed me that I was to leave the school premises forthwith and not to return. Shortly after that, I was interrogated for the first time in my life. . . . In retrospect, I think that if they had been calmer, or more intelligent, tried to be a little more friendly. . . . what do I know? I could have been one of them. . . . They helped me by being so stupid. They made it so easy. The way they acted forced me to explode and the explosion blew me across to the other side of the barricade. One loses one's work and finds that it becomes, strangely, very easy.[35]

The dissident subculture did produce a "parallel information system," disseminating everything from policy reports to officially unsanctioned literary work. Unlike the relatively sophisticated Polish underground press, which had its own press agencies, newspapers, and even books (sometimes printed clandestinely at state printing houses), Czechoslovakia's opposition remained a "typewriter culture," reliant on carbon paper rather than personal computers, photocopying, or mimeographing. This difference is in part a reflection of greater controls in the ČSSR, but it also reflected the intent to conduct a direct dialogue with the regime rather than "widespread conspiratorial distribution of these materials to the public"; public circulation of unauthorized material was, of course, a criminal offense. So was unauthorized reproduction of materials by photocopying or mimeographing. The typewriter was presumed to be legal, and the policy reports and manifestos were addressed to the regime—such communications were also theoretically legal. If these documents were copied and circulated as well, so be it. That was a secondary concern.[36]

This approach to the expression of unauthorized views differs from the approach of Solidarity in Poland in more ways than the form of production. Solidarity was consciously building a "second society" aloof from the communist government; much of its underground activity was designed to ignore the government rather than to confront it. Although Charter 77 activists, too, spoke of a "parallel" society,[37] they pursued a somewhat different strategy; they were calling their own government's bluff, playing by the formal rules of what was legally acceptable. If there was no hope of getting a response, at least the repression of technically legal activity would unveil official hypocrisy. Charter 77's strategy, of course, left the dissidents more isolated than were those in Poland. But that relatively greater isolation may have been more a reason for choosing the strategy than its consequence. Before it was forced underground by martial law in 1981, after all, Solidarity had enjoyed a mass base larger than any that Czechs and Slovaks could ever hope to achieve.

However, the consequences of the Prague Spring were not only significant for the dissident community at home and in the region. Rather ironically, the Czechoslovak communist leadership was straitjacketed as well. After 1968, the Husák leadership undertook a rather thorough housecleaning; two years of "normalizing" purges of the party's ranks cleansed it of reformist thought. Whereas there had been considerable reformist energy lurking within the party waiting for its opportunity under the surface of the Novotný regime, the party of the 1970s and 1980s was a chastened and compliant group. Moreover, it lacked the options even of its communist neighbors in responding to mounting problems. The postreform leadership of 1969 essentially remained in power until the Velvet Revolution; any genuine leadership renewal might open the doors to a reconsideration of the past and reprisals against those responsible. The aging KSČ leaders doggedly clung to their posts to prevent just such an unpleasant result. Worse still, the long Prague winter after the spring was politically inhospitable to policy reform as well. Gorbachev, a new leader unimplicated in the policies of the

Brezhnev era, could castigate his predecessors for an "era of stagnation." It was too much to expect the Czechoslovak leadership to do the same, to critique and reform policies over which they themselves had presided and for which they bore the blame. The Gorbachev reform effort after 1985, which bore a strong resemblance to Dubček's "socialism with a human face," was therefore a severe trial for his Czechoslovak comrades.

Was Soviet perestroika a vindication of 1968? "Was Dubček wrong in substance or merely in timing? How big and reprehensible a sin is being prematurely correct?" Thus Otto Ulč succinctly presented the dilemma facing the Czechoslovak leadership before 1989.[38] Ensconced in power by the will of the Soviet invaders two decades before, Husák could hardly plunge with enthusiasm into a glasnost that would reopen to scrutiny the sensitive past or rally to Gorbachev's implicit disavowal of the Brezhnev Doctrine, which had justified the 1968 invasion. Nor could he readily explain why the Prague Spring was counterrevolutionary and Gorbachev's perestroika was true Leninist socialism. During Gorbachev's visit to Czechoslovakia in 1987, he was asked to respond to a political riddle: "What is the difference between perestroika and the Prague Spring?" The answer, given by a Soviet spokesman, was "Nineteen years"—a riddle, but hardly a joke to the KSČ.[39]

For both the rulers and the opposition, then, the Prague Spring's legacy defined Czechoslovak politics for the next generation. Fear of a reckoning made the leaders unduly rigid, even as the failure of the Prague Spring catalyzed a much more far-reaching critique of socialism than before. As long as the Soviet Union remained committed to the maintenance of communist governments in the region, however, and willing to back up that commitment with force, there was stalemate.

The National Question

The communists failed as thoroughly as their interwar predecessors to come to terms with the problem of Slovak identity. This failure was not for lack of attempted solutions. Rather, the Marxist approach—that is, the economic development program that was intended to assuage Slovak grievances—did not achieve its purpose. In fact, political scientists are by now quite accustomed to the previously heretical idea that economic development may nurture rather than subdue nationalist sentiment.

The political dimension of the assault on nationalism took a more tortuous path. The 1945 commitment to establish Czech-Slovak relations on the basis of "equal with equal" might sound like a federalization program, but it did not turn out to be one. Instead, Slovakia received its own institutional forum—a Slovak National Council and executive board and its own subsection of the KSČ, all subordinate to the center. There was no Czech National Council or Czech bureau of the Communist Party. This constitutional asymmetry comprised a much stronger base for Slovak leaders than they had possessed in the interwar Republic, but it was also rather ambiguous in its consequences. Slovaks came to feel that it threatened to produce a situation in which the Czechs viewed the statewide government as their own, while consigning Slovaks to the reservation. Czechs countered that Slovaks had their own institutions and were thus privileged in the communist state. In short, there was continuing friction over the balance of national power within Czechoslovakia.

As in the past, the issue of national representation tended to reemerge in periods of political crisis and reorientation, when politics as usual was suspended and a window of opportunity presented itself to renegotiate the constitutional compact. During the communist period, that critical juncture was the Prague Spring and its aftermath. Dubček was not only a reform communist but a Slovak as well. His protection of Slovak interests during the Novotný years as head of the KSS had been his springboard to leadership of the statewide Communist Party. Although a Slovak had been prime minister briefly in the 1930s and there had been submissive Slovak prime ministers in the communist period, this was in fact the first time in the postwar period that the key leadership post—the first secretaryship of the party—had been entrusted to a Slovak. Thus it is no coincidence that the party's Action Program adopted in April 1968 contained a pledge to resolve the Slovak question definitively by federalizing Czechoslovakia. Federation would mean an end to asymmetry, the establishment of parallel legislative and executive organs in two Czech and Slovak republics, and a statewide governmental framework structured to set limits to *majorisácia*, that is, the degree to which Czechs could outvote the smaller Slovak population on key policy and constitutional issues.

Working committees were still developing the constitutional mechanisms for federation at the time of the Soviet invasion; however, the new system was slated for promulgation in the fall, and after the intervention Slovaks successfully demanded that this reform at least go forward. Czechoslovakia thus officially became a federation on January 1, 1969. There are two broad clusters of reasons why the federalization of the state did not prove to be the long-awaited resolution of the national question. In the first place, the birth of the newly reconfigured state was mired in all the controversy and pain of the failed reform experiment. Czechs expressed doubt all through the reform months that the Slovaks were as committed to democratization as the Czechs; a challenging slogan of the time was "Democracy first, then federalization." These doubts in turn offended the Slovaks; indeed, they were inclined to read these reproaches as Czech disdain for Slovak priorities.[40] Tensions only heightened after the Soviet invasion. The Soviet Union, itself a federation after all, saw a definite advantage in tolerating the federalization of the Czechoslovak state. The implementation of federalism might contribute to "normalizing" the post-invasion situation in Slovakia, a comforting thought to Soviet leaders after they had miscalculated in assuming that it would be possible to find a domestic leadership that dared to take responsibility for "inviting" them in. "Divide and conquer" is an old strategy, no less effective for its frequent application through the ages. To a significant extent, the Soviet line of reasoning proved prescient. Czechs reacted to the federalization of the state as a benefit that Slovaks had extracted from the general tragedy, and they resented them for it. Further, in subsequent years, they would perceive Slovakia as having disproportionate influence in the revised system, although Slovak bureaucrats hardly swarmed into Prague to the extent that Czechs often believed. These shaky beginnings, obviously, did not underpin the federalization process with a basis for mutual trust.

Secondly, federalization did not satisfy Slovak aspirations, and it is not hard to see why. Within two years, the initial constitutional settlement had been gutted by divesting the two republics of the decentralized economic powers granted in the federation instruments. Even had this direct assault on the meaning of the federation never occurred, however, a communist federation—that is, a federation glued together by a "vanguard" Communist Party (a party that itself never federated after 1968)—still sets narrow limits on the autonomy of its subdivisions, whatever the constitution itself may say. No wonder then, that after the Velvet Revolution, the new political leaders launched a quest for an "authentic federation" to heal old wounds and establish a new basis for national cooperation.

The Foreign Policy of a Subordinate State

As in the First Republic, international context was important to the options of the state under communism. But in the communist era, the international context was so overwhelmingly important that it could be said that Czechoslovakia *had* no options. This was as true of foreign policy as it was of domestic policy. It would be no exaggeration to sum up the international relations of the ČSSR in a single sentence: Czechoslovakia's foreign policy revolved around the objectives and orientations of Soviet foreign policy for forty years. What, then, did this mean in practical terms for the country's military and economic interests and for the future?

In security terms, Czechoslovakia's interests were officially protected by the bloc military alliance, the Warsaw Treaty Organization (WTO), also known as the Warsaw Pact, founded in 1955. After Albania defected from the original group, the treaty bound the USSR to six East European communist states: Czechoslovakia, Hungary, Bulgaria, Romania, Poland, and East Germany. Like NATO, the WTO was a mutual assistance pact. Unlike NATO, its dominant partner had virtually complete control of bloc strategy and organization. In wartime, the Soviet high command would serve as the high command of the whole alliance, and the bloc armies would not fight as separate armies under their own high commands; instead, individual units would be seconded to play assigned parts in the Soviet-directed war scenario. This was a more integrated structure than NATO's, in which individual armies retained their separate national organizations. The effect was that the member countries of the WTO, although assigned key roles in "coalition warfare," had no independent defense plans or strategies.[41] The exception was Romania, which remained a member of the pact but did not integrate its military structure or take part in joint exercises. Subservience was not absolute. For example, in the late 1970s, the smaller bloc countries were able to fight back a Soviet proposal for a 5 percent increase in defense spending on the plea of economic hardship. In this and other matters, maximal Soviet control was sometimes sacrificed in the interest of letting the smaller regimes respond to public pressures that might otherwise be destabilizing. However, the WTO operated largely on Soviet definitions of security interests.

The underlying purpose of the pact was more complex than its official rationale of protection against the West. For all practical purposes, one could say that Czechoslovakia was being protected from itself, since the only full-scale WTO operation in its history was the invasion of Czechoslovakia in 1968.[42] Moreover, the stationing of Soviet troops in the region was only partly the result of defense needs against the West. East Germany on the key battlefront and Poland on the supply lines were the two countries central to bloc security. In the 1950s and 1960s, at the height of the cold war, there were no Soviet troops in Czechoslovakia. The "temporary" stationing of five Soviet divisions on Czechoslovak soil came about as a result of the military occupation of the country after the 1968 invasion rather than in consonance with changing defense strategies toward the West. The Soviet Union did not trust the Czechoslovak People's Army (ČLA) to police its own people. The ČLA had refused to intervene in the workers' protests in Plzeň in 1953. In 1968, army liberalization during the Prague Spring deeply concerned Moscow, and the ČLA was subject to the same "normalization" process as the rest of the system afterwards.[43]

The WTO seemed designed as much to keep its members in the bloc as to keep others out. Following the 1968 invasion, the Soviet Communist Party organ *Pravda* printed a rationale for the right to intervene in the internal affairs of a fellow socialist state. What became known as the Brezhnev Doctrine stipulated that it was the duty of the entire socialist community to intervene if necessary in the internal affairs of a fraternal socialist state in defense of "socialist gains in that country" and in "the interests of worldwide socialism."[44] It was clear that the USSR would decide when socialism needed defending, but the vehicle of this defense was the WTO as a whole. However, the official emphasis was on the Western threat, particularly from West Germany, depicted as the successor to the Nazi fascist state and thus a continuing threat to those who had suffered German domination in the past. Whether the Czechoslovak government and its public believed in the reality of this threat is a moot point. In Poland, for example, the German threat had a more concrete form, since western Poland had been German territory before World War II; Poland had a special concern to protect the changed boundary. The genuine anxiety that Czechs and Slovaks may have had about what was known in the bloc as "West German revanchism" certainly faded over time, as publics became increasingly convinced that there was no serious military threat from the West. Soviet troops stationed locally were understood as preservers of the communist regime, not of the country.

In economic terms, being bound into the Soviet orbit meant a massive reorientation of Czechoslovakia's trade and economic cooperation to the East and the evaporation of the historically strong Central and West European component to its trade. This reorientation was common to all states within the Soviet bloc, and was validated by the ideological justification of furthering fraternal cooperation in the building of socialism. The pattern of bloc trade, however, was not fully multilateral. Some scholars have described it as resembling a wheel, with the USSR at its hub and the East European communist states as its spokes. In other words, most communist states traded more with the Soviet Union than with one another. The bloc's coordinating mechanism, the Council for Mutual Economic Assistance (CMEA), never succeeded in its periodic efforts to create a balanced and coordinated joint economic program to lend more coherence to economic interaction.

Czechoslovakia's incarceration within the Soviet economic system was cemented with several specific restraints. First, all countries in the bloc abandoned hard-currency trading, which is to say that their currencies could not be exchanged on the international market for dollars or marks. The Czechoslovak crown (koruna) no longer traded on international currency markets under communism. Any transactions with the world economy, therefore, had to take the form of barter deals, or countertrade, which understandably reduced trade volume. Although some of its communist neighbors made concerted efforts to attract Western trade and investment in later years, Czechoslovakia was more cautious. There was no legal framework for Western foreign investment in Czechoslovakia—even if any corporations had been interested—until 1988.

Czechoslovak trade with the West also declined because of Western security concerns. Why, in Lenin's words, sell communist countries "the rope to hang you with?" The West hesitated to sell military or dual-use (civilian/military) technology to a member of an adversary bloc, for fear of strengthening it at the expense of Western security. Noncommunist industrial countries therefore organized a Coordinating Committee (CoCom) to organize, administer, and update lists of sensitive technology that could not be exported to the East; CoCom restrictions only began to relax after 1989. The United States in particular was often hesitant to trade heavily with ideologically repugnant countries even in outdated or nonsensitive technologies. Why reward a system that one wished to see fail? West Europeans were generally more eager to intensify economic ties with the East in order to diminish international tensions and encourage Eastern moderation.

Most European communist countries eventually developed significant Western economic ties. Poland and Hungary did so in conjunction with efforts to bolster their economic reform programs with infusions of foreign loans and technology. Romania and Yugoslavia traded rather heavily with the West, reaping the rewards of their relative foreign policy independence of the USSR, an independence the West wished to encourage. East Germany developed a special and economically useful relationship with West Germany. Czechoslovakia, however, remained to the end relatively aloof from Western economic ties, avoiding Poland and Hungary's heavy international indebtedness (a positive factor after 1989) and retaining the classic pattern of trade dependence on the USSR (a negative factor after 1989). All of these factors had the effect of fixing Czechoslovakia's economic position within the bloc, and later they combined to complicate the economic outreach efforts of the postcommunist government.

Energy dependence on the Soviet Union was also a powerful economic constraint. Lacking hard currency and alternate energy delivery systems, Czechoslovakia imported over 90 percent of its oil and natural gas from the USSR and was thus vulnerable to possible Soviet supply cutoffs. It was certainly a result of deliberate Soviet policy that communist Czechoslovakia had only sufficient storage capacity for five days' worth of oil and natural gas. A politically motivated pipeline shutdown would have had immediate impact. The price was also right, as Soviet energy sales to fraternal socialist countries were a relative bargain, often at prices well below the world market. As long as its allies conformed, the Soviet Union could regard this energy subsidy as the price of maintaining regional control. After 1989, when this incentive disappeared, Czechoslovakia and other energy-dependent East European countries had to balance their Western-tilting foreign policy agendas against their continued need for Soviet oil and natural gas.

Overall, within the bloc, Czechoslovakia's economic dependence on the USSR and the consistent subordination of its foreign policy interests to Soviet goals were second only to Bulgaria's. Romania had declared significant foreign policy independence in the 1960s and was probably permitted to do so because it did not border a Western country and because of its orthodox, even Stalinist, domestic policies. East Germany, Poland, and Hungary had developed substantial economic ties with the West. Even during the Prague Spring, the reform communists of Czechoslovakia tried to keep the government's foreign policy positions carefully aligned with those of the USSR, and in "normalized times" this loyalty was even more pronounced. Czechoslovakia's leadership followed Soviet foreign policy orientations in disarmament and East-West relations. Czechoslovakia was also an acolyte to Soviet interests in the Third World—and a valuable one, inasmuch as ČSSR military production reinforced Soviet military assistance to favored Third World client states. As the defeated reformers of the Prague Spring subsequently lamented: "Czechoslovakia is the most peace-loving country in the world. It doesn't even intervene in its own internal affairs."

Notes

1. František Soukup, ed., *Ročenka: Ústavodárného národního shromáždění republiky československé, 1946–1947* (Prague: National Assembly and Ministry of Information, 1947), p. 7.

2. Jon Bloomfield, *The Passive Revolution: Politics and the Czechoslovak Working Class, 1945–1948* (London: Allison and Busby, 1979), p. 35.

3. "Revisionists" in the cold war debate tended to argue that there had been no master plan of empire, and that the escalating tensions of the early cold war had pushed Stalin to seizing fuller control of the buffer zone. It is true that the communization process was incremental rather than instantaneous—that Hungary's fate was unclear until 1947, for example, and that Finland was permitted to tread carefully through the cold war by synchronizing its foreign policy, but not its domestic institutions, with Soviet interests. See John Gaddis, *The Long Peace: Inquiries into the History of the Cold War* (New York: Oxford University Press, 1987).

4. Lord Gladwyn, cited in Michael Charlton, *The Eagle and Small Birds: Crisis in the Soviet Empire from Yalta to Solidarity* (Chicago: University of Chicago Press, 1984), p. 14.

5. There is a vast literature on the communist seizure of power, but see especially Bloomfield, *The Passive Revolution,* and Victor Mamatey and Radomír Luža, *A History of the Czechoslovak Republic, 1918–1948,* pp. 387–474.

6. The most exhaustive study of the purges is Jiří Pelikan's edition of *The Czechoslovak Political Trials 1950–1954: The Suppressed Report of the Dubček Government's Commission of Inquiry, 1968* (Stanford: Stanford University Press, 1971).

7. See Carol Skalnik Leff, *National Conflict in Czechoslovakia: The Making and Remaking of a State* (Princeton: Princeton University Press, 1988), pp. 167–170.

8. See Alan H. Smith, *Planned Economies of Eastern Europe* (London: Croom Helm, 1983): pp. 18–53.

9. See Janos Kornai, *The Socialist System: The Political Economy of Communism* (Princeton: Princeton University Press, 1992), pp. 140–145.

10. Personal computers were much more widely available in the somewhat more liberal Hungarian and Polish states.

11. Cited in Bernard Wheaton and Zdeněk Kavan, *The Velvet Revolution: Czechoslovakia, 1988–1991* (Boulder: Westview Press, 1992), p. 10.

12. Communist states had "anti-parasite" laws that required able-bodied citizens to work in state-approved jobs. A citizen who lived off of others, or off of income unrelated to "socially productive" employment, was seen by definition to be a parasite.

13. A. J. Groth, "Worker Welfare Systems in Marxist-Leninist States: A Comparative Perspective," in Stephen White and Daniel Nelson, eds., *Communist Politics: A Reader* (New York: New York University Press, 1986), pp. 346–360.

14. Jan Pasiak, *Riešenie slovenskej národnostnej otázky* (Bratislava: VPL, 1962), p. 8.

15. *East European Reporter* (September-October 1992), p. 4.

16. Sharon Wolchik, "Regional Inequalities in Czechoslovakia," in Daniel Nelson, ed., *Communism and the Politics of Inequalities* (Lexington, Mass.: Lexington Books, 1983), pp. 249–270.

17. "Vzroste podíl Slovenska na jednotný ekonomice," *Rudé právo,* March 17, 1986.

18. Josef Kotrba and Karel Kríž, "Cui Bono? The Common State in Economic Perspective," *East European Reporter* 5:5 (September-October 1992):5.

19. Slovakia's economic authority was curtailed by constitutional amendment in 1970.

20. The most comprehensive account of the Prague Spring is H. Gordon Skilling's *Czechoslovakia's Interrupted Revolution* (Princeton: Princeton University Press, 1976).

21. Dubček himself, as Slovak party secretary in the 1960s, had to some extent protected Slovak interests and fallen out with Novotný as a result.

22. The Action Program of the Communist Party of Czechoslovakia, April 5, 1968, reprinted in Robin Alison Remington, ed., *Winter in Prague: Documents on Czechoslovak Communism in Crisis* (Cambridge, Mass.: MIT Press, 1969), Document 16, pp. 88–137.

23. Starting in the spring of 1968, Czechoslovak newspapers were confiscated in the Ukraine, Poland, and East Germany. See Jiří Valenta, *Soviet Intervention in Czechoslovakia, 1968: Anatomy of a Decision* (Baltimore: Johns Hopkins University Press, 1979), pp. 23–25.

24. Václav Havel, in *Disturbing the Peace: A Conversation with Karel Hvížďala* (New York: Alfred A. Knopf, 1990), p. 98. Havel subsequently doubted the realism of this proposal, acknowledging that he himself was not in a position to act upon his own meditations.

25. "Two Thousand Words to Workers, Farmers, Scientists, Artists, and Everyone," *Literární listy* (June 27, 1968), reprinted in Remington, *Winter in Prague*, Document 29, pp. 196–202.

26. I. Alexandrov, "Attack on the Socialist Foundations of Czechoslovakia," *Pravda*, July 11, 1968, reprinted in Remington, *Winter in Prague*, Document 30, pp. 203–207. The Hungarian case differed in important respects from the Prague Spring, since in Hungary, the Soviet Union intervened in the face of uncontrolled popular rebellion and the stated government intention to leave the bloc and inaugurate a regime based on competitive elections.

27. See Guillermo O'Donnell and Philippe C. Schmitter, *Transitions from Authoritarian Rule: Tentative Conclusions About Uncertain Democracies* (Baltimore: Johns Hopkins University Press, 1991), chapter 3.

28. See Alexander Dubček, *Hope Dies Last: The Autobiography of Alexander Dubček* (New York: Kodanska, 1993).

29. Jiří Dienstbier, "Život není volební plakát," *Mladý svět*, no. 49, 1991.

30. Milan Kundera, "The Tragedy of Central Europe," *New York Review of Books*, April 26, 1984, p. 55.

31. Cited in Mark Sommer, *Living in Freedom* (San Francisco: Mercury House, 1992), p. 49.

32. Rudolf Převratil, "Czechoslovakia," in David L. Paletz, Karol Jakubowicz, and Pavao Novosel, eds., *Glasnost and After: Media and Change in Central and Eastern Europe* (Creskill, N.J.: Hampton Press, 1995), p. 150.

33. Leff, *National Conflict in Czechoslovakia*, pp. 267–268.

34. For further discussion of dissident activities in communist Czechoslovakia, see H. Gordon Skilling, *Samizdat and an Independent Society in Central and Eastern Europe* (Columbus: Ohio State University Press, 1989).

35. Jan Urban, "Czechoslovakia: The Power and Politics of Humiliation," in Gwyn Prins, ed., *Spring in Winter: The 1989 Revolutions* (Manchester, England: Manchester University Press, 1990), p. 110.

36. H. Gordon Skilling, "Independent Communications in Communist East Europe," *Cross Currents: A Yearbook of Central European Culture*, 1986, p. 60.

37. See H. Gordon Skilling and Vilém Prečan, eds., *Parallel Politics: Essays from Czech and Slovak Samizdat*, special issue of *International Journal of Politics* 11:1 (Spring 1981).

38. Carol Skalnik Leff, "The Changing Character of Soviet-Czechoslovak Relations in the Gorbachev Era," in Richard F. Staar, ed., *East Central Europe and the USSR* (New York: St. Martin's Press, 1991), pp. 148–149.

39. See Charles Gati, *The Bloc that Failed; Soviet–East European Relations in Transition* (Bloomington: Indiana University Press, 1990), p. 178.

40. By and large, Western journalism in particular and some academic scholarship has tended over time to take a Prague-centered view of the Slovaks; Westerners have generally been in much closer touch with Czech intellectuals and Czech interpreters of Czechoslovak events, a fact that has always caused frustration in Slovakia.

41. Robin Remington has noted that "the Czechoslovak desire for a more independent military doctrine, presumably one that would avoid destroying 60 percent of Czechoslovak armed forces within the first three days of a limited nuclear war, exacerbated Soviet-Czechoslovak tensions in the Prague Spring." Robin Remington, "Changes in Soviet Security Policy Toward Eastern Europe and the Warsaw Pact," in George E. Hudson, ed., *Soviet National Security Policy Under Perestroika* (Boston: Unwin Hyman, 1990), p. 227.

42. Even this operation was essentially a Soviet one. Soviet divisions performed the key invasion tasks and were the only units to remain after the initial weeks of occupation. Romania refused to send troops at all, Hungary reluctantly contributed 5,000, and Bulgaria only a symbolic contingent. See Gati, *The Bloc that Failed*, p. 146.

43. Condoleeza Rice, *The Soviet Union and the Czechoslovak Army, 1948–1983* (Princeton: Princeton University Press, 1984), pp. 111–196. A more recent critical assessment of the ČLA in 1968 can be found in Jaromír Navrátil, "Dzúrovo velení ČSLA a jeho nástupnická strategie," *Historie a Vojenství* 6 (1991):71–94.

44. Remington, *Winter in Prague*, Document 65, pp. 415 and 416.

PART 2

THE DOMESTIC POLITICS OF THE TRIPLE TRANSITION

3

THE VELVET REVOLUTION OF 1989 AND THE POLITICS OF DEMOCRATIZATION

If Czechoslovakia's history were written as a fairy tale, this chapter would tell the story of the Velvet Revolution of 1989, in which the communist regime collapsed almost without a fight over the course of a few weeks, and close with the assurance that they all lived happily ever after. However, establishing a democratic regime is not simply a matter of defeating its authoritarian predecessor. In the real world, the Velvet Revolution was only a preface to the time-consuming work of reconstructing institutions and mindsets that would allow democracy to function effectively. Accordingly, the core of this chapter will focus on the difficult tasks of the political transition after the collapse of communist power: the creation of a competitive electoral system, the development of a party system to link public preferences with government policy, the design of legislative, executive, and judicial decisionmaking institutions, the fostering of a free press, and the development of a civic mindset supportive of democratic practice.

Postcommunist governments performed these tasks with varying degrees of success. The greatest failure, to be explored in detail in Chapter 5, was the constitutional deadlock over the resolution of the national question that eventually destroyed the state of Czechoslovakia and led to its bifurcation into two new postcommunist states, the Czech Republic and Slovakia, each of which had its own subsequent political transition to pursue. However, the successes and the lapses of the political transition are worth close examination, because they remind us that there is no standardized formula for democratic governance and that the variant practiced in the United States is not the only, or most typical, type.

The Velvet Revolution

As we have seen, the distinctive history of the "normalization" period made communist Czechoslovakia in the 1980s one of the regimes most resistant to Gorbachev's perestroika and glasnost. By the time of the November 17, 1989, student demonstration that launched the Velvet Revolution, however, both Czechoslovak leaders and the public had been through an educational crash course on the drastically altered dynamics of change in the Soviet bloc. In the summer of 1989, they had witnessed the installation of a mixed Solidarity-communist government in Poland, with a noncommunist prime minister. They had read of the Hungarian government's negotiated commitment to competitive elections in September 1989.[1] And many citizens had seen with their own eyes a flood of East German citizens besiege the U.S. Embassy in Prague for safe passage to the West, or pile onto trains, heading to West Germany through Austria (Czech citizens brought them sandwiches and good wishes). The Berlin Wall had fallen in early November. And through these momentous days from June to November 1989, the Soviet Union had, shockingly, done nothing to halt the onslaught of change. The message was clear. Gorbachev's pledge not to interfere in the internal affairs of fraternal socialist countries was not merely rhetorical; the Brezhnev Doctrine was truly dead, replaced, as a Soviet foreign policy spokesman quipped, with the Sinatra Doctrine: I did it my way.

As one East European leadership after another absorbed this ominous lesson, so did their publics. The Czech and Slovak public encountered an increasingly information-rich environment. The government had ceased jamming Radio Free Europe broadcasts by late 1988, part of a larger pattern of response to Soviet glasnost. Western radio and television broadcasts, long accessible to some viewers near Austria and Germany and, increasingly, to those with satellite dishes, now recorded the course of events in neighboring communist countries; even the language barrier could not dilute the impact of televised scenes of the opening of the Berlin Wall.

While domestic policy failures and internal tensions may explain the desire for political transformation, the timing of that transformational moment was certainly a product of regional developments and the ability to witness them, leading to a dawning understanding that Gorbachev, unlike his predecessors, would not play the card of military intervention as a last resort against independent action. When Soviet hard-liners later grumbled about the loss of the East European empire, Gorbachev's foreign minister, Eduard Shevardnadze, snapped, "So, do you want the tanks again?" Unwilling to undermine his growing rapport with the West, Gorbachev sent no tanks. The domestic communist leaderships of the region were thus left naked, forced to rely on their own inadequate resources to deal with whatever political challenges they faced.

On the surface, the existing communist regimes still had strong cards to play. They could not count on Soviet tanks, but they did face the opposition with all the power of the state: their own security and regular police forces, and the military. In theory, any of the regimes could have attempted the "Tiananmen" solution, a reference to the Chinese military crackdown on protesters in Tiananmen Square only months before, in June 1989. In practice, only Romania actually made this attempt, and it failed. Why? A confident leadership facing an isolated or tentative opposition may be able to quell unrest with force. An ideologically bankrupt and divided leadership facing ever growing popular resistance is in a different position. Force may only increase the number of opposition sympathizers, and, worse still, the regime may find that it cannot even rely on the security forces to follow orders to shoot at its fellow countrymen. In Romania, the army defected from Nicolae Ceaușescu's leadership and took a stand with the popular resistance. Ultimately, none of the East European communist leaderships was able to utilize the coercive power of the state to stay in control.

The collapse of communist power in each of the communist countries was, however, distinctive, evolving from the differential contexts of regimes that had grown increasingly diverse in structure and policies since the 1950s.[2] Some of the most important variables were the character of the opposition that mobilized against the power structure, and the character of the leadership that faced the challenge. Where the opposition was weak or nonexistent, as in Romania, and the regime determined and obdurate, the regime transition was accompanied by violence.

Where the leadership proved flexible, a "pacted" or negotiated settlement was possible. In Poland, for example, economic crisis led Wojciech Jaruzelski's regime to agree to negotiate with the underground Solidarity movement, in the hope that co-opting their opposition into political responsibility might serve several functions. First, it would break the deadlock between rulers and ruled that had stalemated even limited communist economic reform efforts in the 1980s, perhaps permitting the government to receive more active public cooperation in dealing with the severe economic crisis. Second, should economic reform fail or prove economically painful even if eventually successful, Solidarity would be complicit in the guilt and have to share popular anger. These regime calculations made its leaders willing to gamble first on legalizing Solidarity and its right to limited contest of elections, and then to engage in a power-sharing agreement after Solidarity's impressive electoral showing. Ironically, although this gamble might appear to have failed in the short term, it is less obvious that it failed completely. As the communists had hoped, the exercise of power did damage Solidarity's credibility and ultimately contributed to its disintegration as a unified movement. Moreover, the political costs of economic transition were sufficiently painful that by 1993 the ex-communist Democratic Left Alliance was voted into power in the context of a parliamentary system. They were not "back" in power, for the system and the party itself had changed too much for their return to be described as a return of the communist system. But, by the same token, they had maintained a strong foothold in the new institutional order, a result that would have shocked many observers in the fall of 1989.

The Hungarian communists, too, pursued a strategy of survival by accommodation. Jettisoning János Kádár and a septuagenarian leadership that had lost credibility by the late 1980s, the reform communist leaders who emerged from the party plenum of May 1988 began to build bridges with the opposition. Over the course of the next sixteen months, a roundtable process evolved that resulted in an agreement between opposition parties and the communists to hold competitive elections in the spring of 1990. Hungarian communists hoped to reap popular credit for their responsiveness, and hoped further that the rewards would be electoral.[3]

In the Hungarian and Polish cases, it is important to note that it takes two to negotiate a binding agreement for transition; regime incentives to negotiate were based in part on the existence of recognizable opposition forces whose participation in bargaining would help to defuse conflict and lay the groundwork for a smoother systemic adjustment. In that sense, the character of the opposition— its visibility and coherence—were every bit as important as the regime itself. Where the communist government in power did not face a vocal and coherent opposition, the transition took a somewhat different path. Bulgaria was such a case. Reading the evidence of regional turmoil all too clearly, younger Bulgarian party leaders apparently consulted with Gorbachev to gain his approval for what has been described as a "palace coup," in which the elderly leader Todor Zhivkov was deposed and a transition was merely proclaimed, on terms unconstrained by a potent opposition and highly favorable to the communists. Lacking a strong preexisting opposition and able to devise the transition largely on its own initiative, the renamed Bulgarian Socialist Party won the first election handily.[4]

In Czechoslovakia, the year preceding the collapse of communist power had been a year of more daring dissident challenge and unprecedentedly large and frequent public demonstrations that marked every sensitive historical anniversary, from the founding of the republic in 1918 to the Soviet invasion of 1968.[5] The regime became increasingly anxious about the widening impact of dissident ideas on other intellectuals and on the public. Police crackdowns and arrests failed to have the anticipated effect; in fact, the detention of Václav Havel following a demonstration in January 1989 unleashed a storm of protest that went well beyond the circle of established dissidents to draw in a much larger group of intellectuals and artists who had not previously taken public action. Small opposition groups began to proliferate.

These warning signals, however, met with a different response in Czechoslovakia than in Hungary and Poland. The regime made no effort to negotiate with the protesters, alternating repression with empty conciliatory gestures. The leadership that had been installed long ago by the Soviet invasion could not make credible promises of reform; it was difficult enough to adjust to Gorbachev. The current government was "a prisoner of the legacy of the invasion of 1968 not only as regards policy but also respecting the selection of personnel," as Wheaton and Kavan have argued.[6] The thoroughly purged party had no credible alternative cadre of reform communists, and the current leaders had no credentials for reform. They were thoroughly tarnished by their own suppression of the Prague Spring a generation earlier. This dilemma was paralyzing, and party leaders appeared capable only of ad hoc responses to the mounting challenges. By the late fall of 1989, their backs were against the wall. Polish and Hungarian communists had negotiated "pacted" transitions with the opposition; the Berlin Wall had opened; and even Bulgaria had reconstituted its leadership and promised free elections.

The beginning of the final crisis in Czechoslovakia was the brutal suppression of a student demonstration on November 17. The demonstration itself was an example of the double meanings—and layers of meaning—that surrounded so much of communist culture. On the surface, the occasion was a commemoration of the death of Jan Opletal, a student victim of the Nazi crackdown on Czech universities fifty years earlier. This was an impeccably politically correct event—a repudiation of fascism. However, the subtext was less acceptable; it was easy to see the link between fascist repression of education and the behavior of the communist successor regime. Everyone remembered another Jan, Jan Palach, the student who set himself on fire in January 1969 in a suicidal gesture of protest against the destruction of the Prague Spring. And the message of freedom from repression applied universally. The slogans of the day invoked these universal values in the current context, demanding variously free elections, academic freedom, and "genuine perestroika."[7] The student march spilled over from the approved parade route, headlong into confrontation with the police.

Later investigations of this critical night would raise perhaps unanswerable questions about a possible conspiracy underlying the event. There was certainly evidence of security police State Security or StB provocation; the reported death of a student named Martin Šmíd in the clash seems to have been a stage-managed drama manufactured by the security police. But why? To lure the opposition into circulating misinformation and thus discredit them? To stir up further anger and outrage to topple the regime? The second purpose may seem incredible, but the first parliamentary investigatory commission in early 1990 suggested this possibility. The conspiratorial scenario centered on the idea that the KGB (the Soviet State Security Committee) and the StB were working, in the interests of preserving socialist rule, to rid Czechoslovakia of its hard-line rulers and permit more accommodating rulers to take over the helm, as in Bulgaria.

The debate on this subject continued, but in one sense it does not matter. The broader causes of regime collapse—the relaxation of Soviet interventionism and the internal sources of discontent—are still the important explanatory factors, and it is impossible to imagine that Czechoslovakia could have remained immune to the massive changes in the bloc even without a hypothetical push from the StB. What is also important is that the violent suppression of the student demonstration triggered a chain reaction of oppositional response. An isolated demonstration could never have toppled the government. What did topple the government was the steadily broadening base of the opposition. Prague is actually an excellent place for a revolution. In the United States, different types of power and influence are rather dispersed. The political center is neither an industrial center nor the cultural heart of the country. In Prague, however, the core of the intellectual and cultural communities, the country's major university, the politicians, and a major concentration of industry are all packed into a single urban space. On a smaller scale, this is also true of Bratislava in Slovakia. Mobilizing an opposition coalition and confronting government power was accordingly an exercise that could be compressed in time and space. Ultimately, rapid broadening and deepening of the opposition encompassed most of the significant social forces in the country. Some communist party leaders complained that they could not negotiate a stable agreement with the opposition, whose demands kept escalating. This was quite true. The opposition had not started with any clear sense of the boundaries of the possible and first demanded a party leadership shuffle, an investigation of police brutality on November 17, and the release of political prisoners. Ultimately, the opposition would demand and receive the elimination of the dominant role of the party, an interim government of communists and opposition figures, and free competitive elections.

The initial phases of the challenge to communist power were quite literally a drama, for the theater troupes and musicians had gone out on strike with the students and turned their stages over to the opposition. It was in Prague's theaters that dissidents gathered to deliberate on how to respond to the crisis. The ad hoc convocation became the Civic Forum.[8] It was as the most visible and compelling spokesman for Civic Forum that Havel emerged from the dissident ghetto to the central arena of political influence. His news conferences encapsulated the broadening goals of the movement, and his presence on the balcony of Melantrich publishing house overlooking Wenceslas Square was a magnet for the growing crowds who gathered daily in protest against the regime.

From this base, the core of protest in Prague reached out to industrial workers, truly the last hope of the Communist Party. These workers had been relatively privileged, and the party leaders harbored the false but not irrational hope that they would not find common cause with the Prague intellectuals. To expect enthusiastic support for the regime from the working class might be unrealistic, but neutrality and the acceptance of limited change might be enough to buy time for the party's efforts to remain in power. This hope dimmed with the broad, although by no means total, worker participation in the symbolic two-hour general strike at noon on November 27; the brevity of the strike was designed to encourage participation and to avoid disrupting production—revolution on the lunch hour, it was called. Having lost the workers was perhaps the critical last straw. Nor would the People's Militia mobilize to protect the regime. Efforts to prevent information from leaking out of Prague also proved unsuccessful; striking film studios and film academy students created and distributed thousands of copies of still-photo documentary coverage of events for dissemination to the provinces. In less than a week, the official media had broken with censorship, and Czechoslovak Television was broadcasting news of developments in Prague to the country at large.

The week following the strike saw the most definitive steps to a genuine power transition. On November 29, the Federal Assembly rescinded Article 4 of the constitution, abrogating the legal base for the leading role of the party. However, the government's original version of a "new look" in the leadership was hardly a breakthrough; on December 3, there was massive outrage when it was announced that the new twenty-person cabinet included only five noncommunists and fifteen communists. Reinvigorated demonstrations and a threatened second general strike drove eleven of the communist holdovers from office in days. Meanwhile, thousands of party members were resigning, the trade unions were reorganizing, and new parties were forming. The government agreed to a more representative cabinet, balanced between communists and noncommunists: a government of National Understanding to preside over the interim period between December and the scheduled elections in June 1990. The Federal Assembly was partially remodeled through the recall or resignation of the most notorious "normalizers," and delicate negotiations and maneuverings culminated in the resignation of President Husák and his replacement with Václav Havel, whose credentials were his integrity, his visibility in the Velvet Revolution, and the favorable and potentially valuable international image he had received from adulatory Western press coverage.

In several respects, Czechoslovakia was still what the dissidents had called "Absurdistan." Leaders like Slovak dissident Ján Čarnogurský went from prison to a government position in weeks. Jiří Dienstbier, a Charter 77 spokesman and former journalist, was working as a boiler stoker as the penalty of his dissidence. One morning in early December his coworkers worried when he did not show up for work—had the regime arrested him? They were relieved to learn that his absence had been necessary for him to attend his swearing-in ceremony as the country's new foreign minister! He did, however, return to the boilers in the evening, because a replacement had not yet been found.

Western journalists tended to neglect the independent but parallel Slovak mobilization in the weeks following the initial crisis. Public Against Violence (PAV), founded on November 20, three days after the initial student demonstration in Prague, played a similar role in Slovakia to that of Civic Forum in the Czech Republic. Its leadership was composed of religious and intellectual dissidents, cultural figures, and even the symbol of earlier reform efforts, Alexander Dubček. PAV's demands paralleled those of the Civic Forum as well, with the very significant exception of the pronounced emphasis placed on the rectification of Czech-Slovak relations in a more democratic federation. By late November, Civic Forum and Public Against Violence were dealing jointly with the communist government, and in early December the two groups were promising a joint slate of candidates in the projected elections. A Slovak coalition government, composed of communists and noncommunists in roughly equal numbers and headed by former communist Minister of Justice Milan Čič, was sworn in on December 12. [9]

Dubček played a critical role during the transitional period in bridging the gap in communication and confidence between Czechs and Slovaks, traveling to Prague early in the protest period to stand alongside Czech dissidents and speak to the crowds in Wenceslas Square—his first such public appearance since the Prague Spring period. The Communist Party leadership attempted to foment division between the Czech and Slovak opposition by encouraging Slovak claims and Dubček's candidacy for the presidency; the Slovak communist newspaper *Pravda* spearheaded the effort. Dubček eventually defused this issue by withdrawing his candidacy for the presidency in favor of Havel and accepting the post of Federal Assembly leader instead. As the federal government emerged, the key leadership posts were thus divided between Czechs and Slovaks, with the Czech Havel as president, the Slovak Dubček as chairman of the Federal Assembly, and the Slovak Marian Čalfa as prime minister.

Most of us will never live through a revolution and may be somewhat misled by the neatly packaged textbook summaries, which tend to give such events an aura of inevitability. It is important to recognize, however, that there was no such feeling on the part of the participants. They were improvising and taking risks. Students could not know that their strike actions would end with government collapse; it was a real possibility that the end would be expulsion from the university and the destruction of a career. As theater director Arnost Goldflan said as the opposition groped for a strategy, "the inescapable fact is that every one of us will have to decide for himself. Take a risk and believe that everything will work out, and if it doesn't, then reconcile yourself to the fact that you are in for it."[10]

On the other side of the fence, the Czechoslovak Communist Party's efforts to find a way to halt the erosion of its power base also suggest improvisation and an initial failure to recognize the endgame. Party leaders tried to temporize by jettisoning their discredited leaders and promising reform. In a gesture that clearly misread the temper of the times, they invited the reformers purged during "normalization" back into the party; one of the purged, a former journalist, described this as a "senseless ritual": "They would like *me* to legitimatize them."[11] The party failed to see that it was too late to salvage power by such overtures.

Political scientists who have studied the social psychology of mass protests against repressive governments see the East European revolutions as a good case study of the changes in attitude that occur even as the protest develops. They describe a kind of chain reaction in which different social groups watch the regime responding to the first protests, continuously reevaluate the costs and benefits of joining in, and ultimately reach a "tipping point" that pushes them into opposition. What starts with uncertainty on all sides ends in widespread opposition that the regime cannot control. Though in hindsight the government collapse seems inevitable, at the time everyone played a constant guessing game about actions and consequences.[12] This was true in Czechoslovakia. The government did not know how far it would have to go to quell the protest, and it made ever-increasing concessions until all was lost. The dissidents did not know who would follow their lead; they had no real legitimacy to bargain with the regime if they lacked popular backing. The crowds cheering them in Wenceslas Square were essential; their presence told the communist leadership that the Civic Forum had popular acceptance and gave its demands a credibility that nothing else could have.

Finally, and perhaps most importantly for the long run, the public did not have a clear sense of the scope and direction of the change it desired. It would be misleading to think that in the course of the drama of regime collapse the citizenry already had its sights firmly set on a Western parliamentary democracy with a capitalist market. For example, public opinion polls from early December 1989 showed only 22 percent supporting wholesale privatization of industry, and only 13 percent favoring privatization of agriculture. About 45 percent wanted to see Czechoslovakia follow a reform socialist path, only 3 percent favored a capitalist path, and the single largest group (47 percent) favored a "third" or middle way. While rejection of the leading role of the party was widespread (82 percent) and the public favored personnel changes in the party leadership and real perestroika, many had obviously not yet grasped that much more was possible. A revolutionary change, even a broadly popular one, is not marked with clear signposts, particularly when the opportunity appears suddenly and everyone must abruptly shift focus to an entirely new agenda. The euphoria of the Velvet Revolution was obvious, but the inevitable vagueness of its specific policy direction would cause political difficulties in the future.

Engineering a Political Transition

Elite Transformation

The tone of the Velvet Revolution was set by the dissident community, many of whom bore the marks of long-ago exposure to the West in the brief period of openness surrounding the Prague Spring. It was the West of the late 1960s, awash in countercultural influences, that they had directly encountered. Havel, who had visited New York at that time, felt an affinity with that spirit; it showed in the picture of John Lennon on his apartment wall, his visit with rock musician Frank Zappa, the unusual presidential meditation session with the Dalai Lama, and the selection of a rock musician as his presidential chief of protocol. The events of the transition were celebrated not only with a mass at St. Vitus Cathedral but also by folk and rock concerts. Musical luminaries of the 1960s such as Joan Baez and the Beach Boys came to celebrate the new era. One of the anthems of the transition was "We Shall Overcome," sung in Czech and English. In the spring of 1990, a stroll through Wenceslas Square led one past a collage of American culture: a guitarist singing American and British rock songs, a determined accordionist belting out "Home on the Range," and Hare Krishna chanters. Despite its seriousness of purpose, the early Civic Forum retained an almost playful character. The movement's logo—the initials OF for Občanské fórum—were enlivened by a smiley face sketched inside the *O*.

Beneath this surface, the transfer of power—both in Czechoslovakia and elsewhere in the region—was considerably more complex than the displacement of the ruling communist elite by the highly visible dissidents who had spearheaded the Velvet Revolution. Just as the early communist regimes had struggled with a "red versus expert" dilemma—the problem of finding trained professionals to staff government and economic positions who were also loyal to communism—so too did the postcommunist transition require politicians and bureaucrats who had more professional experience than the political novices of the democratic counterelite. And in fact, almost from its inception, the "steering committee" for the Velvet Revolution was a motley crew, composed of former dissidents and their former jailers (or at least those members of the communist elite who were sufficiently unsullied and flexible enough to work in harness with old antagonists and new allies).

Joining them were technical, legal, and academic experts who had never overtly challenged the regime before but who had played by the rules while quietly dabbling in political and economic unorthodoxies in research institutes, publishing houses, or cultural institutions. The elites of this intermediate position were often characterized as living in the "gray zone" between orthodoxy and resistance. The Hungarian political scientist Ákos Róna-Tas characterized them as having occupied "parking orbits" in the former political system, positioned not for dissident political action but for the acquisition of skills and approaches that would "suddenly become valuable for direct participation in high-level politics" after the collapse of the communist regimes.[13]

One way of making the distinction between the dissidents and those in the gray zone is to look at the political careers of two prominent Czech politicians, Václav Havel and Václav Klaus. Václav Havel's path to the presidency of Czechoslovakia and subsequently of the Czech Republic led through political opposition and jail. Born in 1936 the son of a Prague architect and building contractor, Havel's suspect "bourgeois" class origins had barred him from a university or even regular secondary education during the communist period; as a lifelong outsider, he has said, the dissident's isolation was less a burden that it might otherwise have been. Havel gravitated to the avant-garde theater that had begun to emerge in the late 1950s. In the more relaxed climate of the 1960s leading up to the Prague Spring, several of his absurdist plays were performed at home; after the invasion, his later work could only be performed abroad.[14] Before 1968, he had been an iconoclast at a time when there was still a marginal place for iconoclasts in the system; after 1968, an iconoclast had the choice of conformity or dissidence. Havel's activities with Charter 77 made him a public enemy; he was imprisoned in 1977, and again for an additional six weeks the following year, and again in 1979—for four years.

Václav Klaus, however, as heterodox as his economic views proved to be, was never an open dissident. "I have always respected any chair I was sitting on," he is reported to have said in describing his formal adherence to the rules of the old system.[15] Fifty-one at the time that he became prime minister of the Czech Republic in 1992, he had been trained at the University of Economics during the 1960s and benefited from the thaw of the Prague Spring with a study tour in the West. The normalization of the post-Soviet invasion period demoted him from his position at the Economics Institute of the Academy of Sciences (ČSAV), but not to window washer. After sixteen years at the state bank (a lesser position that nevertheless corresponded with his professional training) he was reinstated at the Academy in 1988, in the newly founded Institute for Prognosis (its denizens would be tagged the economic "prognosticators"). During these years, he was to develop a strong affinity for the ideas of Milton Friedman and brought both his training and these strong market views to the service of the transition in the position of federal finance minister. Lacking strong ties to the dissident core of Civic Forum, Klaus was much more successful in appealing to the broader base of newly sensitized political activists within the movement, and in the autumn of 1990 he gained leadership of the Forum in a highly contested mission to whip it into shape as an organized political party. He has proven to be a somewhat unlikely but very successful politician—self-assured, programmatically committed, and no-nonsense in manner.

Klaus and Havel, then, were the most prominent representatives of two groups from which the postcommunist leadership drew heavily. There were similar contrasts in the new Slovak leadership—between the jailed religious dissident Ján Čarnogurský, for example, and Vladimír Mečiar, an expelled Prague Spring communist who worked quietly as a lawyer until the late 1980s.[16] But the third important group, the communists themselves, became the subject of prolonged and heated controversy, a controversy that paralleled, in more dramatic and emotional form, controversies in neighboring countries.

How does a democratic regime treat its former rulers? The Civic Forum was initially tolerant—ironically, more tolerant than much of the public would prove to be, despite the persecution of many Forum members by the former regime for their dissident activities. The government did not move to place on trial the most visible communist leaders, as Germany did in its prosecution of party boss Erich Honecker and others, or as Bulgaria did with Todor Zhivkov.[17] The sole significant exception was Prague party leader Miroslav Štěpán, who was prosecuted for his part in suppressing the November 17 demonstration. Attempts to investigate the suppressors of the Prague Spring reform as traitors who had collaborated in the Soviet-led invasion of their country did not initially lead to any prosecutions, because the twenty-year statute of limitations had expired. The Hungarian government revised the statute of limitations in order to investigate crimes of the 1950s, but the Czechoslovak government at first contented itself with the public identification of the culprits, including sixteen party and state officials still living and five who had died. Among them were Miloš Jakeš, head of the KSČ, and his predecessor, Gustav Husák, who died in 1990. By the summer of 1995, however, a tougher climate prevailed in the Czech Republic, and five surviving former party officials were charged with treason for complicity in the Soviet invasion. No comparable effort was made in Slovakia.

The Forum also failed to embrace the Prague prosecutor's effort in the spring of 1990 to ban the Communist Party as a "fascist" organization under the old communist law prohibiting such organizations. Rather, the interim government recognized that the former opposition was too thinly spread and inexperienced to run the bureaucracy without the contributions of its existing communist specialists. Civic Forum leader Jan Urban calculated in 1990 that the core strength of the dissident community in the 1980s may have amounted to only about 250 people.[18] Many of the needed specialists, who had joined the party for career reasons anyway, had little motive to undermine the new government in loyalty to a dead cause. Extensive purges would hobble the transition effort. Rather, the strategy was to "parachute" noncommunists into the top slots in the new regime and count on them to monitor the good behavior of their subordinates. Longtime dissidents like Havel were also, in many cases, sufficiently attuned to human frailty and to the moral ambiguities of the communist period to feel that healing was more important than retribution in building the new order. Heartily agreeing, the communists themselves argued that true democracy required the toleration of all views, including theirs. "No pluralism without the communists," became their election slogan. Some might gag on the self-serving character of this belated conversion to "true democracy," but many agreed with the philosophical point.

There was never a strong consensus on this issue, however. In particular, many were concerned that the new system could be delegitimized by the government service of too many tarnished holdovers of the past regime. Ironically, much of the popular anticommunism embraced both the disgraced party members of 1989 and the reform communists of 1968 who had long since been expelled from the party. Even those ex-communists who had suffered job demotions and other punitive actions had to watch their step in the new political environment. The detractors of Slovakia's post-independence president, Michal Kováč, who had been expelled from the party in 1970, criticized him for "conspicuously spending his weekends in church." The implication was that he was hypocritically trying to "disinfect" himself of the stigma of his culpable former views. Even Alexander Dubček was repeatedly called upon to resign his post as Federal Assembly chair because of his communist past.[19]

Especially unacceptable, however, was the likelihood that some of the new democratic converts might prove to be as yet unidentified StB informants. Not only would such people damage the system's legitimacy, but also individual politicians with such a past were clearly subject to blackmail. The StB had been abolished in January 1990, and the departments that were not abolished were being reorganized; yet its files remained a time bomb planted within the political system, and there was heated controversy about how to deactivate the threat they posed.

The effort to weed out informers was initially rather unsystematic, relying primarily on informal and voluntary party agreements to submit their electoral candidates for screening. From the first, however, the screening process seemed unsatisfactory. Key leaders were subject to exposure at politically calculated moments. The ad hoc character of these politically determined revelations, which their targets sometimes heatedly rejected as a political smear campaign, certainly raised civil liberties issues and provoked a protracted and not always illuminating debate over who was to blame for past regime failures. One side deplored the divisive "witch-hunts" for informers while the other accused their opponents of being in league with the old order—soft on communism and contributing to the perpetuation of "leftist" influences. The attempt to resolve this debate with comprehensive legislation satisfied no one, however. In 1991, the Federal Assembly passed a screening law that barred former high officials of the party, StB agents and informers, and members of the People's Militia from top economic and political posts for five years. All prospective officials needed an affidavit from the Ministry of Interior certifying a clean bill of political health. After agonizing over this enactment, President Havel signed this violation of his personal principles and offered suggestions for modification that went unheeded. Although Havel had wanted a regularized approach to this cleansing process, known as lustration (*lustráce*), he had not intended to countenance a law that barred "entire categories of people" from public service or that operated on the principle of guilty until proven innocent.

In Slovakia, the lustration law met with resistance from the government of Prime Minister Mečiar, who tried after Slovak independence to gain a constitutional court ruling that it was unconstitutional. Appreciation of Mečiar's solicitude for civil liberties in this case was tempered by the feeling that his own Movement for a Democratic Slovakia (MDS), heavily populated by ex-communists, might suffer from the law's rigorous enforcement. However, it was also true that enthusiasm for lustration was generally less pronounced in Slovakia, where past history loomed less large than current economic and national issues. The issue remained controversial, and unresolved, and the law was not enforced.

The most contested issue in the new legislation proved to be the question of informer collaboration with the StB. The public and leadership revulsion against the harboring of such collaborators in public life is understandable. However, the fairness of the lustration of informers rested on the completeness and accuracy of the surviving StB files and on the exercise of due process in the revelation of their contents. Both issues were in doubt. The evidentiary value of the files was challenged by many, who questioned whether they had been kept secure and protected from StB tampering and whether the sometimes obscure or ambiguous notations in the files could adequately distinguish between those who had actually collaborated and those who had given information unwittingly or merely been approached, unsuccessfully, for collaboration.[20] These critics also queried whether a dissident who had served jail sentences for regime opposition but who had also "cooperated" with a single investigation in his youth under threat of deportation or expulsion from a university was actually a threat to democracy. Ironically, the dissident community was a special target of StB searches for informants, since dissidents had been particularly vulnerable to StB pressure for their activities and particularly useful to the regime in informational terms. Citizens who had sat back passively during the communist period were far less likely to be pressured to turn informant, and tended to be highly judgmental of those whose superior courage had subjected them to StB pressure because of their dissident activities.[21]

Critics of lustration were perhaps even more dismayed by informal leaks and abuse of confidential information by the media than they were by formal government procedures. Activists who felt that only a complete revelation would purify the system gained access to the government database; the subsequent unauthorized publication of "wild lists," often full of errors and even deliberate fabrications, began in the spring of 1992. The published lists included those of current journalists thought to have collaborated in the past. The critics found the cleansing process a socially divisive and equivocally effective washing of dirty linen in public that, in the final analysis, tarnished the political process more than it purified.

Supporters of lustration, while sometimes acknowledging the drawbacks cited by their critics, nonetheless stood firm on the principle that sweeping past crimes under the rug was politically damaging—"a cancer within Czechoslovak society" that would undermine public confidence in new institutions. Petruška Šustrová, deputy minister of interior in the Czechoslovak federal government in 1991, rejected the pejorative "witch-hunt" label: "The analogy is misleading. The women burned at the stake centuries ago as witches were innocent; witches never existed. But secret police and their collaborators existed in a very real and proven way."[22] She and others detailed the procedures by which collaborators were listed in StB files and argued that the specificity of the files made falsification unlikely and distinguishing between informants and subjects of surveillance an adequately accurate procedure. She concluded by insisting that lustration was not a punishment or revenge—that what was at stake was not one's livelihood or freedom but only the right to hold public office.

This view, representative of the defenders of lustration, differed from the critics' view by placing primary emphasis on the right of the public to know and to protect itself rather than on the civil rights of the accused to due process. It is a controversy that could not be resolved to everyone's satisfaction; rather, it is likely to fade away, unsettled, over time. At the present, however, it remains a live political issue in the Czech Republic. In September 1995, as the end of the five-year period designated in the original lustration law for the barring of communists from public office drew closer, the parliament voted its extension to the year 2000. This time, President Havel vetoed it, arguing that Czech democracy had become secure enough not to need such precautions, but his veto was overridden. What remains is one of the classic civil liberties dilemmas of any democracy, that of how to strike a balance between the merits of public protection against the merits of individual civil liberties.

In a sense, both critics and defenders of lustration were right. The communist legacy of repression and informants would have damaged the legitimacy of the new regime whether the files were opened to identify informants and officials (with the certainty that some would be unjustly accused and that the seamy revelations would tarnish political institutions) or remained closed (with the certainty that the public would retain unresolved doubts concerning the placement and influence of former informants in new structures). The inflammatory debate itself was assurance enough that any policy adopted would be muddied by the controversy. It is hard to accept the assurances of lustration supporters that no serious miscarriage of justice would transpire, since loss of reputation from a mistaken charge would surely be a punishment. But it is also hard to imagine that the insistence on tolerance and privacy would not have opened a gulf of suspicion between rulers and ruled. It may be that certain transitional costs are unavoidable, regardless of the policy adopted.

Amidst the sound and fury of the lustration debate over informers and top party officials, the communist elite as a whole was not as vulnerable as one might think, especially in Slovakia. Many resigned their party memberships and realigned with other political movements. The communist party itself jettisoned the more odious leaders of the past, and ran in free elections with a younger and less compromised leadership and a party program tailored to the new environment. The party retained enough support to win parliamentary seats.

The Slovak communists generally proved more flexible than their Czech counterparts. After the KSČ "federalized" into two separate Czech and Slovak parties in the fall of 1990, the Czech branch clung stubbornly to the label "communist" in the new Communist Party of Bohemia and Moravia. The Slovaks, like every other communist party in Eastern Europe, went further in reconfiguring both their name and their image, becoming the Party of the Democratic Left (PDL) under the leadership of a young lawyer, Petr Weiss, who gained credibility from his past willingness to defend dissidents in court during the former regime. The greater reformist energy in the Slovak party, coupled with greater economic stress in Slovakia, did not initially make the PDL more electorally successful than its Czech counterpart (both ex–ruling parties won about the same share of the vote in the 1990 Republic elections), but it did make it more respectable in the long run. The Party of the Democratic Left became the strongest left-wing party and eventually even won a place in a Slovak government coalition in 1994, as we will see.

Meanwhile, the Czech Communist Party floundered, with its leader resigning in frustration over failed efforts to revamp the party's program and image, and with a new, hard-line Communist Party emerging under the leadership of Miroslav Štěpán. The divisions and nonrepentance of the communists had a unique result: The noncommunist Social Democrats became the leading left-wing party in the Czech Republic. Virtually everywhere else in the region, the ex-communists dominate this position on the political spectrum, as they do in Slovakia—an interesting fate for what was once the most powerful communist party in interwar Eastern Europe.

The postcommunist leaderships of the Czech Republic and Slovakia, then, were not noncommunist; they were a composite group drawn initially from the ranks of communists and ex-communists, dissidents, and trained professionals. Of the three, however, it is ironic that it is the dissidents who have proved most politically vulnerable. The form that the Velvet Revolution took would have been inconceivable without the engagement of committed intellectuals who in effect volunteered to focus their energies on the political task of negotiating the transition and consolidating the new regime. In this they followed the path trodden by their colleagues of earlier eras, echoing the political engagement of intellectuals in the Czech and Slovak national revival efforts of the nineteenth and early twentieth centuries and state-building efforts of men like Tomáš Masaryk.

Yet this did not prove to be a permanent role. The Civic Forum had initially functioned around a nucleus of former dissidents in the period of crisis; as the emergency passed and politics began to settle into more normal institutional patterns, some of the musicians and composers and novelists returned to their life's work, which in some cases had been interrupted as long ago as the Soviet invasion of 1968 or even earlier. Those who remained political activists faced the task of adjusting to politics-as-usual. But now they operated alongside the new politicians, often younger, usually trained in economics, administration, or law, who had functioned in the gray areas of the former regime neither as communist partisans nor as dissidents.

The watershed was the second election, in 1992. In that election, the most visible Czech dissidents, especially luminaries such as Foreign Minister Jiří Dienstbier or Czech Prime Minister Petr Pithart (who had created the Civic Movement after the Civic Forum's schism), lost their bid for parliamentary representation. In Slovakia, the most visible former dissident, Prime Minister Ján Čarnogurský, remained chairman of the Slovak Christian Democrats in the Slovak National Council but also lost ground to Mečiar's Movement for a Democratic Slovakia, a breakaway party from the Public Against Violence, whose top leaders were ex-communists. Much of the remaining dissident core of PAV lost its political platform when it contested the 1992 elections as the Civic Democratic Union and failed to surmount the electoral threshold. The party dissolved in November 1992. When Catholic dissident Václav Benda lost his leadership of the Czech Christian Democrats to a "new-breed" politician, only Čarnogurský and Václav Havel were left from the cohort of dissident leaders in visible leadership positions. Journalistic commentary on Benda's departure cited it as "further proof that the revolutionary period is over: one of the most courageous dissidents must clear the field for an ambitious thirty-year-old politician of the new generation."[23]

What had happened to the heroes of the Velvet Revolution? In their post-mortems of the 1992 elections, the dissidents described themselves as having failed to adapt to the demands of politics-as-usual. Under communism, they had followed a vibrant East European tradition of intellectuals as the "voice of the oppressed . . . the writer as priest, prophet, resistance fighter and *substitute* politician."[24] Their formative political experiences in the dissident movement before 1989 had put a premium on uncompromising moral stances, straight talk, and loose organization—very un-politician-like behavior that came to be described in the dissident era as "anti-politics." They later concluded that "anti-politics," essential to the confrontation with the communists, made very bad politics in more normal conditions. In dissolving the Civic Democratic Union, one of its leaders said that the party was dissolved "as an example of how to quit the past—all our mistakes, our unpolitical behavior, the so-called anti-politics."[25]

Some of these dissidents will adapt and continue to be engaged in the political arena. Many of them remain individually more popular than their parties; they could regroup and recoup some of their losses. But it is probable that the dissidents—as a community with a common identity—were primarily a transitional elite, a bridge between systems. The political future belongs more to the younger generation of communists and ex-communists, and to a new breed of professional politician recruited from the ranks of economists, lawyers, and other specialists with politically relevant skills.

Parties and Elections

Free elections were the first item on the agenda of the postcommunist political transition, since all subsequent institutional choices would benefit from the electoral legitimation of the transitional leaders.

Free elections are an essential component of a truly democratic system, but they are also problematic in a number of respects. For one thing, a free press and a free electoral competition comprise a platform for people to voice all their concerns and fears, including those of the intolerant, the ultranationalist, and the demagogic. Freely expressed prejudices and paranoia can gain democratic expression through electoral politics. Democracy always carries this risk—the problem that the *New York Times* described as the problem of "freely elected tyrants," politicians who gain power to pursue their undemocratic values through democratic electoral channels. In the Czech Republic, the prime example of this phenomenon is Miroslav Sládek's rabidly nationalist and antiforeigner Republican Party, which holds seats in the post-1992 Czech National Council (ČNR).

No established democracy is free of this risk (remember the inability of the Republican Party in Louisiana to avert the primary victory of David Duke, a Ku

Klux Klan leader, or Italy's 1994 election of a neofascist leader), but the danger is even higher in transitional politics, where the electorate has not yet had a chance to judge the responsibility and realism of the political alternatives and where there are no rooted political identities and track records for the competing forces. Add to this a perilous economic situation, and you have the formula for potential trouble. On the whole, the electorates of Eastern Europe have not given full rein to extremists. While they have consistently retaliated against the party in power as punishment for economic strain, they have turned largely to other mainstream parties as the alternative. Paradoxically, this mainstream includes reformed communist parties themselves, who have experienced considerable political success in capitalizing on economic discontent to promise social justice in the transition. Yet as they have "returned to power" in Lithuania, Poland, or Hungary, their policies have represented only marginal shifts in emphasis. They have not tried, or have not been able, to reject the market transition or free elections.

A second interesting feature of the "democracy quotient" of free elections is that in some ways they do not produce a legislature more representative of a cross-section of the public than did the communist-era elections. A prime example is the representation of women. Communist electoral politics had been a carefully calibrated exercise in demonstrating that the party represented the whole people. With a quota-like inclusiveness, the legislatures included party apparatchiks, exemplary workers, farmers, celebrities from the arts and popular culture, and a substantial showing of women and ethnic minorities, all to demonstrate the workings of socialist democracy. Of course, this carefully stage-managed display of representativeness was possible, and completely safe, because communist legislatures were largely powerless rubber-stamp organizations for party policy. No matter who sat in the Federal Assembly, each deputy would vote as expected, regardless of gender, ethnicity, or occupation. In fact, the legislature was not where the action was, and an ambitious politician looked elsewhere for status and influence.

Free elections were an entirely different matter, because the legislature now mattered, and representation in it conferred a measure of power and influence. As soon as that happened, the stakes of the game shifted, and the politically ambitious pursued legislative positions with a new interest. Predictably, in Czechoslovakia as elsewhere, the new legislative elite reflected the change. Almost a quarter of the federal deputies in the ČSSR in the 1980s had been women. After the first postcommunist elections, that number dropped to a mere 11 percent.[26]

Elections, of course, cannot be held without making some basic decisions about the rules of competition. The designers of postcommunist electoral laws in Czechoslovakia chose to follow their own interwar model and the practice of many Western states by adopting a system of proportional representation, which tends to facilitate the emergence of multiparty systems—as it had in the interwar period. In planning for the first postcommunist elections, in fact, opening the field to multiple party competition seemed to be the only sensible solution to the problem of deciding just who had a right to run for office after years of communist suppression of diversity. Eventually, voter preferences would be clarified, but initially the emphasis was on low thresholds to the emergence of new political forces. Because it was so unclear just who these forces would be, and because fledgling parties needed financial support to confront the well-funded communists, the state defrayed some of the start-up costs and remitted a small sum per vote for any party with sufficient appeal to gain more than 2 percent of the vote in the first election. Many of the new partisan entries into competition were mere "couch" parties—that is, parties conceived in someone's living room while the would-be leaders sat together on the couch—and would vanish after failing to make a mark. But only electoral competition itself would prove which of the party hopefuls were politically viable.

The transitional legislature did make one important concession to controlling the proliferation of parties; as elsewhere in Eastern Europe, the Federal Assembly borrowed from the German electoral system the idea of an electoral threshold. A party that did not gain 5 percent of the vote failed to qualify for parliamentary seats. The votes registered for failed parties were reallocated, roughly proportionally, among those who did succeed in crossing the 5 percent threshold. The effect of this attempt to prevent total electoral fragmentation was significant. Neighboring Poland did not establish any threshold for its first fully competitive elections in 1991 and found itself with more than two dozen parties in the Sejm (the lower house of the legislature), the largest of them receiving only 12 percent of the vote. But even with threshold rules in effect in the Czech and Slovak Republic elections, the result was a multiparty system. In 1990, seven parties and coalitions gained representation in the Federal Assembly. In 1992, six Slovak-based parties and six Czech-based parties won seats out of a field of forty.

It can be tough to govern with a multiparty system, but it is also difficult to vote in a multiparty election. In 1990, the voter could cut corners; two-thirds of them opted either for the old communist party or the Civic Forum/Public Against Violence coalition. By 1992, the disintegration of the anticommunist movements produced a less clear-cut environment in which the full complexity of voter choice became apparent. First of all, the voter had to participate simultaneously in three different legislative elections: the two chambers of the Federal Assembly and the Czech or Slovak National Council. Prior to the election, each voter received the ballot lists for any of the forty competing parties who had filed candidate lists for that electoral district. A conscientious voter had to scrutinize these lists carefully, for his job was not only to select his preferred party, but also to rearrange the candidate lists if he did not approve of the party's ordering. If individual voters did not change that ordering by exercising their "preferential" voting rights to circle up to four candidates lower on the list, the elected candidates would be those on the top of the party's official list.[27]

By now, it would be logical to conclude that the one thing more unintelligible than *living* in such a complex system is to be the outsider *studying* it. The complexity of the infant multiparty system and the fluidity created by the formation and re-formation of new parties are comparable to the travails of many of the other new postcommunist electoral systems, of course. But here there is the added complication of an additional republic level of power, a level we cannot ignore because the republic-level politics contributed to the dissolution of the state; republic-level politics also became the base for the politics of the two new states after 1992. The parties and individual politicians in charge changed several times from 1990 to 1994, following two federal and Czech Republic elections (1990 and 1992) and three Slovak Republic elections (1990, 1992, and 1994), all of which changed the composition of the governments. In addition, the Slovak governments twice fell in votes of no confidence and were replaced between elections (1991 and 1994). In the coming years, the political systems are likely to stabilize; already, parties are beginning to last long enough to be identifiable to voters, and the period between elections may well lengthen. In the meantime, it will probably be helpful to look at Box 3.1 from time to time to keep the chronology and cast of characters of this transitional period in some kind of order.

The first competitive elections in most communist countries were revealing, largely as a referendum on communist rule. Opposition parties were torn over the best tactics to use. On the one hand, they desired to consolidate an electorally legitimate position for themselves in the new order; no one had "elected" them spokesmen for democracy. On the other hand, there was real concern that early elections would leave the opposition scrambling for organizational and financial resources against a Communist Party amply supplied with both. This concern was fully justified. In the initial, "founding" elections, the Communist Party acted much like an old-time U.S. city machine, mobilizing voters in the countryside behind promises of safe and gradual reform, in contrast with the "radical experiments" of the democratic opposition. In the southern tier of states in the region (Albania, Bulgaria, Romania, Serbia), the rural population was sufficiently large, and communist manipulation of national divisions sufficiently adroit, to secure electoral victories in the first balloting. Throughout the region, the subsequent pattern was generally to punish whoever won the previous election for the dislocations and economic pain of the transition. Anticommunist victories in Lithuania, Poland, and Hungary, for example, gave way to the return of the reform communists to power in the next contest. Meanwhile, in the south, in Bulgaria and Albania, the noncommunist opposition rallied to win the second set of elections.

This general pattern tells us several things and does not tell us others. Public retaliation for economic loss or other dislocation is a familiar occurrence in established Western democracies as well. In fact, scholars of democratic elections see nothing odd in the idea of an election's serving as a plebiscite on previous regime performance. "It's the economy, stupid" was a watchword of the 1992 U.S. election in which seasoned leader George Bush was defeated in a period of economic sluggishness. What is different about the postcommunist elections is the operation of this dynamic in a transitional period in which fluctuations in

BOX 3.1
The Governments of Czechoslovakia and Its Successors, 1990–1994

I. *Governments Prior to the 1990 Elections*
   Mixed communist/nonpartisan transitional governments
   Federal prime minister: Marian Čalfa (Slovak ex-communist)
   Federal President: Václav Havel (Czech dissident)
   Federal Assembly chair: Alexander Dubček (Slovak ex-communist)
   Foreign minister: Jiří Dienstbier (Czech dissident)
   Czech prime minister: Frantisek Pitra (communist)
   Slovak prime minister: Milan Čič (ex-communist)

II. *Governments Following the 1990 Elections*
   Federal Government: Coalition of Civic Forum, Public Against Violence,
      Christian Democratic Movement
   Prime minister: Marian Čalfa (PAV, Slovak)
   President: Václav Havel
   Finance minister: Václav Klaus (Czech, Civic Forum)
   Foreign minister: Jiří Dienstbier (Czech, Civic Forum)
   Economics minister: Vladimír Dlouhý (Czech, Civic Forum)
   Federal Assembly Chair: Alexander Dubček (Slovak, PAV)
      (Disintegration of Civic Forum in early 1991 did not change composition of
      the government)

   Czech Republic Government: Coalition of Civic Forum, People's Party, Movement
      for Self-Governing Democracy/Society for Moravia and Silesia
   Prime minister: Petr Pithart (former dissident, Civic Forum)

   Slovak Government:
   June 1990–April 1991: Coalition of PAV, Christian Democratic Movement, Slo-
      vak Democratic Party
   Prime minister: Vladimír Mečiar (Public Against Violence)
      (Dissolution of PAV in conjunction with Mečiar's ouster)
   April 1991–June 1992: Coalition of Christian Democratic Movement, PAV
      remnant
   Prime Minister: Ján Čarnogurský (Christian Democratic Movement)

III. *Governments Following the 1992 Elections*
   Federal Government Until State Dissolution January 1993: Coalition of Civic Dem-
      ocratic Party (Czech), Movement for a Democratic Slovakia (Slovak), Christian
      Democratic Union/People's Party (Czech)
   Prime minister: Jan Stráský (Civic Democratic Party)
   President: none. *Havel resigns after reelection failure without replacement*

   Czech Government, 1992–present: Coalition of Civic Democratic Party, Christian
   Democratic Union, Christian Democratic Party, Civic Democratic Alliance

Prime minister: Václav Klaus (Civic Democratic Party)
Government remains unchanged following the dissolution of the state, with the exception of the merger between the Christian Democratic Party and Civic Democratic Party in 1996.
President since February 1993: Václav Havel

Slovak Government
June 1992–March 1994: Coalition of Movement for a Democratic Slovakia, at times in cooperation with Slovak National Party
Prime minister: Vladimír Mečiar (Movement for a Democratic Slovakia)
(Mečiar government falls after no confidence vote, March 1994)
President, March 1993–present: Michal Kováč
March 1994–November 1994: Coalition of Democratic Union, Party of the Democratic Left, Christian Democratic Movement, several minor parties
Prime minister: Jozef Moravčík (Democratic Union)

IV. Slovak Government Following the 1994 Slovak Elections
November 1994–present: Coalition of Movement for a Democratic Slovakia, Association of Slovak Workers, Slovak National Party, minor parties
Prime minister: Vladimír Mečiar (Movement for a Democratic Slovakia)

Note: The Czech and Slovak Republics had no presidents until their establishment as independent states. Presidential offices are nonpartisan.

---

party strength occurred against a broader background of flux and transition. The good news about these electoral transitions is their very occurrence. In all cases, the losers accepted the victory of the winners as sufficiently legitimate that there was no challenge to the outcome. Reform communists and their opponents yielded to the popular verdict. Many definitions of democracy emphasize the orderly transfer of power after competitive elections as an essential component of democracy itself. It is a major threat to democratic stability—and a major symptom of regime crisis—if the electoral verdict is greeted with protests, street violence, coup attempts or political boycotts. To this extent, at least, most of the fledgling East European democracies have passed one critical test—the test of playing by the basic rules of the game in transferring power after elections.

This having been said, the party/electoral politics of Czechoslovakia since 1989 are not a textbook case. The first election did, to be sure, fall into the "northern" or Central European pattern of communist repudiation—the Civic Forum and its Slovak ally PAV won the electoral contest with 47 percent of the statewide vote. The Civic Forum had not initially intended to contest the first elections at all, seeing itself as an honest broker of the transition rather than a permanent aspirant to political power. An overwhelming majority of the Forum's supporters did not want it to become an ordinary political party. However, the need to present a broad-based front against the communists led the Forum into the first elections. Still, the dissident leadership of 1990 tended to regard the movement as a "primary school" for politics and politicians during the gestation period of democracy. After that, it might refocus attention on regional or grassroots activity.[28]

The communists came in a distant second, with a significant but as yet marginal parliamentary base built around the votes of 14 percent of the electorate. They had campaigned with pledges of a reformist change of heart, new and less tarnished younger candidates, and the reminder of their own far greater political experience. This outcome strongly resembled those of Hungary and East Germany, and of Poland at its first fully competitive election in 1991.[29]

The referendum character of the election was further enhanced by the strong similarity of party platforms, all of them—even the communists!—pledging commitment to democratization, marketization, and a return to Europe. The victorious CF/PAV coalition had made a point of linking these three ideas, stressing the message that internal transformation would pave the way to a reintegration into the European culture from which Czechoslovakia had been shielded by the iron curtain. PAV election posters carried the party's slogan, "A Chance for Slovakia," superimposed on a map of Europe, and the CF appealed to voters to go "With the Civic Forum into Europe."

However, the 1990 elections told an additional story, and it is worth examining what that story was. The notable thing about Czechoslovakia's adherence to the "northern pattern" of electoral retaliation against the communists is the incompleteness of that parallel. What is missing from the picture is the second striking pattern in that election, the emergence in Czechoslovakia of what amounted to two different party systems, one in the Czech Republic and one in Slovakia. Table 3.1 demonstrates the lack of overlap between the Czech and Slovak electoral constituencies.

With the exception of the Communist Party (soon to be federalized into two separate organizations, each with its own autonomous leadership), the electorally successful parties were all regionally based rather than statewide. One can find an institutional rationale for this outcome; Czechoslovakia's federal structure and the simultaneity of statewide elections to the parliament and regional elections to the Czech and Slovak National Councils facilitated separate organizational efforts in each republic. However, politics in a federal system does not necessarily dictate separate, regionally based parties. The United States and Germany are prominent contemporary examples of federal states with effective statewide parties. In fact, East Germany's first postcommunist election did not produce a separate party system for that country. Instead, the existing party system of West Germany "colonized" the east, much as the Czech parties had been able to parlay their organizational assets into a foothold in Slovakia in the interwar Republic.

A federal system alone is not necessarily a formula for decentralized regional parties, and in the case of Czechoslovakia we need to look further for an explanation. After 1989, there was no Czech democratic opposition party with the organization and following to gain a head start and preempt Slovak party development, or vice versa. The Czech Christian Democrats, for example, did not

Table 3.1 1990–1992 Elections to House of the People of the Federal Assembly of the Czech and Slovak Federative Republic

| | 1990 | | | | 1992 | | | |
| | Czech Republic | | Slovak Republic | | Czech Republic | | Slovak Republic | |
Party	% Votes	Seats	% Votes	Seats	% Votes	Seats	% Votes	Seats
CDM	—	—	19	11	—	—	9	6
CDU	9	9	—	—	6	7	—	—
Civic Forum	53	68	—	—				
Communists	13	15	14	8	14	19	14	10
Hungarian Parties	—	—	9	5	—	—	8	10
PAV	—	—	33	19	—	—	—	—
Sl. National Party	—	—	11	6	—	—	9	6
Czech Social Democrats					8	10		
CDP alliance					34	48		
Liberal Social Union					6	7		
Republican					7	8		
MDS							34	24
MSD/SMS	8	9	—	—	—	—	—	—

Key: CDM=Christian Democratic Movement; CDP alliance=Civic Democratic Party/Christian Democratic Party; CDU=Christian Democratic Union; HCDM=Hungarian Christian Democratic Movement; PAV=Public Against Violence; MSD/SMS=Movement for Self-Governing Democracy/Society for Moravia and Silesia; MDS=Movement for a Democratic Slovakia

Sources: Compiled from Jan Obrman, "Civic Forum Surges to an Impressive Victory in Elections," *Radio Free Europe Report on Eastern Europe* 1:25 (June 22, 1990):13–14, and Jan Obrman, "The Czechoslovak Elections," *RFE/RL Research Report* 1:26 (June 26, 1992):12–19.

swallow up the Slovak Christian Democrats. What seems to be a crucial element in the equation is the national sensitivity of the smaller Slovak electorate. Where regional institutional bases are bolstered by ethnonational divisions, as in Czechoslovakia, Yugoslavia, and the former USSR, the historical learning process since the establishment of these states after World War I "taught" the smaller nations to protect their own interests. A party with a clear ethnonational identity and an institutional base on which to build could do very well amid the chaos of early efforts to organize a party system. Voters responded to the opportunity to express *both* their national identity and their desire for change.

Note that it is the combination of institutional bases and ethnic diversity that facilitates the emergence of separate party subsystems. Minority parties without a constitutional-territorial power base to capture, that is, without a federal structure, do gain electoral followings and parliamentary representation (throughout Eastern Europe, ethnically based parties have prospered electorally) but have no way of translating this into decisionmaking authority, even when the minority is geographically concentrated. But in Czechoslovakia, Slovaks were not dependent on the Czechs. Each republic had its own legislature, and even the Federal Assembly was subdivided into chambers where each republic's representatives had veto power over important constitutional issues. There was therefore a political incentive to organize party politics at the republic level.

The first election, therefore, established a political context more complex than that of ethnically homogeneous Poland and Hungary. Voters had signaled that the agenda of transition in the newly named Czech and Slovak Federative Republic (ČSFR) included a national question that awaited resolution. Until it was resolved, the politics of the postcommunist state would be hostage to the priority attached to the Slovak search for a secure and effective national base and for recognition of the importance of substate identities. We will examine how this conflict led to the disintegration of the Czechoslovak statehood experiment in Chapter 4, but in the context of Czechoslovakia's political transition, what is important is that voters and politicians were acting on a calculation of public choice that included, but also transcended, the question of economic transformation and democratization. Czechs might find the Slovak resistance to a common agenda of change a source of irritation or helpless resignation. But there was no evading the problem, in party politics or in any other institutional context.

The second election, in 1992, found the regional subsystems further entrenched, as Table 3.1 demonstrates.

By 1992, with two years of inconclusive negotiations over the appropriate form of a noncommunist federal state behind them, the two republics conducted two separate electoral campaigns side by side. Czech Prime Minister Petr Pithart looked toward this election in frustration at the way the national question was distorting the electoral process; he expected the election to be a "plebiscite on the ordering of the state,"[30] and he was half right. The Czech electorate and its parties skimmed over the issue to focus on the acceleration and completion of the economic transition. Their Slovak counterparts devoted virtually exclusive attention to the protection of Slovak interests; this did indeed amount to a second referendum election in Slovakia, not a referendum on communism this time, but rather a referendum on which party could best fight for Slovak rights. There was little common ground between the competing Czech and Slovak priorities—they were not even on the same policy scale. Impatient Czechs wanted the Slovaks to shape up and commit to the agenda of economic change. Like their predecessors in the First Republic and even in the communist regime, they tended to see the Slovak agenda as obsessively and parochially fixated on symbolic grievances and national self-assertion. Czech politician Václav Klaus did not consider that the Slovaks really *had* a party system: "Slovakia's union with the Czech Republic in a federation results in the problems of Slovak political development being trivialized to the question of nationalism vs. federation. I think that a potential split of Czechoslovakia will be a chance for the creation of a normal political spectrum in Slovakia."[31] Although his tone was derogatory and condescending (federation was hardly a trivial issue), he did have a point. Slovaks could not and would not focus on what the Czechs deemed to be the central axis of party division and debate—the economic system—without first securing fundamental safeguards for national identity and for the protection of Slovak economic interests.

So some of the central issues of Czechoslovak politics were on hold until this stalemated issue was resolved. Ultimately it was decided that the issue *could not* be decided within the boundaries of a common Czech/Slovak state, and the regional party subsystems became the statewide party systems of two new states, the Czech Republic and Slovakia.

A look at the evolution of these two party systems since the 1990 elections will be a good introduction to postcommunist politics. The first elections did not give a clear sense of the future shape of the party system. Many competing interests and divergent policy outlooks were all huddled together under the umbrellas of the Civic Forum and Public Against Violence, maintaining an artificial unity in confrontation with the communists. These "grand coalitions" were too diverse to survive long once the immediate need for unity against the communists had passed. Like Solidarity in Poland, the broad movements in Czechoslovakia began to disintegrate once they had fought and won the first elections. There was both sadness and bitterness in the parting of the ways of comrades-in-arms, some of whom had fought together for more than a decade against the communist regime. However, even many of the movements' participants understood the inevitability of the change. The defeat of the old regime created a new policy agenda and a need to govern. Negotiating that agenda created new divisions; anticommunism was not a policy program in itself and could not unify movement politicians who now had to design economic institutions, revamp the educational system, or reformulate foreign policy.

In the Czech Republic, the subsequent party alignment came closer than in Slovakia to the left-right continuum pervasive in the West. The political spectrum included right-of-center parties that espoused rapid economic transformation and a less paternalist state, centrist parties, and a cluster of left-wing parties concerned with the preservation of the communist-era safety net to buffer ordinary people against the pain of economic transition. To oversimplify a complex reality, the different clusters initially corresponded roughly to the new experts on the right, the dissident-based movement in the center, and the communists and ex-communists on the left.

This alignment began to emerge in the aftermath of the 1990 election. Civic Forum had remained intact as long as the central issue was confronting communist power. Once that goal had been achieved, however, the unwieldy and diverse Forum faced a crisis of mission. Klaus felt that the movement should become a moderate "right-wing party of clear political orientation," since centrist views would only confuse the public and blur the sense of policy direction, particularly on the economic transformation that was so central to his own political agenda. He and his adherents described the existing Civic Forum orientation as "illegible." In the fall of 1990 Klaus fought for and won the chairmanship of the Forum, beating out rivals who wanted to preserve its broad movement character. In February 1991, the Forum split into subgroups, which continued to cooperate in the government coalition in order to preserve continuity.

For the 1992 elections, the Civic Democratic Party (CDP) that emerged from Civic Forum became the vehicle for the right-of-center Klaus perspective. Two additional offspring of the original Forum also retained the parental adjective "civic" in their names: the Civic Democratic Alliance, a right-of-center libertarian party allergic to tight organization, and the centrist Civic Movement, also loosely organized and banking on the popularity of its leading politicians. Klaus had been right; his party's organization and "clear political orientation" toward rapid economic transformation preempted the field from the two other Civic Forum siblings, neither of which was able to cross the 5 percent threshold for parliamentary representation. The parties of the left, with programs that were more distinctly differentiated, improved their performance over 1990. The Society for Moravia-Silesia, perhaps because it did not offer a distinctive economic program in an election dominated by that issue, did not repeat its surprisingly strong showing of 1990, instead falling below the electoral threshold and out of the federal parliament (it retained a foothold in the Czech National Council). Although the party system in the Czech Republic remained volatile (in 1992, only the Christian Democrats competed in essentially the same form they had in 1990), economic differentiation did seem to be emerging as a primary axis in the system. Nonetheless, Jiří Dienstbier certainly had a point, as well as a colorful image, when he described all the existing parties as formless "amoebas."[32]

It is harder to be sure how to interpret the party spectrum in Slovakia in 1992. Some analysts have pointed to the reappearance of certain cleavages that governed Slovak party politics in interwar Czechoslovakia; this is especially apparent in the reemergence of nationally and religiously based parties, although there is no strong counterpart to the earlier Slovak Agrarians.[33] However, it is hard to forecast the aftermath of the intense focus on the national question in the period between 1990 and 1992. Public Against Violence broke up in the spring of 1991 when deposed Prime Minister Mečiar went into opposition. He took with him a new party, the Movement for a Democratic Slovakia (MDS), built around a core of PAV deputies loyal to him and to his conception of defending Slovakia from disruptive economic reform and Pragocentrism. Thereafter, up to and beyond the 1992 election, the burning question in Slovakia was the future of the state; the issue was not so much what form it should take—most parties wanted a looser federation, and many of these saw decentralization as a building block for eventual independence, formal or informal. The fight was over which party could best achieve this result, which party was sufficiently steadfast or responsible or pure in its pursuit of Slovak goals. Čarnogurský's Christian Democrats, the ultranationalist Slovak National Party, and Mečiar's MDS all claimed to have the "best" program for defending Slovak interests. The national identity issue, like the confrontation with the communists in 1990, would take a new form in the new Slovak state. Because the ultimate constitutional bargain was a negotiated agreement in 1992 to divide Czechoslovakia into two new Czech and Slovak states, the separate courses of electoral politics and party development after the dissolution of the state will be examined in Chapter 5, which analyzes developments after the breakup of Czechoslovakia in greater detail.

Voters, Parties, and the Realities of Parliamentary Governance

It should already be obvious that competitive elections are a necessary but insufficient condition for establishing stable democratic rule. Those entrusted with popular mandates must also be able to govern effectively and accountably. In fact, even genuinely free elections are a mere façade unless elected officials subsequently have real decisionmaking authority. If someone else is calling the shots behind the scenes (the military, perhaps, or the bureaucracy), then voter choices do not have the importance in practice that they do in theory. And of course if the elected officials prove unable to govern because of divisions and contentiousness, there will be little resemblance between electoral promises and policy outcomes.

Historically, the glue of the democratic system in complex industrial societies too large to be governed by town meetings has been the party system, which ideally is the linkage structure between social groups and the governing institutions.[34] In practice, this link does not fall into place automatically. Postcommunist parties were generally organized from the top down; the elections were an experimental search for a constituency base responsive to the party message. Locating a niche in the new system was partly a process of trial and error, and this experimentation produced some complications for governance.

It is more difficult to govern accountably if the partisan alignments are constantly in flux, as they clearly were in the period of party formation after the Vel-

vet Revolution. Evidence of the fluidity of current Czech and Slovak party alignments lies in the parliamentary game of musical chairs played by elected deputies
since 1990. In the 1990 election, eight parties and coalitions won seats in the Federal Assembly. By the next election, defections and schisms had produced more
than twenty parties and factions and a core of independent deputies who abandoned their initial party labels without acquiring new ones. In the Slovak National Council, seven parties grew to eleven in the same period.[35] The central reason for party growth in the Slovak case was the split in Public Against Violence
in the spring of 1991, triggering the collapse of the Slovak government. The party
alignments of the 1992 elections proved no more stable, at least in Slovakia. A series of defections from the ruling MDS into a new party eventually contributed
to the collapse of the government by early 1994 and the announcement of new
elections.

Although the Czech ruling coalition in the Czech National Council did not fall,
this is not because the party alignments remained stable. On the contrary, by
1994 there was only one party in the Czech National Council that had the same
delegation it started with after the 1992 elections. The Czech government remained in power because all the membership reshufflings gave the coalition a net
gain of two seats. The most dramatic realignments occurred in the opposition.
Overall, the number of parties increased from nine to eleven in two years, there
were ten new independent deputies, and some parties had lost as much as half of
their delegations.[36] The changes are not just the result of individual deputies
repositioning either. Not only have new parties emerged to contest each election,
but existing parliamentary parties have undergone frequent schisms as well. A
more orthodox hard-line Communist Party split off from the Czech Communist
Party as it struggled with a moderate reformist identity after 1992. The Movement for Democracy/Society of Moravia-Silesia ultimately regrouped into the
Movement for Silesian-Moravian Unification, losing membership in the process.
These examples could be multiplied.

This kind of volatility is unusual in contemporary American politics, where a
congressional representative's shift in party affiliation grabs headlines. Party splits
are rare in Western Europe, too, and party discipline in parliamentary voting is
much more pronounced. What do the constant shifts in party identity tell us
about the Czech and Slovak party systems and the nature of democratic accountability? First, the Czech and Slovak cases are not unique. Every postcommunist party system has experienced this pattern of regrouping to a greater or
lesser extent. In the Czech and Slovak cases, as elsewhere, these continuous shifts
suggest that the parties do not yet reflect clear, well-organized political orientations rooted in stable voter constituencies. Strong links between voters and parties and strong party organization would tend to discourage frequent switches of
party affiliation as well as periodic party schisms. In the beginning, however, the
voter had no guarantee that the party supported in one election would even exist
by the next and that candidates pledged to the program of that party would have

retained the same partisan affiliation between elections. So with each election, there have been new parties, new acronyms (CDP? CDU? CDA?) for voters to decipher. The many unfamiliar landmarks in the electoral landscape certainly made it difficult and time consuming for voters to choose intelligently and probably made them more vulnerable to demagogic appeals and alienation.

The difficulties of governance with a multiparty coalition already posed obstacles to accountability, even in the absence of further defections and internal schisms. But the fluidity of party lines was a heavy additional burden. It was hard for governing coalitions to count heads to deliver a majority on any given issue, since deputies tended to develop their own stance on the burning issues of the day, and even to quit. To a far greater extent than in the West, deputies in all postcommunist parliaments have tended to act seriously on constitutional provisions (also present in some Western constitutions) that stipulate the right of the deputy to vote according to his or her conscience,[37] and thus, by inference, the right to flout party discipline on a regular basis. Although these constitutional provisions are a legalistic reaction to the regimented voting of the communist period, the practical basis for low party discipline has been the initial inability of fledgling parties to police and enforce that discipline with the tools available to Western parties, particularly in a fluid electoral environment where barriers to new party formation are still low. A multiparty system can be very complicated to govern, but it is doubly complicated when it lacks party discipline in legislative voting.

The eventual stabilization of these volatile party systems might be a measure of the consolidation of the democratic process. Greater continuity would indicate that the political battle lines are finally beginning to settle into more predictable patterns that reflect more consistent issue orientations. This would make election campaigns easier for the voters to "decode," and legislatures easier to organize. In other words, it might signal that the parties were no longer floating free at the top of the political pyramid. Instead of elites shifting allegiance at will, they would be more closely bound to a constituency that would demand predictable, consistent behavior. At that point, the lines of accountability between the public and the government would be far more defined, and there would be a greater chance that what you see is what you get.

It is quite reasonable to suppose that this stabilization process was delayed in Czechoslovakia by the disintegration of the state. But instabilities are also likely to continue, since the class structure of the postcommunist states is still undergoing the changes associated with economic transformation. Even after new social groupings begin to appear, however—a protracted process in itself—political scientists warn that the result may not be party alignments as durable as those that occurred earlier in the West. They point out that the bases for stable party identities are currently eroding in the Western postindustrial societies; the heyday of the party system may be over, and postcommunist polities may be emerging in a period where the party can no longer perform its traditionally understood linkage role even in an established system.[38] The difficulty with this, of course, is that democratic ingenuity has yet to provide a satisfactory substitute.

In Search of a Democratic Mindset

If the party systems are still in their infancy, so is the mindset that permits effective bargaining and compromise among rival political orientations. Institutional design can be a difficult task for the architects of democratic transition, but political attitudes are probably even more difficult to reconfigure. One of the most important components of the democratic mindset is the idea that those who disagree with you politically are not archfiends whose ideas threaten the very foundations of the new democracy.

It is understandable that it has been difficult for governments to accept the concept of a loyal opposition and for the opposition to view its disagreement with government policies as less than a cataclysmic struggle for the soul of the state. After all, decades of communist insistence on the one ideologically correct approach and intolerance of opposition views are not a good training ground for democratic tolerance. Even the dissidents had been engaged in moralistic struggles of good versus evil with the regime, struggles in which it was morally dangerous to compromise one's beliefs. Added to these previous experiences were the uncertainties of the transition period itself. Even paranoids may have real enemies, and some of the critics of new policies are indeed critics of the democratic process itself. Fear of communist subversion of the new order was clearly part of what made the lustration controversy so emotional. This only makes it harder for politicians to sort out Traitors from Worthy Opponents, to adjust perspective to view one's political rivals as meriting respect, negotiation, and compromise. Perhaps politics should be a sacred trust, but if it becomes a chronic moral crusade against evil, then the cooperation and give-and-take necessary to democratic politics-as-usual will be hard to achieve.

The essence of the attitudinal problem, a problem that new democracies must confront if politics is not to degenerate into name-calling chaos, is to be able to accept the idea of a loyal opposition—political opponents who accept the democratic rules of the game even if they disagree on specific policies. The concept of the loyal opposition underpins the ability to bargain and compromise, or at least to refrain from attacking opponents whose mandate from the voters was achieved just as yours was. In the 1994 Slovak elections, Slovak President Michal Kováč appealed to the contending parties to remember this. His words are a good summary of the attitudes that help to stabilize democratic politics; the election campaign, he pleaded,

> should not turn into a life-or-death struggle, where the sole aim is the moral and political destruction of opponents. Let us remember that even after the election we will meet and cooperate with those whom we might have unnecessarily insulted. . . . Esteemed citizens! I would like to appeal to you to respect the results of the election

even if your party or movement does not win or does not achieve the results you hoped for. In a democratic system, the minority must accept the majority view and respect it. In some future elections, the losers now may be winners, and it is therefore proper and correct that they respect each other."[39]

The absence of a conception of a loyal opposition and respect for opponents is not harmful merely because the inability to compromise blocks political debate and undermines policymaking, although the personalist politics of unrestrained rivalry does have exactly that effect. Worse still, the spectacle of rival politicians viciously mauling each other is one that dismays and repels the public and undercuts the legitimacy of democratic institutions and leadership. Postcommunist citizens have become even more cynical about politics as they witness such behavior; they might have been alienated from the previous communist regime, but they had been accustomed to a communist façade of harmony and unity, and the subsequent rough-and-tumble disagreements have therefore been particularly jarring. Although public confidence in some individual leaders and the cabinet governments remained high following the first elections, confidence in parliament took a nosedive, descending from an unrealistically high 90 percent in June 1990 to a lowly 26 percent two years later. Public opinion polls recorded a popular impression that parliamentarians were largely concerned about their own benefit and self-aggrandizement rather than the public good.[40]

Despite these costs, achieving a more moderate outlook has not come easily to postcommunist politics. President Havel issued an eloquent plea to the voters before the first elections: "Vote for people who are modest, who are matter-of-fact, who are decent, whom you trust. Do not vote for loud-mouths. . . . In my view it is not essential which flag is waved by a loud-mouth. The essential fact is that he is shouting. What is necessary is a discussion."[41] The proceedings in the Federal Assembly, however, were not always a forum for reasoned discussion. They have been characterized as "marked by the emergence of a less rational and more emotional and personalized, 'semi-responsible opposition,' with debates quite often degenerating into personal mud-slinging and character assassination, rather than reasoned discussion of the matter at hand."[42] Parliamentary rules gave free rein to contentiousness, granting the unrestricted right to propose amendments on each bill as well as the right to speak to an unlimited number of deputies. The media, not guiltless itself, began early on to intersperse its political commentary with appeals for "fair play" (the term was rendered in English, perhaps to underscore the point that the idea seemed "foreign" to Czech and Slovak politics). But there is still the tendency in the Czech Republic and Slovakia, as elsewhere in the region, to deal with political disagreements by assaulting the character and integrity of one's opponents. Aren't "They" soft on communism? In Slovakia, integrity issues still center on the adequacy of one's "Slovak" credentials. President Kováč's critics have assailed him for being a "lukewarm patriot" who "wanted to arrive at Slovak statehood gradually," and whose East Slovak accent is cited for its "transgressions against the Slovak language."[43]

No politics is free of this kind of personalist innuendo, a lesson Americans relearn in the negative campaigning of every election. But it is especially damaging in a newly established system that has not been legitimated by time and custom and has yet to prove its capacity to perform in meeting public needs. How can the electorate trust politicians who clearly do not trust each other? This syndrome should cause dismay, but it is hardly unique to the postcommunist states. New democracies must always become accustomed to the idea of opposition, rotation in power, bargaining, and compromise. The theorists of democratic transition have been realistic about this attitudinal problem, arguing that democratic institutions come first. They are in effect saying that democracy may start without democrats and that the democratic mindset can evolve with time and practice. In the short term, the most that can be hoped is that politicians will play by the democratic rules of the game and see them as the only acceptable game in town. From that limited start, greater tolerance and cooperation may grow. In the meantime, however, the impediments to governing under such conditions are obvious. In this, as in other respects, democracy is not simply a matter of holding free elections.

Designer Democracy: Engineering the Decisionmaking Institutions

A commitment to free elections is only the first fundamental step to constructing a democratic political system. There is no generic model for democracy, but there are several basic institutional choices to be made before the outlines of a system are clear. These choices are not made from behind a "veil of ignorance," in the Rawlsian sense of abstract justice and fairness. The choices are made by politicians whose own interests and historical-cultural learning are entirely relevant to the outcomes. In East Central Europe, there were no separate constituent assemblies like the U.S. Constitutional Convention; the first freely elected parliaments were intended to do double duty as constituent assemblies, which meant in effect that elected politicians were designing their own job descriptions and selection process, while simultaneously coping with the demands of economic transformation and other pressing public policy issues that could not wait until the constitution caught up with them.

These political cross-pressures and burdens almost assured that, as Stephen Holmes put it, "the political process in the new democracies takes the form of an ongoing constitutional crisis," with the constitutional product delayed in achieving completion, or subject to additional revision and fine-tuning. While it might be theoretically desirable to ratify an instantly hallowed constitutional document, the delays and revisions are not necessarily a drawback. Rather, in Holmes's analysis, there may be considerable value in incorporating the political experience of the transition process into a document that eventually reflects not only "negative" constitutionalism (the construction of a system that guarantees rights and limits government in reaction to the previous communist experience) but also affirmative attention to creating a system that functions effectively and has sufficient power to enforce its decisions.[44] Holmes might have pointed to Poland's so-called "little constitution" as an example of a learning process; the "little constitution" was a provisional understanding on the division of legislative-executive power passed in 1992, which both provided groundwork for a future final settlement and incorporated the experience of the first three years of legislative-executive conflict.[45]

As it transpired, constitutional postponement was the norm in the new post-communist states, except in Romania and Bulgaria, where continuing communist influence was sufficient to crack heads together and achieve a quicker, if less democratic, resolution. Czechoslovakia's constitutional postponement was in some respects a special case, however, because the national question deadlocked deliberations, as we will see in Chapter 4. Nevertheless, the Federal Assembly made significant institutional choices even before the constitutional question was "resolved" by the breakup of the state and the rush to form constitutions for two new states before the January 1993 independence deadline.

Czechoslovakia shared with its neighbors the need to make two basic choices—the type of electoral system and the distribution of institutional power within the regime. As we have seen, the architects of democratic institutions had to design the electoral system first—just weeks after the transition began. As for the balance of institutional power, the starting point was a European parliamentary system, in which the prime minister leads a cabinet government whose tenure in office is dependent on the will of the parliament.

The presidency occupies a peculiar position in this kind of system. The federal presidency occupied by Havel was modeled on the interwar presidency but with substantially less power. The Czech and Slovak successor states adopted variants of this model. As in the interwar state, it is important not to be misled by the word "president" into imagining an office like the U.S. presidency. Perhaps the best way to understand what a presidency means in this different context is to compare the office in the Czech Republic and Slovakia with the more familiar U.S. presidency. First of all, in both the ČSFR and the successor Czech and Slovak Republics, the presidents are elected by the legislatures rather than the public and therefore have no direct popular base. The popular election of the U.S. president, by contrast, gives the holder of the office a special electoral mandate to speak for the country as a whole. The desirability of a directly elected president was debated, but ultimately each legislature, retaining its own preeminence, voted to retain the indirect parliamentary selection of the presidency. The presidents are also subject to removal by the initiative of the legislature during their five-year terms, although the cause of removal, as in the U.S. case, must be a serious challenge to the constitutional order: "high treason" in the Czech Republic, and in Slovakia for "activities against the sovereignty and integrity of the Slovak Republic or a conduct aimed to destroy the democratic and constitutional regime."[46]

The president may be head of state (the ceremonial office) but does not hold the supreme executive power that a president does under the U.S. constitution; supreme executive power is vested in the government—the prime minister and his cabinet. Therefore, even though the Czech and Slovak presidents appoint the prime minister, that appointment is ultimately dependent on the confidence of the legislature; a president cannot appoint and dismiss cabinets at will, and his legislative veto can be overridden by a simple majority (of the whole parliament in the Czech Republic and of the members present in Slovakia). In fact, the Czech president can exercise his most important powers (as commander in chief and treaty-maker, for example) only with the countersignature of the prime minister.

Another source of institutional weakness is the presidents' relation to the party system, or rather the lack of it. Throughout the region, even directly elected presidents are expected to renounce their party affiliations once they have been selected for the presidential office. Although this act is supposed to ensure that the president will act in the interest of all the people, the most obvious political effect is to cut the presidency off from a political power base. The U.S. president often has difficulty influencing Congress even when he can count on some support from members of his own party. Imagine how hard it would be without that base of support. In the Czech and Slovak Republics, therefore, the prime minister is the real political strongman, and this is the office that the most electorally powerful political figures in each republic, Václav Klaus and Vladimír Mečiar, chose to fill in 1992.[47]

Overall, then, a Czech or Slovak president has nothing approaching the power of the U.S. president, and the influence of the office depends significantly on the influence of the incumbent and the existing political system. The Czech and Slovak presidencies reflect this fact in differing ways. In Slovakia, the tumult in the Slovak parliament and within the government itself was so continuous that even the limited presidency was a key element in the balance of power between competing factions; the president cooperated with Mečiar's opponents to help oust his government in 1994. Mečiar declared, in response to such interference, that the Slovak presidency had too much constitutional power, and that the president abused what power he had, thus hinting at the possibility of a messy investigation of presidential activities that would tip the balance further toward the prime minister's office.[48] The Slovak presidency has been embroiled in constitutional controversy ever since his inauguration, as we will see later.

Czech president Havel has not had the political leverage of divisions in the government, since Prime Minister Klaus has maintained a relatively united governing coalition. Havel, however, has resources in his considerable political popularity and standing as the voice of the Velvet Revolution, and these can be thrown into the balance at specific times and on specific issues. Generally, however, the relative power of the president is dependent on the unity or disunity in the legislature; a united governing coalition with a majority in parliament has a good chance of outmaneuvering the president every time. This, of course, is what the framers of the Czech and Slovak constitutions intended, not only because they were the deputies of the sitting parliament, but also because a parliamentary system was the goal.

In fact, many scholars of institutional design agree with the framers of the Czech and Slovak constitutions; they do not consider a strongly presidential system very desirable for a new democracy either. Cross-national studies suggest that new democracies whose architects opt for a presidential rather than a parliamentary system end up with higher failure rates.[49] In the postcommunist countries, the less stable and generally less democratic post-Soviet states have presidential systems, while the more democratized East European states generally have weaker presidents and stronger parliaments.

Of course, there is the chicken-and-egg question here: Are presidential democracies more failure-prone *because* they are presidential and thus potentially dictatorial, or do the constitutional architects opt for the strong individual leadership of a presidential system in the first place because the country faces such political strife that any system might fail? The Russian example illustrates the point well. In 1993 the Russian electorate voted for a strong president in the constitutional referendum in large part because they feared anarchy and chaos, and hoped that Boris Yeltsin and his presidential successors would be able to bring order. The Russian case also raises the possibility that states with strong authoritarian traditions gravitate toward the prospect of stronger individual leadership under a presidential system; thus, a system already burdened with a less democratic political culture may opt for presidentialism because it conforms more closely to the previous pattern of strong leadership and initiative. The Czechs and Slovaks, with stronger democratic traditions and laboring under less volatile political conditions, did not have the same reason to insist on a strong presidency. And if the Czech and Slovak democracies end up being more stable than the Russian, there is no reason to assume that the reason is presidentialism as such rather than the differences between the political climate and political culture that inspired the institutional choices in the first place.[50]

A second question, the problem of whether and how to share power with the regions, was unresolvable until the Czech-Slovak controversy was resolved; even then, the problem remained. Although Czech and Slovak local and statewide government institutions were specified in the two new constitutions of 1992, the question of an intermediary regional institutionalization was so controversial that it defied immediate resolution. It was left to the post-independence governments to determine what, if any, significant power would go to a regional level between the state and the local government. In deciding this issue, both republics appeared all too sensitive to the lessons of their own breakup: Both Czech and Slovak governments were wary of according power to regional bodies and equally conflicted about how to draw regional boundaries.

In the Czech Republic, the sticking point was whether to give institutional recognition to Moravian identity. The historic Czech lands had consisted of two components, Bohemia and Moravia. Both are linguistically Czech, but different enough in interests and culture to inspire Moravian demands to be recognized as a separate subgroup, or even as a separate nation altogether. Politicians of the central government, many of them Bohemian Czechs, did not want to encourage that outlook. They certainly did not wish to create a new "Slovakia" syndrome in which Moravian politicians developed a strong institutional power base from which to challenge the center. The Civic Democratic Party leaders in the ruling government coalition therefore preferred to divide and conquer: They proposed to divide the country into eight regions, trisecting Moravia and thereby diluting its political clout. The Moravian autonomists were insistent that Moravia as a whole should be institutionally recognized as a single region, preferably in a federal form. The central government recoiled from this counterproposal in dismay. One federal experience, it would seem, was enough. Unable to decide this issue in time for independence, Czech politicians deferred it for future political wrangling. Indeed, Klaus appeared willing to defer it indefinitely.

In Slovakia, as well, the question of regional divisions touched a sensitive cord because of the territorial concentration of the Hungarian minority in southern Slovakia. Any regional arrangement that gave this minority a solid power base was just as unacceptable to the Slovak government as recognizing Moravian claims was to the Czech government. The existing Slovak regions therefore remained in receivership under the direction of the Ministry of the Interior until new regional boundaries could be agreed upon. The sole exception was Košice in eastern Slovakia, a powerful industrial center that has its own regional government and a reputation for championing the continuance of the Czechoslovak state as well as for opposing Mečiar's political stance, which has been seen locally by many as a repugnant brand of "Bratislava centralism" worse than Pragocentrism.

In theory, the basic institutional design of the Czech and Slovak political systems was complete with the passage of the constitutions in 1992. In practice, we have just seen that there were several important postponements, particularly regarding the power of the central government in each state in relation to its regions. In fact, however, the institutionalization process is even less complete than that, especially since a few years hardly qualify the framing constitutional documents as sacred texts hallowed by time. As we will see more clearly when examining the performance of the post-independence Czech and Slovak governments in Chapter 5, the barriers to revising the existing constitutions are far from insurmountable, and even the constitutionally mandated balance of power between the president and the parliament in Slovakia is still open to revision.

Democratization and Freedom of Information

Most definitions of democracy include clauses on freedom of speech and freedom of the press as the guarantor of the accountability of government. Government policy that cannot be freely criticized cannot be readily subjected to electoral scrutiny either. In a democratic system, the citizenry cannot be dependent on the government's own interpretation of its goals and achievements. Czechoslovakia had had no system of official prepublication censorship since the passage of the press law of 1967. However, postpublication scrutiny of the press, the self-censorship of media officials, and party control of media appointments all assured that the party would exercise continued control over journalistic output.

In Czechoslovakia, the rebuilding of open channels of public information began with the Velvet Revolution. Existing media began to comment more freely, and the amendment of the press law in March 1990 permitted privately run newspapers to publish, although the electronic media remained state-owned and regulated. In the following months, exile journals such as *Listy* and *Svědectví* were publishing back home in time for the first election campaign. "We Are Home Again!" proclaimed the *Listy* editorial introduction in the first edition of the journal to be legally disseminated domestically in twenty years. Like its new domestic counterparts, it pledged to continue the "battle for democracy, freedom, and social justice," and to help "open the door to Europe."[51] *Svědectví* published a compendium of significant previous articles on a range of historical subjects in its homecoming edition, whose title bore the inscription, "Published legally in Czechoslovakia for the first time."[52] Other journals emerged from the underground to publish openly that same spring, such as *Lidové noviny*, which was initially the preferred reading of liberal intellectuals, though Czech Prime Minister Klaus now has a weekly column in it.

These papers were joined by established communist-era journals. Though a number of specialized party journals soon ceased publication, most of the best-known mass dailies eventually established editorial boards that were independent of direct official control; some of them retained a readership with more open editorial policies. The communist youth newspaper *Mladá fronta dnes*, for example, is still widely read and respected. Vladimir Kusin described the party's official daily *Rudé právo* as evolving "from a confused and defensive mouthpiece of the party's central committee" to "an independent left-wing newspaper that no longer toes the party's line"—all in the course of 1990.[53] It remained the Czech Republic's largest-circulation "serious" daily through 1994, respected for its professionalism. And of course several dozen completely new papers emerged in the early months of the transition; by late 1990, there were more than fifty general-interest dailies and weeklies in circulation in the major cities and in the provinces, thirteen published in Prague and ten in Bratislava. Just as the proliferation of parties differentiates Czechoslovakia and other postcommunist states from the Western pattern, so too does the parallel proliferation of the print media.

The resurgence of free media commentary did not produce a form of journalism recognizable to Americans overnight. In fact, most Americans are not accustomed to the pattern of journalistic practice as it emerged in the East. For one thing, contemporary U.S. newspapers are largely local in circulation; the overwhelming majority of U.S. cities now have only one newspaper attempting to serve the needs of the broadest possible segment of that local community. This pattern tends to produce a rather moderate journalism, designed to inform without offending.

Central European journalism before communism was rather different, even in the interwar period, when it was largely uncensored. It was a journalism of opinion rather than fact; there was a wide range of papers with national circulation in interwar Czechoslovakia, but each of them targeted its own audience. Each party had its own daily or weekly, as did important sociopolitical organizations such as the trade unions and agricultural cooperatives. The journalism that emerged in Central Europe after the collapse of communism has been closer to this pattern of free press than to the U.S. model.

The postcommunist journalism of opinion has not been without its flaws. Above all, postcommunist journalism was in some instances every bit as opinionated as communist journalism had been; the essential difference was in the number and variety of vigorously expressed opinions. And these opinions were not labeled and confined to an editorial page. Each story tended to bear the editorial stamp of the paper in which it appeared, and coverage of the same political developments played very differently in ideologically differing papers. There was a tendency to print as fact what had not been substantiated as fact, creating a whole spectrum of world views, each listening primarily to itself.

Media experts such as Rudolf Převratil of Prague's International Journalism Institute noted the frequency with which even the "quality press" descended to "petty politicking and the spreading of rumors."[54] The Czechoslovak government also began, a bit uncomfortably, to protest some of this exuberant but freewheeling and sometimes irresponsible journalism; President Havel's press spokesman, Michal Žantovský, stirred media resentment when he suggested that there was such a thing as too much free speech, and that open opinion should be tempered by journalistic responsibility. The dilemma of ensuring responsible journalism without suppressing free expression has been a pervasive problem. But, as Převratil suggests, the bickering and excesses of the media are not a uniquely journalistic phenomenon; as we have seen, journalism only mirrors the divisions and contentiousness of politics itself.

Free expression has been most explosive in the area of national and ethnic conflict. The media were now free to print stereotypic assertions that Jews had too much power and gypsies were dirty thieves; the Slovak media was free to charge the Czechs with the intent to suppress Slovak autonomy, and the Czech press was free to vilify Slovak leaders and denigrate the seriousness of Slovak commitment to democracy, comparing present-day politics with that of the tarnished wartime Slovak state.[55] "Hate speech" has prompted limits on what can be printed. The anti-Semitic magazine *Politika* was shut down in 1992 after it published a list of "Jews and Half-Breeds Active in Czech Culture"; *Politika*'s publisher later went on trial for inciting racial hatred and received a seven-month suspended sentence.[56]

In the journalistic realm, the fact that Czechoslovakia was a multinational and multilingual state also meant that Slovaks reading Slovak-language papers, Czechs reading Czech-language papers, and Hungarians reading Hungarian-language papers were living in different cultural-political worlds, each insulated from the outlooks of the others, which were instead translated through their own media sources.

There were more mundane journalistic problems as well. The communist state had controlled not only what was written but also its printing and distribution; until privatization was well advanced, the state would continue to regulate these essential institutions. In fact, the early "small" privatization that released many newsstands into the private sector actually complicated distribution, since these new entrepreneurs preferred to carry a more limited selection of the better-selling papers rather than open counter space to all comers. New newspapers were just as dependent as the established ones for printing facilities and newsprint, the cost of which skyrocketed as price subsidies were eased out; a 22 percent sales tax on the press increased the difficulty of breaking even. The smaller-circulation minority press was sustained partly by government subsidies after the tax was imposed.

In the West, the major source of media income comes from advertising; advertising was still in its infancy in the transitional, largely state-owned Czechoslovak economy, however, generating insufficient revenue to keep the first newspapers afloat. In fact, a Western study of the emerging East European press found that Czechoslovakia lagged behind its neighbors Poland and Hungary in generating advertising revenues for the new media, presumably because economic reform in those countries had begun to permit private economic activity even before 1989.[57] The new Czechoslovak press also initially lacked a source of funds that the Hungarian press had courted and won: foreign investment, which in the Czech Republic started with the regional press. By 1995, this situation had changed, with sixteen of the twenty-five major Czech dailies owned by foreign media conglomerates, particularly those based in Austria, Switzerland, and Germany.[58] With the exception of two major dailies, Slovak media are largely domestically owned. Foreign financial support, of course, is a mixed blessing in democratic terms, since it raises the question of foreign influence on the channels of democratic communication.

Given the financial woes of the print media, the greatest threat to free expression in the Czech Republic may be commercial. After the initial explosion of very political journalism, the best-selling newspapers of the second stage increasingly came from the ranks of the tabloid press. Screaming headlines of sex and scandal reminiscent of the titles stocked at American supermarket check-out lines are a novelty in Eastern Europe, and the human interest angle—complete with horoscopes and celebrity gossip—compete well against more serious journalism. One of the most widely read papers in the Czech Republic after independence was the sensationalist tabloid *Blesk*. This trend has been visible in cultural life generally, to the distress of the intellectuals.

In Slovakia, the tensions between press and government have been more overt than in the Czech Republic and reached a critical point after the second Mečiar government took office in the summer of 1992. Mečiar's mission was to insist that journalists "tell the truth" about Slovakia. In practice, this meant the truth as he saw it; the incentives to be "truthful" included punitive taxes, the selective withdrawal of state subsidies, and the restaffing of editorial boards with his own loyalists. He encouraged the establishment of a rival journalists' association with the vivid name Club of Journalists for a Truthful Picture of Slovakia; its members could count on access for interviews and notification of press conferences to which his critics were not admitted. In fact, government critics were even accused of being in the pay of unspecified foreign interests. The planned privatization of some printing facilities and publishing houses was suspended, leaving them in state hands. Commentators on the Slovak political arena felt that the Slovak media had become "less free than they were two years ago [in 1990]."[59] The Slovak government changed hands four times between the 1990 elections and early 1995. Each new government purged the media policy officials appointed by the previous one, and control of government media agencies has been one of the most visible sources of controversy between the government and opposition since Mečiar's return to power in the fall of 1994. By the following spring, the Mečiar cabinet was pursuing a policy of boycotting all press conferences as a signal of displeasure at media coverage of the government. Although the MDS has its own paper, *Slovenská republika*, a variety of views is still available in the press. Some of the subsidies available for minority-language newspapers, however, have been diverted to fund the translation of government-supported newspapers into Hungarian.[60]

In all the former communist countries, however, the slowest change occurred in the electronic media—radio and especially television. This is an area in need of government regulation in any case, since someone must allocate the broadcast frequencies and assure that the licensees are worthy of the privilege of occupying limited airwave space. However, the broadcast media are also especially sensitive because of their potential political impact; as in the West, most citizens of the East get their news from television.[61] Television's political salience therefore has made governments especially reluctant to give up control of the airwaves, and though there was immediate discussion of a new regime for broadcast media after the collapse of communism, all postcommunist countries have been slow to license private commercial television networks. There was general agreement that one channel should be retained as "public" television, with politicians pointing to Western examples like the prestigious BBC to legitimate the idea. However, most Western public television operates with relatively independent boards at the helm. In the postcommunist countries, the composition of these boards has generally been determined by the government or the legislature. In practice, this means a great deal of air time devoted to official views and a perception that television is in the hands of the ruling parties. The resultant bias varies widely; in Milošević's Serbia, for example, the state-controlled television is popularly known as Miloševision for its faithful replication of his views.

However, problems and controversy abound even in more democratic states such as Czechoslovakia. The federal broadcast law of 1991 established a Federal Broadcasting Council to oversee the operations of the official broadcast media. The council's membership consisted of representatives of the parliamentary parties: three chosen by the federal parliament, and three each by the Czech and Slovak National Councils. Political squabbles over personnel and the accurate depiction of Slovak views immediately ensued. Plans to expand and diversify television programming beyond the public channel have been less expeditious. There is an international commercial station, OK3, scheduled to be awarded to a private licensee only after 1995. Since it is basically an entertainment channel, the issues it raises are less about foreign political influence than about the station's contribution to the country's inundation with foreign cultural influences. Before the disintegration of the state, a third channel broadcast two national (Czech and Slovak) public programs. In the Czech Republic, that channel is now privatized, a joint venture of Czech banks and a U.S.-Canadian firm known as CET (Central European Television) 21. The Czech TV Nova became in February 1994 the first statewide commercial television station in the former Soviet bloc; it is essentially an entertainment channel, with an American-style mix of imported and domestic soaps, game shows, sports, and movies.[62]

In Slovakia, state regulation of television is one of the most inflammatory issues in current politics. Critics of Mečiar have repeatedly decried his appointment of political allies to key positions and what they see as his stranglehold on televised political coverage. In June 1995 the former Slovak Communist Party journal *Pravda* published an analysis of television news coverage that calculated an imbalance in coverage of government versus opposition viewpoints in the lopsided ratio of 47 to 3.[63] President Kováč is lucky if his statements are broadcast after midnight unannounced, and ownership of the major new private station appears to be linked to the MDS. The government has no such dominance in the print media.

Postcommunist Culture:
The Commercial Price of Freedom

The regimented culture of the former communist state has given way to a new form of censorship, many intellectuals feel: the censorship of the marketplace and of what is commercially viable. Under the communist system, the state provided extensive subsidies to art and culture—at a price, of course: the price of creating what was acceptable to the state and what would support its needs. A Hungarian dissident described the fate of the officially sanctioned artist under communism as that of a "velvet prison"—the velvet lining was a steady income, recognition, even privileges, in exchange for conformity.[64] The boundaries of the permissible varied considerably from state to state, with Czechoslovakia among the more orthodox and restrictive, but whatever the boundaries, the writer who transgressed them would not be published, the painter would not be exhibited. Such artists, forced into official silence, could write or paint "for the drawer," as the saying went, or could become overt dissidents, circulating work underground or publishing and exhibiting it abroad. The dissident performing artists were especially hard hit, since illegal underground concerts or plays were considerably easier to police than circulated manuscripts. President Havel only once saw his plays performed at home in the eighteen years between the onset of normalization and the Velvet Revolution.[65]

A telling—and prophetic—dissident adage of the communist period was "over here, nothing is permitted and everything matters; in the West, everything is permitted and nothing matters." In the East, dissident cultural expression might be the only vent for political frustration and political commentary. This kind of expression carried grave risks; one's artistic work was subject to intense scrutiny by the local equivalent of the KGB (in Czechoslovakia, the StB), and punishment for transgressions might mean loss of employment, imprisonment, and retaliation against one's family. However, the very intensity of the regime's pursuit gave one's work a transcendent significance. Why would a novel be forbidden, and its author punished, if it were not important? As voices of conscience, dissidents were clearly important enough to threaten the state. In a real sense, the intellectual dissidents of the communist period could feel that they were carrying on a historically sanctioned political role. As Václav Havel described it:

> The idea that a writer is the conscience of his nation has its own logic and its own tradition here. For years, writers have stood in for politicians; they were the renewers of the national community, maintainers of the national language, awakeners of the national conscience, interpreters of the national will. This tradition continued under totalitarian conditions, where it gains its own special coloring; the written word seems to have acquired a kind of heightened radioactivity—otherwise they wouldn't lock us up for it![66]

Therefore, a committed dissident could rightly feel that he or she was engaging in a conflict of fundamental moral significance. Enemies of censorship and repression were confronting a clear-cut evil, with the universal task of "telling the truth to power," as Václav Havel put it, even if—or exactly because—that truth was unpleasant and unwelcome. Cultural expression was therefore a political act but also fundamentally anti-political. It was anti-political in its complete rejection of the existing communist regime, as well as in its mindset. Conventional politics bargains and compromises to achieve a policy goal. The battle against communist power had to be uncompromising; the objective, realistically, was not to defeat one's opponents and achieve one's goals, but to accept public defeat and its punitive consequences stalwartly, never to give up, and to make one's sacrifice a visible tribute to everything the regime tried to destroy—above all, free expression.

There was not even a reward in public approval. In Czechoslovakia, the public was encouraged to regard dissidents as troublemakers who gained adulation in the West in exchange for disrupting the lives of their own citizens; many ordinary people accepted this view, even those who themselves disapproved of the regime but did not see the point of hopeless opposition.

The postcommunist setting was entirely different. Dissidents were now free to find whatever mode of self-expression fit their needs. But in the changing environment, bold political messages encoded in fiction or art were no longer as necessary. People could read bold political messages in their daily newspapers. The measure of value of artistic work was no longer its political worth, therefore; the artist no longer had to defend art against politics. Ironically, however, the politically engaged artist now exchanged political censorship for commercial censorship. State subsidies for culture began to dry up as soon as the new governments began to face the expensive tasks of pursuing economic and political transition. Symphonies, ballets, and writers' associations have lost their state sponsorship and must raise prices and seek out patrons. Publishers want to print what will sell.

There was an initial rush to print the previously forbidden, filling bookshops with novels and historical works that had only been available abroad during the communist period. But once the public appetite for the previously forbidden had been saturated, it was far more common to see bookstores full of the offerings of mass culture: horoscopes and new age writings, detective stories and romances and science fiction, self-help books and English or German phrase books, works on economic management and business practices, and translations of foreign popular fiction. Serious political magazines jostled for newsstand space with the Czech editions of *Cosmopolitan, Elle,* and *Playboy.* Foreign films predominated among the movies shown in Prague; in May 1996, of thirty-two films showing in the Prague cinemas, only six were Czech, and no fewer than twenty-four were American, including *Dumb and Dumber, Natural Born Killers,* and *Dead Man Walking.* Documentary programming on television was less attractive than soap operas, American sitcoms and drama, and game shows.[67] All these very popular foreign offerings competed with domestic cultural output, raising concern about the viability of Czech and Slovak culture even among those who eagerly devoured the foreign alternatives. For very different reasons from before, serious artists with principles have found it almost as difficult to make a living as under communism. Everything is permitted, but nothing matters?

Education suffered special problems in adjusting to the postcommunist environment.[68] Every communist government had devoted serious attention to the ideological purity of the educational system; schoolchildren would grow up to be "new socialist men" (and women). Teaching "political correctness" started at the earliest possible age and continued for a lifetime through periodic political orientations at the workplace. The Boy Scouts and Girl Scouts were outlawed for their subversive bourgeois values; they were relegalized only in 1990.[69] In their place, a hierarchy of socialist youth organizations channeled young Czechs and Slovaks from the earliest red-scarfed Pioneers through the older and more elite membership of the Czechoslovak Union of Socialist Youth.

But it was the schools themselves that carried the greatest weight of responsibility for "socialization" to socialist values. All curricula were permeated with the proper ideological worldview, even to mathematics problems concerning the number of NATO tanks that threatened Czechoslovakia. And, of course, mandatory age-appropriate instruction in Marxism-Leninism continued through university graduation, with entire departments devoted to the topic! Ideological content and the heavy communist emphasis on technical subjects (less sensitive ideologically and necessary for the building of socialism) severely stunted study of the social sciences and humanities; in all disciplines, however, there were likely to be many teachers and professors who owed their positions to ideological conformity rather than competence.

By the late communist period, this ideological programming had lost much of its fervor. Students parroted the proper phrases necessary to getting through the political courses, and went on their way, much as students wade through required courses everywhere. Nevertheless, the curriculum at all levels was in critical need of "depoliticization" after the collapse of the communist regime. Every textbook, particularly those in previously restricted disciplines like history and the social sciences, needed revision. Faculty needed reeducation. The earliest educational reforms were also the cheapest: the removal of mandatory ideological courses from the curriculum and the closing of departments of Marxism-Leninism at universities.

However, most of the restructuring of education cost money the government did not have.[70] Public education has remained free through secondary school, but the education budget is so austere that some schools supplement government funding by renting out extra classrooms to businesses, selling advertisement space on school fences, and using cafeteria facilities to provide meals to retirees in the community. Of course, parents who choose instead to send their children to the new religious or secular private schools have a new cost to bear. The costs of university education, previously borne by the state, are now partially the citizen's responsibility; starting in 1994 and 1995, all Czech universities began to charge tuition, with dual-track fees that were lower for Czech citizens than for foreigners (including Slovaks who did not hold Czech citizenship) but still substantial.

The flow of ideas and creativity in the postcommunist Czech and Slovak Republics has thus lost most of its previous political constraints. With the significant withdrawal of the state from the support of cultural activity, however, polit-

ical constraints have been replaced by those of government budgetary limitations
and the demands of commercial viability.

Conclusion

The Czech and Slovak political transitions from authoritarian rule proved to be
protracted and complicated. Voter turnouts of over 90 percent in 1990 and the
initial popularity of the heroes of the Velvet Revolution were misleading as indicators of the smoothness of the process of constructing workable institutions, not
least because the constitutional framework broke down entirely in the process,
leading to the dissolution of the state. Despite the eventual ratification of Czech
and Slovak constitutions and the establishment of electoral competition, these
transitions are clearly incomplete. Both republics still need a more balanced and
temperate journalism and more balanced and temperate leaders, greater stability
in their party systems, and clearer links between public and leaders. If there is any
one lesson from the Czech and Slovak experience of this period of political experimentation, it is a very old one that can always bear repetition. No country
achieves relatively democratic government solely by blueprint, by finding a workable institutional design and simply legislating it. The blueprints and the legislation are necessary, of course. However, it is rather shocking to discover, for example, that holding elections solves relatively little. You may be thinking that the
Czechs and Slovaks made governing unnecessarily complicated for themselves by
adopting a system of proportional representation that permits such a cumbersome multiparty system. Václav Klaus, incidentally, would agree with you on
that. With the largest and best financed party in the Czech political system behind him, he has suggested that it is time to turn to an American-style winner-
take-all system. Not unnaturally, the other, smaller parties disagree. Tinkering
with the electoral system, however, would not have made the early politics of
transition any smoother. The Czech political system may grow in a direction that
would permit a two-party system. But it probably could not have started that
way. Where were the two parties? Where were their constituencies? The messy
process of trial and error by which proportional representation has reflected and
refined initially unfocused public attitudes may actually have been useful as a
sorting-out process.

   In any case, these growing pains should not obscure the achievements. Governments have changed hands without provoking coups and countercoups. Despite the legislatures' wrangling, they—and the Czech legislature in particular—
have produced substantial bodies of legislation in support of political and
economic change. Extremist antisystem parties remain marginal, and successful
politicians, even the demagogues among them, generally choose to advance their
careers through the electoral process rather than in the streets. These are not
minor achievements.

These political changes have not occurred in isolation from the changes in the economic and nationalist agendas. In this chapter, we have already seen evidences of these interactions. Slovakia's greater political instability has run in tandem with its greater economic hardships. Political change was more disjointed because of the deadlock over the distribution of power between the Czech and Slovak Republics, and still more so as a result of the division of the state along national lines. The texture of these interactions will become clearer still in subsequent chapters, which analyze economic change and the battles over national identity that destroyed the state and produced two new political systems.

Notes

1. In fact, Hungarian legislation legalizing the formation of political parties in February 1989 actually predated the Polish roundtable agreements.

2. A good overview of the communist period that emphasizes the differential developments in the region is Joseph Rothschild's *Return to Diversity: A Political History of East Central Europe Since World War II*, 2d edition (Oxford, England: Oxford University Press, 1993).

3. As in the Polish case, this strategy initially appeared to have been misguided, since the opposition parties won the first elections handily. However, the Hungarian reform communists were also to share the electoral success of the Polish party in the subsequent election of May 1994. The short-term payoffs of flexibility were dubious, but the longer-term effect was to preserve a power position for the communists in the new political system.

4. Interestingly, this party lost the second election to an amorphous opposition alliance. The lesson here seems to be that those who are initially victorious get to preside over the agonies of transformation; this party, whether communist or noncommunist, will then face the electoral penalties. This kind of retrospective voting, in which the party in power pays electorally for the economic pain of its tenure, is of course exceedingly common in the West as well.

5. Czechs and Slovaks may have been expecting something momentous in 1988, for it had long been remarked that years ending with eight had been critical landmarks for the state: the founding of the republic (1918), the catastrophic Munich agreement (1938), the communist seizure of power (1948), and the Prague Spring (1968). The events of 1988 were only an omen of things to come, however. When 1989 proved to be the critical moment, the slogan became "'89 is '68 upside down."

6. Bernard Wheaton and Zdeněk Kavan, *The Velvet Revolution: Czechoslovakia, 1988–1991* (Boulder: Westview Press, 1992), p. 35.

7. Ibid., p. 42.

8. See Timothy Garton Ash, *The Magic Lantern: The Revolution of 1989, Witnessed in Warsaw, Budapest, and Prague* (New York: Random House, 1990), pp. 78–130.

9. The new federal government took office December 10, and the Czech Republic government on December 5.

10. Wheaton and Kavan, *The Velvet Revolution*, p. 53.

11. Amos Elon, "A Reporter at Large: Prague Autumn," *New Yorker*, January 22, 1990, p. 130.

12. Rasma Karklins and Roger Petersen, "Decision Calculus of Protesters and Regimes: Eastern Europe, 1989," *Journal of Politics* 55:3 (August 1993):588–614.

13. Ákos Róna-Tas, "The Selected and the Elected: The Making of the New Parliamentary Elite in Hungary," *East European Politics and Societies* 5:3 (Fall 1991):369–372.

14. In December 1989, in the midst of the Velvet Revolution, the ban was broken with the stage-reading of his play *Audience.*

15. Jaroslav Veis, "King Klaus," *East European Reporter* 5:5 (September-October 1992):12.

16. Mečiar, however, is not a "textbook" example, because he was one of the young Communist Party members of 1968 who was ousted during the normalization purges.

17. Romania's court-martial and execution of Nicolae Ceauşescu is a special case, as it was part of the revolutionary process itself, undertaken in haste to dishearten the persistence of violent resistance to the new regime by Securitäte officers and others. Albania tried ten former politburo members for corruption, and Hungary passed legislation in 1993 that lifted the statute of limitations for crimes committed during the suppression of the Hungarian Revolution of 1956.

18. Keith Crawford, "Problems of Institutionalization of Parliamentary Democracy: The Federal Assembly of the Czech and Slovak Federative Republic, 1990–1993," in Lawrence D. Longley, ed., *Working Papers on Comparative Legislative Studies* (Appleton, Wis.: Research Committee of Legislative Specialists, International Political Science Association, 1994), p. 252.

19. Dubček's future as a political figure in post-independence Slovakia must remain permanently in doubt. In the 1992 elections, he had given a big boost to the Slovak Social Democrats by affiliating with them (the disintegration of the PAV had left him in search of a party identity). However, his political service was tragically cut short when he died following a car accident in the fall of 1992.

20. The lustration appeals commission was inundated with cases of so-called "Category C" collaborators, who were listed in StB files as having been brought in for a "talk," for potential recruitment. Most of these were eventually cleared, but delays in processing the "acquittals" could cause great personal damage. In November 1992 the constitutional court nullified the "Category C" provisions of the lustration law.

21. Havel reproached those who vocally called for all communists to "hang from the lampposts": those who "served the totalitarian regime . . . are the loudest today." Cited in *Foreign Broadcast Information Service–East Europe* FBIS-EEU-90-101, May 24, 1990, p. 17.

22. Petruška Šustrová, "The Lustration Controversy," *Uncaptive Minds* 5:2 (Summer 1992):129.

23. *Mladá fronta dnes,* December 13, 1993, reprinted in FBIS-EEU-93-241, December 17, 1993, p. 10. Benda subsequently became head of the Office for the Documentation and Investigation of the Crimes of Communism.

24. Timothy Garton Ash, "Prague: Intellectuals and Politicians," *New York Review of Books,* January 12,1995, p. 36. Ash makes it clear that the debate over the role of intellectuals in politics remains very much alive.

25. Petr Tatar, cited in the *Prague Post,* November 25–December 1, 1992.

26. For a fuller discussion, see Sharon Wolchik, "Women and the Politics of Transition in the Czech and Slovak Republics," in Marilyn Rueschemeyer, ed., *Women in the Politics of Postcommunist Europe* (Armonk, N.Y.: M. E. Sharpe, 1994), pp. 3–27.

27. This preferential vote to modify the individual candidate lists, incidentally, is generally the only chance an ordinary voter has in the Czech and Slovak electoral systems to vote directly for individual candidates for national office rather than for a party. Parties set their own slates, although a few parties have experimented with primaries for the 1996 parliamentary elections.

28. Jan Urban, "Czechoslovakia: The Power and Politics of Humiliation," in Gwyn Prins, ed., *Spring in Winter: The 1989 Revolutions* (Manchester, England: Manchester University Press, 1990), p. 124.

29. Poland's first transitional election in 1989 had been conducted under rules that restricted the number of seats opposition parties could contest.

30. "Už nie som optimista," *Národná obroda*, February 17, 1992.

31. Czechoslovak News Agency (ČSTK), June 30, 1992, in FBIS-EEU-92-127, July 1, 1992, p. 13.

32. Gordon Wightman, "The Development of the Party System and the Break-up of Czechoslovakia," in Gordon Wightman, ed., *Party Formation in East-Central Europe: Post-Communist Politics in Czechoslovakia, Hungary, Poland, and Bulgaria* (Brookfield, Vt.: Edward Elgar, 1995), p. 72.

33. Ibid., pp. 62–63.

34. For a discussion of this role, see Geoffrey Pridham, "Southern European Democracies on the Road to Consolidation: A Comparative Assessment of the Role of Political Parties," in Geoffrey Pridham, ed., *Securing Democracy: Political Parties and Democratic Consolidation in Europe* (London: Routledge, 1990), pp. 1–41.

35. *Nový čas*, June 3, 1992.

36. *Mladá fronta dnes*, August 31, 1994, p. 7, reprinted in FBIS-EEU-94-177, September 13, 1994, p. 9.

37. Such provisions occur in the constitutions of Bulgaria (Article 67), Croatia (Article 74), the Czech Republic (Articles 26 and 27), Estonia (Article 62), Lithuania (Article 59), Macedonia (Article 62), Romania (Article 66), Slovakia (Article 73), and Slovenia (Article 82).

38. Political scientists began to debate this point in the 1970s, as signs of decreasing party loyalty began to appear in both the United States and Western Europe. See, for example, Russell J. Dalton, *Citizen Politics in Western Democracies: Public Opinion and Political Parties in the United States, Great Britain, West Germany, and France* (Chatham, N.J.: Chatham House, 1988), pp. 188–192; and Michael Gallagher, Michael Laver, and Peter Mair, *Representative Government in Modern Europe*, 2d edition (New York: McGraw-Hill, 1995), pp. 209–241.

39. From the election address of President Michal Kováč, broadcast on Bratislava STV 1 Television, September 6, 1994, reprinted in FBIS-EEU-94-174, September 8, 1994, p. 11.

40. "Jak lidé důvěřují institucím," *Rudé právo*, July 1, 1993.

41. Cited in FBIS-EEU-90-101, May 24, 1990, p. 17.

42. Crawford, "Problems of Institutionalization," p. 253.

43. *Slovenská republika*, September 3, 1994, pp. 6–7, reprinted in FBIS-EEU-94-174, September 8, 1994, p. 11.

44. See Stephen Holmes, "Back to the Drawing Board: An Argument for Constitutional Postponement in Eastern Europe," *East European Constitutional Review* 2:1 (Winter 1993):21–25.

45. See Louisa Vinton, "Poland's 'Little Constitution' Clarifies Walesa's Powers" *RFE/RL Research Report* 1:35 (September 4, 1992):19–26.

46. Article 65 of the Czech constitution and Article 106 of the Slovak constitution, in *The Rebirth of Democracy: Twelve Constitutions of Central and Eastern Europe* (Strasbourg: Council of Europe Press, 1995), pp. 137 and 534.

47. "Survey of Presidential Powers: Formal and Informal," *East European Constitutional Review* 3:1 (Fall 1993–Winter 1994), pp. 64–68 and 81–94.

48. Mečiar, interviewed in *Lidové noviny*, September 29, 1994, p. 7. See also Chapter 5.

49. See, for example, Alfred Stepan and Cindy Skach, "Constitutional Frameworks and Democratic Consolidation: Parliamentarism vs. Presidentialism," *World Politics* 46:1 (October 1993):1–23.

50. For arguments about the dangers of presidentialism, see Juan Linz, *The Failure of Presidentialism* (Baltimore: Johns Hopkins University Press, 1994); Stepan and Skach, "Constitutional Frameworks and Democratic Consolidation: Parliamentarism versus Presidentialism;" and Guillermo O'Donnell, "Delegative Democracy," *Journal of Democracy* 5:1 (January 1994):55–69. For the counterargument, see Stephen Holmes, "The Post-Communist Presidency," *East European Constitutional Review* 3:1 (Fall 1993–Winter 1994):36–39.

51. Jiří Pelikan, "Jsme opět doma!" *Listy* 20:2 (April 1990):3.

52. *Svědectví*, Spring 1990.

53. Vladimir V. Kusin, "Czechoslovakia: Media in Transition," *Report on Eastern Europe*, May 3, 1991, p. 8.

54. Rudolf Převratil, "Czechoslovakia," in David L. Paletz, Karol Jakubowicz, and Pavao Novosel, eds., *Glasnost and After: Media and Change in Central and Eastern Europe* (Creskill, N.J.: Hampton Press, 1995), p. 162.

55. The problem was not unique to Czechoslovakia. Although an ethnonationally opinionated press was most poisonous in the former Yugoslavia, it raised the political temperature throughout the region.

56. Jiri Pehe, "The Media in Eastern Europe: Czech Republic," *RFE/RL Research Report* 2:9 (May 7, 1993):27.

57. *Emerging Voices: East European Media in Transition* (New York: Gannett Center for Media Studies, October 1990), cited in Kusin, p. 7.

58. A notable exception is the former communist *Rudé pravo* (Red Justice), which remains in domestic hands. In September 1995 it dropped the controversial adjective "Red" to become simply *Pravo*, and it is now more closely associated with the Social Democrats. See Steve Kettle, "The Czech Republic Struggles to Define an Independent Press," *Transition* 1:18 (October 6, 1995), p. 4. Foreign ownership often bred tensions over the perception of interference with editorial autonomy. The editor-in-chief of *Lidové noviny*, Jaromír Šetina, resigned in January 1994 in protest over the management practices of the Swiss publisher Ringier AG, which he saw as compromising the paper's independence.

59. Jan Obrman, "The Media in Eastern Europe," *RFE/RL Research Report* 2:19 (May 7, 1993):33.

60. Sharon Fisher, "Slovak Media Under Pressure," *Transition* 1:18 (October 6, 1995):9.

61. It is no coincidence that the key upheavals in the former Soviet Union always included an effort to gain control of broadcast facilities—the television station or the radio tower. It is a mandatory target for the modern coup plotter.

62. Kettle, p. 5.

63. *OMRI Daily Digest,* June 13, 1995.

64. Miklós Haraszti, *The Velvet Prison: Artists Under State Socialism* (New York: Noonday Press, Farrar, Straus and Giroux, 1987).

65. Václav Havel, *Disturbing the Peace: A Conversation with Karel Hvížd'ala* (New York: Alfred A. Knopf, 1990), pp. 124–125.

66. Havel, *Disturbing the Peace,* p. 72.

67. The international craze for game shows had already begun to penetrate communist countries before 1989, but, as one pioneer game show producer recalled, the first show he worked with offered as the grand prize—after a two-year round of competition—a VCR! And it is almost too good a reflection of the disappointments of communist consumer life that the winning contestant discovered the VCR to be broken, and the warranty expired, when he got it home. The proliferating new game shows offer more frequent and lavish prizes, bolstered by the fact that enterprises in the new capitalist environment are willing to donate prizes to acquire some free publicity.

68. Sharon Wolchik offers a good capsule summary of the former education system and the early changes after 1989 in her book, *Czechoslovakia in Transition: Politics, Economics, and Society* (London: Pinter, 1991).

69. Scouting had also been briefly resurrected during the Prague Spring.

70. Douglas Lytle's book, *Pink Tanks and Velvet Hangovers: An American in Prague* (Berkeley, Calif.: Frog, 1995), offers the perspective of one of many young Americans who settled in Prague after the Velvet Revolution; the year he spent teaching English in the Czech schools offers some sense of the changing education system from a Western perspective.

4

NATIONAL IDENTITY AND THE DISINTEGRATION OF CZECHOSLOVAKIA

On January 1, 1993, the Velvet Revolution was supplanted by the Velvet (although hardly "no-fault") Divorce between the Czech Republic and Slovakia, creating two new states in Central Europe (see Map 4.1). The emergence of new states in the established late-twentieth-century international environment, particularly the *peaceful* emergence of new states, is a rare occurrence. In the last century, regime changes within countries have occurred with great regularity, but the appearance of new states had been largely confined to the consequences of imperial collapse. James Mayall defined three major modern waves of state creation: in nineteenth-century Latin America, in East Central Europe after World War I, and in the Third World following World War II, "all associated with the collapse of empires." He added that "there are no empires left to collapse, and therefore very limited opportunities for further state creation by this route." A bias toward the status quo in the international state system, he argued, had tended to "freeze the territorial map."[1]

Yet soon after this analysis was published, the postcommunist transitions confounded expectations by generating twenty-two new states on the territory of the

---

Some of the material in this chapter has appeared in a different form in Carol Skalnik Leff, "Could This Marriage Have Been Saved? The Czechoslovak Divorce," *Current History* 92:599 (March 1996):129–134, and is used here by permission.

MAP 4.1   The boundaries of the Czech and Slovak Republics after independence

former countries of Yugoslavia, the Soviet Union, and Czechoslovakia. What was
wrong with Mayall's analysis? It is quite possible that his argument was essentially
correct but that he was not thinking of the Soviet hegemonic system as a neoim-
perial system whose collapse would generate propitious conditions for new state
formation. This is not at all a far-fetched conception. Scholars and politicians did
routinely refer to Eastern Europe as part of the Soviet empire, and the territory
of the former Soviet Union itself, with its immense ethnic diversity and complexity, was after all an imperial inheritance from the period of tsarist empire; it
was, in that sense, the "last" European empire. It may have endured longer because, unlike the colonial holdings of Western Europe, it was territorially con-
tiguous to the Russian core and held intact by an authoritarian government.
Throughout the region, with the exception of Germany and the Baltic states, the
communist power structure had retained the existing state entities (although the
postwar boundaries often changed); the system's collapse created an opportunity

to renegotiate fundamental assumptions, including the type of political and economic system and even the boundaries of the states themselves.

However, this general interpretation, while it helps to account for the conditions under which new states could emerge, does not stand alone, because it is not only the structure of the international system but also the structure of the states themselves that is distinctive. Nine European communist states felt the impact of postcommunist transformation politics; the three that disintegrated, and only those three, were federations. The unitary states have remained intact. Are federations less stable than unitary states? What common features do they share that could account for their demise?

A starting point is national diversity. As we have seen in the case of Czechoslovakia, the federation of the state in 1969 was a conscious effort to accord political recognition to the existence of two distinct Czech and Slovak national groupings and thereby satisfy Slovak concerns for the safeguarding of national identity and interests. Federations are not always based on this kind of territorially concentrated national difference; the U.S. federation certainly is not. For that reason, scholars of nationalism sometimes use the term "ethnofederalism" to designate cases in which the federal organization reflects a form of bargain between two or more nations coexisting on the same state territory. Czechoslovakia, Yugoslavia, and the Soviet Union can all be described as ethnofederal states; in each case, the boundaries between republics within the federation corresponded roughly to the existence of territories settled by a dominant national grouping that gave its name to the republic. In all three cases, the ruling communist party intended the federalization of the state as a solution to ethnonational diversity, a way of stabilizing relations among nations and providing a delimited recognition of their national aspirations within the territory of the existing states. As long as the communist authority remained intact, the federal "solution" to the national question also remained intact.

The erosion or collapse of communist power, however, reopened the question of the adequacy of the national bargain on which the state was based. Donald Horowitz argued that a general constitutional change tends to provide "an auspicious setting from which to consider new territorial arrangements to cope with ethnic problems."[2] If this constitutional change is in the direction of greater democracy, the demands to renegotiate the existing ethnonational bargain may be even greater, because of the opening of the system to broader popular influence. This recognition is a starting point from which to consider the subsequent disintegration of the communist federal states in general and Czechoslovakia in particular. Since 1918 there had been continued tension over the identity of the state and over the relationship of Czechs and Slovaks. This unresolved identity issue now reached its final crisis.

The specific case of Czechoslovakia raises two additional questions—the riddle of the peaceful dissolution of an established state, and the paradox of a state that disintegrated even though the majority of its citizens favored its continuance.

New states do not usually emerge without a fight; war, revolution, and violence had accompanied the creation of the new European states in the peace settlements after World War I. The later decolonization process was accelerated by World War II and often accompanied by local conflict. Yugoslavia's violent disintegration is a tragic headline story, and even the negotiated dissolution of the Soviet Union has been accompanied by serious regional violence. The fact that both parties to the Czech-Slovak divorce failed to contest it is indeed a rarity.

But it is the second paradox that truly marks Czechoslovakia's divorce as uniquely demanding of explanation. Why voluntarily dissolve a state that most citizens said they wanted to preserve? Why especially when free elections presumably permitted those citizens a deciding voice in the most significant decisions of politics? Could this marriage have been saved? A closer look at the Velvet Divorce should help to answer these questions and provide some reasonable explanations for some puzzling political dynamics.[3]

State Breakdown

The storm warnings of future trouble were not acute in the early euphoric days of the Velvet Revolution. Initially, it seemed that a rational and workable balance of power between the Czechs and Slovaks, between the central government and the two republic governments, was an issue that would be resolved with goodwill in a democratized framework—a challenge, of course, but a challenge to be confronted along with the rest of the challenges of transition. All the major movement politicians agreed that a satisfactory resolution of the national question was long overdue, and that the communist federal solution had been, by its authoritarian nature, no real solution at all. What was needed, in the phrase of the time, was an "authentic federation" with genuine power vested at the republic levels. Surely well-meaning politicians could negotiate the national question in the process of negotiating a general democratic constitutional bargain. Negotiations, in fact, started almost immediately after the first free election in 1990 and were scheduled for completion in the two-year tenure of the new Federal Assembly.

The first clear sign of the fragility of consensus on the national question predated the June 1990 elections, however, erupting in a parliamentary quarrel in the spring of 1990 over what some unwisely dismissed as a mere question of punctuation: the "hyphen" war. The opening for conflict stemmed from a symbolic change that was occurring throughout the region, where decommunizing regimes were intent on ridding themselves of some of the political markers of communist power even before a freely elected parliament could tackle definitive constitutional revisions. Characteristically, most parliaments passed resolutions eliminating the constitutional guarantee of a "leading role" for the Communist Party. But the communist identity of these states was also encapsulated in the official names of the countries themselves; Czechoslovakia, for example, was officially the Czechoslovak *Socialist* Republic. It was understandable, therefore, that the Federal Assembly in Czechoslovakia should take under advisement the amendment of the state's designation as the *Československá socialistická republika* (ČSSR) to delete the word "socialist."

It was then that consensus began to yield to overt conflict. Slovaks seized the occasion to challenge the accuracy of the remaining words in the state title. "Československá," they argued with some justification, was ethnically misleading. It implied that there was a "Czechoslovak" nationality that merged Czechs and Slovaks; as an example of the imprecision of this term, Slovaks could point to the longtime Western journalistic tendency to abbreviate the polysyllabic and space-consuming word Czechoslovak to the supposed shorthand "Czech." Political leaders of Slovak extraction, such as Dubček and Husák, thus regularly appeared in the American press as "Czech" leaders, and in the process a small but distinct Slovak nation lost its international identity. Slovaks therefore argued that as long as the country's name was undergoing reconstructive surgery, the time was ripe to resolve this ambiguity and clearly distinguish Czech from Slovak. Enter the hyphen, a seemingly innocuous punctuation mark that the Slovaks had championed periodically since the founding of the republic in 1918. In the nomenclature Czecho-Slovakia (Česko-Slovensko), the hyphen could be both a bridge and a divider, announcing the distinction between two nations in a common state.

Czechs resisted this assault on the "integrity" of the state. An ugly and apparently trivial battle ensued, to the increasing embarrassment of the government, as Western media devoted sarcastic column-inches to the unseemly controversy. Eventually, the new state officially became the Czech and Slovak Federative Republic (ČSFR) and controversy subsided. The symbolic character of the political battle does not make it silly, however. It was a clear signal that past legacies of mutual suspicion continued to color national relations and that the Czech and Slovak conceptions of the state might prove to be rather different once serious constitutional deliberations began.

This proved to be the case. Dozens of political summit meetings between the summer of 1990 and the elections of 1992 failed to produce Czech and Slovak consensus on a formulation of "authentic federalism" that could satisfy both national councils and hope to pass muster in the Federal Assembly. A hard-won provisional division of competence between the center and the republics in December 1990 left several key issues unresolved and did not pave the way for a definitive settlement. As elections approached in 1992, the final attempt at agreement failed to gain approval in the Slovak National Council (SNR) by a single vote. All parties to the negotiations then agreed that a final resolution would have to await the outcome of the June 1992 elections. Not surprisingly, the atmosphere of an electoral campaign was an unfavorable political environment for further progress.

Yet the 1992 elections only finalized the stalemate. In fact, it is hard to imagine a mutually acceptable solution under the prevailing circumstances. The electoral campaign in each republic slid past the critical issue of the state's continuance, each in a different sense. On the one hand, virtually every party platform pledged allegiance in 1992 to an at least temporary perpetuation of the common state except the independence-minded Slovak National Party. On the other hand, the electoral priorities in each republic were incompatible with an effective resolution.

In the Czech Republic, the leadership contest centered on the pace and scope of economic reform and on the leadership capabilities of rival Czech parties, with Václav Klaus and his CDP winning handily. The constitutional issue was secondary to his agenda. In Slovakia, where the constitutional/national issue was quite central, Mečiar's MDS made its successful bid for power on a platform that promised the best deal for Slovakia in a more decentralized confederal state. Although Czech observers interpreted the MDS electoral program as "nothing more nor less than the end of Czechoslovakia,"[4] it was not at all a clear independence platform. Voters who supported the MDS held a variety of views on that issue; their concern was the protection of Slovak interests. But the electoral debate did nothing on either side to shed light on how Czechs could be reconciled to Slovak preferences or vice versa; the accent was, as is not unusual in any electoral campaign, on general promises rather than the details of accomplishment.

The elections thus produced clear winners in each republic, but different and incompatible winning coalitions in each case. Klaus's commitment to wholesale economic reform and tighter federation was greatly at odds with median Slovak preferences. Mečiar's decentralized confederation was totally unacceptable to Klaus. Without conscious effort to destroy Czechoslovakia, the two electorates, by focusing on republic-level concerns, had nonetheless elected leaders who could not, and did not, reach agreement on how to continue the state.

In light of the long history of Slovak efforts at self-assertion, and despite the widespread tendency of Western journalists to describe the disintegration of the state as a "Slovak secession," in the final act it was actually the Czechs who short-circuited the negotiations and torpedoed the joint state project. Shortly after the elections, Klaus announced that it was clearly impossible to reach compromise on such divergent views: The federation, he predicted, was dead. It was a self-fulfilling prophecy. Slovak Prime Minister Mečiar cried foul, claiming that Klaus and his CDP had "decreed the disintegration of the state after forty minutes of discussion," forcing both republics into independence.[5] President Havel resigned from his post after failing to achieve reelection in the new parliament; he refused to serve as a powerless interim president who would preside over the disintegration of the state.

The process of dividing the state was shorter but no less complex than the failed effort to negotiate its continuance had been. The federal government did not initially have the votes for the three-fifths majority in each of the Federal Assembly chambers necessary to assure the appropriate constitutional revision. In October 1992, Mečiar's MDS even joined with Czech opposition deputies to pass a nonbinding resolution that would investigate a new "Czech-Slovak Union," designed to bridge the period leading up to European integration. In form, this entity was a confederal structure such as Mečiar's party had previously championed as the preferred institutional form of Czech-Slovak statehood. Since Czech Prime Minister Klaus utterly rejected such a structure as antithetical to Czech interests, the proposal was stillborn. It did reflect, however, a lingering interest in preserving some form of joint political destiny. This time it was the governing Czech majority who blocked the opening for the preservation of the state.

Klaus essentially argued that it was too late, that the only responsible action was to pursue a smooth dissolution—a "velvet divorce"—and that any alternative was destructive and obstructionist. When the Federal Assembly finally agreed on November 25, after two failed attempts, to dissolve the federation, the action was greeted with relief even by many who had favored continued joint statehood, since an anarchic breakup would have benefited no one. Opposition deputies who had criticized the dissolution of the state without a popular referendum as undemocratic were beaten back with the argument that it was too late; even Havel, who had earlier appealed for such a procedure, felt it "no longer made sense" by the fall of 1992. Czechoslovakia ended without a military battle, without an independence referendum, without a clear secession, and without even a widespread independence movement in either republic. We need to understand why.

Structural Conditions for the Disintegration of the State: The Political Consequences of Czechoslovakia's Federal Inheritance

Political groups can make demands for recognition and policy change and can be ignored if they lack real political access. Under communist rule, this was of course true for a wide range of potential issue constituencies, whose demands and interests could only be considered if the government found them acceptable. However, the situation is dramatically different when a dissatisfied group has an institutional base in the structure of power, and when democratization permits the utilization of this power base. This was the case with Slovak demands. Democratizing the existing structure gave them not only a voice but also veto power over any constitutional settlement. Why? In a nonfederal state, such as the interwar Republic, the Slovaks were a minority in the only power structures that had real decisionmaking power, the parliament and the government. As we have seen, it was frustratingly difficult for Slovak autonomy demands to gain a hearing in that structure. In the communist state, even a formally federalized one, power remained concentrated in the center. Federation *plus* democratization, however, was a power equation. Now the federal structures of the former communist state gained real significance. Slovak contestants for the republic-level legislature, the Slovak National Council, could "capture" a legitimate political base and use that official position as a launching point for policy change. Backed by an electoral constituency that lent democratic legitimacy to their positions, Slovak politicians were a force to be reckoned with.

This opportunity structure—the possibility of harnessing electoral support to a formal institutional position in the power structure—was the common denominator in the dissolution of all three communist federal states. In Yugoslavia, the Croatian and Slovenian competitive elections in 1990 gave newly elected governments a legitimized power base to challenge the center; the new legislatures were used to validate the eventual secession from Yugoslavia. In the USSR, republic-level elections also brought nationally assertive governments to power in the Baltic states, Georgia, and elsewhere. It is much harder to ignore a governing coalition than an unaffiliated opposition dissident group or even a parliamentary opposition. The center's opponents now carry the titles of republican prime minister or president. So the communist federal solution to the problem of ethnonational diversity ended up providing an arena for national reassertion under changed conditions.

This chance to gain an official power base was open in all three communist federations. The institutional advantages for Slovak politicians, however, were in some ways even stronger than those of nationally assertive republic leaders in Yugoslavia and the USSR. The newly elected Czechoslovak parliament of 1990 was expected to serve as a constituent assembly, to draft and approve a new democratic constitution during its two-year tenure. In order to pass, however, the constitution would have to obtain not one but three parliamentary majority votes, one in the House of Peoples, and one in each chamber of the House of Nations, both the Czech and the Slovak. Failure in any one of these three votes would defeat the constitution. This was the source of Slovak veto power. Any constitutional draft that the Slovaks refused to pass in their chamber of the House of Nations would not be approved, regardless of the size of the vote in other chambers. This was true veto power; if the proposed constitutional draft did not allocate power between the center and the republics in a way that leaders of *both* republics accepted, the draft would fail, even if the Czech majority supported the plan overwhelmingly. Hence the communist federal constitution, designed for a different regime in which the central party could quash any possible resistance, now gave the minority a powerful bargaining position. The Czechs faced a catch-22 situation. They could not break the deadlock to change the communist federal structure without a constitutional revision. And they could not gain a constitutional revision without Slovak approval.

From the very beginning of constitutional negotiations, therefore, it was obvious that progress on a settlement was dependent on the agreement of both the Czech and Slovak governments; only this could assure a favorable vote in the necessary chambers of parliament. Accordingly, in 1990, for the first time in the history of the state, regular high-level summits between Czech and Slovak government delegations became the norm. Ultimately, the Slovak National Council exercised veto power by rejecting the proposed settlement of February 1992, and the Czechs exercised veto power over the reopening of the question in the fall of 1992.

The federal structure of the state did more than grant veto power, however. It also, as we have seen, shaped the whole party structure. In general, the new parties in search of a reliable base of support concentrated their efforts on the republic level. It was easier to organize at that level—necessitating a smaller candidate roster and a more efficient concentration of limited resources. It was also easier to target an appeal at that level, with the immediate reward of being simultaneously positioned for both statewide and republic-level elections. Statewide parties faced higher organizational costs in the larger arena, and risked losing ground to more focused regional appeals. The simultaneous election of both statewide and republic-level representatives in June 1990 and 1992 seems to have clinched the case. The electorally victorious parties were those with a base in one republic or the other. No parties that won seats in the Czech National Council were also successful in the Slovak National Council. The exception was the KSČ in 1990; with its entrenched statewide organization already in place and its broad bureaucratic base, the Communist Party had a special position. After the federalization of the KSČ later in 1990, however, it too evolved into two essentially separate republic-level organizations with differing programs.

The division of the party system along republic lines was also important to the context of the constitutional settlement. What it meant was that the key party and government leaders spoke for constituencies in one or the other republic, but not both. There was no overarching party with a statewide base to represent the interests of the whole country in the negotiation process. Imagine trying to pass congressional laws in the United States if each state had its own specific party system. The existence of two broadly based parties pulls together regional interests only with difficulty as it is. In the segmented Czechoslovak party system, any politician who tried to speak for the interests of the whole country, as well-meaning Czech Prime Minister Petr Pithart tried to do, was vulnerable to attack as a betrayer of his own republic's interests. And federal officials who tried to transcend their party affiliation to talk of overall interests were likely to be accused of serving the bureaucratic interests of a central government bent on preserving its power.

The segmentation of the party system, therefore, divided the negotiators even more clearly between "us" and "them." Party lines, of course, coincided roughly with ethnic divisions as well. Everywhere in East Europe, in fact, voters in search of clarity in the confusing new electoral environment gravitated to the banner of national identity; ethnically based parties were highly successful in gaining the loyalty of co-nationals even in nonfederal states. Jack Snyder has called this gravitation toward national identity politics the "default option" in cases of transition because new political institutions and interests are still weak and the cultural ~~ional identity is a clear landmark on the political landscape.[6] The~~ Czechs would have supported Czech-based parties and Slovaks ~~arties was therefore strong even had the state not been a federa-~~

tion. Proportional representation, after all, permitted the formation of ethnically based parties throughout East Central Europe, even where there were no federal structures. However, the republic divisions reinforced such tendencies and gave them additional political meaning.

Had the negotiating parties agreed on the general outlines of a distribution of power, divisions in the institutional structure might have been surmountable. The sticking point, however, which became glaringly apparent over months of negotiation, was that Czech and Slovak ideas of a viable constitutional arrangement were basically incompatible. In general, Slovaks wanted a looser federation, with maximal power concentrated in the hands of the two republics rather than the central government—what is called a confederation.[7] The Czechs generally favored a "tighter" federation, with more key powers concentrated at the center. Slovaks were skeptical of this "Pragocentrism," whereas most Czech leaders found it impractical and disruptive even to contemplate any decentralization that might damage policy coherence and further complicate an already complex transition effort. Ultimately, neither side was willing to compromise sufficiently on its basic conceptions of the state to win approval from both the Czech and Slovak National Councils and to pass all chambers of the Federal Assembly.[8]

Czechoslovakia's dilemma, then, was the need for a new constitution in circumstances in which it could only be approved with both Czech and Slovak support under the surviving communist federal arrangement. The battle lines were clearly drawn between two republic-level governments and between two ethnically and territorially distinct party systems, each championing a different conception of the state unacceptable to the other. It was a clear formula for bargaining deadlock, and deadlock persisted. It was not merely a Czech-Slovak settlement that was on hold, either. A country without a constitution cannot stabilize its general political development. Nor can a coherent economic transition go forward without any specification of the allocation of economic authority between the center and the republics. Bureaucratic reorganization remained tentative pending the knowledge of which government bureaucracy, at which level, would be performing which functions. In other words, the delay in resolving the Czech-Slovak relationship effectively held hostage important components of the economic and political transitions as well.

The interaction of all three components of the triple transition—politics, economics, and identity—was thus part of the dynamic by which the state fell apart. This was especially true since the Czech and Slovak differences in conception of state organization were paralleled by differences in emphasis regarding the economic agenda. Most Czech politicians were inclined to insist on the logic of a *centrally coordinated* grand strategy of rapid marketization. Yet the dislocations of economic change hit Slovakia proportionally much harder. The only economic index on which the Slovaks ranked higher than the Czechs in 1992 seemed to be unemployment. Hence Slovak public opinion and Slovak leaders were more skeptical of the radical reform program associated with federal Finance Minister (later Czech prime minister) Klaus. Support for these reforms on the eve of the 1992 election registered at 49 percent in the Czech Republic but only 28 percent in Slovakia.

Slovak economic hardships and the resulting resistance to economic reform only made a looser federation doubly attractive, since it would mean greater control over the character and pace of economic reform in Slovakia. As it was, many Slovaks saw themselves as victims of shock therapy—all shock and no therapy, as the saying went in the region. Many Czech officials thought this attitude shortsighted and felt the Slovaks were disregarding the benefits of both federal subsidies and stable economic policy.[9] The prospect of a separate Slovak economic program, in turn, appalled many Czech officials, who envisaged the nightmarish prospect of two simultaneous but conflicting economic transitions under way on the territory of a single state. "We cannot have two different reforms in a single economy!" protested the federal minister for strategic planning.[10] This unwelcome possibility only reinforced Czech insistence on preserving real authority at the center.

But if the issues of the economic transition in some respects intensified the deadlock, in other respects it had the more radical effect of undercutting the desirability of any joint settlement at all. As the stalemate dragged on, it is clear that some Czech leaders began to see Slovakia as an ever increasing liability.[11] The unsettled national question slowed economic reform and tarnished the country's image abroad (see Box 4.1). The attractiveness of cutting one's losses and moving ahead more freely with the other elements of the triple transition ultimately hardened the Czech position to the point where it was clearly a matter of tighter federation or no federation at all. It is primarily this consideration, and particularly the freeing of Klaus's cherished economic reform agenda from political constraints, that appears to have shaped his loss of interest in further negotiations with the Slovaks after the 1992 elections and led to the final breakdown of efforts to preserve the state. The Czechs clearly did see benefits in a separate transitional road by that point. Looking back on the split, a Czech journalist captured the Czech attitude: "When the split came, the Czechs got rid of all the bad parts. We got rid of the old weapons factories, we got rid of the unemployment, we got rid of the old Soviet frontier. We got rid of all our problems, and we gave them to the Slovaks."[12]

Popular Support for the Continuance of the State: A Failure of Democracy?

The preceding discussion of the breakup of the state focuses on the calculations and preferences of political leaders in their institutional setting. What do we make of the public opinion polls that showed friendly relations among the two nations and consistent popular support for the continuance of the state in both

BOX 4.1
The International Dimensions of the Dissolution of the Czechoslovak State

In the face of any internal crisis of statehood, the first inclination of the international community has generally been to support the status quo and to encourage the continued integrity of the existing state in the hope of halting the spread of destabilizing conflict (even in Yugoslavia, major foreign powers supported the continuance of the common state until after the outbreak of military conflict there). The negative international response to the possible failure of the Czechoslovak statehood experiment was therefore not surprising; in fact, the desirability of the continuation of a common Czechoslovak state seemed even more compelling when seen against the backdrop of broader developments in the region. Remember that during the period of stalemate and breakdown of Czech-Slovak negotiations in 1991 and 1992, Western governments were monitoring, and trying to respond to, two additional state failures, in Yugoslavia and the Soviet Union. By early 1992, these parallel state redefinitions had reached their crises in the outbreak of war in the former Yugoslavia following the secession of Slovenia and Croatia in June 1991, and the collapse of the USSR in December 1991. The spring of 1992 would find Bosnia-Hercegovina embroiled in the post-Yugoslav conflagration. The last thing any sensible external actor wanted to see was yet another postcommunist state dissolution, and the major Western powers all expressed deep concern over the Czech-Slovak stalemate. Yet there was a contradiction between the undoubtedly sincere Western desire to avoid an additional state failure, and the impact of external pressures on the Czechoslovak negotiations. In practice, the Czech desire to rejoin Europe, which could be achieved only through conformity with Western standards of political and economic behavior, drove Czechs and Slovaks apart rather holding them together. Western-style economic reforms pursued by the Czechs raised levels of political dissatisfaction in Slovakia, while Slovak resistance to the transformation process increasingly convinced Czechs that the return to Europe would be delayed if they remained in harness with the Slovaks. Therefore, what the West had to offer in terms of integration into Europe was paradoxically at odds with what the West wanted in terms of the continuance of a single Czechoslovak state. The European Community did, however, maintain pressure for an orderly transition and was particularly insistent on the establishment of what proved to be a short-lived customs union and other mechanisms to mitigate the economic impact of separation.

---

republics?[13] Were politicians blindly battling for their own political advantage in blatant disregard of public wishes? On the face of it, the answer is yes. From 1990 all the way through November 1992, when the official parliamentary vote on dissolving the state was taken, polls showed at least a plurality of citizens in each republic favoring the continuance of the state. On the eve of the definitive 1992 elections, 81 percent of the respondents in the Czech Republic and 63 percent in Slovakia rejected the idea of separation. In fact, overwhelming majorities in both republics subsequently apportioned a share of the blame for the breakup to power politics—politicians abusing national differences to pursue their own ends.[14] What appears worse still is that in Yugoslavia and the Soviet Union citizens in the secessionist republics at least had the chance to vote on independence in referenda. Czech and Slovak citizens never got that chance. It would certainly appear as if the disintegration of the state was at odds with popular wishes, a profoundly undemocratic outcome.

However, abstracting simple answers to a simple question from opinion surveys or even referenda can obscure the complexity of public opinion. A closer look at what the Czechoslovak surveys can tell us about popular attitudes suggests that public opinion on the national question was not as different from the divisions at the leadership level as it might at first appear. From the outset, Czech and Slovak opinion surveys showed that each national group tended to view the existing situation inherited from the communist era as one in which the *other* nation had been the primary beneficiary, an attitude that did not breed a climate of ready understanding of the other nation's grievances and concerns. Even more telling is that although respondents in both republics supported the continuance of a common state, they differed significantly on what that state should look like, as Table 4.1 demonstrates.

In Slovakia, a more decentralized union of some sort was the preferred option, whereas respondents in the Czech Republic favored a tighter federation or even a unitary state. The difference in perspective is even more dramatic when one takes into account the fact that the Hungarian minority in Slovakia tended to

Table 4.1   Public Opinion on the Preferred Form of Czech-Slovak State Relationship (in percent)

	Unitary State	Federation	Confederation	Independence	Other/Don't Know
June 1990					
Czech Republic	30	45	—	12	13
Slovakia	14	63	—	13	6
November 1991					
Czech Republic	39	30	4	5	22
Slovakia	20	26	27	14	13
March 1992					
Czech Republic	34	27	6	11	22
Slovakia	13	24	32	17	14

Sources: Hospodářské noviny, June 26, 1990, p. 2, reprinted in *Foreign Broadcast Information Service* in FBIS-EEU-90-126, June 29, 1990, p. 26; *České a Moravskoslezské zemedelské noviny,* November 22, 1991, p. 3; Sharon Wolchik, "The Politics of Ethnicity in Post-Communist Czechoslovakia," *East European Politics and Societies* 8:1 (Winter 1994):180.

favor greater central power as a counterweight to their minority status within Slovakia; this suggests that Slovaks themselves were even more supportive of a decentralized solution than the overall poll results in Slovakia would indicate. Czechs and Slovaks may both have wanted the continuance of the state. On the proper *form* of that state, however, public disagreement ran along the same lines as leadership disagreement. This is the more complex reality that lay underneath the superficial appearance of consensual support for a common state in the public opinion polls.[15]

This is a problem that democracy alone could not solve. Had there been a referendum on statehood, as a number of politicians had urged at different stages of the process, it might well have produced a vote for continued statehood, as the opinion polls suggested.[16] However, that alone would have done nothing to answer the question of what kind of state should continue—the question that had deadlocked negotiations. And politicians despaired of finding a formula that would reduce the alternative possible state forms to a set of simple referendum options. That is the kind of detailed issue that may need negotiation by political leaders; that is their job as representatives. Of course, a clear-cut referendum outcome might have given the governments a clear negotiating mandate. However, given the differences between Czech and Slovak popular preferences on the form of the state, a referendum on constitutional alternatives could very well have resulted in a Slovak vote for confederation and a Czech vote for a tighter federation. Then what? Back to the conference table for leadership negotiations on a formula that could pass the Federal Assembly. A seemingly democratic device like the referendum, although it is increasingly common globally in the late twentieth century,[17] raises democratic questions of its own (see Box 4.2).

The interpretation of popular preferences is incomplete without the addition of another dimension. The polls on statehood did not measure the intensity of commitment to continuing the existing state; nor did these polls make it clear what trade-offs the public would prefer, for example, between joint statehood and rapid economic reform. The long history of Czech-Slovak disagreement over national questions had undoubtedly weakened mutual trust and undermined emotional commitment to a "Czechoslovak ideal"—in fact, the very idea of "Czechoslovakism" had officially been politically incorrect since the 1940s. It is very possible that both Czech and Slovak publics cared about the continuance of the state, but not enough to insist on a leadership resolution of the conflict at all costs.

However, although the absence of fervent Czechoslovak patriotism may have been the death warrant of the state, it also had one very positive consequence, which is that no group in the state felt intensely enough about its continuance to raise violent objections to its demise. This may be part of the explanation of the peaceful character of the state disintegration. Several other possible explanations will be discussed in the following section.

BOX 4.2
The Political Problem with Referenda

We tend to define democracy in terms of voting, with the citizens' ability to choose what policies and leaders they want. The problem is that a simple, numerically tabulated "yes-or-no" vote does not necessarily resolve anything. It can even make things worse and lead to questionably democratic outcomes, particularly in multinational states. A good example of this dilemma is the referendum held on Bosnian independence in the spring of 1992. Bosnia had three major national groups: Serbs, Croatians, and Bosnian Muslims. Two of these groups, Croatians and Muslims, voted for independence, while the Serbs rejected this choice. The vote "decided" Bosnian independence. Or did it? In fact, nothing was decided. A simple vote could not alter Serbian rejection of the new state or produce a workable compromise (among the potential compromises was the possibility of territorial revisions); in the event, despite the referendum, Serb resistance soon led to a horrible civil war. What is more, the Bosnian referendum raises a serious question about democracy. Is it truly democratic to enforce a solution on the Serbs just because they are a minority that can always be outvoted? Likewise, it would have been equally undemocratic to allow the Serbs to veto the majority preference for independence. In retrospect, and even to many observers at the time, it seemed that the only chance for a stable and fair solution to Bosnia's problem was for leaders of each group to negotiate a settlement that all three parties could agree to.

Complicated questions can sometimes be "decided" by adding up ballots in a referendum, but they often cannot be stably resolved that way. All over the multinational territory of the postcommunist states, this problem appears in variant forms.

Why a Peaceful Dissolution?

Ironically, the dissolution of the state was rendered feasible by the very factors that also made it peaceful. Whereas in the past either side might have been impelled toward concessions (as in the fall of 1938 or the postwar period) by a threatening or coercive international environment, the emerging post–cold war Europe was primarily an environment of opportunity rather than of threat. The international liabilities of a possible separation did not include the risk of absorption by a larger neighbor; post-unification Germany was not Nazi Germany, and the former Soviet Union had lost much of its coercive leverage on Czech and Slovak political calculations.[18] Instead, the primary international considerations centered on the consequences of alternative courses of action for rapid integration into Europe. The question of eligibility for the European Community (EC— now the European Union, or EU) *did* provoke lively debate, as Czechs initially chided Slovaks for their provincialist self-assertion in an era of greater continental integration. In the long run, however, this issue probably cut the other way, as Klaus began to calculate that protracted negotiations on the national/constitutional question would only impede acceptance into the EC, and that the Czech Republic would move into Europe more quickly without Slovakia.

A second factor in the peaceful dissolution was a concern with maintaining stability. The violent Yugoslav breakup that was unfolding at the same time, though not a likely scenario for Czechoslovakia, was nonetheless a potent image. All politicians, regardless of their personal attitudes toward the existing state, were averse to a protracted period of indeterminacy. Once negotiations for a joint state had clearly failed in the summer of 1992, the pressure mounted for a peaceful, negotiated, and timely separation. Failure to agree on separation would only create policy stasis and an anarchical and chaotic breakup; it therefore seemed irresponsible to drag out the process, even by referendum. A vote for continued statehood at that point would only plunge the country into confusion and raise the risks of confrontation.

A third factor that eased the separation and enhanced its peaceful character was the nature of the stakes of dissolution. A key source of friction in the Soviet and Yugoslav cases was the imperfect fit between the distribution of national groups and the boundaries of the republics. Some 25 million Russians, for example, found themselves outside the Russian Federation after 1991, and this has been the cause of continuing tension. The partial mismatch between borders and national groups in Yugoslavia was even more divisive. It is significant that Serbia did not persist in challenging the Slovene secession from Yugoslavia; Slovenia was overwhelmingly Slovenian in ethnic composition. But Bosnia-Hercegovina and Croatia both possessed sizable ethnic Serb minorities, and Serbian championship of their cause has been a primary source of bloodshed during the disintegration of Yugoslavia.

The Czech and Slovak case was very different. Only about 1 percent of the population of the Slovak Republic was Czech, and only 4 percent of the Czech Republic's population was Slovak. Neither minority was seen as a threat to the majority in either republic. The small numbers had even less political importance because much of this moderate intermixture was of very recent vintage. In particular, most of the Slovaks in the Czech Republic had arrived there only during the communist period; they had resettled voluntarily, had (with the exception of Slovak Romanies) assimilated relatively well, and were in a position either to return "home" or settle permanently in the Czech Republic. There was therefore no real sense of ancestral belonging or of being ripped away from the motherland, no ancient territorial right. Most Czechs in Slovakia were in Bratislava, and most Slovaks in the Czech Republic were in Prague, often as a result of service in state agencies; there were no compact settlements of Czech or Slovak minorities to encourage the demand for major border revisions, as was the case in Yugoslavia. No one would go to war over the status of these minorities; the question of citizenship for these "displaced" Czechs and Slovaks simply became an item on the agenda for negotiating the dissolution of the state.[19]

If these conditions had been different, if the minorities had been large enough and beleaguered enough to inspire the protective instincts of their co-nationals, a peaceful dissolution would have been much less likely. In short, the emotional temperature of the ethnonational dispute in Czechoslovakia was considerably lower than in Yugoslavia or the Soviet Union—lower in fact than in several heterogeneous West European states. This may not have been a truly "velvet" divorce, but it was certainly facilitated by absence of the dangerous cross-boundary ethnic ties that complicated the dissolution of other postcommunist federations.[20]

In the final analysis, however, none of the answers to the riddle of the Velvet ·
Divorce is complete without some acknowledgment of the legacy of distrust and mutual incomprehension that fed into the negotiation process and helped to poison it.[21] Again, Czechoslovakia was not Yugoslavia. Polls repeatedly showed that Czechs and Slovaks did not hate and fear each other or even dislike each other. However, most Slovaks did not trust Czechs to treat them as equal partners.[22] There was a fairly wide gulf in understanding between the two groups regarding central priorities, a misunderstanding that had a long historical pedigree. As had been true during the Prague Spring and earlier periods of regime change, Slovaks tended to feel a lack of Czech comprehension of and sympathy with Slovak interest in safeguarding their national identity. Czechs tended to regard Slovak identity politics as a side issue fueled by elite demagoguery that compromised more important goals of political and economic consolidation.

An exchange that occurred early in the postcommunist debate on Czech-Slovak relations captures much of the flavor of this historically rooted distrust. The exchange was launched by one of the most respected Czech dissidents, the writer Ludvík Vaculík. Although Vaculík was hardly uncritical of Czech behavior toward the Slovaks, he viewed them as caught in an unhealthy dependency syndrome in which they had become inclined to blame Czechs for all their misfortunes. He thus questioned whether either side really needed continued coexistence. A well-known Slovak writer responded to these charges with a rebuttal that emphasized Slovakia's affirmative efforts to assert its identity under difficult historical conditions and that rejected both Czechoslovakism and Vaculík's deprecatory comments on the character of Slovak self-awareness.

This exchange was but the opening round of a public and official debate that was often much more vituperative than the initial writers' dialogue. In the course of the negotiations, it became clear that neither side trusted the good intentions of the other. The Czech press saw Slovaks as pursuing a "secret strategy" of independence under the disguise of constructive negotiations, as trying to "break up the federation" with their economic demands. "Although they claim they want justice for the Slovaks," concluded one commentator, "they are playing for [political] posts."[23] Mečiar was a "country bumpkin," an StB informant, or an authoritarian demagogue in the tradition of the wartime Slovak state. Slovaks protested their "demonic image" as "neofascists, neocommunists and anti-Semites" in the Czech media.[24] These writers did not contribute to the easing of tensions, however; instead they countered with charges of Pragocentric colonization of Slovakia, "secret Czech strategies" of restoring Czechoslovakist ideology, and robbing from the Slovak economy to build Czech prosperity. The atmosphere of charge and countercharge, and the historical experiences that generated such heated exchanges, undermined the constitutional negotiations and impeded the reconciliation of the two divergent conceptions of the state. The renewal of old arguments sparked dismay and even surprise as initial optimism about a solution faded, certainly contributing to a sense, on both sides of the negotiating table, that the existing differences were too long-standing to be amenable to resolution.

Conclusion

The disintegration of the state in 1992 was the culmination of a long history of failed Czech and Slovak efforts to devise a mutually satisfactory arrangement for coexistence in a common state. The oddity of the circumstances surrounding the breakup—the lack of a vigorous independence sentiment on either side, in particular—made the two-year postcommunist effort to preserve the state a distinctive one. However, most of the contextual setting for the negotiations on joint statehood appear, in retrospect at least, to have stacked the deck against success. The federal structure and its minority veto provisions, the segmented Czech and Slovak party systems, the historically conditioned atmosphere of mutual distrust, and the differential impact of economic reform all combined to undercut the chances of a settlement. It is certainly possible, however, that some agreement could have been reached if there had been any way of postponing decision on the national bargain until the political and economic transitions had been more firmly under way. Stabler economic conditions and a more established political leadership might have facilitated negotiations. Ironically, it was probably democracy itself that made this postponement impossible. Competitive elections put the national question firmly on the agenda, and the functioning of a genuinely representative Federal Assembly prevented any move to smother that question. Whether you consider the resultant Velvet Divorce a misfortune or a belated recognition of differing Czech-Slovak interests, however, it is probably valid to say that conditions after 1989 put together the two pieces of the power equation that led to the final dissolution of the state. The interwar Republic had been democratic enough to allow the expression of national grievances without giving Slovaks a power base to force the issue. And the communist state, by federating the state, had provided a potential power base for Slovak interests without being democratic enough to make it usable. After 1989, the democratization of the federal structure set the stage for the final showdown.

Despite continuing doubts about the wisdom of the breakup, particularly in Slovakia in the early months, no significant organized political movement emerged to call for reunification. The central national questions in the two successor republics revolve instead around the treatment of minorities and the search for an international niche that will safeguard the newly evolving national identities of both majority and minority populations.

Perhaps the most striking aspect of the national tensions in Czech-Slovak disputes over the constitutional allocation of power is that these conflicts call into question the Western idea of democracy, which has been based on a theoretical foundation of individual rights and majority rule. The Slovak challenge was to the idea of majority rule. Slovak leaders assumed as a basic article of democratic faith that a system in which the Czech majority could determine policy for Slovakia was no democracy. There was a fundamental problem hidden here. As Sir Ivor Jennings said forty years ago, "The people cannot decide until someone first decides who are the people."[25] Czechs tended to define "the people" as all the citizens of the state, whereas Slovaks insisted on the existence of two peoples, each of which had the right to decide the fate of its own territory. The quarrel about federation was really a quarrel about what democracy should look like in a multinational state.

Notes

1. James Mayall, *Nationalism and National Integration* (London: Pinter, 1989), p. 64.

2. Donald Horowitz, *Ethnic Groups in Conflict* (Berkeley and Los Angeles: University of California Press, 1985), p. 563.

3. The following analysis is largely derived from a paper presented to the Department of Political Science, University of Illinois, Urbana-Champaign, April 1993.

4. Vladimír Mlynář, "Volební program HZDS," *Respekt*, May 11–17, 1992.

5. Vladimír Mečiar, interview with *Le Monde*, July 7, 1992, p. 1, 4, reproduced in *Foreign Broadcast Information Service–East Europe* FBIS-EEU-92-131, July 8, 1992, p. 12.

6. Jack Snyder, "Nationalism and the Crisis of the Post-Soviet State," in Michael Brown, ed., *Ethnic Conflict and International Security* (Princeton: Princeton University Press, 1993), pp. 79–102.

7. There were variations in emphasis from one Slovak party to the next on this question, but the general tendency to support a looser federation is clear.

8. The Czech-Slovak impasse is not unique. Students of U.S. history certainly remember that the relative power of U.S. states and the central government was a critical issue in the Civil War, an issue only resolved by bloodshed. The same issue launched the bloody war in Yugoslavia. Two rather different conceptions of democracy lay behind the conflicting positions. Czechs generally favored a more majoritarian democracy, in which key decisions would stem from the overall balance of power in the center. Too much decentralization would hamper majority rule by allowing the individual republics to go their own way on important policy issues. Slovaks generally saw the need to vest democratic rights not in the citizenship of the state as a whole but rather in the national components of that state. Greater decentralization would assure a Slovak voice rather than subordinating it to a larger Czech majority. The decentralization of authority through federal structures is a special case of the broader demands by ethnic minorities in postcommunist East Europe to negotiate some form of institutional protection for minority rights.

9. Josef Kotrba and Karel Kríž, "Cui Bono? The Common State in Economic Perspective," *East European Reporter* 5:5 (September-October 1992):3–6.

10. *Hospodářské noviny*, May 2, 1991, p. 4, reprinted in FBIS-EEU-91-091, May 10, 1991, p. 9.

11. The Czech public, as well, tended to believe that the Czech Republic subsidized Slovakia, although they disagreed with the proposition that an independent Czech state would surmount economic difficulties more quickly on its own. Poll results published in "Jako bychom se míjeli: Veřejné mínění Čechů o Slovensku a Slováků o Češích," *Právo lidu*, December 6, 1992.

12. Quoted in the *Chicago Tribune*, October 12, 1994, p. 1.

13. "Vztahy Čechů a Slováků," *Rudé právo*, April 7, 1992.

14. "Jako bychom se míjeli," *Právo lidu*, December 6, 1992.

15. An excellent survey of divergences in Czech and Slovak public opinion may be found in Sharon Wolchik, "The Politics of Ethnicity in Post-Communist Czechoslovakia," *East European Politics and Societies* 8:1 (Winter 1994):167–186.

16. During the fall negotiations on the dissolution of the state, only 36 percent of the public in each republic reported that they would have cast a referendum vote to end Czechoslovakia, even though they considered its end inevitable.

17. See David Butler and Austin Ranney, eds., *Referendums Around the World: The Growing Use of Direct Democracy* (Washington, D.C.: AEI Press, 1994).

18. Both sides professed to believe that the other, on its own, would drift into subordination to Germany or the former Soviet Union. Slovaks claimed tauntingly that the Czechs would enter the European Community speaking German. They added that association with the Czech Republic actually impeded Slovakia's integration into the West by allowing the center to absorb foreign investment and deflect it from Slovakia to Czech benefit.

19. In the first four years after independence, more than 370,000 Slovaks did acquire Czech citizenship, a figure that represents the overwhelming majority of Slovaks resident in the Czech Republic at the time of the state's dissolution, including former Czechoslovak Prime Minister Marian Čalfa. In the same period, as many as 80,000 Czechs received Slovak citizenship. The Czech government has continued to resist demands for dual Czech-Slovak citizenship.

20. The absence of cross-boundary ties and ethnic intermixtures was central to the European Community's failure to demand a referendum on the future of the state, as it had done in the case of Bosnia-Hercegovina.

21. For an extended treatment of the negative mutual perceptions that evolved after 1918, see Carol Skalnik Leff, *National Conflict in Czechoslovakia: The Making and Remaking of a State, 1918–1987* (Princeton: Princeton University Press, 1988).

22. In a study of a 1990 poll, analysts reported high levels of distrust; fully 75 percent of respondents in Slovakia voiced the suspicion that Czechs were not dealing with them as equal partners. "Samostatné a demokratické?" *Kultúrny Život*, December 10, 1991.

23. Vladimír Kučera in *Práce*, December 1, 1990, p. 2 reprinted in FBIS-EEU-90-235, December 6, 1990.

24. "Tisíc slov o Slovensku a stanovisko OSN," *Slovenský denník*, December 4, 1991.

25. Cited in Samuel Huntington, "Democracy's Third Wave," *Journal of Democracy* 2:2 (Spring 1991):12–34.

5

POLITICAL AND NATIONAL IDENTITY TRANSITIONS IN THE CZECH AND SLOVAK REPUBLICS

The Czech and Slovak parties that won the 1992 elections and formed ruling governments in their respective republics were the architects both of the dismantling of the old state and the construction of the new ones. Despite the profound differences between the two governments, they were eventually able to work through the Federal Assembly to forge agreements that defined guidelines for the split. At the same time, the new Czech and Slovak leaders had less than five months after the separation agreement to put together constitutions for the successor states. This was somewhat easier for the Slovak government; the Slovak National Council had started work on a constitution for itself (originally intended to be part of the federal solution) back in 1990. The Slovak draft constitution was approved in September 1992. The less prepared Czechs worked on their own constitutional document right down to the last minute; it was approved in mid-December 1992—just two weeks before independence—and even then with certain crucial questions of territorial organization left unresolved.

Given the recentness of the last elections, neither republic tried to elect a new parliament following the formal dissolution of the state at the beginning of 1993. The National Councils elected in June 1992 became the sovereign legislatures of the new states, much as Russia's legislature, elected in 1990, had become the sovereign assembly of the Russian Federation with the disintegration of the USSR in December 1991.[1] The pattern of party support in the republic legislatures differed only marginally from the statewide pattern (see Table 5.1). The parties represented in the Slovak National Council were the same ones that had achieved representation at the federal level. All the Czech parties in the Federal Assembly were represented in the Czech National Council, in addition to two that had failed to cross the federal electoral threshold: the regionally assertive Society for Moravia and Silesia, and the Civic Democratic Alliance.

In anticipation of the final showdown on the future of the state, recall that the leaders of the winning parties in each republic (Václav Klaus and Vladimír Mečiar) had chosen to assume the prime ministerships of their republics rather than enter the federal government. This also contributed to leadership continuity in the move toward independence.

Slovak Politics After Independence

Independence posed a special challenge for Slovak politics, however. Parties that had previously focused on the Czech-Slovak relationship, seeking independence or fuller autonomy within the ČSFR, had suddenly attained their maximal polit-

Table 5.1   Elections to the Czech and Slovak National Councils, 1992

Czech National Council (200 seats) Party	% of Votes	Seats
Civic Democratic Alliance	6	14
Civic Democratic Party/Christian Democratic Party	30	76
Left Bloc	14	35
Liberal Social Union	7	16
People's Party/Christian Democratic Union	6	15
Republican Party	6	14
Social Democratic Party	7	16
Society for Moravia and Silesia	6	14

Slovak National Council (150 seats) Party	% of Votes	Seats
Christian Democratic Movement	9	18
Coexistence	7	14
Movement for a Democratic Slovakia	37	74
Party of the Democratic Left	15	29
Slovak National Party	8	15

Source: Compiled from Jan Obrman, "The Czechoslovak Elections," *RFE/RL Research Report* 1:26 (June 26, 1992):12–19.

ical demands on the national issue: self-determination. The new challenge was to rework the agenda into a form suitable for the tasks of governance rather than confrontation with Prague.

The Movement for a Democratic Slovakia (MDS) under Mečiar, which swept to an easy victory in 1992 as protector of Slovak interests, now faced a delicate political task. Mečiar had been something of a political martyr, a politician whose popularity surged when he was out of power. Now he bore responsibility for the mission of consolidating a new state composed of citizens who on the eve of statehood were not fully convinced that they even wanted an independent state. Their initial discomfort only increased as they were buffeted by the economic dislocations that followed the dissolution of the Czechoslovak state, the impact of which drove production down still further.

The result was politically destabilizing. Mečiar's popularity, and that of his MDS, began to slide in the opinion polls. Moreover, the MDS, despite its large bloc of SNR seats, was soon riven with internal conflict. Internal divisions had already surfaced by the time Slovakia gained its formal independence, six months after the 1992 elections.

A highly visible crisis was triggered by the parliamentary vote to select Slovakia's first president.[2] The need to move rapidly on the selection process was urgent for several reasons. The opposition parties were anxious to see a president in office because Prime Minister Mečiar, whom they deeply distrusted, had added the powers of the presidency to those of his own office on an interim basis until a president could be installed. Moreover, several cabinet ministerial appointments were on hold pending presidential approval.

Despite the need for action on the presidency, however, two rounds of parliamentary voting in January 1993 produced no winning candidate. Part of the problem was that at least some MDS deputies took advantage of the secret balloting to desert Mečiar's handpicked presidential candidate, Roman Kováč. Both the opposition parties and some in the government objected to a president who was not only an MDS member but also a close ally of Mečiar himself. Kováč was also tainted because he had been a candidate member of the Slovak Communist Party. Mečiar had forced this choice even on his own party and lost the gamble that parliament would go along with a Mečiar clone in the presidency in order to avoid a long period of conflict over the empty office. Instead, Mečiar faced a mini-revolt from his junior coalition partner, the Slovak National Party, and from within the MDS ranks as well. His own foreign minister, Milan Kňažko, publicly challenged the choice, arguing that the imposition of party discipline on this issue smacked of past communist authoritarian practice. Ultimately, Mečiar was forced to compromise and to accept as the party's presidential nominee Michal Kováč, whose sympathies were suspected to lie more with Kňažko than with Mečiar. The second Kováč (no relation to Roman), Dubček's successor as chair of the Federal Assembly in 1992, was elected president in February (see Box 5.1).

BOX 5.1
Slovakia's First President

Michal Kováč, sixty-five years old, was no match for his Czech counterpart, Václav Havel, in international stature. He had emerged as a compromise choice from Prime Minister Vladimír Mečiar's failure to win the presidency for his own preferred candidate. Like Mečiar himself, Kováč was a professional and a former member of the Slovak Communist Party who had been expelled during the purges of 1970 for reformist sympathies. Demoted from positions as finance professor and banking official after the Prague Spring, Kováč spent the 1970s as a bank clerk before regaining some of his former status with a research institute position in the 1980s. Elected to the Federal Assembly in 1990 on the People Against Violence platform, his expert credentials and political pedigree of persecution under the communists earned him a cabinet position as Slovak minister of finance from December 1989 to the spring of 1991. Reelected to the Federal Assembly in 1992, this time as Movement for a Democratic Slovakia deputy, he presided as a cochairman of the Assembly during the deliberations over the demise of the state before emerging as Slovakia's first president.

This early confrontation within the party and the legislature was an omen of serious future discord that continued through at least 1995. Mečiar's internal critics of early 1993 eventually became his opposition rivals in 1994. This initial conflict was also indicative of the confrontational climate in Slovak politics as a whole, for Mečiar found himself at odds with virtually every other political force in the new state. The MDS coalition partner, the Slovak National Party, eventually left the government, as did a number of MDS deputies disillusioned with Mečiar's abrasive and controlling style.

The opposition felt equally embattled. The coalition of parties representing the Hungarian minority, dismayed by Slovak national assertiveness, vocally challenged the government's minority policy and were joined in criticism by opposition parties that saw the Mečiar government as a public relations disaster for the new state's image as well as a policy disaster for the transformation program.

Popular dissatisfaction and the defections from the coalition finally reached a crisis point in March 1994, when the Mečiar government fell to a vote of no confidence in the National Council over the government's privatization policies. Maintaining a united front against Mečiar, the otherwise diverse opposition parties moved into the power vacuum with a grand coalition headed by former MDS member Jozef Moravčík that allocated government ministries to MDS defectors (who formed the Democratic Union as their own party), the Christian Democrats, and the Party of the Democratic Left. The core defectors from Mečiar's party included all the key critics of the initial controversy over the presidential nominee, including former foreign minister Kňažko and former MDS chair Rudolf Filkus. Slovak President Michal Kováč, grudgingly accepted as the party's presidential candidate by Mečiar the previous year, also cooperated with his ouster. Mečiar's worst political enemies turned out to be his erstwhile political allies. (See Box 5.2.)

The Moravčík coalition that supplanted Mečiar's government had about six months to establish a record before the critical election of September 1994. The record it wished to establish was clearly one of responsibility, fence-mending, and good Eurocitizenship on key issues that would shape Slovakia's image at home and abroad. The new coalition government finally moved on Hungarian language rights, winning the Hungarian-based Coexistence party's cooperation with the government. This in turn paved the way to smoother dealings with the neighboring Hungarian government, itself newly minted after the victory of Hungarian reform communists in May 1994. Gyula Horn was the first Hungarian prime minister to visit Slovakia since its independence a year and a half earlier, and his visit seemed to promise accelerated action on a treaty of mutual cooperation.

BOX 5.2
Slovakia's Key Politicians

Among the most important figures to watch in Slovakia's post-independence politics have been five party leaders—Vladimír Mečiar of the Movement for a Democratic Slovakia (MDS), Jan Luptak of the Association of Slovak Workers (ASW), Ján Čarnogurský of the Christian Democrats, Jozef Moravčík of the Democratic Union, and Petr Weiss of the ex-communist Party of the Democratic Left (PDL). They have very different pedigrees in the communist period. Čarnogurský is the sole dissident among them, a lawyer and lay activist for religious and political freedom who went directly from jail for his dissident writings in November 1989 to deputy prime minister of Czechoslovakia two weeks later. A member of the Slovak Public Against Violence, he subsequently founded the Christian Democratic Party. While serving as Slovak prime minister in 1991 and 1992, he lost political ground to Mečiar, largely by an excess of responsibility during the statehood negotiations. Mečiar, Luptak, and Weiss are former communists but with very different backgrounds. Mečiar, a communist youth organizer, lost his party membership in 1970 for reformist sympathy with the ideas of the Prague Spring and went to work in a steel foundry. In the more heavily "normalized" Czech Republic, he might have remained in a blue-collar job. In the milder political climate of Slovakia, he was able to complete law school and go to work as a lawyer for a Slovak glass company. Luptak, trained as an engineer, was a member in good standing of the party in 1989; he was elected as a parliamentary delegate of the communist successor PDL in both 1990 and 1992. He was co-founder of the ASW as a civic movement; the ASW transformed itself into a party in 1994.

You have already got a sense of Mečiar's abrasive and flamboyant style; Luptak seems unlikely to stand in his shadow in this respect. Weiss took over the Slovak Communist Party in 1990, giving it a new flexibility and competitive edge that quite surpassed its more rigid Czech counterpart. Politics does make strange bedfellows.

In economic policy, the goal of the Moravčík government was to signal renewed commitment to marketization and privatization, launching a second wave
of so-called voucher privatization (the first since Slovak independence) and
bringing the budget closer to balance. After previous years of a skidding gross domestic product, the 1994 forecast was for a reversal, with slight overall projected
growth. The *Economist* reported approvingly that the coalition government was
"beginning to get the economy right," and the International Monetary Fund
(IMF) apparently agreed, extending $263 million in new credits in July 1994.[3]
What the government could not be sure of was whether its approach would be
electorally rewarded in the September 1994 elections, particularly since the IMF
loan carried the price of Slovak commitments to strict budgetary control.

This electoral campaign, the first since independence, dramatized both the
frailties of the fledgling party system and the difficulties of translating electoral
outcomes into effective government. The coalition that was putting its record on
the line was a rather artificial one, united primarily on the need to block Mečiar
from retaining power but otherwise widely divergent in priorities and political
orientation. In that respect it resembled the earlier Public Against Violence and
Civic Forum in substance if not in form. The core parties included the conservative Christian Democrats, the reform communists of the Party of the Democratic Left (PDL), and the newly formed liberal Democratic Union (DU), in cooperation with the minority party, Coexistence. These were strange political
bedfellows indeed, who could only cooperate by cobbling together compromises
on the basic issues that divided them—including, among other issues, privatization and the lustration law—or by postponing action altogether. These parties
fought the election campaign separately while still defending the government
record against the vitriolic criticism of the MDS and the Slovak National Party.

Mečiar was indeed the central figure of the campaign. In fact, whereas Slovak
politics had previously revolved around relations with the Czechs, it now appeared to have become an intensely personalist politics that revolved around
Mečiar himself. A Bratislava clothing store capitalized on this fact with a bit of
entrepreneurial hustle: Shoppers were offered a choice of two election T-shirts,
one saying "Volím Mečiara" (I'm Voting for Mečiar) and one saying "Nievolím
Mečiara" (I'm Not Voting for Mečiar).[4] Mečiar attacked the government for selling out Slovakia to the West and to the Hungarians, calling for less hasty privatization to avoid "dirty property transfers" and for more domestic self-reliance.[5]
Claiming the political center, Mečiar assured a foreign reporter that this would
"be appreciated by Czech [Prime Minister] Klaus, who would otherwise be
squeezed between Germans and the pink-red belt to the east of the Czech Republic."[6]

The well-financed MDS campaign, better funded than any other in the race,
was run with the aid of Italy's neofascist Forza Italia party—not the most respectable Western supporter! Mečiar repeatedly challenged the constitutionality
of his ouster in March and President Kováč's role in it, foreshadowing a post-

election assault on presidential power. Mečiar's offensive recouped much of the popularity he had lost while in power; this resurgence was reflected in the election results.

Table 5.2 records the results of Mečiar's most recent political comeback as well as the complexities of the new parliamentary alignment. The MDS was the strongest party, and the total number of seats won by the former Moravčík government fell short of a majority.

The political parties that gained seats in the new Slovak legislature were recognizable forces, sometimes hidden under a new coalition name. All five parties that entered the SNR after the previous election returned, in addition to two new groupings, the MDS defectors who had formed the Democratic Union, and the Association of Slovak Workers, led by former communist Jan Luptak.

Superficially, this was a less dramatic partisan shift than the 1992 elections had been and might suggest that Klaus was right in expecting more Slovak political coherence after independence. In a sense, however, Klaus had been too optimistic. Slovakia does not have a coherent party alignment yet, because post-independence politics have revolved around the response to the flamboyant personality of Mečiar. This is a case in which elections by themselves have not decided the identity of government; the results were too fragmented. The resolution of that question depended on complicated post-election negotiations among the leaders of the parties that passed the electoral threshold into the legislature, negotiations which took almost two months, from early October to early December.

Table 5.2   Elections to the Slovak National Council, September 1994

Party	% of Votes	Seats
Movement for a Democratic Slovakia/Agricultural Party of Slovakia	35	60
Common Choice	10	18
Magyar (Hungarian) Coalition	10	18
Christian Democratic Movement	10	17
Democratic Union	9	15
Association of Workers of Slovakia	7	13
Slovak National Party	5	9

Turnout: 76%

Parties and coalitions in italics previously represented in the legislature.

Common Choice: *Party of the Democratic Left* in coalition with Social Democratic Party of Slovakia, Peasants' Movement, Green Party.

Magyar Coalition: Hungarian Christian Democratic Movement, *Coexistence,* Hungarian Civic Party.

Democratic Union: Defectors from Movement for a Democratic Slovakia.

During that period of bilateral and multilateral negotiations, the real inflexibilities of the multiparty system were much in evidence. For example, the Party of the Democratic Left is closer to the MDS on many economic policy issues than to its own former coalition partners. The easiest new government to form would have been an MDS/PDL coalition. But here the tense personal relations that have plagued postcommunist politics came to the fore. The antagonism between the two party chairmen, Weiss and Mečiar, seemed such a roadblock to cooperation that many political pundits predicted during the 1994 campaign that the two parties could only work together if their leaders were replaced. Additionally complicating the task of building a majority was the fact that no Slovak party wanted to risk appearing to collaborate with the electorally successful Hungarian coalition of parties for fear of appearing "un-Slovak."

After weeks of wrangling, the Association of Slovak Workers agreed to join the Slovak National Party and the Movement for a Democratic Slovakia in a coalition led by Mečiar as prime minister. The first sessions of the new parliament, held in November 1994, before the installation of the new government, set the tone for continued confrontation and antagonism, as Mečiar's majority acted to undo recent privatization and personnel decisions of the previous government and to conduct massive purges of sensitive institutions such as the television and radio boards.[7]

The interim between the Slovak elections and the official formation of a new government was a rather lengthy one, but that in itself is not unusual in the unstable postcommunist politics of the region. Governments in Eastern Europe fall more frequently than in Western European countries, last a shorter time (about ten months shorter than in the West), and are more difficult to form in the first place. This is only to be expected, however, in transitional systems in which the parties are new and have no established patterns of cooperation with one another to ease the process of government formation and maintenance.

What is of far greater concern in the Slovak case is the worrisome new political controversies that were spawned in the post-election period. In this interlude, the MDS launched two initiatives that augured further trouble ahead. One was a legal challenge to the participation of the Democratic Union in the elections, a challenge that put in question the DU's eligibility to claim its parliamentary seats and even the validity of the election itself. Further, Mečiar continued to threaten an investigation of President Kováč's exercise of his presidential authority: MDS officials even called for the president's resignation.

Both of these challenges to rival power groups continued after the election. Despite Electoral Commission and Constitutional Court rulings that the Democratic Union had registered properly for the election, a parliamentary commission comprised only of government parties continued to investigate the issue in 1995, and Mečiar continued to accuse his rivals of electoral fraud. In the spring of 1995, the government authorized an additional police investigation; Democratic Union leaders protested that police inquiries of the petition signatories were designed to intimidate their voters.

President Kováč was the target of ever more relentless criticism. In addition to the formal parliamentary investigation of the March 1994 events, his powers of appointment to key offices to media and defense positions were curtailed in overrides of presidential vetoes,[8] and the presidential budget has been repeatedly cut. In May 1995 the president was met with the first of several votes of no confidence (these were purely symbolic, since parliament cannot remove him except by impeachment). By summer, there was little doubt that the government was looking for a way to remove him. His chief crimes, which government coalition partner Slovak National Party wanted to investigate as treason, were objections to government policies and criticism of the government in domestic and international settings. Neither of these two offenses, of course, are considered "treasonable" in the West. No one is demanding impeachment proceedings against President Bill Clinton for disagreeing with Congress and vetoing some of its enactments.

The showdown between the president and the government is interesting and very worrisome in several respects. In the first place, the president's vetoes of government legislation are not a real impediment to the government, since the constitution provides that a veto override requires only a simple majority, which the government already has. What the MDS coalition appears to find objectionable, therefore, is that the presidential office has come to serve as a rallying point for the parliamentary opposition and a politically legitimate platform for criticism of sometimes questionable government policies—restrictions on media operations or the curtailment of the privatization program, for example.

Secondly, the government's response to this politically unpleasant opposition is to identify all legitimate Slovak interests with itself and to characterize the president as a betrayer of Slovakia. The government has repeatedly expressed the demand that he resign, and yet it is unable to remove him by constitutional means because the coalition does not have the necessary three-fifths majority to proceed with formal impeachment.

Kováč's continued refusal to resign seems to have contributed to a series of troubling episodes. In August 1995 police raided the office of a Slovak bishop on suspicion that he was trafficking in illegal foreign art objects; angry protests of this action raised the question of whether the raid could have been mounted simply because the Council of Slovak Bishops had defended the president. In October the MDS newspaper *Slovenská republika* published a copy of a bank account statement purporting to show that Kováč had over 2 million dollars stashed away in an Austrian bank. Kováč denied that it was his account and said that he would be glad to withdraw it and distribute the sum to Slovak orphanages. But he also filed suit against the government paper for libel; the Vienna bank backed up his claim that the account statement was falsified and pointed out, among other things, that the date of the statement was an Austrian public holiday on which all banks were closed.

The most bizarre of the suspected "dirty tricks," however, has spawned a continuing and very serious melodrama. The president's son, wanted for questioning in Germany for his possible complicity in a fraud under investigation, was kidnapped from Bratislava by an unidentified group of thugs, transported to Austria, and deposited in front of a police station, where he was taken into custody as a witness in an ongoing embezzlement case. [9]

The dramatic abduction immediately sparked questions as to the identity and motivation of the kidnappers. Suspicion centered on the possible role of the Slovak Information Service (SIS), a security agency over which the president lost appointment power in the spring, and which was subsequently headed by a government appointee—Ivan Lexa, an MDS loyalist whom Kováč had twice refused to confirm as a cabinet minister.[10] Lexa's SIS now came into conflict with the regular police over the investigation of SIS involvement in the kidnapping; in quick succession, two police officers investigating SIS links to the kidnapping were dismissed. The governing coalition forestalled opposition attempts to launch a parliamentary inquiry, shutting off debate after seven minutes, although an independent commission published findings in March 1996 indicating an SIS link to the abduction.

Since 1994, then, the parliamentary opposition and the president have been aligned in resistance to the government over the president's future. These controversies are not ordinary political squabbles. Taken together, the direct and indirect attacks on the presidency and the opposition Democratic Union add up to a scenario for a major constitutional crisis. As opposition parties repeatedly warn, the allocation of the Democratic Union's fifteen disputed seats among the other parliamentary delegations would give the Mečiar government the three-fifths parliamentary majority to make unilateral changes in the constitution. Given MDS outrage over Kováč's independent presidential power base, it has become clear that likely revisions would focus on further curtailment of the power of the presidency and an expansion of the grounds for impeachment or other means of removing him.[11] In November 1995 the government voted to transfer a key presidential power to the National Council: the power of deciding whether a proposed referendum meets constitutional requirements. The government has made it clear that they are exploring the president's removal by referendum, and gaining control of the referendum process clearly furthers this goal.

After the 1994 elections, Western journalists painted a harrowing scenario of what could follow:

> Mečiar is an unstable autocrat prone to violence. President Michal Kováč, regarded by Mečiar as his mortal enemy, would be ousted if not imprisoned on trumped-up charges. The constitution would be amended in favour of an executive presidency, which Mečiar would then fill, probably dissolving parliament. The country would degenerate into a primitive, corrupt, one-party neo-communist client-patron state— inherently unstable and shunned by the west.[12]

This scenario may be too apocalyptic; Mečiar's prior behavior, after all, has not been this extreme. What this nightmare image does underline, though, is a dangerous situation in which the rivalries of government and opposition politics transcend policy and threaten to penetrate the underpinnings of the constitutional order itself. The government's moves against their parliamentary opposition and the president are not merely quarrels over individual policies but rather center on changing the rules of the game in order to get rid of opponents through means other than the normal electoral process.

Does it matter whether politicians keep tinkering with the constitutional order and questioning the legitimacy of the opposition? American constitutional scholars tend to regard it as a sign of stability that the U.S. Constitution has been amended relatively rarely, and generally only with regard to rather fundamental democratic issues such as voting rights and civil liberties. Fine-tuning a constitution seems to be both legitimate and desirable. However, a new democracy that keeps playing with the rules of the game is liable to undercut popular confidence because the rules start to look like a political shell game that each government will try to manipulate to its own advantage, rather than an enduring expression of political principles.

Whenever a government tries to teach its critics a lesson by rewriting the rules, in other words, it is a clear sign that the political order is still unstable. Slovakia faces the dilemma of a system in which the politicians who try to govern by consensus and cooperation with the West cannot gain a clear electoral mandate to remain in office, and the politician who can and does maintain a strong public following (Mečiar) is unable to govern without crisis and confrontation. Between independence in 1993 and the spring of 1995, Slovakia had three different government coalitions, each beleaguered and controversial. Mečiar's leadership fortunes have followed a repeated pattern of electoral victory and political erosion. Although he was the most popular and trusted politician in Slovakia in the fall of 1994, his public ratings slipped markedly in the atmosphere of post-election contentiousness. By the spring of 1995, confidence in the presidency stood higher than confidence in Mečiar's government.[13] Political tensions thus continue to undermine democratic consolidation. Slovakia is not a protocommunist state, but nor is it a fully democratized one, because policy disagreements have not been routinized. Instead, they remain too heavily personalized on the one hand—revolving around the personality of Mečiar—and too "constitutionalized" on the other—with each confrontation threatening to escalate into a crisis of the whole system. It is all too obvious that both Mečiar and the opposition see their opponents not merely as political rivals but as threats to Slovakia itself. The opposition fears that the pattern of his actions represent a latent authoritarian agenda. Mečiar himself regards this opposition as wholly illegitimate. He has described his ouster in March 1994 as a "parliamentary putsch" conducted by rivals—"groups of personally dissatisfied, ambitious people" who knew which posts they wanted but did "not know what they [would] do in those posts."[14]

This pattern has aroused increasing concern in the West, as we will see later. More important, the current confrontation represents a critical turning point in

Slovakia's democratization effort. The government has tailored the March 1996 law on regional government to its own political ends to reward loyalists and redraw boundaries, further marginalizing the Hungarian minority and undercutting the special status of the capital Bratislava, which is a stronghold of Mečiar's opposition. Additional legislation passed in March to "protect" the political order threatens to criminalize opposition criticism. Both domestic and foreign observers ponder the future of Slovak politics, which appears increasingly less free.[15]

Czech Politics After Independence

The Czech Republic, by contrast, has experienced considerably greater political stability since independence. The major parties were aligned primarily on economic issues, and, with the notable exception of controversies over political corruption, the post-independence governing coalition has rarely lost its stride. The broad policy agenda set by the 1992 elections was not disrupted; the central goal remained to pursue the economic program outlined by Klaus. Bolstered by this coherent program and economic success, the governing coalition built around Prime Minister Klaus and his Civic Democratic Party (CDP) was able to maintain itself in office while successive Slovak governments floundered.[16]

However, several important challenges to Czech democratization remained unresolved. President Havel launched an ongoing debate in his presidential address of January 1994 when he argued for the value of a strong "civil society" of organizations and associations to serve as a buffer between the state and the individual. "Civil society" is social science terminology that has provoked intensive definitional debate. However it is specifically defined, the term captures a larger understanding that democracy does not function on periodic elections alone but flourishes only where broader ongoing public participation in autonomous political and socioeconomic organizations develops to serve societal needs.

Prime Minister Klaus, however, rejected this apparently innocuous idea as "aberrant," arguing that social strength was sufficiently safeguarded by the market economy, the preservation of individual freedom, and political pluralism.[17] His concern was to avoid the loosening of central government control over the processes of economic and political transformation.

In practical terms, what was at stake were several specific issues: the character of legislation to establish nonprofit status for public interest associations and churches, and the decentralization of the government. According special privileges to nonprofit organizations (a common Western practice) struck Klaus as an affront to his commitment to the free market; it is "a mistake," he argued, "to think that nonprofit organizations are something better than organizations that make a profit."[18] Havel, in turn, has vetoed legislation that failed to provide for nonprofit exemptions from administrative fees and taxes. A bill establishing the legal basis for nonprofit organizations finally passed parliament in October 1995 allowing exemptions from property, gift, and inheritance taxes for unofficial undertakings to promote culture, health, education, social and charitable services, and sports.

The decentralization of government was a still trickier issue. In fact, a very focused controversy about fuller democratization revolved around the fact that the Czech government had accrued two so-called "constitutional debts": the unresolved issues of establishing and electing both a new Senate and the regional governments, both of which had been mandated by the 1992 constitution. The government's lack of haste in constituting these two political institutions seems to reflect its contentment with control of the existing government and its unwillingness to hurry into establishing new structures that could carry the risk of voters' upsetting the current balance of political power in elections for new Senate and regional governments. The balance of power in the central government, of course, favored the ruling parties and facilitated the acceleration of Klaus's cherished market reforms. A challenge to that balance is very likely in the case of the future regional governments, in particular since Moravian regional interests would certainly be more strongly reflected in voting at the regional level than at the national.

Klaus saw no need for regional power bases in opposition to his own central power base; his government's proposal in the summer of 1994 for seventeen regions was spurned by other parties, who argued that this was too many subdivisions for a small country. Larger subdivisions, however, would be more powerful, and so the stalemate over decentralization continued, with its resolution deferred until after the 1996 elections. In a political system in which the parliamentary majority is the dominant force in policymaking, this reluctance to build up rival power centers is not unexpected.

The missing Senate posed a potential constitutional problem. The constitution provided that, in the event that the government fell and the lower house had to be dissolved for new elections, the Senate would remain in session to act on matters too urgent to be delayed.[19] Yet until a Senate was created, the lower house performed the duties of both houses and therefore could not be dissolved! Had the Klaus government fallen as Mečiar's had in Slovakia, the Czech Republic might have faced a constitutional deadlock. Fortunately this did not happen, and in September 1995 the parliament finally passed an enabling act setting up the Senate and providing for its election in 1996.

Arcane government squabbles over administrative divisions did not rivet popular attention. A challenge to the establishment of Czech democracy more provoking to the public has been the problem of drawing the line between proper political behavior and corrupt practices. This controversy, which reached a peak in early 1995, even threatened to topple the government. Of course, corruption is a problem even in well-established democracies; electoral fraud, city machine politics, and patronage appointments to bureaucratic office were a visible feature of nineteenth-century U.S. democracy, and conflict-of-interest scandals persist in American politics today. Nonetheless, such scandals have greater impact, and are probably more frequent, in a political system like that of Czech Republic, which is just establishing itself. In the first years after the Velvet Revolution, bureaucrats and party officials operated largely free of constraint by conflict-of-interest laws or other legislative restrictions on behavior. The line between ethical and unethical conduct was hazy and undefined. The temptations were particularly strong because of the simultaneous transitions in politics and economics; radical changes in the economic system provided an open season for profit-making and insider deals.

Not surprisingly, there were highly publicized cases in which government officials appear to have cooperated with, and benefited from, close working relationships with foreign and domestic business interests. In October 1994 the chief administrator of the government privatization program was arrested leaving a restaurant with a briefcase full of Czech crowns, on charges of accepting a substantial bribe for his services in brokering a deal over the allocation of shares in a privatizing enterprise. An additional 1994 scandal involved the German Helbig Brothers company that exports Mercedes Benz cars to the Czech Republic. Facing prosecution for tax evasion in Germany, the Helbig brothers fled to the Czech Republic. Soon the Czech media began to ask why the ruling Civic Democratic Party's deputy chairman (the party official in charge of party fund-raising) was driving a Helbig Mercedes and what other financial support the party might be receiving from that company.

At the root of the Helbig controversy was the problem of Czech legislation on party finance. Corporate contributions to party war chests are quite legal, as they are in the United States. The difference in the Czech Republic is that the corporate sponsors could remain confidential; most Czech parties preferred to keep the identity of their contributors secret, thus reinforcing public doubt about just who is influencing the party leaderships and how.[20] Given the laxity of regulation, very often it was unclear whether it was a case of undue influence or merely the *appearance* of impropriety, but the effect was politically poisonous either way.

In early 1995 the Czech government succumbed to popular pressure and proposed a stricter campaign finance law, which may help to clear the atmosphere of suspicion. In February 1995 the government also banned donations to political parties by state-owned or subsidized enterprises. This action was taken following a public outcry over a fund-raising dinner organized by the ruling CDP, which soon became known as the "meal of fortune"; the function was a $9,000-a-plate dinner attended by both private and state sector industrialists. Since very few dinners are worth a $9,000 tab, it was hard not to regard the CDP invitations to this gala affair as a barter deal granting special access to the party leaders in exchange for financial support. Once the legislation implementing the ban goes through, state sector enterprises will be able to make contributions only to charities and social welfare organizations.[21] As these examples suggest, the largest and most dominant party, the Civic Democratic Party, and its coalition partners have been the major focus of the scandals; the government's predominant influence in politics makes it the natural target for those seeking to affect policy and therefore gives the CDP and its allies the greatest capacity to capitalize on their position. Both the Czech Republic (in 1995) and Slovakia (in 1994) have also passed broader anti-corruption laws designed to control money laundering in the banking system.

Public scandals are not unique to Czech politics; all of the postcommunist states, including Slovakia, have experienced comparable scandals over the use of political power for personal or partisan interests.[22] The communist legacy of closed and often corrupt political dealings did nothing to build a foundation for clear guidelines on political ethics. However, it feeds popular cynicism about *all* politics to see any continuance of such behavior in the new regimes—behavior that is now far more visible because a free press can investigate and publicize it. The cynicism is clearly there: Three quarters of the Czech public believe that widespread corruption is routinely hidden from their view, and most see this as a continuation of communist-era corruption.[23] (Commentators point out that the Czech breach of law and order remains largely financial; the murders and kid-nappings of the former Soviet Union are not a feature of the Czech political land-scape.) The Czech government has, however, begun to react as most of the es-tablished democracies have, by beginning to set legally mandated standards for ethical behavior in politics.

Despite the constitutional debts and recurrent corruption squabbles, public opinion polls consistently reflected continuing majority support for the Czech government. However, an impressive 78 percent approval rating in late 1994 plunged to 52 percent after the corruption scandals broke, and Václav Havel sup-planted Václav Klaus as the most popular political figure in the country. In the meantime, the Social Democrats (a party that displaced the communists, with their stubborn hard-line rigidity, as the primary voice of the left) gained in popu-larity as the government coalition stumbled. It nonetheless caught pollsters and prognosticators by surprise that the June 1996 parliamentary elections produced an indeterminate outcome. The loss of voter support by the coalition partners was marginal, with Klaus's Civic Democrats maintaining their first place position with some 30 percent of the vote, but the leakage was sufficient to cost the government its previous majority. Moreover, disaffected voters rallied around the Social Dem-ocrats, who finished a strong second with almost 27 percent support. For the first time, the Czech elections produced no obvious victor—no logical and desirable governing coalition—and thrust the previously stable political scene into uncer-tainty pending the negotiation of a new governing alignment of forces.

The outcome appeared to be a peculiar Czech variant of the problems of tran-sition elsewhere in the region; popular dissatisfaction about the handling of so-cial and environmental problems seemed to have found electoral expression, to an extent sufficient to destroy the government's free hand in determining policy direction. Environmental concerns have been particularly salient in ravaged northern Bohemia, and broader public concern for the social safety net was evi-dent in a symbolic fifteen-minute warning strike in December 1994 against government plans to raise the retirement age and reorganize social security insurance payments. It appeared before the 1996 election that this discontent was counterbalanced by sensitivity to the government's financial limitations and appreciation of Czech economic progress, but the results suggest more limited patience and more ambivalence than the pundits had forecast.

Clearly the 1996 elections suggest that the Czechs do not yet have a fully formed party system and a well-established "electoral connection" with the voters. It is increasingly possible, however, to make sense of Czech politics in terms of a left, right, and center focused on economic issues—the left-right continuum so central to analyses of Western party politics. This may be a comfort not only to the political scientists, but also to the citizens, who have a much better sense of what they are getting in policy terms when they make their voting choices. Within the governing coalition, the sorting of alternatives proceeded further in 1995. The smallest coalition partner, the Christian Democratic Party, voted to merge with Klaus's Civic Democratic Party effective March 1996. Dissenters from this decision, including half of the parliamentary delegation, are moving into the Christian Democratic Union, so that there is now a single major Christian Democratic voice and thus a streamlining of the center-right. The daily *Mladá fronta dnes* hailed the merger as a step that gave an "impulse to the crystallisation of the Czech political scene" and that would "help voters to choose parties with clearly defined programmes and exercise better control over their implementation."[24]

At the same time, the lopsided political spectrum, in which the right was vastly stronger than the left, also began to reequilibrate during 1995, so that there was a clearer Social Democratic alternative to the governing coalition and a stronger opposition to serve as critic and alternative political choice to Klaus's center-right governmental coalition.[25] The 1996 elections confirmed the new Social Democratic appeal.

Whether or not they win a place in the new Czech government, however, the Social Democrats are unique in the postcommunist political landscape. In almost every other postcommunist state, a strong ex-communist party has persisted or reemerged as the dominant force on the left. In fact, in every other state besides Croatia and Bosnia, that party has been electorally strong enough to gain a place in at least one of the governments after 1989. The obvious explanation for this communist resurgence is probably the correct one; noncommunist governments in other states have failed to perform well enough during the economic transition (particularly in protecting citizens against unemployment) to avoid losing ground to a reformed communist alternative that promises greater social security. The Czech government, even in a narrow defeat, is virtually unique in presiding over an economy with low unemployment, and it has done much to keep hope for the immediate future high. To the extent that it has faltered in delivering on this bargain, Czech voters did not search for an alternative in the ex-communists, who have proved to be considerably less adaptable to the new conditions than communist parties elsewhere in the region. The first postcommunist leader of the Czech Communist Party, the reformist Jiří Svoboda, resigned his position in despair in 1993 after the central committee refused to abandon the communist label and orientation; Svoboda's departure was a protest against the spread of "a regrettable nostalgia for the past."[26] The party split in June 1993, with reformists resigning to form a new, more moderate communist party. In the aftermath of this schism, the party currently electorally dominant on the Czech left is a Social Democratic Party that is not the organizational successor of the communists (its leader, Miloš Zeman, is an ex-communist, however).

If, despite its electoral erosion, the Klaus coalition manages to maintain itself, does this mean that the situation is a potentially undemocratic one in which one group of parties continues to dominate the political scene? Of course that result would be partly a consequence of the government's effective economic performance since the last election. The Civic Democratic Party was, after all, the first-place party in 1996. In the West, cross-national electoral studies suggest that economic performance is a powerful influence on voting behavior, second only to party identification or ideology.[27] More specifically, "economic voters" tend not to vote according to their own pocketbooks (that is, to judge by their personal situations) but rather to respond "sociotropically" to the broad condition of the economy. If a Klaus coalition does return, the Czech Republic will be the first state in North Central Europe to continue a sitting government in some form, and this is consistent with the economic picture, since the Czech Republic has been the only postcommunist state to hold down unemployment during a sustained economic transformation. In that sense, the government has "earned" a dominant position with the voters.

Moreover, there are modern cases in which a government that most observers would call democratic has remained in the hands of the same party or group of parties even for decades. The Liberal Democratic Party, for example, ruled a democratic Japan from the period after World War II until the elections of 1993. For that matter, interwar Czechoslovakia was considered a democracy even though the same core of parties generally formed the government all the way to the Munich Conference.

David Olson suggests that the new Central European party systems are likely to go through three phases: unity, fragmentation, and consolidation.[28] At present, Czech and Slovak politics have not yet reached the consolidation phase. This is especially true because there are unresolved national identity questions in each republic, which we will examine in the final section of this chapter.

The Reconfiguration of National Identity Questions in Slovakia

The question of Czech and Slovak statehood may finally be resolved. In the period since independence, both publics have come to regard the divorce as necessary. In a poll published in January 1995, two years after independence, only about 20 percent of Czechs and one-third of Slovaks regret the breakup.[29] The belated "postmortem" consensus on the dissolution of Czechoslovakia, however, does not resolve all the outstanding questions surrounding state structure and national identity in either republic. Theorists of nationality issues refer to the "Russian doll" problem in national self-determination. Like the Russian *matrioska* dolls, the disassembling of an existing state reveals still smaller minorities nested within the territory of the newly liberated national unit. The achievement of national independence, therefore, often does not bring to an end the problem of national tensions. On the contrary, the smaller minority groups may feel more insecure than before, as they now coexist with a newly dominant national grouping in the process of consolidating its identity. This is the fate of the Slovak Republic. Slovakia was not ethnically homogeneous after it achieved statehood, for south Slovakia remained an ethnically mixed territory with a substantial Hungarian community of more than 500,000 people, some 12 percent of the new state's population.

Past history and the contemporary domestic and international context have burdened this Slovak-Hungarian relationship and recontoured the national question for both national groupings. The Hungarian-Slovak relationship does indeed carry a troubling historical legacy. For Slovaks, the long history of political subordination to Hungary that preceded the emergence of the Czech-Slovak state in 1918 remained a vivid part of historical memory, and the remaining Hungarian minority is a reminder of a narrow historical escape. In turn, Hungarian resentment of territorial provisions of the post–World War I Trianon Treaty of 1920 that tore away one-third of the ethnically Hungarian population from Hungary remains an equally vivid reminder of the past.[30]

In short, the small postcommunist Hungarian minority in Slovakia is not merely a minority—they are seen by Slovaks as the dispossessed former masters of the Slovak homeland, whose intentions and loyalties remain suspect. To make the issue still more sensitive, Hungarian minority interests are championed by a neighboring sovereign state, Hungary itself, and the underlying Slovak nightmare is of a secessionist movement aiming to rejoin southern Slovakia with Hungary.

Tensions between the two national groups were evident from the outset of the postcommunist transition. The first warning signal was the decision of key Hungarian minority leaders (notably Charter 77 signatory and Hungarian rights activist Miklós Duray) that Hungarian interests could not be sufficiently protected by Hungarian representation within broader-based parties and movements. Instead, these activists chose to protect their own interests in a separate electoral movement, Coexistence. Hungarians found resurgent Slovak nationalism especially threatening, and they responded with demands for security guarantees—protection of language and culture in particular. Language, as both a symbolic and practical preserver of identity, soon became a particularly controversial issue, since the Slovaks wished to enshrine their new influence in the democratizing state by establishing Slovak as the official language of the Republic. The Slovak language law that passed in the fall of 1990 achieved that goal[31] while preserving the right of territorially concentrated minorities to use their own language in the public arena. No one seemed satisfied with this compromise. Slovak nationalists thought that their government had catered too much to minority interests, while the Hungarians feared that the practical implementation of the law would fall short of real protection of their linguistic rights.

While Czechoslovakia was still a joint state, Hungarians strongly supported its continuation, and tended to approve the "tighter" federal model, in the hope that the center would exercise a moderating influence over Slovak relations with the minority. Coexistence leader Duray commented that "Hungarians in Slovakia feel relatively secure only as long as Slovakia remains within the framework of the present democratic republic, which makes it possible to control [Slovak!] extremists." The Magyar Independent Initiative defined the "preservation of the unity of Czechoslovakia" as "a vital interest of the Hungarian minority."[32] Mindful of the uncertainty of the future, however, Hungarian political leaders continued to pledge a commitment to Slovakia and an acceptance of the results of negotiations, whatever they might be. Leaders did nonetheless attack Slovak nationalism as such; Duray singled out the Slovak National Party and the Slovak cultural organization Matica Slovenská (which had pushed for the language law) as nationalist culprits, as organizations that were "blindly anti-Hungarian and thus accuse us of chauvinism, nationalism, [and] separatism, although those are all *their* characteristics."[33]

Issues of national identity and language continued to fester in the independent state and in fact increased in intensity under the Mečiar government. An initial bad omen in the fall of 1992 was the alteration of the opening words of the preamble to the new Slovak constitution—"We, the citizens of the Slovak Republic"—to read "We, the Slovak nation," a formulation that seemed to imply that Slovakia belonged only to the Slovaks. Understandably, the national minorities preferred the previous, more inclusive preamble that acknowledged all the peoples of Slovakia. They walked out of the Slovak National Council session in protest when the change was adopted but were unable to influence the decision. There is similar wording in the constitutions of other new postcommunist states, notably Romania and the successor states to Yugoslavia. Robert Hayden describes the mindset behind this identification of the state with the dominant nation as "constitutional nationalism." He warns that it is a symptom of a constitutional order that is so intent on celebrating the national self-assertion of the dominant group that it dangerously undervalues the rights of its constituent minorities, with the potentially tragic consequences that are so visible in Yugoslavia.[34]

There were also heated controversies over restrictions on the use of bilingual signs for roads, towns, and buildings. (The Mečiar government offered several unlikely reasons for banning bilingual signs, including the highway-safety argument that such signs might dangerously distract motorists and the even more un-

likely argument that bilingual signs were too restrictive—they slighted the linguistic rights of Slovakia's unpopular Romany (or Gypsy) population!) Still further controversy erupted over a law that regulated the usage of personal names
according to Slovak linguistic practice; in Slovak and other Slavic languages, male
and female surnames have different suffixes. A man might be named Martin
Navrátil, but as any tennis fan knows, the equivalent woman's name is Martina
Navrátilová. The *ová* or *á* suffix, however, is not used in Hungarian, and the
Hungarian minority strongly objected to appending it to Hungarian women's
names, seeing it as an infringement against the most basic right of personal identity. The Moravčík government acted in June and July 1994 to rescind the offending practices; this gesture pleased the international community and won the
government the tacit support of the Hungarian parties but was unpopular among
ethnic Slovaks.

When a Mečiar government returned to power in late 1994, the language wars
resumed. Hungarians were particularly concerned about draft legislation in June
1995 that further restricted the use of unofficial languages in public institutions
and that established a "language police" who would serve as inspectors to enforce
this provision.[35] Defying Hungarian government and European Union protests,
the National Council passed the controversial bill in November 1995. Like the hyphen war, these issues of language usage may seem primarily symbolic, but they
are in fact part of a larger pattern of tension over the identity of the Slovak state
itself. Is it essentially a Slovak state, or is it truly a multinational state within
which all citizens have equal standing?

The Hungarian minority issue is one that Mečiar's rivals are reluctant to compromise themselves over. Every major Slovak party, including those that served
in the Moravčík government, opposes any form of autonomy for the Hungarians
in south Slovakia. And even Mečiar's opponents voted for the controversial language law after brave words of opposition beforehand. (They were "encouraged"
to do so by a government deputy's unusual demand that each legislator respond
by name and state his opinion during the vote!) The Slovak National Party has
even included a plank in its electoral program for outlawing the Hungarian parties. The Hungarian-Slovak relationship remains too hot to handle through serious negotiation and compromise.

The larger issues of the Slovak-Hungarian relationship thus remain unresolved,
and there are immense insecurities on both sides. Hungarians feel themselves a
disadvantaged minority, but Slovak nationalists are in turn concerned that the Slovaks of southern Slovakia are themselves a minority even within their own country, outnumbered by local Hungarian populations. From these insecurities has developed a debate about the basic nature of democracy. The core Slovak position
has been that democracy is based on individual rights and responsibilities and that
the state will not and should not grant a minority greater rights than individual
citizens of the majority possess: Minorities should have no claims to special representation and access to government.[36] Hungarians argue that minority commu-

nities should be treated as just that—communities—with collective rights as well as individual ones to sustain their distinctive identity. As a Hungarian political activist in the Coexistence movement put it, "How can there be a democracy when 15 percent of the population are considered second-class citizens?"[37]

Since this is an issue that has tormented the postcommunist transition in other states as well, and one that arises wherever several national groups reside under the same sovereign roof, it is worth considering in greater detail. What is a "collective" right? It is a right vested in a group of people rather than in individuals, on the understanding that some rights essential to identity and survival cannot be guaranteed on an individual basis. Language rights fall into this category. To grant language rights on an individual basis would mean that each individual was free to speak his native tongue, or the language of his choice, in his personal life. The problem with limiting language rights to this individual freedom of speech is obvious. Language use is perpetuated by education and public use—in newspapers, books, and public proceedings. A minority language that lacks this larger context is likely to wither and die as the new generation of language speakers turns to the majority language as a bridge to education and advancement. In the United States, most English-speakers tend to regard the idea of a single state-supported language as the natural and efficient public policy, and the introduction of bilingualism in schools and public institutions has been exceedingly controversial. Yet the United States is a nation of immigrants; most citizens came here to a new cultural context and assimilated linguistically.

The protection of language use is seen differently in East Central Europe. The Hungarians of southern Slovakia were not migrants; rather, it was the Hungarian border that migrated south after World War I, leaving them behind. These Hungarians, and other minority nations in Eastern Europe, argued that the historical border shifts should not deprive them of their basic cultural identity. The region is therefore multinational in a different sense than the United States. Hungarians and other minorities want the right to language use guaranteed by government support of Hungarian-language schools and media. They do not see why the vagaries of state boundary-drawing in the region should accord a local majority sole right to government-funded education in their language while minorities pay for their own private schools. This issue provides a window onto the concept of a collective right, which includes the granting of state support for minority culture on the same basis as a majority receives. The third Mečiar government has resisted a full elaboration of this policy (such as supporting Hungarian-language schools), opting instead to promote "alternative" education in ethnically mixed areas—a policy very unpopular with Hungarians.

There are other forms of collective rights, and these too have been controversial in Slovakia. Hungarians asked for certain guarantees of political access to counterbalance their certainty of being outvoted in standard electoral contests, in which all of the citizens' individual votes add up to a permanent majority for the dominant national group. At first these demands specifically did not include regional autonomy, the right of local self-governance. Such a demand was considered too sensitive, too much a signal of possible secessionist motives. However, after Slovakia's independence, the heightening of tensions raised the level of insecurity to the point that Hungarian leaders began to toy with the possibility of presenting regional autonomy as an overt demand. Hungarians feared that an administrative reorganization would result in the gerrymandering of Hungarian districts in order to dilute their concentration and influence. Indeed, Hungarian politicians have protested that none of the seventy-four regions created by the territorial organization bill passed in March 1996 had a Hungarian majority. Of course, new demands only increased Slovak doubts about the loyalty of southern Slovak Hungarians to the state.[38]

The uneasy Slovak-Hungarian relationship imposes a heavy tax on Slovak politics. Not only is the definition of democracy in dispute as a result of the continued disagreement over the kind of action needed to safeguard minority rights, but also day-to-day governance is rendered more complicated by the distance between Slovak and Hungarian parties. Studies of Western parliamentary governments have emphasized the constraints on government stability that result from the exclusion of certain parties from eligibility to participate in governing coalitions. If a key party or group of parties is considered "uncoalitionable," then the number of alternatives shrinks, and it may be harder to form an effective cabinet. In the West, the "uncoalitionable" parties have been the communists, who are regarded as "antisystem" and therefore ineligible to hold cabinet posts in the central government even if (as in Italy) they have renounced unconstitutional methods and have long track records of local and regional government experience.[39] In postcommunist states, minority-based parties also tend to be regarded as antisystem, no matter how they describe themselves; their loyalty to the state in which they are a minority is considered suspect, and it is politically dangerous for the parties of the majority ethnic group to court their support or include them in government. Just as in the West, then, the range of alternative political alliances is restricted by the difficulty of including "suspect" parties in deliberations over important policy issues.

This problem has been evident in Bulgaria, where a Turkish-based minority party has frequently held the balance of power in parliament. It has also been evident in Slovakia. The opposition badly needs Hungarian party support in holding the line against the prime minister; Hungarian parties gave the previous Moravčík government a working majority, and in the current National Council the Hungarian coalition holds just over a quarter of the opposition votes. Yet the Slovak parties in opposition dare not risk too close an association with this Hungarian minority for fear of damaging their own national credentials and giving Mečiar an opening to attack them. As a result, the idea of formally including Hungarian parties in a government coalition cabinet is still taboo. No Hungarian has held a parliamentary office since 1991. The 1994 Moravčík cabinet accepted Hungarian support (and was castigated for it) without daring to contemplate the inclusion of even a token Hungarian cabinet minister, and the search for an alternative to a third Mečiar government after the 1994 elections was forestalled by the fact that no party was willing to negotiate with the eighteen-seat Hungarian coalition—that, a spokesman of the Democratic Left said euphemistically, was "unrealistic."

The irony of the emotion surrounding this issue is that, by most expert accounts, personal relations in southern Slovakia between Hungarians and Slovaks remain relatively peaceful. Local citizens and many scholars tend to regard the visibility of the national issue as a product of electoral politics, in which parties compete for voters by outbidding each other on the purity of their commitment to their respective nations. The dangers of demagogic politicization of the national issue by political leaders are all too evident in the former Yugoslavia, where predominantly peaceful interethnic relations among Bosnian Serbs, Croats, and Muslims were rent asunder and permanently embittered in the interests of "high politics." While this catastrophic scenario does not currently appear likely in Slovakia, it is entirely possible that local relations will increasingly sour under the burden of repeated public controversy, even to the point of sporadic violence. This in turn would hamper the satisfactory resolution of the problem of reaching consensus on just how an ethnic minority should fit into the pattern of democratization.

As in the Czech-Slovak conflict, the Hungarian-Slovak dispute over collective versus individual rights is also a quarrel about the meaning of democracy. In this confrontation, it has been the Slovaks who champion majority rule on their own territory and argue that constitutionally recognized individual rights are a largely sufficient guarantee to the citizens of the smaller Hungarian nation. In fact, any Slovak politician who even shows sympathy for bilingualism is likely to be attacked for betrayal of Slovak interests. The Hungarians, as we have seen, argued that democracy in a multinational state should include the investment of "collective rights" in the state's minority groups in order to preserve their identity and culture.

The Czech-Slovak conflict over the meaning of democracy was settled by the drastic expedient of dividing up the state. The Slovak-Hungarian dispute remains unresolved. Both cases, however, suggest that the national question is more than a separate problem that interacts with democracy. Agreement on the national question actually requires agreement on what democracy means. However, the prospects for mutual accommodation are not strictly an internal matter; in Chapter 7 we will see that the international setting has generated pressures to resolve the Hungarian problem.

National Tensions in the Czech Republic

At first glance, the Czech Republic would not appear to have a similar minority problem of its own. The largest minority is Slovak; Slovak cultural organizations began to form after independence, but Slovak rights have yet to become a burning political issue. Indeed, in December 1994, two-thirds of the Czech population reported a positive attitude to the Slovak minority, and only 7 percent reported negative feelings.[40]

Yet there *are* Czech minority problems, even if not all of them are visible in the census data. The first is the problem of the German minority deported from Czechoslovakia after 1945 under the so-called Beneš decrees. Many of the aging survivors and descendants of the deportation live next door in Germany; their Sudeten German *Landsmannschaft* (Association) has pressed vigorously for a recognition of the injustice of their expulsion and for compensation for their lost property. In a Christmas 1989 letter to German President Richard von Weizsacker, the newly elected President Havel called the deportation a "deeply immoral act" for which he asked German forgiveness. Havel's apology was highly unpopular at home, where more than 70 percent opposed any form of restitution to the Germans.[41] However, neither Havel nor any subsequent political leader has made any moves toward developing a program of legal rectification for past wrongs.[42]

Havel's apology did trigger endless discussion of the problem in the media, which was but a continuation of the debate that had occurred in dissident circles in the 1980s.[43] However, on this issue, the often elusive Czech nationalism has asserted itself; the efforts of former Prime Minister Pithart and other intellectuals and former dissidents to press the government to start reconciliation talks in March 1995 met with adamant government refusal to consider direct contact with Sudeten Germans,[44] although Klaus would clearly like to see the issue settled somehow in order to remove an obstacle to smooth relations with Germany. Government maneuvering room is strongly constrained, however, by the fact that the public at large has expressed approval of the original deportation by margins of three to one and has consistently rejected dialogue with the Germans by similarly large margins. Most Czechs regard the Sudeten German claims as financially rather than morally motivated, and 37 percent in a 1995 survey even expressed fear that the purpose was to reannex border territory.[45]

In light of continued resistance to reconsidering the Beneš decrees, aggrieved Germans have done what Western citizens in this situation do: take the issue to court. A north Bohemian German sued the Czech government for the return of his expropriated property; after losing in the local courts and on initial appeal, he won a remand to the lower courts for reconsideration.[46] This case is significant not only because the issue of German deportation and property confiscation is significant, but also because it represents a method of gaining redress of grievances that was not available under the communist system. In the event that this avenue of approach is exhausted, the only remaining source of pressure would be the Czech-German governmental relationship, which will be discussed in Chapter 8.

Most of the visible conflicts over national identity and national assertion in postcommunist East Europe concern groupings that have one of two advantages in their struggle: Either they have had a federal institutional base, or, lacking that kind of protection, they were nonetheless supported in their claims by a neigh-boring co-national sovereign state. Examples of the latter include Hungarian mi-norities in Slovakia, Serbia, Ukraine, and Romania, all of whom could turn to Hungary as a champion of their demands, and Albanians in Serbia and Macedo-nia, who could turn to the small and impoverished but still sovereign Albania.

There is one prominent national grouping, however, that lacked either of those advantages—the Gypsies, or, as they prefer to be called, the Roma or Romanies.[47] They are a truly marginal group, lacking both protectors and a homeland. As Zoltan Barany has pointed out, whereas some minorities have historically been politically marginal without being economically marginal (the Jews, for exam-ple), the Roma have "since their arrival in eastern Europe some 700 years ago" been "politically, socially, culturally and economically marginalized" to a greater or lesser degree.[48]

Living on the fringes of European societies, less educated and more impover-ished than the dominant national groups, the Roma have historically lacked both political power and social respectability. Regarded by many of the continent's more fortunate citizens as an itinerant criminal class rather than a nation, they are nonetheless present in large numbers throughout all of East Central Europe except Poland; estimates of the number of Roma living on Czechoslovak territory at the time of the Velvet Revolution range from 240,000 to 800,000.[49]

The communist government had made massive efforts to assimilate this large population and had succeeded to some extent in forcing them to settle on the fringes of urban society, without having succeeded simultaneously in raising their socioeconomic status to a level that would truly integrate them into local com-munities. It is hard to conclude that democratization has substantially improved their lot so far. Adrift in the transitional economy, often without basic survival skills, the Roma faced unemployment levels that hovered as high as 60 and 70 percent regionwide. High illiteracy rates in the dominant regional languages and low educational levels had not been remedied in the communist period; in fact, a very disproportionate number of Romany children appear to have been "ware-housed" in the Czechoslovak educational system by placing them in classrooms for the mentally disabled. The current limited education budgets mean that this problem has yet to be seriously confronted in the postcommunist period. And so the vicious circle of poverty and marginality has continued.[50]

Other citizens have tended to blame the Roma for the rise in crime that ac-companied economic and political transition in all postcommunist countries.[51] Even the opponents of the former regime seemed unable to extend their toler-ance sufficiently far to encompass sympathy for the Gypsies; in fact, one opinion poll registered an astonishing 91 percent of Czech and Slovak respondents ex-pressing antipathy to them. When Václav Havel appealed for sensitivity to Ro-many problems, he therefore met with a stony public response.

Nor have the Roma themselves been able to mobilize effectively to defend their interests. As a scattered and impoverished group, the Roma have found it diffi-cult to mobilize the resources to wield political clout even in proportion to their minority numbers. Despite official recognition in the Czech Republic as a national minority (the Slovak government was slower to accord such recognition) and the freedom to organize politically, the results have been very modest. In fact, the initial attempts to organize produced divisions and controversy within Romany groups rather than a unified Romany movement. Low educational and economic achievement has meant that there are few Romany professionals and cultural figures to form the core of a new national leadership, even though Romany national awareness has been on the rise since 1989. Barany concludes that Romany politics is still a small island of activism, isolated both from the political mainstream and from its own popular base. In the Czech and Slovak Republics, the Roma initially achieved representation in the first postcommunist parliament with five Romany Civic Initiative deputies under the banner of the Civic Forum, and three in Slovak electoral coalitions. The disintegration of the Civic Forum was a major blow to Romany access. In 1992 one Romany candidate gained a seat in the legislative bodies.

The disintegration of the state was a further setback. Most Roma held Slovak citizenship, but many of them had long lived and worked in the Czech Republic, and thousands more tried to immigrate there because of the more favorable Czech economic conditions. They have met with rising hostility and discrimination in the Czech Republic in proportion to their growing numbers, including deportation demands and skinhead violence that has resulted in several dozen murders of Romany citizens.

Anti-Gypsy initiatives, however, have not merely been the province of the young and dispossessed. In the Czech Republic, where high crime rates have registered as the top public concern in opinion polls, political officials have done little to alter public sentiment aside from sporadic attempts to control skinhead violence.[52] Right-wing extremist politicians like Miroslav Sládek directly blame the Roma and other "alien" residents for virtually all social woes. Facing popular hostility and limited official response, Romany organizations tried to form volunteer Romany "police" units for protection in 1995. While government action blocked this approach, the Czech government subsequently announced the adjustment of education requirements to allow greater recruitment of Roma to the official police.

The most internationally controversial action regarding the Roma, however, came from Prague, in the form of provisions in the new Czech citizenship law. That law, in setting conditions under which former citizens of the Slovak Republic and other non-Czechs might acquire Czech citizenship, stipulated as one of the requirements the provision that eligible applicants had to demonstrate a clean criminal record for the preceding five years. This limitation did not apply to ethnic Czechs, but rather to all others, even noncitizens born in the Czech Republic. The provision quickly became known as the "Romany clause," inasmuch as it was believed to target the group specifically for its higher crime rates. Thousands of Gypsies therefore lack citizenship in their current country of residence; if born in the Czech Republic, they may lack any citizenship status at all.

Opposition parliamentary deputies filed a lawsuit challenging the citizenship law as unconstitutional, but the rejection of the case by the Czech Constitutional Court did not end the controversy, since the "Romany clause" potentially violates a number of international agreements to which the Czech Republic is party and has aroused unfavorable international attention.[53] In the spring of 1996 the government finally introduced legislation that amended the citizenship law to restrict the relevant criminal records to sentences of more than two years in prison.

The larger Romany population in Slovakia has also been the target of hostility. Lacking political representation in the Slovak National Council, they are no better positioned for political protection than their counterparts in the Czech Republic. Their seat on the government's Council for Minorities is not a power position, since the organization itself is seen as politically marginal and uninfluential. The Roma have rejected Coexistence claims to represent the interests of all minorities. The Romany Civic Initiative has argued all along that "only Romanies have the moral right to represent Romanies" in the Slovak parliament.[54] A Romany effort was mounted in 1995 to unite its diverse splinter parties into a single coalition to speak for Romany interests. It is a measure of their fragmentation that there are no fewer than fifteen Romany parties in this coalition.

Government commitment to Romany rights is certainly doubtful. In 1993 Mečiar provoked a major controversy when one of his population policy speeches seemed to imply the need for sterilization of the country's Gypsies. Following a series of scattered beatings and killings, national attention was riveted by the death of a Romany youth in August 1995 who was attacked and then set afire by skinheads. This horrible incident prompted an emergency session of the Minorities Council and an official condemnation of ethnic hatred and violence, with the promise of greater protective measures in the future. However, in less formal settings, expressions of MDS antipathy to the Roma is fairly common. An MDS deputy commenting on the immolation, for example, dismissed the idea that such attacks were racially motivated; the brutal attack, she argued, was rather a statement "by people who want to live in peace, who oppose those who steal from them, beat them, damage houses, and threaten their children."[55] Romany representatives have expressed the opinion that the only Slovak official who is willing even to talk to them is President Kováč.

Local curfews and restraints are also commonplace in Slovakia, whatever the official state policy. In fact, it is estimated that more than half of Slovakia's Roma live in ghettoized "settlements" (*osadas*) on the outskirts of towns, deliberately segregated from the local public. Public opinion in Slovakia may be even more antagonistic to the Roma than is Czech public opinion; in early 1995, 57 percent of Slovak citizens favored tighter legislative controls on Gypsies, compared with 44 percent of Czechs.[56]

What is striking about antagonism to the Roma is not only its pervasiveness but the openness with which it is expressed. It underlines a dimension of East European ethnonational tensions that U.S. visitors, who are accustomed to an environment in which crude admissions of race or religious prejudice to strangers is socially unacceptable (the prejudice may be there, but it is not openly stated), would immediately notice. Unschooled in Western norms that put a premium on at least the appearance of tolerance, East Europeans in the aftermath of communism can speak very unself-consciously about Jewish international conspiracies or the racial inferiority of the Roma. In fact, feeling against the Gypsies does appear to have a racial component. They are frequently described as racially alien, and even, because of their often darker complexions, as "black." One can find Prague restaurants with "whites only" signs. In his survey of postcommunist ethnic tensions, journalist Paul Hockenos has described the mindset of prejudice against the marginal minorities as a "beer hall nationalism" that has been inflamed by popular uncertainties in the transition period and that finds its release in identifying scapegoats.[57]

The place of Jews in postcommunist societies is less tenuous than that of the Roma in a number of respects, but there remains in Eastern Europe a peculiar phenomenon that Paul Lendvai called "anti-Semitism without Jews."[58] In Czechoslovakia in the early 1990s, for example, only some 15,000 Jews (about 3,000 of them in Slovakia) remained of the vibrant interwar Jewish community of 350,000.[59] The decimation of Jewish populations by the Holocaust did not eliminate the issue. Despite their dwindling numbers and the waning of religious practice, Jewish communities in communist Europe still found themselves stigmatized. The official ideology of the communist regimes was, communist leaders asserted, "anti-Zionist" rather than anti-Semitic, although the distinction in practice was hardly clear. After 1989, the expression of fringe anti-Semitic sentiment reappeared throughout the region, as we saw in Chapter 3. In the Czech Republic, this phenomenon is largely confined to the fringe. In Slovakia, anti-Semitic feelings are more widespread, reflected in a 1993 public opinion poll that shows nearly one-third of citizens expressing fear of "the influence of Jews in Slovak politics and the economy" (even more, however, think the influence of Jews would be helpful!). More than a quarter preferred not to have a Jewish next-door neighbor, and 42 percent preferred not to have a close relative who was Jewish.[60] Most politicians try to distance themselves from anti-Semitic statements, but the Slovak National Party in particular has experienced some embarrassing outbursts. In 1994, for example, the party's chair had to disavow a party supplement published in the government paper that contained several anti-Semitic articles, including a piece entitled "Only Jews Live Well in Slovakia."[61] There is also great defensiveness in confronting the historically volatile question of the complicity of the World War II Slovak state in cooperating with the liquidation of Slovak Jews—only about one-fifth of the population is inclined to assign even partial responsibility to the Tiso regime, preferring to blame it entirely on Hitler.[62]

The scapegoating of Jews and the Roma is the most troubling illustration of the way in which the dislocations experienced along the path to democracy and the market can unleash some very undemocratic forces and even give them, as is the case with the Czech Republican Party, a place in electoral politics.

Conclusion

The insecurities and anxieties of the postcommunist period in both republics have manifested themselves in a series of "internal security issues." Neither republic has immediate cause to fear foreign invasion, but a sense of security and safety does not depend solely on the character of external threats. Economic uncertainties, particularly for publics accustomed to the low-level but consistent economic security of the communist period, translate into insecurity. Economic stress also translates fairly directly into political destabilization. The contrast between the political volatility of Slovakia and the relative political calm of the Czech Republic has much to do with concern about economic direction in the former and confidence in the upward direction of the economy in the latter. But even in the Czech Republic the sense of injustice that flows from evidence of economic corruption in the political process has been highly visible and has weakened the standing of the governing coalition.

Moreover, both economic and political instabilities pile a great deal of excess baggage on the third component of the triple transition, the national identity problem. National divisions create new, almost conspiratorial meaning for economic dilemmas (whose national agenda is forwarded by economic reform? whose national agenda is impeding reform?) and complicate the search for compromise and bargained solutions in politics. In multiparty systems the refusal of one group to bargain with another across national boundary lines intensifies the already substantial stresses of transition. In Slovakia, the pariah status of the Hungarian parties—the fact that no Slovak party wishes to risk appearing "unSlovak" by forming alliances with them—makes it that much more difficult to build a governing majority in parliament.

None of these stresses is absent from established political systems. But established political systems have developed coping mechanisms and some sense of continuity. The juggling act in postcommunist states trying to build new systems is considerably more complex. The extent of this complexity will become clearer in the following chapter, in which the size and scope of the economic transformation task are examined.

Notes

1. The comparison with the Russian case probably ends there, however. In the Russian case, the parliament that carried over had been elected in 1990 in a partially competitive election conducted while the communists were still in power. The Russians did not enact a new constitution until later, thus continuing to operate under an amended communistera constitution until the crisis in the fall of 1993 triggered both new elections and a constitutional referendum.

2. See Jan Obrman, "The Czech and Slovak Presidential Elections," *RFE/RL Research Report* 2:7 (February 12, 1993):15–17.

3. *Economist*, August 13, 1994, p. 47.

4. *Eastern Europe* 8:19 (September 21, 1994), p. 1.

5. First Roundtable Election Debate, broadcast on Bratislava STV 1 Television, September 10, 1994, transcribed in *Foreign Broadcast Information Service–East Europe* FBIS-EEU-94-176, September 12, 1994, p. 12.

6. *RFE/RL Daily Report,* July 13, 1994.

7. Local elections in November 1994 confirmed Mečiar's MDS as the most popular party in the selection of city council representatives, though the largest group of mayors were independents without party affiliation. In general, throughout the region, independents have done well at the local level.

8. Slovakia does not have a civil service law that would protect appointees from removal after a change of government. For that reason, it is of considerable political significance who controls appointment power to the top bureaucratic positions. Staffing of the entire agency may be affected.

9. *Prague Post,* September 6–12, 1995.

10. At the time of the transfer of authority over SIS appointments, in April 1995, opposition deputies had expressed concern that the utilization of the organization would be subject to political abuse.

11. The opposition has been deeply concerned about this scenario. See *OMRI Daily Digest* 20:1 (January 27, 1995).

12. *East European Newsletter* 8:19 (September 21, 1994):2.

13. *OMRI Daily Digest,* May 10, 1995.

14. *RFE/RL Daily Report,* September 23, 1994.

15. See especially the U.S. State Department report *Slovak Republic Human Rights Practices, 1995,* issued March 6, 1996.

16. The government coalition itself executed a streamlining in which the Christian Democratic Party merged with the Klaus Civic Democratic Party. Half of the Christian Democratic parliamentary coalition (five deputies) defected to the Christian Democratic Union in protest of the merger in September 1995, but since the Christian Democratic Union is also in the government, this will not affect its ruling majority.

17. Jiri Pehe, "Czech Republic: A Leader in Political Stability and Economic Growth," *Transition* 1:1 (January 30, 1995):29.

18. Ibid.

19. Constitution of the Czech Republic, Articles 33 and 35, reprinted in *The Rebirth of Democracy: Twelve Constitutions of Central and Eastern Europe* (Strasbourg: Council of Europe Press, 1995), pp. 125–127.

20. *Český deník,* September 24, 1994, p. 3, reproduced in FBIS-EEU-94, October 3, 1994, p. 7.

21. *OMRI Daily Digest* 1:23 (February 9, 1995).

22. Concern over political corruption is also woven into the fabric of Slovak political controversy. In March 1995 the Slovak government responded with a "clean hands" policy, but this has repeatedly been decried as window dressing amid charges of continued government engagement in manipulation of privatization and of inadequate legal safeguards. Corruption as such has played a less central role in Slovak political debate, not because politics is cleaner but because the political agenda is so laden with additional political issues.

23. Findings of the Institute for Public Opinion Research, reported in the *Prague Post,* September 20, 1994, p. 5.

24. *ČTK Press Survey,* November 20, 1995.

25. Earlier concern had been expressed that the Czech Republic lacked a distinct opposition alternative, and analysts speculated during the 1992 election campaign on whether the outcome would be instead a left-right coalition. See Jan Zahradil, "A Czech Political Map," *Uncaptive Minds* 7:3 (Fall-Winter 1994):84; and Petr Nováček, "Budeme mít pravolevou koalici?" *Mladá fronta dnes,* March 26, 1992.

26. Cited in *RFE/RL Daily Digest,* no. 48, March 11, 1993.

27. See especially Michael Lewis-Beck, *Economics and Elections: The Major Western Democracies* (Ann Arbor: University of Michigan Press, 1988).

28. David Olson and Ian M. Fried, "Party and Party System in Regime Transformation: The Inner Transition in Poland and Czechoslovakia" (paper prepared for the annual meeting of the American Political Science Association, Chicago, September 1992), p. 11.

29. Poll results cited in *OMRI Daily Digest* 1:11 (January 11, 1995).

30. See Julius Mesaros, "Hungarian and Slovak History: A Distorting Mirror," *New Hungarian Quarterly* (1992):98–103.

31. Slovak politicians had fought unsuccessfully for the establishment of Slovak as the official language of Slovakia in the interwar Republic and during the reform period of 1968.

32. "Tvrdenie proti tvrdeniu," *Národna obroda,* October 2, 1990, p. 5; and Czechoslovak Radio, March 13, 1991, transcribed in *RFE Monitoring,* March 13, 1991, p. 5.

33. Miklós Duray, cited in "Duray Klame uz aj Mad'arov," *Slovenský národ,* October 13, 1990, p. 2.

34. Robert Hayden, "Constitutional Nationalism in the Formerly Yugoslav Republics," *Slavic Review* 51:4 (Winter 1992):654–673.

35. Four directors of Hungarian secondary schools were removed from their positions after they had objected to government plans. *OMRI Daily Digest,* June 21, 1995, and June 23, 1995.

36. Yet, as Hayden suggests, to a certain extent Slovaks created this issue themselves by insisting on a special place for the Slovak nation in constituting the political order.

37. *Prague Post,* September 27, 1994, p. 9A.

38. The Hungarian protest was reported in *OMRI Daily Digest,* no. 183, September 20, 1995. The political agenda of the most popular Hungarian-based party, Coexistence, is summarized in the party's position paper, optimistically entitled "From Minority Status to Partnership: Hungarians in Czechoslovakia/Slovakia, 1918–1992," Bratislava, 1993.

39. See Giovanni Sartori, "European Political Parties: The Case of Polarized Pluralism," in Joseph LaPalombara and Myron Weiner, eds., *Political Parties and Political Development* (Princeton: Princeton University Press, 1966), pp. 137–176.

40. *Radio Free Europe/Radio Liberty Daily Digest,* December 12, 1994.

41. Milan Hauner, "The Czechs and the Germans: A One-Thousand Year Relationship," in Dirk Verheyen and Christian Soe, *The Germans and Their Neighbors* (Boulder: Westview Press, 1993), p. 256.

42. Václav Klaus has "thought out loud" about the issue, but no concrete action immediately resulted.

43. See "Ankety," *Svědectví* 78 (1986):258–334.

44. The intellectual initiative, known as "Reconciliation 95," also met with editorial and popular resistance.

45. See, for example, the study conducted by the Institute for Public Opinion Research in July 1993, the results of which are summarized in *RFE/RL Daily Report,* no. 141, July 27, 1993; and the study published by the newspaper *Mladá fronta dnes* in July 1995, summarized in *OMRI Daily Digest,* July 14, 1995. Willingness to consider negotiations has increased only slightly over time.

46. This lawsuit emanated from the tiny remnant of the Sudeten German population that remained in Czechoslovakia after the deportation, officially numbering some 50,000, although spokesmen for the group claim the size to be twice as great. November 19, 1995, ČTK Survey of the Czech Press.

47. There is a second stateless minority in Slovakia, the small and embattled Rusyns, whose very existence is questioned by Ukrainians who insist that the Rusyn language is merely a dialect of Ukrainian and that there is no such thing as a Ruthenian national identity. The ceding of the interwar Czechoslovak province of Subcarpathian Ruthenia to the USSR (now in Ukraine) further divided the tiny group. According to the 1991 census, there are 17,000 Slovak citizens identifying themselves as of Rusyn nationality. Under the umbrella of the Rusyn Revival movement, they celebrated the codification of a written Rusyn language in January 1995. The Rusyns in the Transcarpathian region of Ukraine made a bid for autonomy in an unauthorized referendum carried out in December 1991 as an adjunct to Ukraine's referendum on independence from the Soviet Union. The Ukrainian government ignored the results of this referendum, in which 78 percent of the region's inhabitants approved the autonomy measure. The government has also ignored the unofficial Provisional Government of Subcarpathian Ruthenia, formed in 1993, which claims that the region was never legally ceded to the USSR and therefore formally remained part of Czechoslovakia after 1993. See *Moscow News,* September 10, 1993.

48. Zoltan Barany, "Living on the Edge: The East European Roma in Postcommunist Politics and Societies," *Slavic Review* 53:2 (Summer 1994):323–324.

49. It was not until the late 1980s that official estimates of the Romany population were even published. Moreover, census reports and other official statistics may not accurately reflect the number of the Roma, since many of them prefer to maintain a low profile and therefore report themselves in one of the dominant ethnonational categories. Still others are missing in the census count because they do not have a permanent address. The official 1991 census count of 80,000 Roma in Slovakia is acknowledged even by the government as a significant undercount. For more detailed coverage of the Romany plight, see Barany, "Living on the Edge," pp. 321–344; Jiri Pehe, "Romany Migration Causes Legal and Social Problems, *RFE/RL Research Bulletin* 10:4, February 16, 1993, p. 3; "Romové v Československu," *Svobodné slovo,* November 8, 1991; and Jana Blažková, "Nikdo neví, kolik je u nás Romů," *Lidové noviny,* July 2, 1993.

50. Josef Kalvoda, "The Gypsies of Czechoslovakia," *Nationalities Papers* 19:4 (Winter 1991):269–296.

51. In light of their marginal economic status, higher Roma crime rates are not surprising.

52. *OMRI Daily Digest,* April 14, 1995.

53. *Prognosis,* September 28, 1994, p. 6, reprinted in FBIS-EEU-94-202, October 19, 1994, p. 5. A U.S. Congressional commission, the Conference on Security and Cooperation in Europe (CSCE), and the Council of Europe have all criticized the law for its tendency to target the Roma with penalties for crimes committed before the law's enactment.

54. Jan Kompus, chairman of the Romany Civic Initiative, cited in *Slovenský denník*, September 2, 1994, reproduced in FBIS-EEU-94-176, September 12, 1994, p. 11. The Romany Civic Initiative was irate that Coexistence had co-opted a rival organization to speak for Romanies, the Association of Hungarian Romanies in Slovakia (Romanies may speak their own language, or Slovak or Hungarian).

55. *OMRI Daily Digest*, August 3, 1995.

56. Poll results cited in *OMRI Daily Digest* 1:11 (January 11, 1995).

57. Paul Hockenos, *Free to Hate: The Rise of the Right in Post-Communist Eastern Europe* (London: Routledge, 1993).

58. Paul Lendvai, *Anti-Semitism Without Jews: Communist East Europe* (Garden City, N.Y.: Doubleday, 1971).

59. The Holocaust itself is estimated to have claimed the lives of 250,000 of Czechoslovakia's Jews; still others emigrated after the war. In East Europe as a whole, only some 200,000 of the 6 million interwar Jews are estimated to have survived, the largest numbers in Hungary.

60. A 1992 survey recorded still higher levels of respondents who felt that Jews had too much economic influence: 56 percent, compared with 14 percent in the Czech Republic. See "Míra antisemitismu," *Český deník*, May 23, 1992.

61. *RFE/RL Daily Report*, August 1, 1994.

62. This issue is probably the most difficult one for Slovak historians as well as the public in assessing the meaning of the wartime state. James Felak has documented the strain of anti-Semitism in the interwar Slovak nationalist Hlinka Slovak People's Party, the ruling party (in fact, the only legal party) from 1938 to 1945. See James Ramon Felak, *"At the Price of the Republic": Hlinka's Slovak People's Party, 1929–1938* (Pittsburgh: University of Pittsburgh Press, 1994). Jeshayahu Jelinek has devoted considerable attention to the issue in his work, starting with the study *The Parish Republic: Hlinka's Slovak People's Party, 1939–1945* (New York: East European Quarterly Press, distributed by Columbia University Press, 1976).

6

ECONOMIC TRANSITION IN THE CZECH AND SLOVAK REPUBLICS

In the first elections of 1990, all serious political parties, even the communists, announced themselves in favor of a market economy. This electoral platform was, of course, more easily promulgated and voted for than implemented. There were two overwhelming difficulties with constructing capitalism. First, there was the problem of devising and implementing the program itself. There was no historical precedent for the dismantling of bureaucratic state socialism and therefore no tried and tested blueprint for moving from communism to capitalism. A politician in neighboring Poland tried to capture the daunting character of the task by complaining that the communists had taken an aquarium and turned it into fish soup: How to turn the soup back into an aquarium? Second, there was the difficulty of managing the political fallout from the inevitable dislocations of the economic reform process. Politics is the art of the possible, and it simply was not possible to disassemble the socialist economy and reassemble a capitalist one without a rather awkward intermediate period of lackluster economic performance and social suffering. How patient would the public be with still further slippage in their living standards? In this chapter both the Czechoslovak experiment in economic transformation and its political tensions will be examined.

Devising an economic strategy was the first order of business after the Velvet Revolution. Jan Prybyla has cited Paul Johnson's comment that "capitalism merely occurs, if no one does anything to stop it."[1] In practice, however, it is not possible merely to unleash market forces and sit back to await the results. Despite the general consensus on the necessity of introducing something more like a capitalist market economy, political leaders were well aware that the legacy of communism included plenty to stop capitalism, or at least to slow it down. Recent scholarship frequently points out the paradox that it takes strong state action to produce a relatively autonomous free market in place of the heavily bureaucratized network of state-owned socialist enterprises.[2] In Czechoslovakia, therefore, even those among the leadership who were most committed to laissez-faire free markets saw the need for considerable state intervention to channel the process. The debate was over just how to do this.

There are different forms of functioning capitalism (see Box 6.1). In Czechoslovakia, the model to emulate was largely an adaptation of the neighboring Western European market systems. Even for those who agreed with this goal, there were important strategic decisions to make about how to reach it. As a first principle, it was necessary to decide whether to push ahead with the process in radical and rapid fashion—the so-called "shock therapy" approach pursued in Poland—or to proceed with greater caution in a gradual reconstruction of the economy. In this debate, the political elite was often more radical than the public at large in the formulation of remedies and in prescribing the swiftness with which the remedies were to be applied. Czech policymakers in particular were concerned with the need to make a break with the past; the nervous public, in Czechoslovakia and elsewhere, was inclined toward more caution in the hopes that a slower transition would be less disruptive and painful.

Perhaps the single most important figure in shaping the strategy of the economic transformation in Czechoslovakia was Václav Klaus, minister of finance in the first elected government coalition, and Czech prime minister after the 1992 elections. His rhetorical commitment to free market principles was virtually absolute. He fought for what he repeatedly called a "market without adjectives"—not a "socialist market economy" or a "mixed" economy, but a full-blown free-market economy, emphatically not of the sort that the welfare states and economically interventionist governments of Western Europe maintained.

To Klaus, critical of overbureaucratization and large state sectors in the West, even European capitalism was not capitalist enough. He himself sympathized thoroughly with former Prime Minister Margaret Thatcher in her deregulatory policies in Britain and regretted that the Thatcherite "revolution" had failed to spread in the West. He was impatient with gradualism, since it only delayed the reckoning and left the emerging markets heavily contaminated with elements of the old system. He was prepared to take some big risks, too, venturing into uncharted waters, as we will see when examining Czechoslovakia's innovative and unprecedented coupon privatization plan.

The way in which Klaus pursued his economic objectives, however, showed him to be a savvy politician as well. His reform agenda was a workable mix of economic daring and political caution. Although he talked a free-market game and backed the rhetoric with rapid privatization, we will see substantial evidence that the reality was more moderate than the façade. Klaus kept an eagle eye on unemployment, selling the public on patience with lower wages in order to carry

BOX 6.1
The Road Not Taken

In the 1990s there was a vibrant alternative to the emulation of Western Europe; this was the economic strategy of the small, export-oriented Asian Tigers such as Taiwan, Singapore, and South Korea, which started further back developmentally than Eastern Europe after World War II, and then surged ahead on a crest of impressive economic growth. While some post-Soviet states have expressed interest in this Asian model, particularly because the Tigers had accomplished their economic progress under authoritarian governments, Czech and Slovak economists doubted that they could follow such a path. Václav Havel noted that the Tigers modernized under less restrictive international trade practices than the current ones. Czechoslovakia, he pointed out, had obligations to the General Agreement on Tariffs and Trade (GATT), the European Union (EU), and the European Free Trade Association (EFTA) on trade policy, and commitments to observe intellectual property rights. He also acknowledged Asian cultural-historical differences in savings levels and entrepreneurialism. Were the Czechs too "Western" to follow suit?* In a political sense, this perspective is hardly surprising. Popular perceptions of the appropriate economic model were shaped by what they saw next door. The citizenry was like a patient arriving in a plastic surgeon's office, displaying a photograph, and saying "I want to look like *that*." The photo in this case was a picture of a prosperous West European welfare state.

Hospodárské noviny, December 12, 1993, pp. 1, 3, reprinted in *Foreign Broadcast Information Service–East Europe* FBIS-EEU-93-247, December 28, 1993, p. 5.

---

larger payrolls and attract foreign investment. His economic program moved more quickly to transfer formal ownership than to relinquish state control. This careful mixture of politics and economics was very necessary, for the task of economic reform was a formidable one.

The economic restructuring effort required massive and technical reworking of every facet of the economy. None of the standard economic institutions worked under socialism as they did under capitalism. The socialist structure of administered prices had to be transformed into one of market prices, prices that reflected the real costs of production and responded to supply and demand. Banks had to make the transition from being mere bookkeepers and clearinghouses for government resource transfers, to credit allocation institutions that would determine which loans met market standards. The monopoly structure of socialist industry needed a thorough overhaul; any student of introductory economics knows that free-market pricing does not work properly in the absence of competition. A monopoly market is a seller's market in which the monopolist can impose artificially high prices and make a tidy profit regardless of efficiency. The transitional communist economies soon learned this elementary lesson in economics. Freeing prices in a monopoly environment put no pressure on the state firms to cut wasteful expenditures and upgrade quality.

Currency convertibility to facilitate integration into the international economy was also essential to the economic transition. And there were still further problems. The establishment of domestic financial markets to provide capital for growth was desperately needed. So were the restructuring of the tax system to encourage foreign and domestic investment, bankruptcy laws (even chronically unprofitable communist firms did not go bankrupt, as they were subsidized by the state), the construction of a legal framework for commercial dealings, and the devising of a framework for privatizing the large state sector. The list seemed endless.

Because of the complexity and interrelatedness of this ambitious policy agenda, there was a tendency for the government policymaking process, in both Czechoslovakia and other postcommunist states, to shut out broad popular participation on "technical issues" such as economic reconstruction. What Adam Przeworski has labeled the "technocratic style of reform" stems from a leadership perception that the economic issues should be left in the hands of experts.[3] Such issues, they argue, are too abstruse and interrelated to risk "political" tinkering by interest groups or even the legislature itself.

While such an approach may be efficient in the short run, Przeworski finds it counterproductive in the longer term. Economic programs developed without popular input may not self-correct for the negative social impact of unemployment in particular; in fact, economists in the region tended to regard unemployment as a *good* thing, a sign that economic policy was working; to them, rising unemployment meant that factory managers were responding to the profit motive by laying off surplus labor. This kind of reasoning, if taken too far, invites an eventual popular explosion at the ballot box or in the streets.

Observers of the Czech Republic see traces of this technocratic style of economic reform in the arcane debates over economic policy and the attitude that the economy is too important to be subjected to detailed public scrutiny. The popular and durable cabinet minister Vladimír Dlouhý articulated a variant of this philosophy when he tried to describe to the public the way Western states make economic policy: "In the world, an economic program is usually associated with the election cycle. . . . The parties do not usually submit such programs to the "working people" for widespread discussion. Their programs tend to be formulated by experts, and the elected government simply implements them."[4] This formula may work neatly if the government achieves spectacular economic results, but the rougher the transition, the more questionable it is not to involve the public.

If we are to consider the economic pain of the transition, it would help to have a statistical sense of the general trends of the economic transformation period.[5] Table 6.1 offers a summary.

Table 6.1   Economic Trends in the Czech and Slovak Republics, 1990–1995 (annual percentage change)

Czechoslovakia	*1990*	*1991*	*1992*			
Inflation	10.0	57.9	11.8			
Unemployment	1.7	6.6	5.5			
GDP Growth	−0.4	−16.4	−7.2			
Industrial Growth	−3.7	−23.1	−10.0			
Czech Republic	*1990*	*1991*	*1992*	*1993*	*1994*	*1995*
Inflation	9.9	56.6	12.7	20.0	10.7	8.0
Unemployment	1.1	4.4	2.6	3.5	3.5	2.9
GDP Growth	−1.9	−14.5	−7.1	−0.5	2.5	5.2
Industrial Growth	−	−25.0	−10.6	−0.2	2.8	9.2
Slovakia	*1990*	*1991*	*1992*	*1993*	*1994*	*1995*
Inflation	10.3	61.2	10.0	23.2	11.7	7.2
Unemployment	2.4	11.8	10.4	14.0	14.3	13.1
GDP Growth	−2.0	−15.8	−7.0	−4.6	4.2	6.8
Industrial Growth	−2.7	−24.9	−13.7	−13.5	6.4	8.4

Sources: Deutsche Bank; OMRI Daily Digest; *Foreign Broadcast Information Service, Daily Report on Eastern Europe;* World Bank, *World Tables 1994* (Johns Hopkins University Press, 1994), pp. 580–583; Organization for Economic Cooperation and Development, *OECD Economic Surveys: The Czech and Slovak Republics* (Paris: Organization for Economic Cooperation and Development, Center for Cooperation with the Economies in Transition, 1994); Federal Statistics Office report, reprinted in *Smena,* August 19, 1992; *PlanEcon Reports.*

The data in the table make it clear that the initial period of the economic transition in Czechoslovakia delivered a serious jolt to the modest economic security that had been the hallmark of the previous communist regime. The most obvious jolt was the shrinking of the economy; economic growth not only stalled but became negative after 1989. In this respect, Czechoslovakia was quite representative of postcommunist transitions; all of them suffered a major initial decline. Not all of the initial deterioration resulted from domestic economic change. The dramatic collapse of trade in the former communist bloc was itself a major culprit; this collapse probably hit Czechoslovakia harder than most of the other countries, since it had been more dependent on bloc trade in the communist period.

However, the reasons for the economic skid may be less important than the effects. As elsewhere in the region, the public had traded socialist-era shortages for an escalating cost of living; instead of socialist guaranteed employment, ordinary people now faced the uncertainties of competition in the new labor market of a shrinking economy—and here the political and economic transitions intersect. A new political system is very fragile in any case, and all the more so when it must be the bearer, and even the cause, of bad economic news. A Hungarian reformer once described economic reform efforts as a race between politics and economics: Could economic reform begin to pay off before the public became fed up? A troubled economy, as we will see later in a closer look at political instability in Slovakia, can invite populist politics and undermine the legitimacy of the entire system.

We will also see, however, that the reform program of the economic professionals did register some concrete gains and, in the Czech Republic at least, may have won the political gamble of pushing for rapid economic reform. From the outset, the federal government sought a "responsible" macroeconomic profile, achieving balanced budgets (Prime Minister Klaus even wanted a balanced budget law), a stable currency, and fiscal responsibility. This stable environment won the applause of the International Monetary Fund (IMF) and other international institutions and the interest of foreign investors. The freeing of prices did cause an inflationary surge—60 percent in 1991—but the Czechoslovak government cushioned the impact with temporary subsidies to citizens, designed to allow them to adjust to higher costs of energy, food, and housing. In the Czech Republic, unemployment remained low enough to avoid the Slovak government's experience of retaliation by angry voters.

Even the most politically open and responsive economic transformation project, however, could not have eliminated a central political problem of the transition. In postcommunist economies in general, there were winners and losers, and all too often the winners were the managers and political functionaries of the former regime. These "red capitalists" were able to translate their insider knowledge of the system and the rules of the game into major competitive advantages in the new market economy. Throughout the region there were communist factory directors who ended up running their old enterprises after some fancy bureaucratic footwork, government officials who moved laterally into economic entrepreneurship with the collaboration (well-rewarded!) of former bureaucratic colleagues, and clever apparatchiks who appropriated state and party resources to start up their own commercial operations. All of these inspired popular resentment. The way in which the postcommunist states marketized was often denounced as "nomenklatura privatization"—privatization to the benefit of the old elite.

Many government officials were, at least in their public stance, undisturbed by this phenomenon. Their attitude was that scarce entrepreneurial talent should be welcomed regardless of its origins and its financial sources; the new system desperately needed all the entrepreneurs it could generate. The public was less magnanimous; it was frustrating to see the old guard seem to come out on top yet again while ordinary people suffered the shocks of transition. This was yet another sense in which a technocratic, results-oriented philosophy of the transitional government could undermine public confidence in the new policies.

Table 6.1 also reflects the sense that there were effectively two economic transition experiences in Czechoslovakia, even before the disintegration of the state. By almost any available measure, marketization was making greater and less painful progress in the Czech Republic than in Slovakia. There was greater entrepreneurial activity in the Czech Republic; the budget was in surplus; unemployment was between one-third and one-fifth that of Slovakia, and Slovakia suffered from a higher proportion of the chronically unemployed.[6] In 1994, as labor productivity rose, the unemployment rate stood at a mere 3.2 percent in the Czech Republic, the second lowest level in Europe, whereas it registered around 14 percent in Slovakia.

What accounted for this difference? The past is prologue to the problem. In addition to differences in economic development levels and resource endowments that had marked Czechoslovakia from its inception and persisted in diminished form, the well-intentioned communist-era development strategy for Slovakia proved to be counterproductive in the long term. Slovak industrialization had focused heavily on trade with other communist states and particularly on military production—areas that were hit hard by the collapse of interbloc trade after 1989. Reviving that trade was highly problematic, since the former trading partners were also going through a period of economic dislocation and had limited resources to purchase imports. Selling the output at home was equally problematic; Czechoslovakia's defense complex had produced for the bloc at large; the army was in no financial condition to buy the surplus of tanks and heavy armor, even had such purchases been militarily useful. Greater economic pain created pressures to slow down the economic transformation in Slovakia, an option that Czechs felt would only delay the inevitable. In poll after poll, the Slovak public displayed lower degrees of support for economic reform and greater enthusiasm for a mixed economy.[7] Table 6.2, which reflects reform attitudes in 1990, shows that such differences emerged very early in the reform process. Eventually, the differences in economic perspective would contribute to the disintegration of the state.

In the interim, the stress of economic change was fertile ground for disputes over budgetary allocations. Ministers of the Czech National Council, working from the (Czech) premise that past communist budgets had subsidized Slovak development, pledged in the spring of 1990 that each republic would subsequently decide upon the disposition of resources created on its own territory, living "mainly off resources generated" at home.[8] The Slovaks agreed, in the interests of gaining greater control over their own budget. There was no agreement, however, on who would benefit from the change in the old system. Slovak officials reminded the Czech public that "many factories stand in Slovakia, but that the decisions on what they will produce are made in Prague." They accordingly

Table 6.2   Czech and Slovak Attitudes Toward Reform, 1990

	Percent Who Agree in Proposition	
	Czech Republic	*Slovakia*
1. National governments rather than the federal government should formulate and be responsible for the substantial changes in the political and economic spheres.	36	47
2. We should avoid unemployment even at the cost of significantly restraining or even suspending economic reform.	19	34
3. Prefer a harsher and more accelerated version of tightening our belts (to promote economic change).	61	51
4. Willingness to accede to 50 percent price increases in essential goods.	53	39
5. Willingness to accept loss of current employment.	48	37
6. Fears that our situation will turn out as badly as Poland's.	19	33
7. Favor a strike following a considerable increase in the cost of essential goods.	37	50
8. The state should bear complete responsibility for finding employment for every citizen.	32	47
9. The state should bear complete responsibility for ensuring a decent standard of living for every citizen.	34	46

Source: Extracted from Czechoslovak Press Agency, March 31, 1990, reprinted in *Foreign Broadcast Information Service–East Europe* FIBS-EEU-90-064, April 3, 1990, p. 19.

expressed reluctance to maintain the costs of a federal bureaucracy that they saw as unresponsive to their interests.[9]

Predictably, the dissolution of the state was itself initially bad news for the new economies. A major impediment was the flood of new border regulations; the customs union promised at independence collapsed in months, amid a welter of customs barriers, trade licensing requirements, import duties, tax codes, and transit regulations. All of these combined to push trade between the two republics down 30 percent below its former levels in the first six months of 1993.[10] Individual enterprises that customarily used components manufactured in the other republic now stagnated. A case in point was the agricultural sector; since no one had anticipated in earlier years the breakup of the state, food processing industries were primarily located in the Czech Republic, whereas the Slovak agricultural sector produced most of the raw foodstuffs. The appearance of an international border between the two republics thus forced Slovakia to import poultry, dairy and bakery products, margarine, and tobacco, even when the un-processed agricultural goods had originated in Slovakia.

The new Czech Republic appeared to have the economic cards stacked in its favor. The Czech economy had many of the advantages of postcommunist economies (a relatively cheap, well-educated labor force), and some additional ones as well. The Czechs well remembered their advanced industrial base of the pre-communist years and were quick to remind those who had forgotten that the Czechs had once been effective capitalists and could be so again. Czech economic performance seemed to prove the point. Private-sector activity, which had been a minuscule 5 percent of the economy in the late 1980s, grew to a quarter of the annual gross domestic product at the outset of independence in early 1993. The second wave of privatization was expected to raise it to over 70 percent by the end of 1994. The Czech market was in addition conveniently situated at the heart of Europe, almost surrounded by two Western market economies—Austria and Germany, with which there had historically been close economic ties.

Moreover, a comparatively stable political leadership was saying just what West European businessmen and politicians wanted to hear about the virtues of capitalism and marketization. Policymakers in the Czech Republic worked to earn a reputation of fiscal responsibility. The reaction of Heinz Bednar, research chief at a major Viennese bank, is typical: "You can't compare the Czech Republic to western nations yet, but compared with the other countries in Eastern Europe, they are world champs—no ethnic tensions, stable economic policy, stable cur-rency. The transition will take time, but they are headed in the right direction."[11] The government was rewarded with international respect; while Slovakia went begging for investment, the Czech Republic was accruing a lopsided share of the influx of investment and trade into the state after 1989. It was also rewarded with a level of domestic popular satisfaction unique in the former Soviet bloc; despite earning power that is only one-fifteenth that of Germany's workers, more than half of the Czech public considered itself better off than before the Velvet Revolution, and the government of Václav Klaus remained popular. By 1994, Czech economics minister Karel Dyba was inclined to protest the listing of the Czech Republic among the so-called "emerging markets." "Forget it," he said, "We have already emerged."[12]

The most serious shocks of economic transition, however, could still lie ahead. The Czech Republic's low unemployment rates may look like good news, but economists fear that the low number is symptomatic of government reluctance to take the heat for the shutting down of inefficient factories. The existing bank-ruptcy law is not being strictly enforced, and heavily indebted firms continue to operate. In short, Klaus has not really been practicing the unfettered free-market economy that he preaches but instead has allowed continued government sup-port for ailing enterprises. The pessimists in the economic community expect a major political and economic jolt to come, when unprofitable plants go under or prune back their labor forces to survive. Others are more optimistic and believe that the Czechs may have postponed their rendezvous with high unemployment long enough to avoid it altogether. Their reasoning is that if the Czechs wait long enough to lay off workers from the inefficient and overstaffed communist-era enterprises, the private sector may by then have grown enough to absorb the surplus labor. If they are right, the Czech Republic alone among its neighbors will have dodged a particularly dangerous bullet, sidestepped the political repercussions of high unemployment, and won the race between politics and economics.[13]

Slovakia faced a less enviable prospect after independence. Freed from the direct influence of the Klaus program, the ruling Slovak MDS promised a more measured economic transformation and the abandonment of the radical agenda promoted by Czech politicians. The new program was designed to cushion the blows dealt by the first three years of economic transition. In the first months of independence, the accent was on "gradualism," the attempt to build the new economy on a foundation that Mečiar described as "neither socialist nor capitalist." Western observers interpreted this to mean Slovakia's "tilt to the East." The postponement of Slovakia's second wave of privatization in 1994 prompted the *Prague Post* to compare the number of Czech and Slovak privatization projects approved since the 1992 elections: "For anyone who is keeping track, the score goes like this: Czech Republic 1,400—the Slovak Republic 25."[14]

The gradualist rhetoric of the Slovak government, however, soon faded, to be replaced by protestations of unequivocal loyalty to the Western model. By the fall of 1993, Mečiar was assuring listeners of his commitment to rapid economic change and a renewed privatization wave. His government had spent the early summer gaining a renewed Economic Community association agreement and IMF loan guarantees in return for promises of Slovak budgetary and fiscal self-restraint, promises on which the Slovak government has delivered.[15]

The free-market rhetoric would have been more impressive, both at home and abroad, had there been clearer action and better results. In 1993 Slovak gross domestic product fell an additional 14 percent over the declines of previous years. Unemployment, which had fallen slightly in late 1992, rebounded in 1993. Nonetheless, Slovakia's failure to match the economic record of the Czech Republic—particularly in employment—is somewhat misleading, since the Czechs are the bloc "champs."

In comparison with the economic performance of postcommunist Eastern Europe as a whole, Slovakia's record looks much better. Its high unemployment rate was still lower than the levels in Hungary, Slovenia, and Poland, and even below the levels in some of the less developed West European countries, such as Portugal or Greece. Slovakia's double-digit inflation rates fell somewhere in the middle of the pack, comparable to those of the Czech Republic and less than Poland's. And the Slovak economic growth rates in 1994 and 1995 were actually distinctly higher than the Czech rates. Economic indicators began to improve about the time of the ouster of Mečiar's second government in the spring of 1994, but Czech and Slovak economic prospects still diverge, as they have in fact since

1918. It should be emphasized that it has been Slovakia's political instability and Mečiar's foot-dragging on further privatization, rather than its economic performance as such, that have tarnished Slovakia's international image. The election of the third Mečiar government in the fall of 1994 did nothing to assuage international concern about the Slovak intentions and long-term commitment to economic transformation.

Privatization: The Keystone of Economic Transformation

A general look at the economic trend lines after 1989 does not tell us enough about the institutional changes under way. Dominant on the economic agenda was the problem of how to privatize a state economy. Poland and Hungary had made some progress on this issue before 1989 (Poland's agricultural sector had been largely in private hands since 1956, and Hungary had permitted increasingly varied private entrepreneurial activity in the 1970s and 1980s). Czechoslovakia's state sector was, by contrast, nearly all-encompassing, embracing more than 95 percent of all economic activity. The Czechoslovak communist leadership delayed in laying the groundwork for any form of private participation in the economy until 1988, with the passage of a joint venture law that permitted the participation of foreign capital in Czechoslovak enterprises. Thus the new postcommunist government largely had to start from scratch in its announced goal of privatization and marketization.

The first priority was the controversial issue of *restitution*. The communist government had nationalized property and businesses in earlier years without compensation. It therefore seemed legally and morally imperative to restore to the former owners or their descendants something of what had been taken from them. Until this issue could be resolved, the legal title to any given property would remain under a cloud. However, deciding who deserved compensation for past wrongs was trickier than it appeared. The Czechoslovak government was insistent that the right of restitution ought to be granted only to those who had suffered after the installation of the communist regime in 1948. Civic Forum's position was that "we are not and will not be able to redress all wrongs in our history. Easing the effect of wrongs or compensation for losses cannot go beyond the date of the communist coup on February 25, 1948."[16] Specifically, however, the government was afraid that an earlier time limit would open the Pandora's box of property claims from the Germans deported after World War II. Public and elite opinion alike were overwhelmingly opposed to honoring any such claims.

Still, setting the cutoff point for restitution at 1948 caused additional complications. The first was the problem of compensation to the small group of Jewish Holocaust survivors in Czechoslovakia for property seized by the Nazis in World War II: The dilemma was how to grant at least symbolic restitution to them without opening the door to similar treatment for the Germans. The Czech government finally resolved this question in May 1994 with an amendment to the original restitution law extending the right to property return to Jewish families. To preserve the 1948 cutoff, politicians did some fast talking in order to describe this compensation as the rectification of communist era policies; Jews had been promised compensation by the immediate postwar government, they argued, but the communists never followed through on this commitment once in power.

The second problem with the 1948 cutoff, just as deeply embroiled in the politics of Czech-German relations, was the case of the non-Jewish victims of World War II—some 8,200 political prisoners, 3,100 widows and widowers of executed prisoners, and several hundred orphans. Time is running out for these now-elderly victims; over 2,500 died between the initiation of talks on restitution and late 1993. They are currently dying off at the rate of about one thousand per year. The German government has concluded compensation agreements with all its other neighbors but has been hesitant to move on the Czech and Slovak cases for fear of enraging its Sudeten German constituency. The Sudeten German deportees do not want the German government to compensate other Czechoslovak war victims until their own property claims in the Czech Republic are resolved. Hence, the Czech government hit on the expedient of teaching Germany a "moral lesson" by paying a symbolic compensation themselves (a maximum of about $3,700) from the Czech treasury, to be reimbursed by the Germans if possible at a later date.[17]

After these adjustments, the restitution program involved restoration to private citizens of some 100,000 small real estate properties and a far smaller number of enterprises. Still outstanding was the problem of restitution to religious organizations. Churches had been major landholders of fields and forests in the pre-communist period and had held properties as well. After 1989 there was a consensus on restoring church property for religious use, and legislation in 1990 and 1991 restored both churches and monasteries. The most controversial of the property transfers was that of Prague's fourteenth-century Gothic St. Vitus Cathedral, which sits on a hill above central Prague next to the Hrad presidential offices. In early 1995 a Prague court ruled in favor of returning this well-known historical landmark and tourist site to the Catholic Church, prompting a massive public outcry at the "privatization" of a national monument. The case is still in litigation.

But there was more general objection to the return of commercial property and land to the churches, and questions also arose over whether the churches should be obligated to continue to operate socially valuable service facilities, such as hospitals and schools, that had been built on confiscated church land. The controversial question of restitution of church property was therefore separated from the initial restitution law and ultimately was postponed until after the disintegration of the state. The Slovak National Council eventually passed its law providing for restitution of property to religious institutions (including Jewish property) in October 1993; it included provisions to safeguard the lease of property currently being utilized for educational, medical, or other social purposes. There has been continued deadlock on the issue in the Czech Republic, primarily because it divided the parties in the government coalition. The coalition junior partner, the Christian Democratic Union, repeatedly failed to convince Klaus that church land as well as buildings should be returned.

A larger issue was how to dispose of the remaining property, enterprises that were built in the communist period and had never been in private hands. The problems were very real—who had the money to buy up the state's economic holdings? The practical alternatives seemed to be foreign capital or domestic "dirty" money (anyone who had gotten rich under the communist state was probably violating dozens of laws). The idea of buyouts by foreign investors caused political qualms; a massive infusion of foreign investment could very easily give foreigners disproportionate political and economic influence and compromise Czech and Slovak independence. Germany was the particular object of concern here. When German officials spoke of restoring the "traditional" economic role of German business in the region, referring carefully to the nineteenth century, Czechs remembered German economic dominance in the 1930s and 1940s under the Nazis and publicly debated the dangers of becoming an appendage of the German economic giant.

Generally, each postcommunist country has been sensitive about selling off the "family jewels"—traditionally sound enterprises that most citizens feel should remain in local hands. In the Czech Republic, for example, these included the famous breweries that produce Pilsner Urquell and Budweiser (Budvar) beer,[18] as well as the traditional glass industry. The state retains a controlling share—the so-called "golden share"—of Pilsner Urquell, so that the label remains "protected national property." Nonetheless, the Czech government in particular worked hard to attract foreign investment. There is no such thing as "German capital" or "French capital," argued the economics minister. "Capital is capital, and we need it."[19]

The alternative to foreign investment is of course domestic investment. But domestic investors were scarce, and the source of their revenues was sometimes dubious. How could an honest citizen have made a fortune in communist Czechoslovakia? As in other transitional economies, the Czechoslovak plans for privatization therefore ended up a grab bag of alternative privatization routes.

Smaller firms were the first and easier problem to approach. The government auctioned off these enterprises under the so-called *small privatization* law of 1990, which eventually disposed of more than 25,000 small operations (including newsstands and restaurants), mostly by lease or purchase. About a quarter of them were returned to families under the restitution program. However, Czechoslovak enterprises tended on average to be much larger than those in the West, often employing thousands of workers. These socialist dinosaurs, apart from their questionable profitability, were too expensive for purchase or lease by a single buyer. Hence each of these enterprises was mandated to devise a privatization plan for itself, listing assets and liabilities, a schedule for transformation into a suitable corporate structure, and the planned procedure for privatization. Groups of citizens could also submit competing plans. The Czech and Slovak privatization ministries then evaluated the submissions and approved one of the plans.[20]

Even a plan, however, cannot produce acceptable buyers out of nowhere. To prevent the process from dragging on indefinitely, Czechoslovakia pioneered an approach that *did* produce buyers from nowhere, the so-called "*coupon*" or *voucher privatization*. The basic procedure, as outlined in the privatization law of February 1991, was simple. Every adult citizen had the right to purchase a coupon book of vouchers at a nominal fee equivalent to about a week's salary (roughly US$35); the citizen could then exchange these vouchers for shares in state enterprises being put on the market for privatization. When the process was complete, ownership of the enterprises would have been transferred into private hands, and every participating citizen would benefit. Initially, the public was unsure of what to make of this novel scheme, and sales of the voucher books were sluggish. To the government's disappointment, only about 500,000 of the country's 16 million citizens bought voucher books in the first few months of the program.

Then help came from an unexpected quarter. The twenty-eight-year-old, Harvard-educated entrepreneur, Viktor Koženy, came forward with a flashy marketing scheme that included an "ironclad" guarantee that any vouchers entrusted to the investment skills of his Harvard Capital and Consulting fund would be redeemable "a year and a day" later (a phrase frequently used in Czech fairy tales!) at ten times the original price. Those who wished to continue to avail themselves of his moneymaking talent could, of course, choose to leave their investment in his hands indefinitely and reap the dividends. This reassuring message, coupled with an aggressive television sales campaign, spawned a number of imitators and sent voucher sales skyrocketing. Although the government was slightly worried about the soundness of his operation, and Harvard University was more than slightly indignant about the unauthorized appropriation of its name, Koženy's intervention into the voucher program did ensure broad public participation. By May 1992, more than 8 million people had bought into the program, and over 800,000 of those entrusted their voucher points to Koženy's Harvard Investment Fund.[21]

The genius of coupon privatization was that—if it worked—it would accomplish several desirable goals at once. It was a shortcut to the slower process of selling off firms one by one, thus accelerating the transformation. The scheme offered all citizens a chance to buy into the capitalist dream, which gave them an instant stake in the new economic system. And a stock market for future capital investment would be created virtually overnight, as soon as coupons were converted into share purchases. In fact, the Prague Stock Exchange opened on a once-weekly basis in April 1993, immediately following the completion of the first wave of coupon privatization. In September 1994 the Exchange moved to daily trading; with the flood of newly privatized companies, it is now the largest stock market in Eastern Europe.

Of course, there was one significant drawback to voucher privatization. The "sale" of enterprises by this method does not generate any income for the firm or the government, and in fact the new firms are not yet showing any growth in profits. Whereas a foreign investor might bring in a parent firm's resources to refurbish and renovate the enterprise, Czech and Slovak citizens were investing nothing but a nominal fee in exchange for their acquisition of shares. The Czechoslovak government was probably in a better position to "give away" its industrial base in this manner because the country had not accrued huge foreign debts during the communist period. The communist government had not gone into debt at home by running budget deficits either. This gave Czechoslovakia an advantage over Hungary and Poland, both burdened with massive inherited debts from the communist period. The Polish and Hungarian economic planners had to think about generating revenue to pay off this debt; they could hardly afford simply to distribute shares of state enterprises to their citizens. In fact, both of these countries' governments hesitated much longer before deciding on their privatization projects and lost the initial advantage they had held over Czechoslovakia in 1989. Coupon privatization vaulted Czechoslovakia into the lead in the economic transformation process.

Coupon privatization occurred in two "waves," the first launched in 1992, the last year of the joint state. The dissolution of the state temporarily suspended the process; the Czech government held up the conversion of vouchers into stock market shares for several months as a bargaining chip in negotiations with Slovakia over the settling of financial accounts between the states. The second and final wave was completed in the Czech Republic by the end of 1994. Subsequent enterprise sales would proceed by more conventional methods; the Czech government announced in 1995 that it would continue to sell off the residual shares held by the state and to liquidate the shares—a 5 to 10 percent stake in already privatized companies—still held by the National Property Fund. The state was projected to complete a radical scaling down of its share holdings by 1997.

In Slovakia after independence, however, coupon privatization was a more controversial issue. Many Slovaks had purchased shares in Czech enterprises in the first wave, and their rights to those shares were held up for months in the spring of 1993 while the Czech and Slovak governments argued over the financial terms of the separation agreement. A greater controversy surrounded the Slovak government's ambiguous stance on coupon privatization, which repeatedly delayed any action on their second wave. Prime Minister Mečiar's rhetorical commitment to privatizing was somewhat diluted in practice by the way he qualified his enthusiasm. "I support privatization," he said during the 1994 electoral campaign, "but gradual privatization, after a few years, after proper conditions have been established for it."[22]

In his various periods of service as prime minister, Mečiar was frequently accused of stacking key positions, including industrial management, with his own
loyalists and of maintaining tight personal control over privatization agencies. In
early 1994, for example, he was simultaneously prime minister, minister of privatization, and chair of the Fund for National Property. His ally, Deputy Prime
Minister Julius Toth, was both minister of finance and chair of the Fund for
National Property. This concentration of positions came in handy; during their
last days in office in the spring of 1994, this team was accused of hurriedly privatizing some fifty enterprises—the so-called "midnight privatizations"—and
placing them under the control of cronies. In one highly publicized case, Mečiar's
chauffeur acquired a meatpacking plant for an estimated one-twentieth of its real
value. The interim Moravčík government suspended these eleventh-hour deals
pending investigation; more than a dozen of them were subsequently canceled
(Mečiar's chauffeur is no longer a factory owner). An opposition critic described
Mečiar's privatization as "a way to concentrate political power instead of a means
of economic transformation."[23]

The Moravčík coalition government that replaced Mečiar and the MDS in
March 1994 was divided on some privatization issues. In particular, there was
considerable disagreement about whether key sectors such as the state gas and oil
monopolies ought to be included in the second wave of privatization.
Nonetheless, Moravčík hurried to restart the privatization process; voucher
coupons to launch the second wave of privatization went on sale in September
1994—but perhaps not soon enough, because a return of Mečiar to power after
the September elections meant further delays. Mečiar heatedly criticized his predecessor's privatization efforts as hasty and even a "robbery of the people." In late
1994 the new parliament canceled the Moravčík government's privatization deals
(an action later overturned by the courts) and postponed the completion of the
second wave of coupon privatization, despite strong evidence of popular interest
(90 percent of those eligible chose to buy vouchers in the second wave).

The voucher sale, rescheduled to take place in the summer of 1995, was gradually whittled away and eventually canceled, dogged by controversy at every step.
The government decision to scale back the number of enterprises on the auction
block by as much as 50 percent raised howls of protest. Both trade unions and
opposition parties criticized the revised program for its limited scope and the lack
of "transparency" about behind-the-scenes maneuvering for ownership control.
Further outrage followed parliament's complete abolition of the second wave in
July 1995 (instead, coupon holders are to receive government bonds—*after* the
next elections!). Opponents of the Mečiar government's policy, aware that only
3 percent of the public fully approved the government's action, have threatened
both a referendum campaign and a legal battle over the abolished program; the
government countered with populist charges that the original program permitted favoritism to insider interests.

In raising doubts about fairness, the Mečiar government was indeed responding to a broad sense of malaise over the equity of the economic transformation process. Earlier the Association of Slovak Workers and a breakaway faction of the ex-communist Democratic Left had capitalized on this often-justified popular suspicion of corruption in the privatization process by forcing a referendum on the "dirty money" question. The referendum was an advisory vote on whether the government should pass legislation retroactively requiring participants in the privatization process since 1990 to disclose the source of their finances. The referendum, held on October 22, 1994, mobilized a determined minority that cast over 90 percent of its votes in favor of disclosure. The measure failed because less than 20 percent of the electorate went to the polls, but it made clear nonetheless that a substantial proportion of the population was deeply suspicious of the equity of privatization.

Although Slovak hesitations and inconsistency in pursuit of the privatization process contrasts rather sharply with the radical Czech initiative, the difference between the two should be seen in the context of the larger pattern of politics on the privatization issue in postcommunist states. In that context, it is the Czechs who appear atypical. In most other states debate over privatization has dragged out over years, plagued by the sort of disputes over equity and effectiveness that are so manifest in Slovakia—and that mark Czech politics as well, although without actually halting the process. Despite Poland's initial head start, for example, the successive Polish governments continued to wrangle over the privatization procedures well into 1995. Other countries have followed the Czech lead, with both Bulgaria and Romania adapting the coupon privatization model to their own conditions.

Economists have tended to be more worried about the effectiveness of the privatization process than about its equity. They are troubled not only by the hesitant progress in Slovakia but also by the pattern of Czech privatization. What they are seeing in the Czech case is that the large investment companies that came into being during the first wave of voucher privatization now dominate ownership of the newly privatized companies. These investment funds, in turn, are primarily directed by banks, some of which are still in the state sector. The Czech model of privatization, therefore, is very much bank-controlled. Why did this happen? Economists are not surprised. They see the banks as moving into a vacuum created by the weakness of the financial markets—by the absence of a well-established stock market, for example. The Prague Exchange was established relatively late and is dominated by the bank investment funds and by significant trading on a very limited number of companies.

What difference does it make where the money comes from and who controls it? The predominance of banking interests in the new private sector creates something of a built-in conflict of interest; as lending institutions, banks are in effect judging the creditworthiness of firms in which they also hold an ownership interest. In short, it is easy to imagine a bank's being tempted to grant loans to prop up floundering firms rather than rewarding solvent ones, all in the interest of averting a banking crisis that might stem from the failure of bank-owned firms. Since banks are also poised to move heavily into another critical sector, the management of pension funds, it is not hard to see why there is concern among experts. An economic system so dependent on the health of the new banking industry is clearly vulnerable. This uncertainty is important in itself, but it is also a powerful reminder that postcommunist capitalism is not evolving in a simple pattern that merely reflects the adoption of a standard Western model. The ways and means by which the new postcommunist governments are constructing their private sectors will leave a mark on the new economies for years to come and make their versions of capitalism somewhat different from Western versions.[24]

Finally, concern among economists about banking dominance in the new economy has also stemmed from the belief that the newly privatized enterprises will perform efficiently only if they are forced to operate in a truly competitive economic environment. All over the former communist bloc, governments have succumbed to the pressure from workers and managers to bail out floundering firms, to continue the communist-era subsidies. Of course, a private firm that is propped up by the government or by a bank loses the profit incentive, just as the state-owned sector had during the communist years. For a firm to be efficient, there must be real penalties for operating at a loss, including the threat of bankruptcy. The Czechoslovak parliament passed its first bankruptcy law in 1991, but the government was not anxious to push failing companies under, and economists still wonder what will happen when the bankruptcy laws are truly enforced. Meanwhile, the investment funds that dominate ownership of the newly privatized sector do not have experience with restructuring companies to generate profits, and trading on the stock market is depressed and insufficiently regulated; there is insufficient information for potential investors in the market, and insider trading and other abuses are relatively common in this early stage of the game. In sum, then, the privatization process in Slovakia is incomplete, and in the Czech Republic it is still proceeding with substantial growing pains.

Social Stresses

The economic transition was a psychological shock to almost everyone. Even though unemployment remained relatively low by Western standards in the Czech Republic, this was a jolt to people who had never lived with unemployment at all under communism and never had to compete on the job market. The soaring Slovak jobless rates brought the insecurities even closer to home. In fact, under the socialist regime, many state-funded benefits—housing, vacation allowances, medical care delivery, child care—were channeled through the workplace, so the loss of one's job could have even greater consequences than in the

West. The unemployment compensation system was new and unfamiliar. Such a thing had been unnecessary under the former regime.

Crucial economic issues affecting labor were negotiated in a tripartite council—the Council for Economic and Social Agreement—a voluntary arrangement among trade unions, managers, and government officials, so there was an official worker input.[25] However, the Council members knew that they were essentially consultants or advisers; the government frequently voiced the opinion that this guidance mechanism had outlived its usefulness. Trade unions were not going to be able to exercise significant influence on the government's broad economic program, and representatives of labor did not have a decisive voice. After all, keeping wages low gave Czechoslovakia a competitive edge in attracting foreign investment. The trade unions, still tarnished by their communist-era reputation for subservience to the regime, were a very junior partner. As late as 1994, the government could amend the labor law to constrict labor prerogatives, and the Czech minister of the economy, Karel Dyba, could still scoff, "Trade unions? What is that?"[26]—and get away with it politically. His government then had a two-thirds approval rating in the polls. Growing restiveness in key sectors was more visible in 1995, however, as doctors, teachers, and rail workers all went on strike in protest of wage levels and working conditions.

The costs of transition, psychological and practical, weighed most heavily on ordinary citizens. In the Czech Republic and Slovakia, as elsewhere in the region, the old rules are changing or evaporating, and, as George Kolankiewicz describes it, everyone had to "cash in" whatever assets and experience they had acquired from the old system that might be convertible to the new: "The neighbor who was a mere bookkeeper suddenly became an accountant, the brother-in-law who was a bureaucrat emerged as a property dealer, the derided shop-assistant became a part-owner of a supermarket. . . . Class was being created next door and looked you in the eye every day."[27] People worried that they were too old to change with the changing job market, too young to break into it (unemployment was particularly high among recent high school graduates), too unskilled to adjust to rapid technological change. It was a very stressful experience.

Most citizens felt like spectators, and the spectacle they saw was sweetheart deals between government officials and their allies—bribery and scandal. A system in flux is vulnerable to corruption; the interlude between the breakdown of the old order and the institutionalization of the new is a fertile field for practices that would be more closely regulated by law in an established economic system. As it is, the public has become all too accustomed to headlines proclaiming a securities scam at Banka Bohemia, the granting of contracts or licenses by favoritism, questionable privatization deals in publishing and real estate, and party finance scandals.

Further undermining the public faith in the integrity of the transformation process, as mentioned earlier, is the fact that those best able to play the new game, with or without rules, often seem to be those who had profited under the old system. Communist Party members with established positions in the old bureaucracy could build on their former connections and expertise to convert political power into economic power much more easily than an ordinary citizen could. The new entrepreneurial class seems to have more than its share of "red capitalists" or "nomenklatura capitalists." Unfortunately, this is another visible lesson in the lack of fairness of the new capitalist market economics—and the lesson for many is that "they" are still in control, even if "they" may have slightly different positions in the new order, converting political assets into economic ones. Citizens emerged from the initial stages of the transition with the feeling that ordinary people—workers, women, and young people—had too little influence on the political decisions that affected them.[28]

If several categories of citizens have special advantages in the economic transition period, others are clearly disadvantaged, lacking suitable resources and skills to cash in on new opportunity structures. Pensioners face the unpalatable fact that their incomes do not keep pace with rising price trends. Government efforts to subsidize certain important goods and services during the transition were a temporary expedient; in the longer term, market prices have increasingly been phased in, leaving pensioners feeling that they are too old to adjust by retooling their skills and yet financially strapped by their failure to adapt.

Women have also felt the erosion of their economic position. Under communism, almost all women of working age were in the labor force. Sharon Wolchik captures well the essence of this apparent equality when she describes it as basically instrumental. That is, the promotion of women's participation in the communist workforce was a means to an end, a support to the regime's pursuit of maximum production, rather than an abstract commitment to equality. Socialism needed a large labor force, and women were a natural reserve of additional labor. Equality of entry into the job market in numerical terms, however, did not result in economic equality. Women were paid less than men, to a significant extent because they were concentrated in less prestigious and less remunerative professions and industries (oddly enough to the Western eye, these "feminized" professions included medicine). Nor did full-time employment lessen the traditional emphasis on the woman as keeper of the home and children. Women therefore suffered under the "double burden" of a full-time paid job and full-time domestic responsibilities. All the same, their paychecks had been an essential supplement to family income.[29]

In the postcommunist period, the impact of unemployment fell quite unequally on men and women, with women in some regions up to four times as likely to be jobless as their male counterparts. In part, the response to this pattern of layoffs was ambivalent. The emphasis of Western feminism on a woman's equal right to fulfillment through her career choices played differently in countries where women were *obligated* to work and where the double burden made that obligation still more onerous. When the Czechoslovak postcommunist government began to speak of helping women to fulfill their traditional feminine role in the home, many women were quite receptive.

However, it would be a distortion of the issue to consider the declining participation of women in the work force as simply a relief to the carriers of the double burden. Westerners are generally a bit shocked by the open expression of discriminatory attitudes in the new market economies of the East, where employment ads specify that women applicants must be "attractive" and where the sexual requirements of the job may be encoded in the same ads. A Prague human rights group, Nová Humanita, conducted a seminar in assertiveness training for women in the workplace. One of the speakers noted the case of a legal colleague passed over for an important assignment because, she was informed, her legs were not "nice" enough. Another woman reported being told by a prospective employer that the firm was not interested in employing women because they might leave if they become pregnant. Besides, he added, he would feel guilty if she did not have time to find a marriage partner because of her work![30] Fair-employment legislation bars discrimination on the basis of race, sex, religion, or ethnicity; gender discrimination in the labor force, however, is often very overt despite the laws and contributes to a climate in which the massive economic dislocations fall disproportionately on women.

Another rallying issue for Western feminism, the question of reproductive rights, also has a different resonance. As in all communist states except Romania, legal abortion had been available in Czechoslovakia since the 1950s. In an economy plagued by shoddy goods and limited supplies, contraception was inadequate; as an unfortunate consequence, abortion became the primary mode of birth control. Abortion was not available "on demand," however. The termination of pregnancy was subject to review by an abortion commission that not only approved the abortion procedure but also set its cost; abortions for socially acceptable reasons (advanced age or impending divorce) were cheaper than those undertaken by the unmarried. The commission review could be more harrowing than the abortion itself. Nonetheless, under this system, it was estimated that by the late communist period, nearly every other pregnancy ended in abortion; there were eighty-seven abortions for every one hundred live births. Whereas in the United States, the typical abortion seeker might be a young single woman, in Czechoslovakia, the most common case was that of the married woman in her mid-twenties with two children already and without the income and living space to support a third. Most surveys suggest that families in socialist countries often had fewer children than they would have preferred but were deterred by the daunting logistics of child care without consumer conveniences and by cramped housing.

Regime policy responding to this problem was a bit contradictory. On the one hand, declining birth rates since the 1950s raised concern about shrinkage of the future labor force and market base. Some pro-natalist policies, such as paid maternity leave (now expanded to paternity leave) and children's allowances, responded to this problem. On the other hand, the state very much encouraged labor market participation by reproductive-age women, and legal abortion was just one—slightly uncomfortable—concession to that end.[31] The new dimension in the equation after 1989 was popular concern with the morality of abortion, mobilized by the Catholic Church. Catholic activists had criticized regime abortion policies even before the regime change and, as in Poland, hoped to gain fuller consideration for the church's stance. Success is more likely in religious Slovakia than in the more secular Czech Republic.[32]

All of the public is affected by the deterioration of the social safety net that remains the most popular feature of the former communist regime. The priority of economic transformation channeled budgetary outlays away from communist-era subsidies, so that services that were formerly free now have a price tag, and services that were formerly cheap have become expensive. Budgetary cuts have shut down many of the state-funded child care facilities and pared back expenditures on education just at the time when massive expenditure is necessary for revised instructional materials. Social welfare policy has moved from a philosophy of universal provision of benefits to the narrower criterion of who is in need. But needs outstrip the budget and leave many citizens strapped to provide for themselves services that the state formerly did.

Both the Czechs and the Slovaks have thus far escaped the soaring death rates—up 20 to 30 percent between 1989 and 1991—that have amounted to what population researchers are calling an unprecedented peacetime demographic catastrophe in the other postcommunist states.[33] Since the former Czechoslovakia suffered the same environmental hazards, alcohol and tobacco abuse, and deteriorating medical facilities as other countries, scholars have speculated that the reason for the lower Czech and Slovak death rates is that the psychological stress of transition is lower in these two cases. This is, of course, a theory that is difficult to prove.

In the field of health care, the privatization of medical institutions has begun, at least in the Czech Republic. In late 1994 the Czech Republic was in fact the only postcommunist state that had set up regulations allowing physicians in private practice to receive insurance reimbursement. However, five years after the transition started, neither former Czechoslovak state had developed a detailed plan for a new health-care insurance system.

Other social welfare benefits are also in limbo. A number of state-subsidized programs, such as day care facilities or vacations, have been slashed or eliminated altogether. Housing units and energy costs are moving, after a temporary subsidy period, toward their market values.[34] However much the governments may wish to preserve the social safety net, budgetary pressures work against it. In fact, previous programs are even being squeezed out by the new welfare costs of providing unemployment compensation and funding pensions for the growing number of senior citizens in a graying population. In the last year of the joint state 17 percent of the federal budget went to pensions alone. This hefty allocation is reminiscent of the substantial share of the U.S. budget devoted to social security, with the important difference that the U.S. economy is far stronger. Moreover, the socialist states had been more generous with early retirement, so that a communist country with the same age structure as a Western one has more pensioners.

Social stresses like these can have serious political repercussions. Even in the more fortunate Czech Republic, we have already seen the dislocations fueling support for right-wing extremists and the search for minority scapegoats. The Czech government proposal in 1994 to reduce the pension budget by raising the retirement age sent 40,000 trade union members into the streets in protest, a demonstration described as the largest in Prague since the Velvet Revolution.

In Slovakia, the cost of economic and social dislocation has been still higher. It has undermined support for economic reform and increased the risks for responsible politicians, who were attacked as salesmen of the national wealth abroad or as purveyors of human suffering. The losers, those who found no stake in the economic system, have become alienated from politics as well. In most public opinion surveys, those who see themselves as most hurt by the economic changes are less likely to vote, less likely to trust government, and less likely to declare a commitment to a political party. In a new political system that already faces considerable dislocations, this is an unwelcome additional burden.

In the Slovak elections of 1994, the only new party to enter the parliament was the Association of Slovak Workers (ASW), led by dissatisfied deputies from the Party of the Democratic Left who felt that "no one defended the interests of the workers" after the Velvet Revolution. "We, the workers, supported the changes by a general strike and, were it not for us, the actors and students could still be standing in the squares and winning nothing," commented ASW chair Jan Luptak. His own depiction of the postcommunist state was a portrait of a leadership that had forgotten its public: "Of course, we didn't know then that the workers would be worst hit by layoffs and that their wages would decrease incessantly, while prices would continue to grow. We had no idea then that deputies, ministers, bankers and enterprise managements would grant themselves large salaries and live in comfort, while people living from labor of their hands would struggle in poverty."[35] The anticorruption platform of the ASW included planks on requiring the disclosure of the source of money used to purchase the property being privatized, as well as conflict-of-interest laws to nail government officials who benefited from sweetheart deals. This challenge to the special privileges and immunities of the newly rich was sufficiently resonant with the public to propel the ASW into the legislature despite the communist pasts of many of its leaders. Clearly, there is considerable class resentment of those who, by hook or by crook, have prospered under the postcommunist system.

The Energy Dilemma

Czechoslovakia shares an additional economic problem with its neighbors. Where hydroelectric power is lacking, there are really only three energy options for Central Europe: petroleum (oil and natural gas), coal, and nuclear power. None of these options is without drawbacks for Czechoslovakia. The problem with petroleum and natural gas is simple: Czechoslovakia does not have any. These fuels must therefore be imported, at considerable expense to the hard currency account.

Historically, the Soviet Union was Czechoslovakia's primary supplier of oil and natural gas. Forgoing its own potential hard currency earnings on the world market, the USSR sent a substantial share of its petroleum exports to the bloc at prices favorable to the recipients, gaining in return a certain amount of additional political and military leverage. Czechoslovakia was dependent on the Soviet Union for 95 percent of its natural gas and oil, although at reasonable cost.

After 1989, this relatively advantageous situation changed dramatically. Once its allies had abandoned their communist regimes, the economically strapped USSR had little political incentive to provide cheap oil to Eastern Europe, particularly with its own oil production falling and its own need to earn hard currency to purchase Western products. Why should the USSR sacrifice a valuable commodity to benefit an ungrateful region that no longer acknowledged Soviet hegemony? In 1990 the Soviet negotiators and Moscow's former East European allies agreed that all regional trade would be placed on a hard currency basis effective January 1991. Although this agreement continued, in practice, to allow for other kinds of exchange, it was a signal to East European countries to try to diversify their oil imports. The need for diversified supply was especially urgent because the contracted Soviet deliveries were increasingly subject to delay and renegotiation as the Soviet economy and its oil production capacities continued to decline. The collapse of the Soviet Union hardly improved Russian reliability as a supplier, particularly since the oil pipeline now runs through the independent Ukrainian state. Periodic interruptions of Russian fuel deliveries to the Czech Republic and Slovakia were still occurring in early 1995.

Reorienting the supply networks was, of course, no less expensive. Petroleum products cannot be airlifted in at will. Their delivery depends on the existence of an effective distribution system of pipelines and tankers. Landlocked Czechoslovakia has no ports to receive delivery from the Middle East, and its only pipeline network was connected with the Soviet Union. It took time to construct an effective alternative delivery system. Several regional pipeline projects are now under way. An additional problem has been whether to incur a new form of energy dependence by allowing the big multinational oil companies to buy into local refineries. The Czech Republic is considering this step, but shares of Slovakia's monopoly oil importer and refiner, Slovnaft, are going on sale on the New York Stock Exchange in an effort to finance independence from foreign corporations. The politics and economics of petroleum supply continue to vex the postcommunist governments.

Coal was a different problem. There was plenty of it in northern Bohemia and Moravia, so supply was not an issue. But at what price? Coal mining regions produced heavy pollution, and an economy powered by coal, and especially brown coal, was highly pollutant as well. Atmospheric contamination from burning coal was a primary source of health and environmental damage throughout the Central European industrial region known as the "black triangle," which included parts of northern Czechoslovakia, East Germany, and Poland. In this sense, the abundance of coal was not an energy bargain. Its health effects alone were disastrous. Alone among the world's industrial states, European communist countries faced rising death rates; a prime culprit was the toxic effect of air pollution. In some parts of Bohemia, government programs sponsored annual "vacations" from pollution for young children, sending them to "cleaner" locales as temporary relief from the poisonous atmosphere.

Finally, there was the nuclear energy option, attractive for its being the cleanest of all and in the long term possibly the cheapest for a country like Czechoslovakia, which has its own domestic uranium supplies—*provided that it was safely produced*. And there lay the problem. Czechoslovakia's nuclear power program, which got off to a halting start in the 1950s, accelerated in earnest in the 1970s and after. A nuclear power program based on Soviet technology, however, raised the specter of multiple regional Chernobyls, even though the specific technology that went awry at Chernobyl in 1986 was different from the Soviet technology in place in Eastern Europe. (That was the good news; the bad news was that the alternative water-pressurized technology was regarded as possibly even less safe than Chernobyl's!)

In fact, Czechoslovakia was better off than some of its communist neighbors. In the 1970s Czechoslovakia had insisted on having some say in the modification of the Soviet reactor design and on manufacturing its components domestically. This success made Czechoslovak nuclear installations a bit safer than those of Bulgaria, for example.

Nonetheless, the initial postcommunist reaction to nuclear power was rather hostile. In Czechoslovakia as elsewhere, the response was heavily colored by the very recent Chernobyl disaster and the sense that nuclear power was a prime example of regime indifference to the environment and the safety of its citizens. Environmental concerns had mobilized considerable opposition to the communist regimes throughout the bloc and was the most frequently cited policy concern in early public opinion polls after the collapse of communist power. The harsh realities of energy dependence—most of these states had been dealt poor cards in the matter of energy alternatives—seems to have shifted public and government opinion in favor of greater reliance on nuclear power, a shift noticeable in the Baltic states and Ukraine as well. By November 1990, a ČSFR government spokesman was arguing that "The only alternative to the traditional way of producing power from brown coal is the use of nuclear energy."[36] As an example of this shift, the Mochovce power plant survey of local citizens conducted in 1991 found that only about one-third of them approved of the further development of nuclear power in Slovakia and of the Mochovce power plant in particular; two years later, over one-half approved.[37]

The partial relaxation of domestic concern over nuclear power, however, did not resolve its fate. The nuclear power controversy, like all others, was interwoven with both Czech-Slovak and international tensions. The government of the Czech Republic, for example, balked at putting nuclear energy facilities on-line in its own territory that were primarily designed to service Slovak energy needs. Moreover, Czechoslovakia's neighbors, particularly Austria (a nonnuclear state surrounded by nuclear power plants in neighboring countries) flinched and protested plans to extend Czechoslovakia's nuclear power grid further, characterizing the Czechoslovak nuclear industry as "a Chernobyl at Vienna's gates."

Hence it became important, in order to allay domestic and foreign concern, to demonstrate progress toward nuclear power plant safety. The Czech government accordingly solicited bids from major Western firms to provide technological input to improve the safety and reliability of its controversial Temelín plant, which has drawn environmental protests from Greenpeace and local activists as well as from Austria, whose capital is 120 miles downwind from the plant site (Prague is a mere sixty miles away). The winning bidder, Westinghouse, had much at stake. America's relative abundance of electricity and the nuclear safety controversy had chilled the firm's domestic market. The last completed contract for a new U.S. power plant was awarded in 1974. A Western firm that gained a foothold in the postcommunist nuclear industry could reap a tremendous windfall—Temelín was not a unique case. There was an urgent need to improve safety standards of functioning enterprises and those under construction throughout the region, and the Temelín contract could lead to considerable additional business. Westinghouse was also bidding on four Hungarian nuclear projects in the same period.

The successful Temelín bid, however, opened the door to problems that are general to investment in the region and specific to nuclear energy issues. Since the investment was underwritten by the U.S. Export-Import Bank, several U.S. congressional representatives raised the question of liability. What if Temelín suffered a nuclear disaster? Would U.S. financing mean U.S. liability for the costs? In the early stages of economic restructuring, foreign investors face many such cases of legal uncertainty, although few as symbolically potent as the fear of another Chernobyl; starting in 1992, the Czechoslovak government began to demand the inclusion of environmental audits in all purchase proposals, with the Czech Republic promising to reserve half of an enterprise's purchase price for any necessary environmental cleanup. These measures were no insurance against future liability lawsuits, however; in practice, liability questions in the privatization process have been settled rather cumbersomely, on a case-by-case basis.[38] In the

Temelín case, the Czech government promised to obtain international agreements to protect contractors from financial liability before the project—slated to go on-line in 1996—gets under way. As of the spring of 1996, these agreements had yet to be completed.

Slovakia has also faced international controversy over its nuclear power program. Several years of Slovak governmental efforts to gain a $300 million loan from the European Bank for Reconstruction and Development (EBRD) to complete the Soviet-designed Mochovce nuclear power station and upgrade its safety erupted into controversy in the spring of 1995. Not only was the Slovak government hesitating between an EBRD and a less restrictive Czech-Russian partnership in the project, but also the EBRD itself faced overt resistance to its financing scheme. Debate raged over the wisdom of patching up safety flaws in the Soviet design rather than building new plants with safer Western designs. Neighboring Austria threatened to withdraw support from the EBRD if the project went through. Mochovce raises the larger issue of dozens of suspended Soviet-designed nuclear plants in postcommunist countries; the EBRD precedent—its largest loan to date and the first loan by any multinational development institution to finance a new nuclear power facility—raised the prospect of additional such refurbishing in other postcommunist countries, most of which are heavily dependent on nuclear power for affordable electricity production. Eventually the EBRD suspended consideration of its loan, and Slovakia has concluded a financing and technical deal with the less persnickety Russian government. Sensitive to such controversies, but reliant on nuclear power, neither the Czech nor the Slovak successor governments have been able to develop a coherent long-term strategy for nuclear power development.

The tribulations of the search for safe and affordable nuclear power suggest that the postcommunist energy dilemma went deeper than the matter of bad luck in the endowment of fuel sources. Just as important were the defects of the economic system that utilized the resources. The notoriously wasteful and inefficient Soviet-type economies meant that a communist enterprise used twice as much energy to produce a unit of industrial output as a Western firm.[39] This inefficiency not only strained budgetary resources but also produced disproportionate amounts of pollution in heat and power production. The communist emphasis on heavy industry made the pollution problem a great deal worse than it would have been with a higher concentration of service industries.

Unlike in the West, which had responded to the oil shocks of the 1970s with greater conservation efforts, there was no comparable shock to East European countries, as they continued to receive relatively cheap fuel from the Soviet Union. A factory that could command fuel as a part of its planned allocation of inputs does not need to worry about conserving it. Pollution control technology was also primitive and often disregarded. A factory polluting in excess of Czechoslovakia's misleadingly strict environmental standards could merely include the resultant fines in its budget. Overall, there was no incentive to curb pollution built into an economic system centered on production and still more production, without serious regard to cost or efficiency.

Capitalist economies, of course, are hardly immune to the problems of environmental pollution. An individual firm, left to its own devices, might well be tempted to avoid the expense of waste processing and storage or of filtering equipment to reduce air pollution. However, what was missing from the equation in communist states was the counterweight of public opinion. In Czechoslovakia, the press did not even begin to report systematically on the environmental crisis until the mid-1980s. Government reports on the problem were so routinely withheld from the public that Charter 77 and other opposition groups considered the dissemination of such documents to be their public duty. Even then, ordinary people, who were not plugged into the dissident information network, had no solid information on which to base a demand for action. If they had been able to acquire such information, however, it would have been impossible to pressure the government to act on it under the prevailing authoritarian controls on popular mobilization. In the West, environmentalist movements have played an important role in raising public consciousness and alarm about pollution and in generating a climate for government regulation. In the East, such organizations were generally illegal, although the more liberal climate in Hungary did permit an environmentalist Danubian Circle to pressure the government on its policies. The political constraints in Czechoslovakia were stricter than in Hungary, however. For example, police persecution quickly aborted attempts in 1985 to organize a citizen's group to press an environmental agenda in heavily polluted northern Bohemia.[40]

After the Velvet Revolution, environmental consciousness and organization began to increase. In Slovakia, a Green Party even won seats in the national council. However, the new governments still gave first priority to economic growth and transformation. There have been repeated demonstrations in northern Bohemia for greater government commitment to ameliorating the environmental disaster there. Throughout postcommunist East Europe, in fact, the financially strapped governments have tended to back away from the immense budgetary outlays that would be necessary for a wholesale environmental cleanup.

Conclusion

The legacies of the communist period showed up in most dramatic and concrete fashion in the efforts to revamp the aging and inefficient socialist economy. Despite the advantages of a cheap and educated labor force, good geographic location, and the pre-communist history of economic development, postcommunist governments in the Czech and Slovak Republics needed to devote a major part of their energies to a massive, uneven reconstruction that remained incomplete five years after the transition. While economic growth appears to have resumed in both republics, it has yet to make up the ground lost since the 1980s.

Moreover, this resumption of growth has yet to result in substantial improvement in unemployment levels. In the Czech Republic, it is not yet clear whether higher unemployment levels lie ahead. In Slovakia, economic instabilities have clearly contributed to the instability of government. This is a politically volatile syndrome, evident in Poland and Hungary as well, because the apparently good news in economic growth that cheers the governments and the IMF is not paralleled by popular perceptions that personal economic security has accompanied that growth. Instead, the growth figures seem hollow measures of how well *someone else* must be doing in the transition period. In Poland and Hungary the combination of renewed growth and continuing unemployment toppled the governments and paved the way to a reform communist victory—in Poland in the fall of 1993 and in Hungary in the spring of 1994. The race between politics and economics continues.

Notes

1. Jan Prybyla, "Out of Socialism: Easier Said Than Done," in Joan Serafin, ed., *East Central Europe in the 1990s* (Boulder: Westview Press, 1994), p. 88.

2. Michael McFaul looks at the Russian case from this perspective, arguing that Russia's economic travails were a result of the state's weakness and inability to enforce the discipline necessary to establish market competition. See Michael McFaul, "State Power, Institutional Change, and the Politics of Privatization in Russia," *World Politics* 47:2 (January 1995):210–243.

3. Adam Przeworski made these points in an essay highly critical of the Polish economic transformation. See his "Economic Reforms, Public Opinion, and Political Institutions: Poland in the Eastern European Perspective," in Luiz Carlos Bresser Pereira, Jose Maria Maravall, and Adam Przeworski, *Economic Reforms in New Democracies: A Social Democratic Approach* (Cambridge, England: Cambridge University Press, 1993), pp. 132–198.

4. Bernard Wheaton and Zdeněk Kavan, *The Velvet Revolution: Czechoslovakia, 1988–1991* (Boulder: Westview Press, 1992), p. 163.

5. Readers should keep in mind that the reliability of economic statistics cited for the postcommunist economies is undermined by a number of factors. Price distortions, for example, make it difficult to measure the value of production, the levels of inflation, and other basic variables. Moreover, many economists suspect that figures on the decline of national income may be unduly pessimistic, since it is likely that a significant but elusive share of economic activity simply goes unreported in order to avoid taxes and other forms of economic regulation by the state. The new states have yet to develop effective economic policing methods, and this makes it easier to underreport income than it would be in Western economies.

6. John Ham and Jan Svejnar, "The Emergence of Unemployment in the Czech and Slovak Republics," *Comparative Economic Studies* 35:4 (Winter 1993):121–134.

7. See Sharon Wolchik, "The Politics of Ethnicity in Post-Communist Czechoslovakia," *East European Politics and Societies* 8:1 (Winter 1994):181–184.

8. *Svobodné slovo*, May 25, 1990, reprinted in *Foreign Broadcast Information Service–East Europe* FBIS-EEU-90-105, May 31, 1990, p. 25.

9. *Zemědělské noviny*, May 11, 1990, reprinted in FBIS-EEU-90-097, May 18, 1990, p. 12.

10. By the end of 1995, the last remnant of the special Czech-Slovak economic relationship was scheduled to be dismantled; since independence, the two economies had operated under a special clearing agreement for payments. The Czech and Slovak governments were negotiating in 1995 for payment arrangements between the two states to shift over to a hard currency basis.

11. Cited in Ferdinand Protzman, "Czech Republic: Doing Well for Now," *New York Times*, June 22, 1994, C4.

12. Cited in the *Economist*, October 22, 1994, p. 23.

13. Readers with some background in economics will find it useful to look at the first three issues of the journal *Eastern European Economics* in 1995, which are devoted to in-depth study of the Czech economy during the transition, with some comparative references to the Slovak case.

14. *Prague Post*, March 3–9, 1993, p. 5.

15. See Sharon Fuller, "Economic Developments in Newly Independent Slovakia," *RFE/RL Research Report*, 2:29 (July 23, 1994):42–48; and "Slovak Economic Monitor," *PlanEcon Report* 12:9–10 (April 18, 1996):2.

16. Czechoslovak Press Agency, November 6, 1990, reprinted in FBIS-EEU-90-217, November 8, 1990, p. 16.

17. *Denní telegraf*, December 2, 1993, p. 3, reprinted in FBIS-EEU-93-232, December 6, 1993, p. 14. The formal compensation law was passed in December 1994.

18. American beer drinkers probably know Pilsner Urquell. Although Budvar has the largest export volume of any Czech beer, it has not been marketed in the United States because of a trademark controversy with Anheuser-Busch over the use of the name "Budweiser." Czechs argue that they were brewing Budweiser/Budvar before the United States was even founded, but Anheuser-Busch has the trademark rights to the name in the United States.

19. See, for example, "Kapitál neznamená germanizáci," *Mladá fronta dnes*, February 6, 1992; "Chceme do Evropy a ne do Němĕcka," *Rudé pravo*, February 6, 1992; and "Bude Československo kolonii Západu?" *Lidové noviny*, February 4, 1992.

20. This procedure was mandated in the Large Privatization Act no. 92/1991, approved in February 1991.

21. See John McIntyre, "Ex-émigré Entrepreneur Viktor Kožený and the Harvard Group," in Daniel S. Fogel, ed., *Managing in Emerging Market Economies: Cases from the Czech and Slovak Republics* (Boulder: Westview Press, 1993), pp. 158–160. Kožený might have captured an even larger share of the voucher market had the government not acted to put a ceiling on the holdings of any individual investment fund.

22. *Slovenská republika*, September 12, 1994, p. 1, reprinted in FBIS-EEU-94-179, September 15, 1994, p. 17.

23. *New York Times*, February 13, 1994.

24. For a discussion of the Czech Republic's "banker capitalism," see Karla Brom and Mitchell Orenstein, "The Privatised Sector in the Czech Republic: Government and Bank Control in a Transitional Economy," *Europe-Asia Studies* 46:6 (1994):893–928.

25. The official communist trade union organization was abolished in March 1990, and an umbrella organization—the Czech and Slovak Confederation of Trade Unions—was established in its stead, with Czech and Slovak subsections. After the breakup of the state these separate Czech and Slovak labor confederations continued to function as the principal labor organizations of the new states. Although there are a number of independent unions, the confederations have been the recognized labor spokesmen in the tripartite advisory councils. ČTK Press Archive, March 23, 1995.

26. Cited in FBIS-EEU-94-027, February 9, 1994, p. 5.

27. George Kolankiewicz, "Elites in Search of a Political Formula," *Daedalus* 123:3 (Summer 1994):151.

28. Polls in 1992 recorded popular perceptions of powerlessness for these groups. See *Lidové noviny*, May 13, 1992.

29. Sharon Wolchik, *Czechoslovakia in Transition: Politics, Economics and Society* (London: Pinter, 1991), pp. 201–203.

30. *Prague Post*, May 5–11, 1993, pp. 3 and 9.

31. See Alena Heitlinger, *Reproduction, Medicine, and the Socialist State* (New York: St. Martin's Press, 1987).

32. In the census of 1991, the proportion of religious believers in the Czech Republic was 44 percent, whereas 73 percent of the population of Slovakia professed religious beliefs. Statistics reported in "Obyvatel'stvo ČSFR podle národnosti a náboženského vyznání," Dokumentační přehled ČTK, no. 32 (1991), pp. H1–H3.

33. See Nicholas Eberstadt, "Demographic Disaster," *National Interest* 36 (Summer 1994):53–57.

34. This trend, of course, is occurring in other socialist states at the same time. The early government responses are discussed in Bob Deacon, ed., *The New Eastern Europe: Social Policy Past, Present, and Future* (London: Sage Publications, 1992). Wage regulation was also a feature of the transition period; controls on wages, designed to stabilize the economy and improve the environment for foreign investment, were in place from July 1993 to July 1995 (*OMRI Daily Digest,* July 12, 1995).

35. *Rudé právo*, October 3, 1994, p. 20, reprinted in FBIS-EEU-94-191, September 28, 1994, p. 18.

36. Cited in John M. Kramer, "The Nuclear Power Debate in Eastern Europe," *RFE/RL Research Report*, 1:35 (September 4, 1992), p. 60.

37. Generally, environmental concerns have begun to take a back seat to economic growth across a range of issues. In the first months after the Velvet Revolution, environmental pollution was listed as the number one problem of the state by more than half (55 percent) of the citizens polled. The economy quickly supplanted it as the number one concern. Poll data from *Rudé právo* (February 14, 1990), p. 15, reprinted in FBIS-EEU-90-033, February 16, 1990, p. 22.

38. *Prague Post*, November 25–December 1, 1992, p. 7.

39. Gertrude E. Schroeder, "Economic Legacies of Communism: A Common Inheritance," in Serafin, *East-Central Europe in the 1990s*, pp. 60–61.

40. Jan Bugajski, *Czechoslovakia: Charter 77's Decade of Dissent* (New York: Praeger, 1987), pp. 59–60.

PART 3

THE INTERNATIONAL DIMENSIONS OF DOMESTIC TRANSFORMATION

7

THE SEARCH FOR
A NEW SECURITY ORDER
IN INTERNATIONAL
RELATIONS

Under communism, Czechoslovakia was at best a semisovereign state with very limited control over both its foreign policy agenda and the character of its domestic institutions. After 1989 the new Czech and Slovak leaderships started from scratch in a radical reformulation of foreign policy goals in an effort to satisfy the security needs of a small country and to develop an approach to the international community that would reinforce the domestic policy agenda of radical change. Adapting to the international environment was particularly difficult at a time when the post–cold war international environment was itself changing so rapidly, particularly in Europe itself. More than one scholar has used the metaphor of changing a tire while the vehicle is moving to describe the dilemma of reconstructing the European order after communism. In Czechoslovakia this dilemma was all the greater because the breakup of the state necessitated starting over yet a second time in order to redefine Czech and Slovak interests after independence.

In this chapter the focus of attention is the reorientation of Czech and Slovak security policies as defined in the traditional military sense: defense policy. Students of international relations have become increasingly dissatisfied with the narrowness of this understanding of what constitutes national security. They argue that true security is inseparable from broader considerations, including political stability, economic viability, and environmental safety, among other concerns. In short, there are profound internal and external threats to national survival and well-being against which no army can defend and for which no military defense policy is adequate. The boundaries between domestic and foreign policy have become increasingly porous.

Problems with a narrowly defined conception of security are especially apparent in the transitional postcommunist states. Many of them face more direct and profound *internal* threats to survival and stability than any that could be offered in the current international setting. In addition, their international policies revolve around the agenda of domestic transformation. In effect, the triple transition in postcommunist domestic politics is the substance of foreign policy as well. This is true for several reasons. In the first place, most of the postcommunist domestic transitions were from the beginning national liberation movements from Soviet hegemony. Soviet hegemony not only had represented a dependence of client states on an external power, but it also took the form of an external "military veto on political reform." No Warsaw Treaty Organization (WTO) member state was free to experiment with alternative forms of governance and economic organization—that is, free to launch a triple transition—as long as the Soviet Union exercised the control over its domestic structure as well as its international posture. The reclamation of sovereignty from the Soviet Union was therefore also a license to engage in internal transformation.

The triple transition was the substance of foreign policy in another sense. The cold war bipolar system had been one in which the foreign policy divisions between East and West were paralleled by divisions between two distinctive kinds of domestic political and economic systems. The Soviet bloc into which Czechoslovakia was locked after 1948 was defined not just as a foreign policy alignment among states, but as a socialist community. The WTO security alliance of 1955 was designed not only to "protect" the sovereignty of individual states, but, even more, to protect their domestic socialist character. Soviet and East European communist leaders saw the socialist community as a guarantor of political stability based on party leadership, economic stability based on state control, and defense capability based on coordinated military strategies.

This community faced a Western community that was almost its mirror image. In the West, the NATO foreign policy alignment forged in 1949 was explicitly recognized in its charter as an alliance of democratic states committed to mutual security cooperation as well as close (capitalist) economic cooperation. In the West, too, therefore, the foreign policy security community was seen as an alliance sharing similar domestic economic and political institutions. NATO was only one of a complex of Western institutions with interlocking memberships that U.S. and European foreign policy architects regarded as making a joint contribution to security broadly defined; this included political stability based on democracy, economic prosperity based on increasing integration of capitalist economies, and defense capability based on coordinated military strategies. Over time this Western alliance achieved its goals to a much greater extent than the socialist alliance did.

After 1989, when Czechoslovakia and other former communist states adopted domestic programs of transformation, we have seen that West Europe was a reference point. But it was not simply a model. The former communist states were not merely seeking to be *like* the West; they wished to be *part* of it. The "return to Europe" was often described as "joining" Europe, quite literally, by gaining admission to Western supranational organizations: the European Union (formerly the European Community), NATO, and the Council of Europe. In fact, Czechoslovakia and other postcommunist countries feared that their domestic revolutions would fail if they were left alone in a "gray zone" outside of Western institutions. They often spoke of a "security vacuum"—a limbo in which they lacked political, economic, and military protection for the domestic transformation.

The means of escaping this vacuum was to convince the West that Eastern states could be valuable partners in Western institutions. And admission to those institutions was possible only by demonstrating steady progress in the domestic transformation effort. Why? Because the multiorganizational Western alliance defined itself as a community of democratic capitalist states, and each Western organization, even a military organization like NATO, had admission standards that emphasized these domestic criteria for eligibility. This context is what so closely connects the domestic and foreign policies of postcommunist states like Czechoslovakia. The logic of this connection was a closed circle. The triple transition was supposed to produce stable democratic capitalist states. Affiliation with Western institutions would further this cause. And in turn, only stable democratic capitalist states would be welcome in Western multilateral institutions.

This is the context in which we must analyze the international environment of the Czech and Slovak Republics during their effort to make a transition from communism to democratic capitalism. The focus in this chapter on the traditional core issues of defense and security is complemented by the focus of the following chapter, which targets the international dimensions of the triple transition directly. Taken together, these approaches help to define the Czech and Slovak quests for security in a broader sense. The search for economic security through affiliation with West European economic institutions such as the European Union, the search for political stability in relations among national groups, and the search for a secure military and diplomatic position in a new European order are all interconnected, with one another and with the domestic transformation efforts. The ultimate objective of these final chapters is to gain a fuller understanding of the way in which these issues interlocked. The first order of foreign policy business for Czechoslovakia in 1989, however, was to bring foreign policy reality into line with the effort to assure that a democratizing Czechoslovakia would be a sovereign state rather than a Soviet satellite. The task of extricating itself from the remnants of the old order was a necessary preliminary to Czechoslovakia's finding a secure place in a new European order.

Disengagement from the Soviet Bloc

The first foreign policy priority of the leaders of the Velvet Revolution was to establish Czechoslovakia's sovereignty after long decades of Soviet hegemony. To that end, the spokesmen of the Velvet Revolution demanded and quickly received an apology from Soviet leaders for the 1968 invasion, which Soviet leaders now acknowledged to have been "unjustified." Mikhail Gorbachev made a ready admission that the Prague Spring had been an authentic search for socialist democracy, but he stopped short of turning Soviet archival material on the invasion over to the Czechoslovak government. Russian President Boris Yeltsin would do so later, after the Soviet collapse.[1]

The rehabilitation of the Prague Spring served several purposes simultaneously. It reaffirmed Czechoslovakia's right to its own independent development; it rehabilitated the reform efforts of the "men of 1968," who could no longer be labeled counterrevolutionaries; and it reconciled the Czechoslovak socialist reform effort of 1968 with the Gorbachev policies they so strikingly resembled.[2] Because of the strong parallels between the Prague Spring and Gorbachev's reforms, the admission that the 1968 invasion was a mistake was a much easier concession for Soviet leaders to make than any comparable concession of malfeasance regarding the Soviet intervention in Hungary in 1956. The Hungarian Revolution, unlike the Prague Spring, had evolved into a direct repudiation of the Soviet bloc and of communist rule, something Soviet leaders would be reluctant to forgive as long as the USSR remained committed to socialism. Three years would pass after the breakup of the Soviet Union and the final collapse of communist rule in Russia before Yeltsin would finally offer an apology to Hungary for the Soviet intervention of 1956.

A symbolic apology, of course, did nothing to reposition Czechoslovakia in the new post–cold war order. A more protracted and complicated reckoning with the existing institutional framework of Soviet power lay ahead. The targets were the military arm of the bloc, the Warsaw Treaty Organization, and its economic coordinating mechanism, the Council for Mutual Economic Assistance (CMEA). The Czechoslovak government wanted to defang these institutions, to neutralize the most coercive elements of the old control system, but without unduly upsetting the USSR in the process. Soviet leaders had accepted declarations of sovereignty from one country after another during the fall of 1989, but they remained quite paranoid about the possibility that this could lead to Soviet isolation from Europe. Hence East European leaders tried to curtail the military operational functions of the WTO and negotiate the withdrawal of Soviet troops from their forward positions in the region without suggesting that the new enemy was the Soviet Union itself. Concern with the political consultative functions of the alliance was therefore at first of secondary concern to the problem of Soviet military presence in the region. The new Czechoslovak leadership even touted the political value of the WTO as a forum for further arms control discussions and as "an instrument to keep the Soviet Union within the European process."[3]

The problem for the immediate future, however, was the removal of Soviet troops from Czechoslovak soil. The Red Army's presence was a double insult to sovereignty, for it had not been installed for the purposes of military defense;[4] rather, it had arrived as an invading force and then been "temporarily" stationed in Czechoslovakia for decades, as a consequence of the Soviet invasion of 1968. Czechoslovaks were being protected from *themselves* and the heresy of the Prague Spring, and none too temporarily either. When this symbolic message is added to the practical import of having foreign troops on one's territory, it is not surprising that there was an immediate demand for complete Soviet evacuation. After all, if Gorbachev had acknowledged that the original invasion was illegitimate, then what legal or moral basis remained to justify the continued presence of Soviet troops?

Therefore, as soon as the Soviet leadership apologized, Czechoslovak leaders added the issue of Soviet troop withdrawal to the foreign policy agenda. The Soviet leadership was quite receptive; the Velvet Revolution had virtually erased the political and security rationales for stationing troops, and their continued presence was an expensive measure that had no justification in Gorbachev's policy of cooperation with the West. By February 1990 negotiators on both sides had agreed on a timetable for complete withdrawal of the nearly 74,000 Soviet troops by the end of June 1991, a deadline the Soviet forces eventually honored with days to spare. The event was marked by both personal and collective celebration. In Wenceslas Square in Prague, several dozen men shaved off beards that they had started to grow twenty-three years earlier in protest of the invasion. It was perhaps appropriate that the public celebration was a rock concert with fireworks, since the Czechoslovak parliamentary supervisor of the pullout was a former rock musician (who expressed disappointment that the Soviet troop commander had declined the invitation to attend and to lend a note of drama to the occasion with his departure by helicopter from the concert grounds).

The official response of the Czechoslovak government to the completion of the withdrawal was low-key in comparison to the public celebrations. Czechoslovak officials were appreciative of the cooperation of Gorbachev and Soviet Foreign Minister Eduard Shevardnadze on the troop withdrawal issue, and reluctant to thumb their noses at Gorbachev's government in a summer of Soviet crisis—what turned out to be the last summer of the Soviet Union before its disintegration. ČSFR Defense Minister Luboš Dobrovský summarized his government's sentiment in commenting—both on the troop withdrawal and the protocol dissolving WTO that was signed days later—"I felt at that moment that the sovereignty of Czechoslovakia as an independent state was fully restored."[5]

Winning agreement to the withdrawal of Soviet troops was the first stage of Czechoslovak disengagement from Soviet hegemony. The second important part

BOX 7.1
What Does One Do with an Abandoned Soviet Military Site?

The eastern installations in Slovakia had some immediate security value. During the cold war, the bulk of Czechoslovak military forces were based in the west, oriented toward defense against the presumed NATO threat. The postcommunist defense posture, by contrast, did not assume a security threat from any specific state or alliance and therefore mandated an "even deployment" of military forces across the whole of what was then a single Czechoslovak state. As a result, the evacuated Soviet sites could be used to house the redeployment of the Czechoslovak army to eastern Slovak sites in the republic. After the disintegration of the ČSFR, Slovakia in turn used the former Soviet bases to help house its own fledgling defense establishment.

In most other respects the military sites were worse than useless. Many were environmentally contaminated and in some cases carelessly dismantled. The Czech and Slovak press was rife with stories of children playing with abandoned machine guns on the sites, and of the poisonous effects of toxic chemicals that had been inadequately disposed of and fuel supplies that remained behind to contaminate soil and ground water. This lingering damage was the subject of protracted Soviet-Czechoslovak negotiations.

---

of the process of restoring sovereignty was the dissolution of the Warsaw Treaty Organization. The fact that the last Soviet troops withdrew in the same month that the WTO dissolved is somewhat misleading. Soviet leaders were much quicker to agree to troop withdrawals; in fact, Gorbachev acquiesced in the dismantling of the Warsaw Pact only in the spring of 1991, more than a year after the withdrawal agreement. The end of the troop withdrawal process only coincided with the dissolution of the Pact because the logistics of troop withdrawal were more complicated, and took longer, than the act of dissolving a treaty.

Why was the dismantling of the WTO organization so much harder for the Soviet Union to accept than the removal of their military forces from East European soil? This question remains relevant because Soviet sensitivities about Eastern European security alignments have continued to be of major importance in post–cold war international politics. The Warsaw Treaty Organization had from its inception in 1955 been a response to the perception of a Western threat embodied in the NATO alliance that had formed some six years earlier; NATO had included the Federal Republic of Germany in its membership just months before the signing of the WTO. In its most basic form, the WTO sent the message that the Soviet Union was not alone; between the USSR and the Western threat was interposed a buffer zone of allied socialist states. To accept the dissolution of the Pact was to accept not only a loss of allies but also the prospect of isolation.

Even after Gorbachev accepted the removal of Soviet troops, therefore, he was very reluctant to accept the idea of completely separate East European security policies; he continued to insist that the Soviet state shared common interests with its neighbors and that the Soviet Union retained vital interests in the foreign policy orientations of these neighbors. The persistence of the WTO would have validated that view. Its survival was of particular concern in light of the fact that NATO, an alliance that had been created to counter Soviet power, showed no signs of dissolution. Abandoning the WTO left the field to NATO. Worse still, it left the former Soviet allies in limbo in between East and West; the possibility that they might spurn neutrality to gravitate into the Western sphere of influence, even joining NATO and extending that cold war enemy up to the borders of the Soviet state, remained a Russian nightmare even after the collapse of the USSR. The nightmare was the vision of a Soviet isolation as profound as that of the 1920s and 1930s.

In the cold war period, the American political essayist I. F. Stone liked to say that the Soviet Union was the only country in the world almost completely surrounded by hostile communist states. He was of course making the point that the West did not face a united communist threat. But after 1989, the Soviet leadership concluded that recalcitrant and restive communist neighbors were less threatening than the specter of an international united democratic capitalist front poised on its borders. These fears have repeatedly reasserted themselves since 1989; the delay in the dissolution of the WTO was only the opening phase of the Soviet and post-Soviet nightmares about NATO, for disengagement from the Soviet bloc was only part of the Czech and Slovak foreign policy agenda—the negative component. The affirmative thrust of that policy was to find a place in Europe, which (as Gorbachev had feared) meant finding a place in the major institutional structures of Western Europe.

The Search for Security in Europe After the Cold War

The broader objective of security policy remained the effort to escape from the "gray zone" of exclusion from European security institutions and to avoid what Václav Havel called a "new Yalta" dividing Western and Eastern Europe. Convinced that small European states could only find security in the context of a larger, inclusive post–cold war European security regime, the Czechoslovak leadership never seriously considered neutrality as an effective defense option, even though it was initially popular with the public; Czechoslovak foreign policymakers sought to "remain within the system of European security" and to seek broader security guarantees within that system, just as they sought to gain admission to the European Union to protect the economic transition. The task, as Foreign Minister Jiří Dienstbier put it, was to "transfer security on the Continent from a bloc basis [NATO versus WTO] to an all-European one."[6]

Czechoslovakia's desire to participate in a framework of collective security after the cold war was seriously complicated by the nonexistence of such a framework. In the unlikely event that Czechoslovakia had been able to break from the Soviet bloc all by itself, it might have been able simply to switch sides from WTO

BOX 7.2
Demonstrating Global Citizenship

Compiling a good record of cooperation in international crises became a primary concern in the foreign relations of postcommunist states as the basis for integration into some form of European defense and security community as well as for economic reasons. The affirmative component of foreign relations was the attempt to establish sufficient international credibility to merit integration into the larger international economic and security networks. We have already seen that progress in consolidating a democratic capitalist system was important in establishing a credible international image, and we will explore this point further later. However, in addition to building a domestic order compatible with the Western values and international institutions, there were also litmus tests of good behavior in foreign policy. Prime examples were the East European response to two early crises of the postcommunist international order: the Gulf War and the Yugoslav crisis. Iraq's invasion of Kuwait came on the heels of the first round of postcommunist elections and represented an early chance for the reconstituted regimes to demonstrate their cooperation in the new world order. Obviously, major troop commitments were not expected of these relatively small countries. What *was* expected, and was largely forthcoming, was compliance with UN-imposed sanctions against Iraq. This compliance was in many cases economically burdensome, since Iraq had been a Soviet client state with ties to other, European Soviet allies. Indeed, cooperating with sanctions meant the loss of opportunity (if indeed one existed) to collect on outstanding Iraqi debts. In addition to complying with UN sanctions, the East European states also tried to maintain a symbolic presence by assigning small support units to the UN contingent assembled in Saudi Arabia. In the case of Czechoslovakia, this assistance took the form of chemical warfare units and medical units.

The Yugoslav crisis was a more direct and critical challenge to good behavior. Once again, the litmus test of good behavior was compliance with UN-imposed embargoes on arms shipments to the Federal Republic of Yugoslavia and on economic traffic with the unrecognized rump Yugoslav state comprising Serbia and Montenegro. Czechoslovakia was in a less sensitive geopolitical position than some of its southern neighbors who bordered directly on the conflict zone. For example, Romania was under particular pressure to regulate shipping into Serbia on the Danube River, and Hungary's borders with Serbia and Croatia drew NATO requests to the Hungarian government to allow NATO flyovers. Nevertheless, the Czech government in particular could point to contributions to security: its service on the UN Security Council during the Yugoslavia crisis, its cooperation on refugee flow management, and the service of the Czech battalions in the NATO Implementation Force (IFOR) mission sent to enforce the Dayton accords of 1995 for a Bosnian peace settlement. The Czech and the Slovak armies are organizing rapid deployment forces, because responsible European citizens will be expected to be able to contribute to European security in this manner in the future.

to NATO. But Czechoslovakia's was not an isolated democratic transition; it occurred simultaneously with the collapse of the entire European communist bloc and its institutions. The whole postwar security architecture of Europe was either defunct or seeking a new mission. The WTO was gone by 1991, and NATO was in search of a new role in Europe after the collapse of bipolarity. The *Western European Union* (WEU), the underdeveloped security arm of the European Union, was not an operational military alliance.

The Czechoslovak government therefore first tried to promote the emergence of a completely new security framework as part of the process of its own defense policy orientation. Officials did not initially favor the extension of the NATO umbrella; they even suggested the desirability of its dissolution in conjunction with the demise of the WTO. Despite its past contributions, NATO seemed to them part of the old order that would now have to change. This was an extension of the thinking of the previous dissident community that initially dominated the postcommunist government. During the communist era, they had identified the division of Europe as the primary threat to peace, and they visualized a Europe without blocs, whether NATO or WTO.[7]

The ambivalence about NATO was related to one foreign policy concern that has remained fairly constant from 1989 to the present in both the Czech and Slovak Republics, namely, the fear of isolating the Soviet Union, and later Russia. Dienstbier, the first foreign minister, emphasized that his party's campaign pledge of a "Return to Europe" should not be simplistically understood as a move to the West. The goal was rather to realize Gorbachev's image of a Common European Home, inclusive of East and West. This lofty goal had some very practical underpinnings. Any policy move that might alarm the Russians with the prospect of isolation would raise tension in the area and undermine the very purpose of creating a security framework in the first place. The public, too, was decidedly lukewarm toward NATO, with only 5 percent favoring NATO membership in the early months of the transition.[8]

It was very obvious that the possible extension of NATO membership to Eastern Europe did indeed alarm the Soviet Union. In reconstituting relations with Eastern Europe after the demise of the Warsaw Pact, the USSR delayed the signing of new bilateral cooperation treaties with its former alliance partners by insisting on language that would bar the signatories from joining any alliance "hostile" to the other—and no one doubted that this language might be applied to NATO. Although Hungary, Poland, and Czechoslovakia refused to accept such a restriction (Romania initially agreed), the message of Soviet paranoia about NATO came through loud and clear.

With NATO initially a problematic candidate for an inclusive security alliance, the Czechoslovak government's first institutional choice for the task of building a security framework was the *Conference for Security and Cooperation in Europe* (CSCE). The CSCE seemed attractive because it *was* inclusive—the only organization that could claim membership of all the European states "from the Atlantic to the Urals" and beyond (some spoke of a security community extending from Vancouver to Vladivostok—in essence, all the way around the northern hemisphere). Countries of both cold war blocs had used the CSCE since the 1970s as a forum for the discussion of a range of security and confidence-building measures, and Czech dissidents had long viewed this "Helsinki process" as the kernel of a new European order.

The promising inclusiveness of CSCE membership, however, was matched by some formidable drawbacks. Chief among them was the problem reflected in the organization's title: The CSCE was more a floating "conference" than a true organization, meeting periodically in major European cities to discuss important issues, but dependent on a consensual search for unanimity to achieve any concrete results and lacking in institutional structures that would make it more than an itinerant discussion and negotiation forum. With these liabilities in mind, Czechoslovak foreign policymakers first promoted a larger role for the CSCE with the proposal that it be institutionally developed (not at all incidentally, with a headquarters in Prague).

Through the next several years the CSCE did maintain its inclusive character, expanding from thirty-five states in 1990 to more than fifty with the admission of successor states to the defunct federations of Czechoslovakia, Yugoslavia, and the USSR. And it developed institutionally as well, in response to the changing needs for consultation on regional change and conflict. More frequent meetings were convened on a regularized schedule. Three standing offices were created in November 1990 by the Paris summit of CSCE chiefs of state: Prague got its headquarters for the permanent CSCE secretariat, Vienna housed the new Conflict Prevention Center, and Warsaw was the base for the Office of Free Elections, later expanded into the Office of Democratic Institutions and Human Rights. The CSCE began to reformulate its consensual procedures in a format described as "consensus minus one" to allow at least for a discussion of security crises even when the member or members involved refused to welcome outside consideration.[9] The CSCE has continued to develop as a forum for the discussion and monitoring of European tensions. As of January 1995 it became the OSCE—the *Organization* for Security and Cooperation in Europe—in recognition of its gradual evolution from a floating conference to a more structured institution.

The CSCE still lacked military enforcement power, however, and was helpless to stem the momentum of the Yugoslav tragedy, which was well beyond its capacities to resolve. But even before the Yugoslav conflict, Czechoslovak foreign policy officials had been sobered by the growing tensions in the USSR and began to reassess the attractiveness of NATO. Increasingly, most other East European states also saw NATO as the desirable institutional counterpart, in military security terms, of the European Union's perceived haven of economic security. The benefits of association with NATO were clear: To come under the NATO umbrella would mean protection by a sophisticated and integrated military apparatus far more capable of enforcing its security guarantees than any other existing or proposed alliance. Whatever regional tensions might threaten destabilization, a revamped NATO offered the best chance to deter and control them.

Furthermore, NATO seemed more attractive than a security system based solely on European countries. For Czech experts, the continuing presence of the United States as a key architect of any subsequent security policy was a valuable counterweight to Germany's regional power. Advisers in the Czech Institute for International Relations (generally considered the key government think tank on security policy issues) particularly stressed this factor, arguing that the alternative was a German-based security concept that might reduce Central Europe to a German sphere of influence.[10]

Accordingly, Czech and Slovak governments began to pursue a closer relationship with NATO institutions, with the eventual goal of inclusion in the alliance.[11] Similar policies crystallized in Hungary, Poland, and elsewhere. This direction was the product of a fairly broad political elite consensus, pursued despite the public's still lukewarm enthusiasm.[12] In the Czech Republic, where President Havel has taken the lead on the issue since Czech independence, only the Left Bloc parties overtly opposed any government decision to join NATO, arguing instead that such a weighty matter should be decided by popular referendum. The Czech and Slovak left wing remained committed to a security system centered on the CSCE, with Jan Luptak's Association of Slovak Workers explicitly favoring neutrality. Czech and Slovak Prime Ministers Klaus and Mečiar both support NATO membership, although Mečiar has devoted considerable energy to creating a "special relationship" with Russia and Klaus has been more concerned with the agenda of economic integration; in his worldview, economics always has taken first place.

The problem with East European interest in NATO was obvious. What seemed to be an excellent solution for the evolving East was an open-ended formula for complications for NATO itself. Even as it struggled to define its own post–cold war identity, NATO was being asked, in effect, how it would like to absorb a large group of politically and ethnonationally unstable and economically struggling states, who could offer in return only an opportunity to practice peacemaking and peacekeeping.

NATO countries were also aware that extending the alliance east was certain to affront Russia, whose sensitivity to the perception that the rest of Europe was ganging up on it was both consistently and vocally expressed. In September 1993 Yeltsin sent a letter to NATO members urging them to refrain from any eastward expansion, and this soon became a standard refrain. Yeltsin warned that such a step would be viewed by many Russians as "a new kind of isolation of our country" and suggested instead that NATO and Russia might together serve as coguarantors of East European security.[13] This overture was hard for the West to disregard, particularly as it coincided with the major confrontation between Yeltsin and the Russian parliament—a crisis in which the West was reluctant to act in a way that would undercut Yeltsin's position.

The ongoing Russian political crisis was also, of course, an incentive to East European countries to move closer to NATO. These aspiring NATO members could not convincingly pretend that Russian instability was not a consideration in their petitions for membership—especially after the collapse of the Soviet Union and the continuing turmoil in Russia. As a Slovak Foreign Ministry official said, "We get scared easily. This is why we want to join NATO." But regional officials rejected the idea that Russia, as Havel put it, retained any legitimate "sphere of interest" in Eastern Europe sufficient to block their alliance choices.[14]

Although NATO countries might not want to take on the expense and uncertainty of Eastern allies, and though they certainly did not want to step into a brawl with Russia over the issue, there was another side to the story. Weighing against this unpleasant picture was an equally unpleasant one—the possible consequences if NATO did not exercise this opportunity for damage control in the East. Western countries clearly would benefit from measures to defuse tensions and deter upheaval in the neighboring Eastern regions. The security environment had changed dramatically between the 1980s and the 1990s. In the 1980s, even prior to Gorbachev's accession to power in 1985, the East-West divide in Europe was increasingly seen as a diminishing threat to Western security. Publics and policymakers alike saw war as a receding possibility, and the cold war confrontation had settled into an almost cozily domestic pattern of predictable and routinized negotiations. Gorbachev's "new thinking" relaxed the sense of threat still further. After 1989, however, the level of uncertainty escalated again, and it would be a shortsighted policymaker who could feel that it was prudent simply to ignore the possible consequences of Eastern tensions.

The West decided to temporize. The result of these conflicting considerations was a compromise: NATO policy attempted to modulate tension and appease East European demands with a series of improvised arrangements in an effort to satisfy East European states with something short of full NATO membership. There have been two major initiatives of this kind. The first was the creation in 1991 of a consultative body called the North Atlantic Cooperation Council (NACC), which embraced most of the new postcommunist states, including the Soviet Union (and later its successor states) in a form of NATO observer status.

The second initiative was President Bill Clinton's Partnership for Peace (PFP) plan, articulated in the fall of 1993 and accepted by the postcommunist states in the following months. The Partnership initiative made no guarantees about future admission to NATO, but it did broaden and intensify cooperation on security issues between NATO and the East and held out the nonspecific promise of eventual membership. Some disappointed East European critics rejected the whole concept as a "gimmick" and a "pacifier." Nevertheless, the Czech and Slovak Republics joined the group of twenty-four additional postcommunist signatories to the project and in 1995 were among the nine countries whose individual PFP plans had received approval.

While both Czechs and Slovaks accepted the PFP initiative, they reacted to it somewhat differently. The Czechs saw the whole Partnership for Peace initiative in the context of the larger historical canvas; in particular, they protested Yeltsin's initiative to NATO over their heads as inappropriate "because it is we and our security who are being talked about, but the talks proceed without us." In a clear reference to the Munich accords, radio commentary on the Russian intervention stressed that "the policy of sacrificing small countries in the interests of larger ones, and perhaps, even in the interest of peace, was once very unlucky for Europe."[15] Moreover, critics tended to see the Partnership plan as a rejection of the Czech Republic's European credentials; it placed the Czech Republic, said these critics, "on a par with entities who do not have a democratic tradition, do not respect human rights, and are socially and economically at the bottom."[16] Notice that the Czechs were defining their eligibility for NATO not as a military power but as a democratic capitalist state, in line with the logic of the Western security structure.

In fact the critics were saying approximately the same things that the government was saying in accepting the Partnership for Peace. The government regarded the Partnership plan only as an interim step to eventual full alliance membership; official Czech acceptance of the Clinton plan was coupled with warnings of its long-term inadequacy. Interestingly, both the public and official Czech responses were not narrowly related to military security concerns but more broadly to the question of the country's readiness to join the European community of nations. The pervasive disappointment expressed with the gradual evolution of NATO's self-definition, therefore, was compounded by the desire to break away from the rest of the postcommunist pack, a measure of hurt pride that Czech special worthiness had not been recognized, and the frustration of the effort to move from the category of object of security policy to coarchitect of European security policy.

Because Czechs continue to see security as a pan-European question, they have also not been interested in pursuing regional military alliances and security commitments that would supplant the guarantees of a larger continental system. The Czech perspective is in fact rather condescending, reflecting a desire not to be held back by any regional alliance that might cause the Czech Republic to be lumped together with other NATO aspirants who have a lesser chance of early admission. In rejecting a regional security alliance, the Czech Christian Democratic spokesman made an analogy that was rather demeaning to the Czech Republic's regional partners, referring to them as "unreliable riders en route to the same destination." "I am sorry," he said, "but Poland, Slovakia, and Hungary have let themselves be pushed into the role of three drowning men who are trying to grasp the coattails of a fourth one. The representatives of the Czech Republic, however, do not belong to those who cannot realize that three drowning men are too much for one rescuer. It must be hoped that the drowning men know how to swim, at least a little."[17] The smugness of this attitude grates on Czech neighbors, but shared interests continue to bolster certain basic forms of economic cooperation despite the competitive undertones of the dialogue.

This sense of superiority and unique entitlement was not shared by all Czech participants in the debate, for many thought that any marginal advantages to be gained from going solo were outweighed by the fact that the Central European countries shared "the fate of the small in the game of the large"—that is, each had an interest in a solidarity of small countries trying to avoid exclusionary great-power negotiations about their status. Nonetheless, the key decisionmakers were anxious both to pursue full NATO membership and to preserve the possibility of gaining it ahead of the rest of the postcommunist pack. As a result, the Czech approach while "waiting for NATO" has been to pursue bilateral military agreements with both Western and Eastern countries that provide for consultation, information exchange, and technical cooperation without any of the formal regional commitments to mutual assistance that would accompany a true alliance.

Differences in the Slovak approach to NATO membership and the Clinton Partnership plan reflect differences in Slovakia's eligibility and geographic position. While Czech politicians tended to assume the eligibility of their republic,[18] it is quite striking that the Mečiar government in power in Slovakia during the Partnership discussion paid much greater attention to the threshold political eligibility requirements. Mečiar's particular concern was that the criteria for involvement in a closer relationship with NATO included observance of minority rights. Reams of Czech commentary on the Partnership plan contain no mention of this requirement, but it was a sensitive issue for Slovakia. Any security arrangement that might lead to further external pressure on Slovak policy toward its Hungarian minority would have been quite unwelcome, and Mečiar claimed to have received assurances from Clinton that a proper observance of minority rights did not require the Slovaks to grant "collective" rights to its Hungarian citizens. All partnership adherents were required, however, to pledge to respect the inviolability of borders. Since this is a pledge that Slovakia wishes to extract from neighboring Hungary every chance it gets, its inclusion in the Partnership requirements was enthusiastically cited.[19]

Slovakia has not been as resistant to a common security concept for Eastern Europe as the Czechs have been. For Slovakia, after all, the U.S. and West European tendency "to perceive central Europe as one unit" is all to the good— it places the country "in the first group" of NATO eligibles; Slovakia is not on the Czech fast track—it does not want to "race towards Brussels [NATO headquarters]" against others in the region[20]—and its identification with a larger regional grouping would not slow its integration into Western security structures. The Slovak stance rejects the Czech interest in individual admission, advocating instead that the regional cooperation group Visegrad Four (composed of Slovakia, the Czech Republic, Hungary, and Poland) should enter NATO as a bloc. Slovak

Foreign Minister Juraj Schenk repeatedly objected to any "partial, individual approach."[21] The differential emphasis of the two states in their generally parallel security goals is a reflection in international policy of the same kinds of differentiated approaches that were evident in domestic policy.

Nevertheless, for the time being, the Czech and Slovak states are in the same boat with regard to their security goals. In the event of regional war, the two countries would have to rely on general NATO promises of "consultation" concerning security threats and assurances that violations of their state sovereignty would not go unnoticed. In all of the maneuverings, Slovakia and the Czech Republic must comfort themselves with being on the "short list" of postcommunist states mentioned in the West as potentially eligible NATO members.

The effort to gain admission to NATO fit together with broader Czech and Slovak efforts to join Western institutions in several respects. First of all, the two governments regarded NATO as the security pillar of the Western European institutional architecture and the only operational military organization in a position to defend the gains of domestic transformation. However, even after the governments expressed a clear commitment to work for admission to NATO, they continued to see it as part of an architecture of interlocking security institutions. They expressed interest in associate membership in the Western European Union and continued to press for the development of the OSCE, in which they already held membership.

Beyond NATO's status as part of a larger security framework of institutions (admittedly the first among equals), Czech and Slovak officials recognized that gaining NATO membership was intertwined with the components of the triple transition. Slovakia clearly understood the requirements of the Partnership for Peace initiative in this light when it emphasized the Partnership standards on the democratic handling of national minority issues and when it acknowledged that NATO would not welcome members who could not peaceably negotiate their differences on the national minority question.

More broadly, it has repeatedly been made clear that NATO membership is only available to democratic capitalist states. In September 1995, when NATO approved its "enlargement study," the stated requirements for membership included several explicitly political and economic criteria: a commitment to democracy, human rights, a free-market economy, and democratic control of the military. The Czech Republic staked its claim for membership in just those terms. There was even discussion in both the Czech and Slovak Republics of the possibility that entrance into NATO would accelerate entrance into the European Union, another recognition of the interconnectedness of Western institutions. Entrance into the security institutions of the West, therefore, would be further proof that a postcommunist state was eligible for full participation in all Western supranational institutions. As the search for protection under the NATO umbrella continued, Czechoslovakia and its successor states also worked to reorganize their own military establishment in line with Western conceptions of the military position in a democratic society and in line with the needs of a post–cold war military capability.

Democratizing Defense

What kind of defense establishment does a small postcommunist state need? Obviously, there is little practical sense in—or even possibility of—maintaining a huge military force capable of defeating foreign invaders. A country like Czechoslovakia cannot fight alone. In fact, too vigorous a defense buildup is likely to produce a classical "security dilemma" by alarming or offending neighboring states. Moreover, the limited budgets of new East European states were already fully committed to coping with the demands of their internal reform efforts. Nor did the public or the government initially perceive, in post–cold war conditions, a direct military threat to their country. In 1990 only 18 percent of those polled in a statewide survey thought that Czechoslovakia faced an external danger, and fully one-fourth questioned whether any army was necessary at all under these conditions.[22] These practical considerations aside, the dissidents who initially came to power in Czechoslovakia had long been critical of what they saw as a "militarized" state, and they had a pronounced disinclination to support military priorities. In March 1990 the transitional government began a series of steps that, taken collectively, tended to reduce the size of the military establishment.

The most controversial government stance was an early pledge to withdraw from the arms trade. Led by the powerful Skoda conglomerate, founded in the nineteenth century, Czechoslovakia's development as an armaments manufacturer long predated the communist period. The interwar state was armed to the teeth. Under communism, the state remained a major international arms producer and exporter within the framework of bloc needs and interests. Czechoslovakia's heavy exports both to WTO countries and to "politically correct" Third World countries gave its military-industrial complex a weight in international affairs far out of proportion to the state's small size. The arms trade seemed essential to national defense; a small state cannot efficiently produce a range of armaments for itself alone; its own army is not a big enough customer. If it produces military goods for domestic defense, it must export them as well. In the late 1980s, Czechoslovakia was the seventh largest arms exporter in the world, ranking just behind West Germany and the major military powers—ironically the five permanent members of the UN Security Council charged with maintaining international peace! Exports went to a number of sensitive conflict zones, including armored personnel carriers, tanks, trucks, ammunition, and spare parts to Iran during the Iran-Iraq War.

The postcommunist transition completely reconfigured the all-important export market in two ways. First, sales to former communist buyers began to shrivel up; budgetary stringency and the search for new defense policies had the immediate effect of slashing military procurement budgets throughout Eastern Europe and the Soviet Union. Second, the former Third World customers were both political and economic liabilities—economically because they were frequently in arrears on payments (a shortfall no longer compensated by Czechoslovak government subsidies), and politically because Czechoslovakia's shift in political orientation ruptured the political ties with radical or dictatorial regimes that had previously been major purchasers.

At the same time, an emphasis on arms exports was embarrassingly out of step with the humanist profile of the Velvet Revolution. Parliamentary deputies pronounced themselves "appalled and immensely ashamed" at Czechoslovakia's participation in this "plot against world peace."[23] In January 1990, Foreign Minister Dienstbier promised an end to Czechoslovakia's reliance on military production to enhance the foreign trade balance sheet. The tone of his promise reflected the early idealism of the Velvet Revolution: "It seemed that some things could not be done because they had never been done before, but they can be done if people do them. For instance, Czechoslovakia will simply end its trade in arms without taking into account what the pragmatists will say . . . it will simply be done and weapons just won't be sold anymore. We can stop that actually even without knowing how big the trade was." All arms exports would end immediately, the government hastily clarified, after current contracts were honored. Thenceforth, Czechoslovakia would produce only for the needs of its own defense establishment and export only what was needed to generate revenues for purchasing defense equipment not produced domestically.

This worthy-sounding action elicited howls of protest from a key segment of the economy, a military-industrial sector already hard pressed by the collapse of the Warsaw Pact arms market, which had formerly represented two-thirds of export sales. By 1991 arms exports had fallen to one-eighth of their former levels, both to Third World buyers and to the neighboring countries of the Warsaw Pact. Assembly lines shut down, and the industry that had represented 3 percent of the gross domestic product was in a state of collapse. This economic crisis had the further political impact of exacerbating Czech-Slovak relations because of the disproportionate Slovak share of the military-industrial complex and the concentration of less salable heavy military equipment in the Slovak economy.[24]

The government was thus forced to backpedal on its striking gesture of renouncing arms sales and instantly found itself wrestling to maintain the delicate balance between domestic economic stability and international reputation. A 1991 tank deal with Syria, designed to rescue Slovak tank-producing enterprises that had run out of orders, triggered U.S. presidential protests, eliciting Czechoslovak assurances that profits from the sales would be used to foster the conversion of military to civilian production. This promise was accompanied by pleas for U.S. support in the conversion process. Earlier, officials in charge of conversion had conceded that the state was in no financial condition to fund the retooling of 98 of 111 military enterprises slated for conversion without outside help.[25] Still struggling with this problem after the breakup of the state, both the

Czech and Slovak governments further relaxed export controls, with the announced intention of ruling on arms sales on a case-by-case basis that would avoid sales to clients in the most conflict-sensitive global regions. The West has been particularly concerned that Iran figures among the countries' potential clients.

A highly sensitive but more limited issue was the production and export of Semtex, an industrial explosive designed for quarry and mining operations but widely used in terrorist bombings; it was the suspected culprit in the 1988 crash of Pan-Am Flight 103 at Lockerbie, Scotland. In the communist era, Czechoslovakia exported massive quantities of the explosive to the Libyan government, which is known to have distributed it to terrorist organizations. Since 1989, when general sales abroad were banned, Semtex has been exported mainly to Kuwait for use in its Gulf War cleanup and in small quantities to Great Britain and other countries for research purposes in their counterterrorist programs. Beyond that, Semtex does not have a respectable international market, and its production does not enhance Czechoslovakia's image abroad. In 1991, the manufacturer of Semtex altered its composition so as to make it readily detectable to electronic security devices. Older stocks of the undetectable variant, however, continued to disappear from mining and quarry sites in the Czech Republic, and monitoring this supply will be an international relations headache for the government until the older supplies degrade to the point of unusability.

In general, the relative sophistication of the Czechoslovak military complex, and the opportunities for export abuse during the transition period, provoked Western wariness over the destination of exported munitions. Wherever Skoda business delegations travel, there is concern in the international intelligence community over the purpose of the trip; for example, were the Skoda representatives in Iran in January 1994 to explore technological contributions to Iran's nuclear program? Were other "freelance" Czech and Slovak entrepreneurs illegally diverting arms to sensitive countries? Responding to such concerns, the Czech government once again tightened export licensing requirements and stiffened the rules on the revolving door: Former government officials dealing with the arms trade must wait three years before working for enterprises that produce or sell armaments. Here, the government has walked a tightrope, trying to strike a balance between economic needs for export revenues and the risk of alienating the West and losing support for its broader foreign policy agenda.

Even if there were no political ramifications to the sale of arms abroad, however, the markets have dried up. The relatively advanced Czech Republic has begun, cautiously, to recover from its initial slump in arms trade; in 1994, foreign sales were up 16 percent over the previous year.[26] Slovakia's trade dependence on arms exports, however, was particularly awkward. Russian purchases of East European military equipment plunged; as the Russian economy continued to flounder, exports from Slovakia fell by half from 1992 to 1993, recovering slightly in 1995. Worse still, Slovakia found itself in competition in the world marketplace with its former WTO allies, in particular with cheaper Russian and Polish military equipment. The Slovak product might be of higher quality, but it was increasingly difficult to sell. Ninety-nine percent of Slovak arms exports in 1993 were tanks.

The desperate Slovak search for new markets is reflected in its courtship of military cooperation with the People's Republic of China, a tempting market newly opened to Russia and its former allies by the shifts in alignment of the post–cold war period and by China's expanding defense budget. Slovakia is also trying to upgrade its military technology to meet NATO standards for marketing in the West. A new howitzer design compatible with NATO ammunition specifications was scheduled to be in the manufacturing stage by late 1994; ZTS of Dubnica nad vahom, the manufacturer of the new howitzer, however, must simultaneously juggle this new project with the complexities of both privatization and conversion of other assembly lines to civilian goods. And in the process, it has not generated a single order from the financially strapped Slovak army. In the long term, conversion to domestic production will probably need greater priority, but in the short term, the huge military industrial complex represents a large chunk of the economy with limited prospects.

The arms production dilemma is an object lesson in the problems of transition, with all of the now familiar problems of economic and political change in general. It illustrates the sensitive intersection of domestic and international policy: A change in the security environment has had catastrophic consequences for a major domestic industry, but efforts to maintain that industry run up against international disapproval that could damage efforts to join Europe. The arms production problem also illustrates the practical complications of adaptation to rapid changes in both foreign and domestic contexts and the impossibility of building a security complex confined within the borders of small countries, where one's own army cannot absorb domestic production, and where the alternative of export sales is a treacherous one.

A Democratically Controlled Army?

Most theories about the necessary conditions for democracy include a reference to the requisite of subordinating military control to civilian authority, a goal that the Partnership for Peace program and the NATO enlargement study also insisted on.[27] Obviously, even a freely elected government cannot truly be democratic if the military can override the popular mandate and get what it wants through coercion, through the use of force or the threat to use it. This has been a more fundamental problem for the Latin American countries trying to make a democratic transition from military dictatorship, where a very central problem is getting the soldiers back in the barracks.[28] Communist regimes historically were notable for the party's ability to control the military, to work in harness with the defense establishment, and to monitor its conduct through political penetration of ideology and personnel.[29] Moreover, the European military establishments of the Warsaw Pact were significantly subordinate to Soviet organizational penetration and Soviet strategic concerns; that was an undesirable situation, but it nonetheless further undercut the military's ability to behave as an independent political actor.

Although the potential military threat to democracy is somewhat different in the postcommunist cases from in Latin America, the goal is the same; as Eric Nordlinger characterizes the task, a democracy must allow the military its professional autonomy and thus a measure of respect in its sphere of expertise but must also establish accountability to civilian control at the highest level.[30] Threats to the success of this task did and still do exist in postcommunist countries. In the immediate aftermath of the collapse of communism, the new East European political leaderships were concerned about the army as a lingering stronghold of communist, antidemocratic sympathies; a lopsided majority of the military officers were party members. Policymakers declared it a priority to depoliticize the military and to outlaw partisan activity within it, establishing civilian control on the model of Western states.

In addition to concerns about party holdovers in the military, the transition itself was destabilizing for army-society relations. It is clear in the case of the former Soviet Union that governments presiding over a strife-torn transition may find an angry and demoralized military to be a genuine threat to civilian governance. This has been a burning issue in the Russian military intervention in Chechnya and Moldova.

On the whole, Czechoslovakia was more fortunate in its democratization experience than some of its neighbors. In the past, the military had made only sporadic and ineffective attempts to intervene in civilian affairs, either in the interwar Republic or later, under communism.[31] There was no history of praetorianism. In the transition period of the early 1990s, as well, there were no sustained outbreaks of violence to embroil the military in politics, and the peaceful and negotiated dissolution of the state gave no opening for military involvement either.

The reconstruction of the Czech and Slovak armed forces, therefore, never made the headlines in the West but was nevertheless a critical part of the reorientation of defense policy.[32] The rebuilding of the armed forces, to be sure, was somewhat hampered by the absence of a proud or heroic military tradition in defense of the republic. In demanding a rationale for the army, journalists asked pointed questions about a military force that had failed to fight foreign occupation in either 1938 or 1968, and the defense minister acknowledged that critics had confronted him with the fact that no Czech or Slovak army had fired a shot since the Battle of White Mountain in 1620! This was rather unfair, since the decision not to offer military resistance in the past had been made by civilian leadership,[33] and Slovak partisans did fight the Germans at the end of World War II.

However, the paucity of recent military heroism did deprive the army of a model comparable to Masaryk's democratic example in the political sphere.

The goal nonetheless was a modern defense establishment democratically subordinate to the elected government. This demand was part of the original program of Civic Forum during the Velvet Revolution. In fact, all party organizations were banned from activity in the army in December 1989.[34] Two personnel issues were central to the subsequent reorientation: the rethinking of the citizen's obligation to serve, and the dilemma of working with the overwhelmingly communist officer corps (an estimated 80 percent of the officers held party membership).

After the Velvet Revolution, the conscripted "citizen soldier" had a novel and welcome choice to make; even those already in service could refuse to serve on the basis of religious or moral conviction and opt for a period of alternative service instead. By the fall of 1990, when over 14,000 currently serving recruits applied for this attractive option, the army sought and won the amendment of the new law to provide that recruits could only opt for alternative civilian service *before* induction. Nonetheless, Czech petitions for alternative civilian service had reached the 40,000 mark by the end of 1993, and the government reacted in 1994 by proposing that alternative service be made less attractive by extending the term from one to two years.

Particularly in view of the alternative service option, efforts were also made to "humanize" military service by shortening the conscription period (first to eighteen months in 1990, and then to twelve months in 1993 in both new states) and by barring the use of troops in agricultural work. The communist army had frequently sent its conscripts as "volunteers" to help harvest the crops; apart from the fact that this duty was unpopular with the troops, it also violated international agreements on the use of military personnel for forced and compulsory labor. Off-duty soldiers are now permitted to attend religious services as well.

These improvements in the conditions of military service have not made it very much more popular, however. Even though virtually no one expects to fight during his term of service, the greater enemies are disrupted career patterns, the sheer boredom of routine drill, and an excess of empty time.[35] Said one veteran of military service, "Before you go into the army, you should spit your brain out onto a little plate and put it into the refrigerator until you come back home, because otherwise it will turn green."[36] With the attractiveness of service low and enforcement mechanisms lower still, draft evasion is rife. It is clear that the morale of the rank and file remains a pressing problem in both states even after the Velvet Divorce.

The officer corps presented a different set of problems, and in particular the problem of de-communization. It was not possible to decapitate the army by dismissing the entire officer corps, so the effort to "democratize" it focused on "competence checks" that would identify and weed out the incorrigibles, a process under way in civilian bureaucracies as well. Many officers chose to retire with up to six months of salary, and others deemed unfit were reassigned or mustered out. As early as mid-1991, more than half of the senior officer corps had retired.[37] The military-political apparatus that formerly served as liaison between the army and the party and supervised morale and ideological education also had to be reorganized. Many of the former communist political officers, however, remained in the educational apparatus to teach democracy, a makeshift arrangement that even the Defense Ministry acknowledged to be "not the most fortunate solution."[38]

The adequacy of these measures, first conducted under a defense minister, Miroslav Vacek, who was a career soldier and Communist Party member,[39] were subject to debate and controversy. Critics cited evidence that the armed forces had contemplated a Chinese-style Tiananmen solution to the November 1989 crisis and expressed fears that mere competence testing would not eliminate those who lacked the "civic aptitude" for command in a democratized army. Dissatisfaction mounted until the appointment in the fall of 1990 of a noncommunist civilian defense minister who pledged a more rapid and radical shake-up of the army command structure and competence testing that would include an "ethical" dimension. The debate over putting a civilian in charge of defense has surfaced in other postcommunist countries as well. The hope is that a civilian defense minister will feel a first loyalty to the government rather than to the military. The fact that the post-independence Slovak government reverted to a career military officer for defense minister received unfavorable comment in the Western press.

The new service rules and purges created an immediate shortfall, and the Ministry of Defense found itself short 40,000 soldiers by the fall of 1990.[40] However, the long-term goal was in any case to downsize the army substantially from the 1989 level of about 200,000. The projected size was scaled back first to 140,000 and later to 100,000, only to face still further paring after the new Slovak and Czech armies emerged.[41] The Ministry of Defense also pledged to work toward the elimination of conscription and toward the establishment of a professional army by the year 2000. This hope has foundered, however, on the high costs of paying a professional army; conscripts can be paid much less for their required service, and the current expectation is that there will be a continued presence of draftees for the foreseeable future.[42] Both the Czech and Slovak governments therefore now speak of "gradual professionalization" of the military, with Slovakia aiming for a military that is 60 percent professional by the turn of the century.

The most serious political tensions in the military prior to 1993 probably revolved around the Czech-Slovak conflict. Slovaks were dissatisfied with their underrepresentation in the Ministry of Defense (Slovak presence in the ČLA officer corps itself was proportional to population size), the assignment of Slovak conscripts to service in the Czech Republic, and the speed with which defenses were being built up in Slovakia. The tensions in the military, in fact, were a microcosm of the general national tensions in Czechoslovakia.

Decisionmakers in Prague were in turn appalled in July 1991 by Slovak proposals to set up its own home defense force. Although the direct inspiration probably came from observation of the territorial defense forces then emerging in Yugoslavia (an unfortunate model to emulate), Slovaks described this idea as comparable to the U.S. state-based National Guard units. To Czechs, however, the Home Defense proposal seemed a challenge to the federal government's responsibility for military security. It also seemed uncomfortably reminiscent of the politicized paramilitary forces (Hitler's storm troopers were only the most internationally known example of the phenomenon) that had characterized the street politics of East Central Europe—and Slovakia—before World War II. The wartime Slovak state had institutionalized such a force as a Home Guard. After heated polemics, the Slovak National Council narrowly defeated the bill. The Home Defense controversy was only part of a larger pattern of tension over the relationship between civic patriotism and national identity in the military.[43]

The dissolution of the state resolved that tension but in other respects represented an additional challenge to the coherence of the military establishment. The division of personnel went relatively smoothly; career officers were given the option of which successor army they wished to join, and the draftees served out their time wherever they had been assigned. Subsequent recruits, of course, now serve according to citizenship. The main military equipment redistribution was accomplished in a mere six weeks during November and December 1992, with some Slovak military supplies remaining temporarily in the Czech Republic pending the construction of Slovak storage facilities.[44] However, the necessary restructuring of two separate forces was estimated to take an additional three years. The Czech and Slovak armies have adapted to the new order slowly, but they have not represented a serious threat to civilian control. The substantial erosion of military morale and cohesion, which would be potentially catastrophic in the event of the need to defend against invasion, is less disconcerting in light of the current absence of such a threat. The post-independence militaries, therefore, had breathing space in which to regroup, and defense policymakers could concentrate on the peacetime tasks of rebuilding the armies along lines of command and control favored by the West. The biggest security problem lay elsewhere, as we have seen, in the mismatch between new conditions and old alliances in Europe.

Conclusion

What external dangers do Slovakia and the Czech Republic face? In the aftermath of the Velvet Revolution, the official view was that the state had no international enemies, no neighbors whose ambitions might culminate in war. Instead, the perceived security threats have taken a broader form.

Czechoslovakia, while highly nervous in the face of the dislocations of the Soviet collapse, was not concerned with any short-term Soviet effort to reconquer its lost East European empire. After the breakup of the USSR, Russian military power seems even farther away, with Ukraine intervening geographically. The current post-Soviet threat is nonetheless real. What if a nationalist regime in Russia comes to blows with Ukraine? What if violence in the successor states escalates? At minimum, the instabilities of the former Soviet Union threaten its neighbors with refugee flows. Russia still possesses economic leverage as well, since no modern state considers the interruption of the flow of its energy supplies as anything but a security threat. Russia's potential market is also economically important, as is the fact that Russia still owed the Czech Republic and Slovakia some $5 billion in past debts at the time of the Czech-Slovak divorce.

Perhaps the most direct security threat that Russia can pose to the Czech and Slovak states in the 1990s is its capacity to block security arrangements it finds unacceptable. After failing to convince the Czechoslovak government to sign a bilateral treaty limiting Czechoslovakia's accession to "hostile" alliances, the Russian government subsequently intervened directly with NATO to discourage East European membership, as we have seen. Thus, even after Soviet troops have withdrawn, and direct military intervention has become a very distant possibility, Russia continues to represent a perceived threat to regional sovereignty of countries seeking to find a voice in their own security arrangements.

Notes

1. Gorbachev's first admission came as early as December 1, 1990. The East German, Hungarian, and Polish governments had already apologized for their part in the invasion.

2. Public anger about the presence of Soviet troops was a response to the role they played in constraining Czechoslovak sovereignty. But the hypocrisy of the jargon that surrounded their presence, the pretense that these troops somehow protected the citizenry, added insult to injury. The incident of the "pink tank" added a longer historical dimension to the Soviet military occupation. One of the many memorials to the Soviet "liberation" of World War II scattered through the territory of Eastern Europe was a monument to the liberation of Prague, a Red Army tank alleged to have been the first to enter the Czechoslovak capital in the spring of 1945. In the spring of 1991, an artist painted the controversial tank pink, an act of protest that scandalized and insulted Soviet officials. After the local government restored the tank to its original color, parliamentary deputies who wished to emphasize that Czechoslovakia was now truly liberated—this time from the USSR—took advantage of their parliamentary immunity from prosecution to revisit the memorial with buckets of pink paint for a second coating. See Douglas Lytle, *Pink Tanks and Velvet Hangovers: An American in Prague* (Berkeley: Frog, 1995), pp. 217–218.

3. Carol Skalnik Leff, "Czechoslovak-Soviet relations," in Richard F. Staar, ed., *East-Central Europe and the USSR* (New York: St. Martin's Press, 1991), p. 154.

4. Strategically, the most important countries in Soviet defense calculations were Poland and East Germany.

5. *New York Times*, June 26, 1991. The financial questions surrounding the withdrawal were less tractable. Soviet military installations had treated the Czechoslovak environment as casually as the Czechoslovak communists themselves had, which is to say that there was massive environmental contamination at the 150 military sites. Czechoslovak estimates put the cleanup costs at $2 million per site. The Soviet Union in turn claimed compensation for the military installations it was leaving behind. The final settlement of these claims lagged behind the actual withdrawal by over a year.

6. Cited in Andrew A. Michta, *East Central Europe After the Warsaw Pact: Security Dilemmas in the 1990s* (New York: Greenwood Press, 1992), p. 111.

7. See Jiří Dienstbier, "Redesigning Czechoslovak Foreign Policy: An Interview with Jiří Dienstbier," in Tim D. Whipple, ed., *After the Velvet Revolution: Voices of the New Leaders of Czechoslovakia* (Lanham, Md.: Freedom House, 1991), p. 126.

8. *Lidové noviny*, May 14, 1990, reprinted in *Foreign Broadcast Information Service–East Europe* FBIS-EEU-90-095, May 16, 1990, p. 18. Faced with increasing instability on the territory of the former states of Yugoslavia and the Soviet Union, the proportion of Slovaks and Czechs favoring NATO membership later rose sharply.

9. See William Korey, "Minority Rights after Helsinki," *Ethics and International Affairs* 8 (1994):119–140.

10. *Mladá fronta dnes*, May 24, 1994, p. 2, reprinted in FBIS-EEU-94-105, June 1, 1994, p. 11.

11. President Havel, however, remained concerned with the need to reformulate NATO's objectives in order to distance it from the cold war alliance mentality. He argued: "The expansion of NATO should be preceded by something even more important, that is, a new formulation of its own meaning, mission, and identity." Cited in *Mladá fronta Dnes*, from *OMRI Daily Digest*, no. 95, April 28, 1995.

12. Less than half of the Slovak and Czech publics (49 percent and 46 percent respectively) favored NATO membership as late as the fall of 1994. See *Národná obroda*, October 7, 1994, p. 3, reprinted in FBIS-EEU-94-199, October 14, 1994, p. 7. Still lower support percentages were recorded in Slovakia in the summer of 1995. See *OMRI Daily Digest*, July 10, 1995.

13. Text of the Yeltsin letter is reprinted in *Mladá fronta dnes*, December 2, 1993, p. 6, itself reprinted in FBIS-EEU-93-230, December 2, 1993, p. 10.

14. Havel, interviewed on Prague Radio Network, February 20, 1994, transcribed in FBIS-EEU-94-035, February 22, 1994, p. 4.

15. Prague Radio Network, October 1, 1993, transcribed in FBIS-EEU-93-190, October 4, 1993, p. 12.

16. *Lidové noviny*, March 18, 1994, p. 6, reprinted in FBIS-EEU-94-055, March 22, 1994, p. 10.

17. *Lidové noviny*, January 25, 1994, p. 6, reprinted in FBIS-EEU-94-018, January 27, 1994, p. 6.

18. In fact, the chairman of the U.S. Joint Chiefs of Staff, General John Shalikashvili, during his September 1995 visit to Prague, praised the Czech Army as having probably the "most mature" relations with the U.S. armed forces of all the postcommunist states taking part in Partnership for Peace. The Czech press agency quoted him as saying that the Czech armed forces were taking a lead in the program in both quality and quantity. *OMRI Daily Digest*, no. 187, September 26, 1995.

19. Bratislava Radio, January 13, 1994, transcribed in FBIS-EEU-94-010, January 14, 1994, p. 8.

20. *Frankfurter Allgemeine*, 9 October, 1993, p. 6, reprinted in FBIS-EEU-93-197, October 14, 1993, p. 15.

21. Cited in *OMRI Daily Digest*, March 30, 1995.

22. Prague ČTK, October 31, 1990, transcribed in FBIS-EEU-90-213, November 2, 1990, p. 19.

23. Bratislava *Pravda*, January 9, 1990, reprinted in FBIS-EEU-90-018, January 26, 1990, p. 35.

24. The Czech arms industry was also in trouble, but some of its more sophisticated equipment (aircraft, small arms, radar) remained potentially competitive in world markets. Czech arms production had therefore fallen by only 30 percent by the time of the disintegration of the state, whereas Slovak production had fallen by 90 percent.

25. Interview with General Jaroslav Kovačík, Bratislava *Pravda*, March 15, 1990, reprinted in FBIS-EEU-90-056, March 22, 1990, p. 22.

26. *OMRI Daily Digest*, 1:26 February 6, 1995).

27. See Samuel Huntington, *The Third Wave: Democratization in the Late Twentieth Century* (Norman: University of Oklahoma Press, 1991), pp. 231–253; and Alain Rouquie, "Demilitarization and the Institutionalization of Military-Dominated Polities in Latin America," in Guillermo O'Donnell, et al., eds., *Transitions from Authoritarian Rule: Comparative Perspectives* (Baltimore: Johns Hopkins University Press, 1986), pp. 108–136.

28. I was puzzled when scholars studying the Latin America military talked about it as "the gorilla problem." It was explained to me that they were referring to the old riddle, "Where does a 500-pound gorilla sit? . . . Anywhere he wants." Scholars found to be this a good description of the Latin American military influence in politics.

29. Eric Nordlinger characterizes this form of civilian control of the military as the "penetration model" in his classic study *Soldiers in Politics: Military Coups and Governments* (Englewood Cliffs, N.J.: Prentice-Hall, 1977), pp. 15–19. The nature of civil-military relations in communist countries has sparked considerable debate, particularly in the cases of the USSR and China. See, for example, Timothy Colton, *Soldiers and the Soviet State: Civil-Military Relations from Brezhnev to Gorbachev* (Princeton: Princeton University Press, 1990).

30. Nordlinger describes this ideal type as the "liberal model" of civil-military relations. See Nordlinger, *Soldiers in Politics*, pp. 12–15.

31. Some elements of the military did appear to have maneuvered, ineffectually, to forestall Novotný's ouster as party chief in late 1967. See H. Gordon Skilling, *Czechoslovakia's Interrupted Revolution* (Princeton: Princeton University Press, 1976), pp. 172–174.

32. For a brief summary of Czechoslovak efforts to depoliticize the military, see Dale R. Herspring, "The Process of Change and Democratization in Eastern Europe: The Case of the Military," in John R. Lampe and Daniel N. Nelson, eds., *East European Security Reconsidered* (Washington, D.C.: Woodrow Wilson Center Press, 1993), pp. 58–61.

33. In 1938, for example, a well-equipped and fully mobilized Czechoslovak army was on alert before the Munich Conference and was prepared to fight, a fact that has generated lively speculation as to the course of World War II had Hitler become bogged down in Czechoslovakia. For a documented viewpoint on this subject, see the article by Czech historian Karel Bartošek, "Could We Have Fought? The 'Munich Complex' in Czech

Policies and Czech Thinking," in Norman Stone and Eduard Strouhal, eds., *Czechoslovakia: Crossroads and Crises, 1918–1988* (New York: St. Martin's Press, 1989), pp. 101–119.

34. See Andrew Michta, *East Central Europe After the Warsaw Pact: Security Dilemmas in the 1990s* (New York: Greenwood Press, 1992), p. 116.

35. The masculine pronoun is used here because the 1990 federal legislation on military service proscribes the conscription of women in peacetime. Women may enlist voluntarily.

36. *Prague Post*, October 4, 1994, p. 8a.

37. Michta, *East Central Europe After the Warsaw Pact*, p. 124.

38. *Rudé právo*, October 4, 1990, reprinted in FBIS-EEU-90-198, October 12, 1990, p. 18.

39. The first civilian Czechoslovak defense minister was appointed to replace Vacek in October 1990. The new minister, Luboš Dobrovský, was a former foreign correspondent and Charter 77 dissident active in the founding of Civic Forum. He served as Foreign Ministry spokesman and deputy foreign minister after the Velvet Revolution.

40. Jan Obrman, "The Czechoslovak Armed Forces: The Reform Continues," *Radio Free Europe/Radio Liberty Research Report* 1:6 (February 7, 1992), p. 49.

41. Slovakia's personnel structuring program is expected to be complete by the end of 1995, bringing the army down to about 47,000 in uniform. Czech debate continues regarding the eventual size of its military establishment.

42. See, for example, Defense Minister Dobrovský's comments in "Profesionální armáda—hudba daleké budoucnosti," *Právo lidu*, December 10, 1991.

43. See especially Obrman, "The Czechoslovak Armed Forces," pp. 53–54. An Association of Slovak Soldiers was formed in 1991 to protect the expression of Slovak patriotism. This kind of Slovak response heightened federal government concern over possible military polarization along national lines.

44. Jan Urban, "The Czech and Slovak Republics: Security Consequences of the Breakup of the CSFR," in Regina Cowen Karp, ed., *Central and Eastern Europe: The Challenge of Transition* (Oxford, England: Oxford University Press, 1993), p. 120.

8

DOMESTIC REFORM
AND INTEGRATION
WITH THE WEST:
THE TRIPLE TRANSITION
AND INTERNATIONAL
RELATIONS

For the Czech and Slovak Republics, as for contemporary European countries generally, foreign policy looms large in state management. In the former Eastern bloc countries, the onerous tasks of domestic transformation are so interwoven with the ties that bind the postcommunist countries to their neighbors as to make it very difficult to disentangle the two. Every domestic policy decision is made with an ever-present concern over how well the decision will conform to the model of the cooperative and responsible Eurocitizen. Even the politicians who play a game of backlash politics by raising the alarm about a sellout to the West are responding to the very real pressures and incentives to seek closer European integration.

The immediate foreign policy problem of the transformation process, therefore, was to demonstrate that all the desirable domestic changes were indeed occurring—hence an almost obsessive concern with international image. "Image" is a broad term, but although it may appear to lack specific content, it is nonetheless a focal concern for all new regimes in the region. How does the world perceive us? The political debate is rife with agonizing over this question. Facing revelations of pervasive corruption, nearly three-fifths of the Czech public in a 1994 survey worried that media coverage of domestic scandals would travel abroad and shame the new state.[1] Slovak domestic politics is a continuous tug-of-war over the definition of the country's standing abroad. Image is a particularly pressing problem for these transitional regimes because they need to remain on good terms with a broad spectrum of international actors who are gatekeepers to global and continental institutions with important incentives to offer.

Why does the image problem loom so large? What incentives does the West have to offer? On what terms? In the broadest sense, the gatekeepers have it in their power to confer respectability or legitimacy on the new regimes. Specific acts of diplomatic recognition and ratification of membership in regional and international organizations are important in themselves as symbolic acceptance of the right of the transitional East European states to belong to the world community and to Europe. More specifically, the interlocking web of memberships is a guarantor of positive consideration for aid, investment, support in negotiating outstanding issues with neighbors, and a share in Western European prosperity and stability.

All of these interests have acted as incentives for good behavior on the part of new states. And what constitutes good behavior? There are several litmus tests. "Good behavior" means tailoring domestic policy to the precepts and operations of Western market democracies. A clear commitment to marketization and privatization, and fidelity to the maxims of budgetary and monetary responsibility, all mark a state that is preparing itself to fit into the existing Western economic network. Stable parliamentary institutions, the capacity for peaceful resolution of internal political conflicts, the absence of pressing claims by minorities and other domestic actors—these are further evidence of European civic-mindedness, sending the message that the state would not be a "problem child" in the new world order.

For pre-1992 Czechoslovakia, whose policies were generally moving in the "right" direction, the particular sticking point was the resolution of the Czech-Slovak dispute, which West European governments were correct to see as an impediment to the stabilization of political and economic policy. We have seen the way that deadlock on the national question stalemated other reform efforts. As a barometer of the effect that this stalemate had on the West, it is interesting to look at the changes in investment risk assessment. Western economic forecasts regularly include assessments of just how risky it is to invest in a given country; these assessments incorporate judgments both on economic prospects and political stability. In the initial year of the Velvet Revolution, Czechoslovakia was privileged to be viewed as the lowest risk postcommunist economy; a prominent risk assessor, the *Economist* Intelligence Unit, placed the country in the mid-twenties to low thirties on a risk scale of zero to l00.

Czechoslovakia's evaluation changed markedly in early 1991, following the first major unresolved controversy over the division of power within the state; the risk assessment levels nearly doubled in only three months. Risk assessment levels remained higher (although still comparable to other Central European countries) until the resolution of the national question in the summer of 1992. Normally, one might expect the impending dissolution of a country to increase risk levels, but this was a case of a peaceful settlement that removed a roadblock to further reform; accordingly, the Czech Republic's risk levels were abruptly halved, returning to the mid-twenties, after it was clear that the state would divide peacefully, and it recovered its former favored position among postcommunist economies (the Russian risk rating was 90, and Hungary's and Poland's hovered around 50).[2]

Although this is only a single indicator, it is a concrete example of the kind of scrutiny East European states were receiving from the West and of the payoffs of dealing with internal problems that troubled Western observers. What we are seeing here is clear evidence that the internal triple transition had an important external dimension as well. Democratization, marketization, and national identity politics interacted at the international level just as they did in domestic politics. Foreign governments and international organizations monitored the progress of the internal transformations in each state and determined the scope of external support and cooperation in large part on the basis of their assessment of that progress. If Czechs and Slovaks wanted significant foreign economic support for new and fragile domestic institutions, they would have to behave themselves by showing respect for Western democratic norms, economic frameworks, and national tolerance. In short, *all* phases of the triple transition counted in Western evaluations of worthiness for economic assistance and inclusion in Western institutions.

Unified Czechoslovakia experienced the weight of Western concern over its unresolved national question. Once the state dissolved, however, the Western response to the two newly independent states diverged. The Czech Republic, vigilant in proclaiming its Europeanness, was considerably less plagued with "image problems" than its neighbors, especially Slovakia. Havel's moral stature and Klaus's highly touted commitment to rapid marketization and privatization made a potent and favorable impression, and the country's general economic progress and political stability raised no alarm signals in the West. The Czech credit rating with Western financial analysts such as Standard & Poor's is by far the highest in the postcommunist region, and the Czech economy ranked twelfth freest in the world in a 1994 Heritage Foundation survey, ranking well ahead of other postcommunist countries and even ahead of Western states such as Spain, France, or Italy (Slovakia ranked twenty-ninth).[3]

Slovakia's situation was less enviable. Marked abroad as the home wrecker in the failed Czech-Slovak marriage—a somewhat inaccurate but pervasive impression—the Mečiar government suffered further erosion of its image after independence. Mečiar's governments were widely perceived as fomenters of political instability at home, and their democratic credentials were impeached by international perceptions that Slovakia had developed an inadequate minority policy and authoritarian tendencies in dealings with critics—the parliamentary opposition, the president, and the media. In economics, Slovakia under Mečiar was seen as dragging its feet on marketization and privatization and equivocal in its commitment to Europe. Since Mečiar's response to the image problem was often to inveigh against the opposition parties as disloyal to "his" state, the image problem persisted. In March 1996 an amendment to the penal code, termed the Law for the Protection of the Republic, raised further international concern that journalists and opposition leaders (especially minority politicians) might face criminal penalties of up to five years in prison for undermining the state with criticism of the government.

In fact, the foreign policy of the new Slovak state did not start with the premise of full identification with the West at all. Mečiar and some other Slovak leaders initially took a different view of Slovak identity in its regional setting. In translating Slovakia's geographic setting and historical ties into a focused policy framework, these policymakers thought it might be rational and desirable to balance between East and West, looking toward relationships with Western Europe as well as with the countries of the former Soviet Union to the east. Mečiar enumerated a number of Russian economic interests in Slovakia, including Slovakia's value as a transit country for Russian trade and energy pipelines to the West.[4]

Was this balancing act too unstable a platform for a country that needed recognition, investment, and assistance from the West—assistance that seemed to have eluded them when they were part of the ČSFR? Perhaps so, because if this initial posture was intended as a declaration of independence, it appears to have been a transitory one. Slovak experimentation with the idea of balancing between East and West had the unsettling effect of troubling the gatekeepers to West Europe, who were inclined to question Slovakia's commitment to a Western-style democracy and market in any case because of its internal problems. Mečiar's subsequent efforts to show the proper attitude to the West, which had clearly emerged by the fall of 1993, never gained full credence, however. In the spring of 1994, the Moravčík coalition government mounted a damage control operation in which most of its policies were oriented toward refurbishing the Slovak image as a responsible partner. As this government took office, President Kováč, its ally, told journalists: "I would like this Government to succeed in raising the political credibility of Slovakia abroad. It should be able to persuade the politicians and the banks and the businessmen that Slovakia wants to be a stable, democratic country, a country that wants to join Europe's political and economic structures."[5] The Moravčík government was more successful than Mečiar had been in reassuring the West of Slovak respect for minority rights and of its commitment to market reform and democracy. The setback suffered by the coalition in the September 1994 elections, however, found Slovakia's third Mečiar government coalition back on the Western doubtful list.

There is due cause for Slovak concern. A government with a reputation for having an uncertain commitment to minority rights or freedom of expression can pay a penalty in flows of investment and international aid. This was the problem of the Mečiar government in Slovakia; for example, the denial of a $246 million loan to the country in November 1994 by the European Parliament was understood as a rebuke to the "unclear and confusing" situation in Slovakia, which appeared to Western institutions to represent a marginal commitment to all elements of the triple transition.[6] In the first quarter of 1995, direct foreign investment in Slovakia hit a postcommunist low, reportedly in response to the unstable domestic situation, although the second quarter recorded a slight recovery. By the fall of 1995, the Western warnings very specifically centered on the possibility that nondemocratic behavior could delay entry into the European Union and result in the suspension of EU aid and the closing of the EU office in Slovakia.[7] Slovakia's recent strong economic performance is all the more striking for occurring despite foreign investor hesitancy.

Since 1989, a number of Slovak politicians intent on forging a solid Slovak identity have said, "Europe can wait." But these politicians have not been happy with the economic consequences. It would not be exaggerating to say that the present transition under way in East Central Europe is a partially "brokered" transition—brokered by the external forces that can exert at least marginal leverage on the process of change by extending or withholding incentives for technical cooperation, institutional membership, and other "carrots." This leverage does not always have the desired effect. Some forces loose in the region, such as the conflict in the former Yugoslavia, have not been amenable to direct pressure and response. In less inflammatory circumstances, however, most of the postcommunist states, including the Czech and Slovak Republics, have modified their domestic policies to some degree to meet European standards. In this chapter, we will look more closely at the interaction of the triple transition and the international environment in the Czech and Slovak cases.

This way of looking at the relevance of the international community has a somewhat negative, coercive coloration. It almost suggests that the postcommunist countries have lost control of their own internal destinies again in their efforts to meet Western standards. There is a more affirmative way to evaluate the impact of the foreign policy environment. After all, Germany after World War II was "forced to be free" by military defeat and allied occupation. This was truly a coercive path to democratization—what Alfred Stepan terms a "democratic imposition" by external powers.[8] However, it was also a path to German revitalization and autonomy. For Central Europeans, the search for revitalization has been substantially less constrained than this and above all has represented an attempt to find a solution to the broad security problem that has plagued the whole region since independence in 1918—the dilemma of how small countries survive and prosper in the shadow of larger powers. The answer of the 1990s is to seek integration in larger and more powerful continental institutions. In historical perspective, this approach to safeguarding security and prosperity is certainly more attractive than the experience of the earlier twentieth century of groping unaided for protection against considerably more malevolent outside forces than any that directly threaten the region today.

International Dimensions of the Political Transition

As we have seen, all aspects of the postcommunist transition in the Czech Republic and Slovakia have had important international dimensions. Meeting the standards of West Europe and conforming to its practices have been important influences on domestic policy, blurring the lines between internal and external issues.

External involvement in encouraging democracy has been a defining feature of the post–cold war era in Europe. A look at the "input" side of East European politics, the linkage institutions connecting elites with mass publics, offers illustrative examples. Western research institutions and foundations have bankrolled an infusion of expertise in public opinion polling in order to improve the quality of surveys of public policy and electoral preferences. Nascent parties have received foreign support for basic equipment (computers, fax machines, campaign materials) and for the formulation of programs and tactics; the sources have included official government programs (the U.S. Fund for Democracy, for example), individual Western parties (the Konrad Adenauer Foundation of the German Christian Democrats, the Fritz Ebert Foundation of the German Social Democrats, Forza Italia for the Movement for a Democratic Slovakia), and international federations of ideologically associated parties. In July 1990 a delegation from the U.S. National Council to Support the Democracy Movements arrived at a Prague conference laden with "democracy kits"—word processors, fax machines, and photocopy machines to be distributed to new political groups to enhance free communication.[9] The electoral systems themselves emerged from a process of institutional design that included technical assistance in drafting electoral laws and election monitoring (drawing, for example, on the legal expertise of the Venice Commission of the Council of Europe). Elected legislators have moved into a parliamentary setting that is institutionally reinforced by external programs of training and resource provision for parliamentarians and legislative staffs (as from the Speaker's Special Task Force on the Development of Parliamentary Institutions in Eastern Europe of the U.S. House of Representatives).[10]

A prime mover in external political influences on the reshaping of domestic politics has been the Council of Europe (CE), the first of the post–World War II European multilateral institutions and the one with the clearest mandate for promoting political and social tolerance and democratic governance. As central guardian of European democratic norms, the Council of Europe became an important target of affiliation for the Eastern states. Admission was a validation of at least a minimal threshold of democratic performance on the part of the admitted state. However, the certification process did not consist of a single act of acceptance. To be certified as a democracy meant to undergo an investigatory process that started with sustained and detailed consultation between the CE and the aspirant member, and that did not cease with admission. Fledgling members were in effect on probation subject to follow-up evaluation pending eventual unconditional membership.

What is most significant about this feedback cycle is its content. Membership in the CE did entail incurring certain international obligations to fellow members, but eligibility hinged equally on the character of a state's internal politics. No state was of course compelled to submit to vetting by the Council of Europe, but those who did aspire to membership mortgaged parts of their sovereignty and agenda-setting autonomy to the organization. Over the course of its almost fifty-year history, the Council of Europe has ratified some 150 conventions binding on its membership, and new members are expected to come into compliance with these conventions. Ratification of CE human rights protocols (the European Convention on Human Rights), for example, entitles individual citizens or groups of citizens in member states to appeal their grievances to the CE Human Rights Committee and to the European Court of Human Rights, which effectively extends the international monitoring process indefinitely into the future.

Membership in the Council of Europe was thus not a single "carrot" or one-time incentive to behavior modification but rather an ongoing process of accommodation with the CE's definitions of constructive democratic behavior, both codified and uncodified. Membership was not only a reward but also a normative structure that set standards and a monitoring structure that evaluated compliance to the standards; it was thus a mechanism for encouraging favorable results on a broad range of domestic and foreign policy issues over time.

Czechoslovakia joined the Council of Europe in 1991, and it faced intermittent CE interventions on such issues as the lustration controversy. Both republics sought CE advice in drafting their new constitutions in 1992. When the Czech and Slovak Republics were recertified individually for CE membership in 1993 after the division of the joint state, both countries continued to be monitored for democratic behavior. In each case, the offer of membership was accompanied by specific, enumerated expectations as to which problem areas for democratic practice remained unresolved. Slovakia, in particular, was expected to act on legislation safeguarding bilingual public signs and to submit to CE review of its treatment of the Hungarian minority at six-month intervals.

Although Western governments and institutions have been heavily engaged in an advisory role during the reconstruction of Eastern political institutions, their influence stems not only from any democratic wisdom and experience they may have accumulated but also from the understanding that only recognized democracies can hope to join NATO and the European Union. Accordingly, membership in the Council of Europe is valuable in itself but still more so for being an indicator of the democratic credentials in the ongoing search for inclusion in the new European order.

What is the West watching for? What is the test of democracy? By and large, most East European countries have passed the test of competitive elections.[11] The West has shown significantly more concern about the routinized daily functioning of government. In the case of the Czechs, the Western countries have expressed little general doubt about political stability thus far. Slovakia is a different case. Western leaders and opinion-makers tend to share with the opposition to Mečiar's government uneasiness both about his confrontational politics and about impediments to a free press. As conflict between the Slovak prime minister and president escalated in the fall of 1995, Western governments began to express strong concern about the need, in the words of a U.S. spokesman, "to reestablish cooperation among the constitutionally established institutions of the state of Slovakia." In October 1995 British Foreign Secretary Malcolm Rifkind warned visiting Slovak Foreign Minister Juraj Schenk that Britain and the other EU members were worried about "the trend of recent political development in Slovakia."[12] In November the European Parliament approved a strongly worded resolution urging the MDS-led Slovak government to respect democratic principles in its dealings with the opposition and the presidency. The MDS did not assuage concerns when a spokesman compared this warning with the ultimatums of Hitler when he "first sent demarches to states and then occupied them with tanks."[13]

By far the greatest international concern, however, lies in the area of intersection between national tensions and democratic politics. A democracy that has not settled its national conflicts cannot be considered a stable democracy. The framers of the U.S. Constitution long ago recognized that representative government had to balance majority rule with minority rights; the protection of minority interests and opinions was built into the separation of powers precisely in order to avoid the "tyranny of the majority." The framers were not thinking specifically in ethnonational terms, of course; in Eastern Europe, though, the guarantees for ethnic minorities are very central to the more general problem of assuring that minority interests will be protected. The international dimension of this problem is the focus of the following section.

National Identity and the International Setting

The impact of external expectations and concerns on the national question is the most sensitive of all the transitional issues. Historically, the principle of sovereignty has meant that each state has formal legal equality with all the others and that interference in the internal domestic affairs of a state is a violation of sovereignty. In practice, even a very powerful state has only limited sovereignty; it has always been true that dependence on the international community has shaped internal policies to some degree.

The difference between theory and practice, however, has been crumbling over time, and especially since World War II. Increasingly, member nations of international governmental organizations have been expected to assume obligations in return for the benefits of international cooperation—obligations that directly restrict sovereign decisions and limit the scope of government behavior. An important example is the UN Universal Declaration of Human Rights, to which all member nations are expected to subscribe. And in general since the founding of the UN, the body of treaty obligations that restrict sovereignty in the area of human rights has been growing.

In Europe, a landmark was the Helsinki Accord, part of a process that started in the 1970s; this process was important because it encompassed both regions of a divided Europe. Although the signatories of the original Helsinki Accord sat down to talk with rather different motives, the Soviet bloc members found that in addition to achieving their own goals (primarily the recognition of the existing borders in Europe), they also had to agree to a set of agreements (the "third basket") that pledged adherence to fair standards of free emigration, free speech, and other human rights. This formal agreement became a nuisance to communist states, as their internal repressive actions were subject to increasing international scrutiny, and as they had to cope with local Helsinki Watch committees organized by dissidents to monitor and document bad behavior. The legacy of the original talks was the ongoing CSCE forum for negotiation and discussion.

The original Helsinki statement of human rights resembled those of other international bodies of the era in focusing on individual rights rather than the collective rights of national minorities. However, the eruption of national tensions in the former communist countries soon inclined the West Europeans to give consideration to the value of the CSCE as an arena for addressing minority questions as well. As this notion came into practice, the CSCE was of course once more moving into an area that had in the past been considered a sacrosanct preserve of state sovereignty.

General European concern with the security consequences of national tensions was reinforced by the fact that two CSCE member states, Russia and Hungary, had intense and specific interest in minority rights. Each of these states had a large co-national population living beyond its own borders (in the Russian case, minority groups of Russians totaling 25 million lived in the fourteen former Soviet Republics separated from Russia after the collapse of the Soviet Union in 1991). In both Russia and Hungary there was strong public concern with the treatment or mistreatment of their kinsmen abroad, and the CSCE seemed a valuable path of influence for both states. Crude and direct individual Russian or Hungarian pressure on the minority issue, by coercion or otherwise, was all too likely to offend the international community. Countries that wished to develop stable relations with the West knew that it would be wise not to throw their weight around too conspicuously. Once the CSCE took up the cause of minority rights protection by establishing a High Commissioner for Minorities, however, the protection of Hungarian and Russian minorities abroad became part of a legitimate international effort rather than the hardly impartial agenda of two individual members. In this guise, it was more difficult for third-party states—those with Russian and Hungarian minorities—to dismiss the investigation of their minority policies as merely the unwarranted intrusion of a nosy neighbor. In the first CSCE session on minorities, in July 1991, the head of the Hungarian delegation hailed the session as confirming "that the national minorities are an international issue, and not merely the internal affair of the countries concerned."[14]

Slovakia, a target of this unwelcome attention because of its sizable Hungarian minority, has tended to resent any form of Hungarian government intercession on behalf of this minority as a violation of its sovereignty. A characteristic expression of this view in the media presented Hungary's stance as "an obvious effort to disrupt the internal territorial integrity of neighboring states" and as an "expansionist policy" that "strives outwardly to adapt to European norms, without, however, renouncing in the least its power objectives."[15] In short, many Slovak politicians and citizens feared the territorial revision of the 1920 Treaty of Trianon that ceded "upper Hungary" to Slovakia after World War I; further, they feared that the ultimate loyalty of the Hungarian minority in Slovakia lay in Budapest. Accordingly, the Slovak government insisted that the long-delayed joint treaty between the two countries include border guarantees.

Hungary in turn regards the treatment of neighboring Hungarian minorities as an important yardstick in determining relations with Slovakia, Romania, Ukraine, and Serbia. Hungary's first postcommunist prime minister, Jozsef Antall, sparked immense controversy when he claimed that he felt himself to be prime minister of 15 million Hungarians. It took only a quick arithmetic calculation based on Hungary's population—ten million—to reach the conclusion that Antall was claiming responsibility for "their" Hungarians across the border. Outraged, Slovak Prime Minister Mečiar responded: "Never in my life would I dare declare that I am the premier of all the Slovaks in the world. . . . I therefore reject out of principle the claim of the premier of the Hungarian republic that he is the premier of all 15 million Hungarians. . . . Our Hungarians have their own government in Bratislava and Prague. . . . To this, we reply that our state border is inviolable . . . this is our country, and it will never again be Upper Hungary."[16] The danger here is not currently a military one, despite Slovakia's repeated questioning of Hungary's territorial ambitions. The most important security damage that Hungary can do to Slovakia is to tarnish its image in the eyes of the West and hence to impede Slovakia's progress into Europe. In fact, Hungary, having achieved membership in the Council of Europe in 1990, was tempted to try to block Slovakia's admission into the Council in 1993 on the grounds that Slovakia had not met the Council's standards for democratic treatment of minorities. The Hungarian government was persuaded to content itself with an abstention on the admission vote after gaining Council approval of the requirement that Slovakia submit to biannual monitoring of the minority situation as a condition of admission. The Council of Europe also obtained Slovak agreement to allow the use of bilingual road signs and the use of Hungarian family names, two issues we have seen to be highly controversial in Slovakia. It was not until the Moravčík government took office the following year that Slovakia took action on these promises, however.

Hungary's pressure on Slovakia is a two-edged sword, since the Hungarian government must pursue the protection of its co-nationals without itself appearing shrill, hypernationalist, and, in short, a bad European citizen. Direct pressure has at times been counterproductive, raising concerns in the West about regional stability—hence Hungary's move to "sanitize" its pressure on Slovakia by channeling the issue of minority treatment through the CSCE process. Thus far the contest between the two neighbors has not produced a clear victor, in that other European states have resisted efforts to take sides and have preferred a more impartial mediating role through institutions such as the CSCE, the Council of Europe, or the World Court, or through individual diplomatic initiatives. The CSCE has held several exploratory sessions with Slovakia on its minority policies.

As for direct relations between Hungary and Slovakia, they remain correct if not cordial, despite the tremendous emotional impact of the minority issue in each country. The Hungarian-Slovak treaty was finally signed in the spring of 1995; the Hungarian government had stipulated as a condition for concluding the agreement that the Slovak government first sign the Council of Europe's Framework Convention for the Protection of National Minorities. The Mečiar government complied, signing the convention in February 1995 and ratifying it in June. The Hungarian-Slovak treaty itself, however, ratified by Hungary in June 1995, faced a year's delay in Slovakia, until March 1996, because of dissension in the governing coalition. The Slovak National Party held out against ratification, and the heavy price of its approval was a series of measures that further alarmed Slovakia's Hungarian minority: the stronger Slovak language law; an unfavorable drawing of regional boundaries; the Law on the Protection of the Republic; and an interpretative appendix to the treaty disclaiming the argument that its minority protection clauses would mandate the granting of collective minority rights. This mortgaging of the treaty commitments stalled the exchange of ratification instruments with Hungary.[17]

Despite these ratification controversies, it is obvious that both governments felt external pressure to conclude a treaty and to demonstrate continued progress in agreement on the minority issue. As Slovak President Michal Kováč put it, "We both know that neither the European Community nor NATO are ready to welcome any new members who would be incapable of putting an end to quarrels."[18] External pressures have thus clearly shaped both the Hungarian recourse to international bodies for assuring minority rights, and the Slovak willingness to accept those commitments, however reluctantly.

In fact, Slovak reluctance demonstrates the limits of international influence on internal policies. While successive Slovak governments have indeed undertaken the commitments required by multilateral organizations for the protection of national minorities, it is far less clear that the spirit of these commitments has been honored. Representatives of the Hungarian minority in Slovakia have repeatedly appealed to organizations like the Council of Europe to protest government actions detrimental to their interests; when they have taken this recourse, the government counters with charges that they are damaging the country's image abroad. In November 1995 the Mečiar government's passage of a new and restrictive language law went through in defiance of Hungarian protests that the law would violate provisions of the pending Hungarian-Slovak treaty and a European Parliament resolution requesting the withdrawal of the law from consideration. Slovak acceptance of general principles, in other words, has hardly meant automatic enforcement of these principles.

The foreign policy dimension of Czech nationality policy is rather different. European multilateral institutions such as the CSCE and the Council of Europe have been critical of Czech treatment of its Roma population. However, the central foreign policy relationship for the Czech Republic is clearly with Germany; Germany is simultaneously the country's leading trading partner, the leading foreign investor, and the primary champion of Czech integration into Western institutions. Yet, as we have seen, all these important roles interact with the "German question" in its varying manifestations. Thus, Germany plays all of these roles while also representing the haven of Sudeten German activists and a neighboring force so overwhelming that the question of Czech sovereignty in the shadow of German political and economic power remains a viable electoral issue and a challenge to Czech statecraft.

Because Sudeten Germans have continued to press for the revocation of the Beneš deportation and property confiscation decrees and to lobby the German government for action, the issue has colored all aspects of Czech relations with Germany, complicating what has otherwise been a largely cooperative economic and political interaction. The treaty of German-Czechoslovak cooperation signed in 1992 (subsequently renegotiated after Czech independence) became a battleground, as the document was scrutinized paragraph by paragraph and word by word to assure that the Czechoslovak government was making no concessions on the Sudeten German question. To Sudeten German demands for high-level official talks with the Czech government, Czech Foreign Minister Jozef Zieleniec sharply responded in 1994 that he had no intention of changing the results of World War II.

Where the Sudeten German question intersects with economic issues, it has produced complications. A case in point is the Ingolstadt-Kralupy oil pipeline, vital to Czech interests if the country is to wean itself from energy dependence on Russia.[19] The pipeline project was contingent on the cooperation of the Bavarian government, electorally constrained to champion the Sudeten German interests of those deportees resident on its territory; most of the deported Sudeten Germans settled in Bavaria, where they created a powerful voting bloc in the dominant Christian Socialist Union—longtime CSU leader Franz Joseph Strauss termed the Sudeten Germans "the fourth tribe of Bavaria." Despite the group's continued political clout, Bavarian negotiators on the pipeline issue have officially denied any connection between the Sudeten question and delays in approving the pipeline project. However, the Czech government, detecting a clear linkage, had begun to explore alternative energy transport routes before the Bavarian government finally accorded official approval to the project in December 1994. If any case illustrates the enduring power of national issues in Central Europe, it is this peculiar case of the influence of a *former* minority on the politics and economics of transition.

The German federal government, although far less wedded to the Sudeten cause, nonetheless behaved circumspectly when facing the potential wrath of the Sudeten electoral constituency before the fall 1994 German elections. Polemics on the issue mounted after the elections, however, and an accord remained elusive following further German challenges to the legality of the deportation. The Czech government, of course, has also been constrained by hostile public opinion on the Sudeten issue. In 1995 more than two-thirds of the Czech public continued to reject an official dialogue with Germany on the matter, and opposition to dialogue was particularly fierce in the northern Bohemian regions where the primary deportations occurred. Yet, until this issue is decided, the larger Czech economic and political goals in the European arena that are served by cooperation with Germany will be impeded, not least because Sudeten German deportees have petitioned the European Parliament not to accept Czech or Slovak applications to the European Union until Sudeten German claims are satisfied and the Beneš decrees repealed. In the long run, however, commonalities of interest in other areas are likely to prove determinant. Either the two governments will find a very carefully worded formula to dispose of the issue, or they will work around it.

On a continental scale, one of the largest national identity problems of the late twentieth century has been the waves of refugees and immigrants that wash against the borders of Western Europe. The existing pressure from the Third World was reinforced in the late 1980s by the prospect of Eastern migration from the former communist countries to the more prosperous and stable West, amounting to the largest population movement on the continent since the displacements of World War II. West Europe has not coped gracefully with this onslaught; rising foreign populations in Germany and France have increased local sensitivity to the possible dilution of national identity, giving new life—and a new issue—to right-wing nationalist extremism. In fact, migration issues are being treated in primarily negative terms as an "internal security" problem, despite economists' arguments that the additions to the labor force in graying populations with a shrinking labor pool could be helpful.

In Germany, a wave of asylum-seekers that had surged to 438,000 a year by 1992 prompted a tightening of Germany's liberal asylum law in 1993 in an effort to control or halt in-migration and to undercut the right-wing appeal on this issue. The largest single influx had entered through neighboring Czechoslovakia. Under the new rules, no asylum-seeker may enter Germany from a so-called "safe country" that observes human rights standards and international refugee conventions. Since all of Germany's neighbors fall into this category, including the Czech Republic, Germany is now legally unapproachable by land (one commentator suggested that the only legal refugee route into Germany was by parachute).

Central Europe has experienced the repercussions of the Western reluctance to absorb additional foreign populations. Although both Romania and the war-torn former Yugoslavia have generated considerable out-migration, the problem is not that vast hordes of Poles or Czechs or Hungarians or Slovaks wish to emigrate. In a 1993 poll, the latter four countries ranked as the least interested in emigration to the West of all the postcommunist states.[20] However, Germany's neighbors, who have signed the international refugee conventions and are obligated to take care of those who arrive, face the problem of coping with migrants from third countries who are headed for Germany but who are stopped at the German border. No Central European state wishes to end up as the default option for frustrated émigrés trying to move west; none of the postcommunist states relishes the status of "receiving" country, particularly in a period of economic transition. The dilemma has spawned a scramble to sign "readmission treaties" with neighbors to facilitate the repatriation of illegal entrants.

The Czech and Slovak Republics have been no exception. Germany negotiated a supplemental refugee agreement with the Czech Republic in 1993 on the matter of returning rejected asylum applicants who had entered through the Czech Republic. Included in the agreement were German commitments for financial compensation for the costs of repatriating rejected refugees and for the fortification of Czech borders against illegal immigration. For Slovakia, which received no such concessions, the agreement created friction because of the "one-sided" tightening of Czech border controls with Slovakia. The new situation was doubly alarming because, in what Czech observers described as a "domino effect,"[21] it meant that the fence to discourage immigration had been moved further east, up to its own borders. At present, however, Slovakia only has a few hundred asylum applicants and a little over a thousand temporary refugees from the former Yugoslav republics.

The Czech Republic has experienced a larger foreign influx.[22] There were over 100,000 foreigners with either long-term or permanent residency in the country at the end of 1994,[23] and 5,000 applicants for refugee status. The Czech police must work overtime tracking illegal immigration. The government reported in late 1994 that police had detained almost 15,000 illegal immigrants in the first half of the year. Although some of this influx consists of refugees attempting to transit from the Third World to Western Europe, 90 percent of the illegal immigrants came from former communist countries. Interestingly, the illegal East European immigrants did not come from neighboring states but rather from the poorer, strife-torn states of southern Europe: Bulgaria, Romania, and the former Yugoslavia.[24] Scholars visiting the Czech Republic encounter a pervasive concern about the consequences of this mounting immigration pressure and are struck by the frequency with which the problem is raised as a security threat to domestic order. Ironically, in the case of refugee policy, it may be the East that is suffering from the national identity insecurities of the West, insecurities that have tightened Western border controls and immigrant admissions policies and allowed spillover migration to come to rest in the more prosperous of the neighboring Eastern countries.[25]

International Dimensions of the Economic Transition

Joining Europe: The Courting of the European Union

If the intercession of foreign actors in national identity politics has been the most sensitive issue, the international linkages on economic policy have been the most powerful. Since 1989, the Czech Republic and Slovakia have gone through a profound reorientation of their external economic ties from East to West. Under the prevailing conditions, the dismantling of Soviet economic control was in a sense all too rapid. CMEA, the bloc's economic organization, was disbanded in 1991 without fanfare. The problem in this case, as will become apparent, was that the fabric of economic relations within the bloc was ripped apart too soon, and too precipitately. The root of this disruptive effect was the continuing Soviet economic skid and the pattern of simultaneous economic dislocation regionwide; taken together, these parallel economic hardships radically cut back bloc purchasing power. The resultant collapse of bloc trade delivered a serious jolt to domestic economic transformation. This startling and abrupt deterioration of economic relations among Eastern countries, of course, pushed the Czech and Slovak Republics even harder and faster into the international economic arena.

In the late twentieth century, it is never really possible to chart a country's economic development in isolation from the global market. Global economic interdependence is not merely a catch-phrase. It is a reality, even for large states with strong resource bases like the United States, but all the more so for smaller countries. For the postcommunist states, economic interdependence has a special importance. In the first place, as we have seen, the economic model that governments wish to adapt could be described as an international one—the model of advanced industrial/postindustrial capitalism. Secondly, both citizens and leaders in the Czech and Slovak Republics repeatedly expressed support for rapid integration into European economic institutions. Virtually every major Czech and Slovak party supports full membership in the European Union. Public opinion follows the same pattern; in a poll conducted in February 1993, 84 percent of the respondents in the Czech Republic and 86 percent in Slovakia expressed support for EU membership.[26] Given this goal, the adoption of a Western economic model was hardly optional. The construction of political and economic institutions that would be compatible with those of the West was the benchmark of "eligibility" for economic integration with the West. Foreign policy and domestic reform therefore merged; progress at home would accelerate progress in meeting foreign policy goals.[27]

At a more specific level, each individual economic policy decision was also colored by the long-term aspirations of European integration. Architects of reform were careful to be mindful of Western standards in each area of economic transformation; the European Union in particular had set hundreds of standards for its members in product quality, environmental regulation, and occupational safety. It was sensible for an aspiring member to work toward meeting those standards to ease the path to acceptance and reduce later transition costs. The federal parliament of Czechoslovakia legislated a legal requirement that all new economic legislation be reviewed for compatibility with existing EU regulations, and special government bureaus were established as monitoring agencies. This effort is a clear reflection of the fact that, for the hopeful future EU member, the most important foreign policy decisions were actually domestic.

Neither the Czechs and Slovaks waited passively to be recognized as viable partners in European economic activity. The joint state, and later its two successors, campaigned continuously for immediate acceptance into West European institutions wherever possible and for intermediate "associate" relations where immediate acceptance was unlikely. This pattern of behavior was visible in both economic and security fields. The Council of Europe, with its restriction to democratic governments, was a promising immediate target of opportunity. Both the Czech and the Slovak governments negotiated vigorously and successfully to gain individual admission after the breakup of the common state.

In some respects admission to the Council of Europe was only a stepping stone. Full integration into Europe, and in particular into the European Union, was the longer-term objective. There was a long waiting list for the European Union, and the richer Scandinavian and Austrian applicants jumped to the head of the line in the early 1990s. The timing of their applications was a consequence of the end of the cold war, in which Sweden and Austria had been neutral. They had previously hesitated to make membership bids to the EU because EU members were also NATO members, and there was therefore a fear that EU membership could embroil neutral countries in cold war security squabbles. The end of the cold war after the collapse of the Soviet bloc removed that obstacle, and the EU admitted Norway, Finland, Sweden, and Austria in the spring of 1994.[28]

The Central European countries must now await the outcome of the EU's internal crisis of direction. If certain core EU countries decide to devote their energies to the closer integration of an inner circle within the EU—a "two-speed Europe" that Eastern European countries see as unfavorable to their interests—then it may be a long wait before still more members are welcome. For the Central European states, the Czech and Slovak Republics among them, EU membership is the highest priority goal in foreign economic policy. Loudly warning of the potential dangers to stability of a new "iron curtain" or "poverty curtain" in a Europe divided by differential economic development levels, they have continued to press for signals from the West that their aspirations are respected.

Although reluctant to open the doors of the EU immediately, the governments of EU member states, in turn, were well aware that a failure to respond to these aspirations could undermine support for reform in the East. Therefore, they tried to temporize and compromise as they had done on NATO membership, first by offering the most promising postcommunist states special status as associate members of the EU. In the company of Hungary and Poland, Czechoslovakia gained an intermediate status of "associate membership" in the European Union in 1991, subsequently renegotiated as separate memberships for the Czech and Slovak Republics in 1993, after the state's dissolution. In addition to special concessions in trade and quota preferences, associate membership carried with it a general acknowledgment of (but no specific commitment to) the goal of eventual full membership for the contracting countries; in return, the new associate members made a commitment to bring their own postcommunist economies into conformity with EU standards.[29]

Associate membership was not a permanent solution. All of the East European states continued to press for a clearer timetable and a more explicit set of guidelines for future eligibility for full membership. In May 1995 the EU fulfilled its December 1994 pledge to develop such guidelines by publishing a preliminary White Paper on East European membership that delineated, in three hundred pages of detail, the legislative standards that the EU's postcommunist associate members would have to meet in order to merit consideration for full membership. Although there have been complaints that the standards are more stringent than many of the EU's current membership can meet, the Slovak government submitted a membership application in June 1995, with a target date for admission set at the year 2000. The Czech government followed suit in January 1996. The Czech Republic has already met some of the economic guidelines; the EU Trade Commissioner acknowledged that the Czechs could boast a balanced budget and unemployment statistics that western countries could envy.[30] But the impatient Czechs pose a problem for the EU in their eagerness to negotiate an early admission, ahead of the rest of the pack; Slovakia, with a less stellar economic track record, is more resigned to seeking entry in the company of other Central European states. In fact, facing increasing criticism from the EU for incipient authoritarian practices, Mečiar warned the Slovak public for the first time in April

1996 that Slovakia's entry into Western organizations might be delayed. Not surprisingly, he has blamed his opposition for misleading external actors about Slovakia's stability and commitment to democracy.

The quest to join Europe in the guise of the EU, then, has been a delicate balancing act for both sides. EU initiatives have consistently reflected an awareness of the need to "keep hope alive" in the East, by demonstrating ever more concretely that there is a path to membership and therefore a powerful incentive to continue economic and political reform. Even so, impatience and disillusionment in the East over EU intentions have not been fully countered, for the path to membership is clearly neither short nor simple, and the EU's continued trade barriers breed doubts about Western sincerity. Eastern pressures and expectations, therefore, push the EU to move slowly closer to accepting postcommunist members. On the one hand, to refuse to respond to these expectations would undercut the reform process. To respond too fully and quickly, on the other hand, would saddle the EU with the problems of partially reconstructed Eastern economies and resentful Western members who are struggling with their own sense of the EU's mission and scope.

Waiting for the European Union: Czech and Slovak Trade, Investment, and Assistance Policies

While they sit in the EU's waiting room, the Czech and Slovak Republics have focused their foreign economic policies on the more immediate prospect of sustaining domestic economic development through foreign assistance, trade, and investment.

Assistance was of particular concern to governments that lacked the expertise in capitalist market relations to make a smooth entry into the global economy. Although Eastern Europe is more economically advanced than many of the countries that have traditionally received international assistance, the expense and disruptiveness of the attempt to marketize has made foreign assistance an attractive supplement to domestic resources. The international community, and particularly the developed industrial nations, have worked through existing assistance organizations such as the International Monetary Fund (IMF) to channel support for the economic transformation in postcommunist countries. Traditionally, the IMF has been the champion of fiscal and monetary responsibility, expecting recipient governments to curb inflation and budgetary deficits and to maintain a stable currency. These expectations have frequently been nightmarishly challenging to Third World countries and to the less stable postcommunist states. Moreover, the impact of these restrictions have been controversial, since fiscal conservatism may dampen economic growth.

Czechoslovakia was fortunate to be able to deliver on the desired fiscal responsibility. This had broad benefits, since the IMF seal of good financial housekeeping often unleashes assistance funds from other organizations and encourages foreign investment as well. Slovak Finance Minister Rudolf Filkus described support from the major international lending institutions as "an indication for the European, and, perhaps, the world economy of the credibility of the Slovak economy, and . . . a challenge to foreign investors to invest in our country."[31] Likewise, Václav Klaus, who cast a critical eye on the IMF's economic prescriptions, nonetheless approved Czechoslovakia's efforts to join it because "it is important for us to have the kind of credit rating that IMF membership would indicate."[32]

Initially, then, the state readily received a multimillion dollar loan from the IMF to facilitate the economic transition. The Czech Republic triumphantly repaid their part of the loan in August 1994, five years ahead of schedule; it was the first former communist country to retire its indebtedness to the IMF. In announcing this coup, the Czech government added that it could handle its own credit needs in the future.

Slovakia, however, with a rockier economic road ahead, still needs the IMF and has already received two grants of additional IMF assistance since independence, one in the summer of 1993, and the second a year later. More recently, the Slovak government gained considerable approbation for forgoing a further IMF loan. It remains to be seen whether Slovakia can deliver on the pledges it made to contain government spending and control inflation in order to qualify for the existing IMF funds.

In addition to existing conduits for international assistance, however, both Western Europe and the United States developed specialized programs specifically focused on the postcommunist countries. Examples include the EBRD (European Bank for Reconstruction and Development) and PHARE, whose acronym stands for "Polish and Hungarian Assistance for the Reconstruction of Europe," a reflection of the program's inception in early 1989, when Poland and Hungary were the only states clearly committed to economic reforms. PHARE currently extends aid to most of the postcommunist countries. The United States developed its own assistance programs, coordinated under the umbrella of the U.S. Agency for International Development. Janine Wedel has emphasized that these aid programs, in contrast to those targeting the Third World, were from their inception not only directed to economic growth but also to the systematic transformation of postcommunist economies and political arrangements.[33] In short, foreign assistance was consciously aimed at fostering the triple transition.

From the beginning, the Czechoslovak government differentiated itself from its neighbors by downplaying the value of foreign aid, deeming it far less important than normal economic interactions in trade and investment.[34] However, it welcomed assistance targeted at specific pressing domestic problems. PHARE, for example, has contributed millions to the task of helping Czechoslovakia and its successor states to fund the development of effective pollution monitoring systems, to construct waste disposal facilities, and to install desulfurization equipment to reduce air pollution. PHARE also funds the technical upgrading of nuclear facilities, helping to subsidize foreign contracting such as the Westinghouse award for the Temelín plant.[35] Environmental assistance supports policy initiatives in an area squeezed by the budgetary priorities of privatization—and in turn benefits West Europe, because spillover effects of Eastern environmental pollution do not respect official borders.

The question of assistance was more complex than the calculation of what the West was willing to spend. Some Western voices called for a new Marshall Plan similar to the post–World War II infusion of financial support for the rebuilding of Europe after its wartime devastation. However, the parallel between Western Europe in the late 1940s and East Europe in the 1990s is not an exact one. West Europe had suffered massive physical destruction after World War II, but the institutions and human skills for a market economy remained as building blocks for the reconstruction period. In Eastern Europe more than a generation later, much more had been lost and much more needed to be done to revitalize the administered economies. Institutional memory, business and management skills, and all the intangible basics of a market economy had been lost in the four decades since East Europe had last experienced capitalism. Rebuilding would be a longer, more expensive process than the Marshall Plan had underwritten, and the recovery of technical know-how was as important as the infusion of cash.

The problem was not, therefore, just to attract enough Western support but rather to attract *useful* Western support. As minister of finance, Klaus declared himself swamped in offers of assistance that he was not sure what to do with: "I have at least ten suggestions for creating a business administration school in Czechoslovakia. I have several foundations suggesting the same. Three or four are American, two are Canadian. Then come France, England, West Germany, saying, 'Well, don't just accept the American way of studying business administration.'" "We have hundreds of Western banks offering scholarships, fellowships, for people in my ministry," he added. "And I say, 'I'm sorry, but I can't make use of your offer because who speaks English at a level that he can spend three months in the finance ministry of Canada?' My assistants are doubly essential to me here, and they cannot spend three months in Canada at this time. I desperately need them here."[36] Klaus was voicing a universal dilemma. The needed skills were spread very thin in the new system, and those most capable of absorbing useful skills were also those most needed for the current operations of the government and economy. The U.S. Congressional Research Service's parliamentary development assistance program ended up running its personnel training sessions in the home country to avoid pulling essential staff members away from their jobs for extended periods.[37]

There were also tensions over the form that Western assistance took. Eventually, East Central European governments complained that some 90 percent of the technical assistance granted them went into the pockets of foreign consultants with highly variable knowledge of the region who often visited for a matter of weeks and made only a superficial impact. Considerable resentment built up over the shuttle of foreign advisers who swooped down to tell transitional governments what to do and then flew out on the next plane. A Czech aid coordinator's letter to a Western scholar in 1994 encapsulates the cynicism bred by the encounter with international donors.[38]

> The salaries paid to foreign assistance contractors advising government ministries are widely known by Czech officials to be stratospheric in local economic terms—it is known, for example, that the European Union PHARE advisers are paid six times more (and upwards) than the Ministers they are paid to assist. This of course causes a certain level of cynicism on the part of the local beneficiaries regarding just who is the intended beneficiary of foreign assistance.

Increasingly, it was felt that a larger proportion of technical assistance should be invested in funding the longer-term and more sustained efforts of local experts whose working knowledge of the problems would yield more concrete results at a considerably lower hourly fee.

Trade posed a different set of problems. Countries of the former Soviet bloc were, of course, anxious to realign their trade patterns enough to foster development and insulate themselves from the negative impact of the foundering Soviet economy. For Czechoslovakia, this was a particularly pressing problem because of its previous heavy dependence on Soviet trade. Reorientation to new markets was somewhat easier for Hungary and Poland, whose trade with the USSR was only about a quarter of overall volume, than for Czechoslovakia, which had depended on the Soviet market for nearly 40 percent of its imports and exports. Yet progress toward the development of Western markets was impeded by the need to upgrade Czech and Slovak production quality and technology to world market standards.

What was frustrating to Czech and Slovak enterprise managers was that even retooling did not always prove to be sufficient. The experience of the Slovak steel industry (described in Box 8.1) is an illustration of the larger problem that the new industry of the East has faced. The EU's grant of associate membership to Central European states has not lowered critical trade barriers in those so-called "sensitive" areas, such as steel, textiles and agricultural production, that Eastern economies are best prepared to sell. In the case of agricultural products, Czechoslovakia and other former communist states are merely facing the same protectionist policies that the European Community has long applied generally. Nonetheless, obstacles of this sort have led East European leaders to reemphasize their pleas with the West not to set up a new, economic "iron curtain" to divide Europe as the cold war did.

Despite the existing trade barrier, there has been a surge in export growth (slowing slightly after 1992, as it did elsewhere in the former Soviet bloc) and a pronounced reorientation of trade to the West. In 1989, about a quarter of Czechoslovakia's imports came from the European Community. Four years later, by late 1992, imports from the same source accounted for nearly half; the countries of the Organization for Economic Cooperation and Development (OECD)

BOX 8.1
The Dilemmas of Dealing with Western Markets: A Case Study

The current dilemma of the restructuring of heavy industrial plants in the region is clearly illustrated in the southeastern Slovak city of Košice, historically a quiet cathedral town in one of the poorer regions of the state. The Stalinist development programs of the 1950s brought the huge VSŽ (East Slovak Ironworks) steel mill to the city. VSŽ employed 15,000 workers and supplied steel to arms manufacturers and other heavy industrial enterprises throughout the bloc. This industrial growth catapulted Košice to the rank of the second largest city in Slovakia before the collapse of the trade bloc after 1989. The VSŽ responded constructively to this challenge, however, investing heavily in modern Western equipment and capitalizing on cheap labor to win a share of the West European market. By 1992 the company was selling 25 percent of its output to European Community countries. Then came the impact of the West European recession, with the EU clapping strict import quotas on East European steel and sending the Košice foundry, which accounts for almost 20 percent of Slovak exports, into a scramble for new but less lucrative markets in Asia. A scheduled easing of these EU restrictions will only partly alleviate the impact of the current quotas.

With the east Slovak region heavily dependent on the plant for employment and export revenues, bitterness over the EU restrictions is understandable. The local ethnic mixture of Slovaks, Hungarians, and Roma is a volatile one, and might prove explosive if massive layoffs by the city's chief employer send shock waves through the economy. There is a strong sense that VSŽ tried to play by Western rules and received a slap in the face because it succeeded.*

---

*_New York Times_, June 19, 1993. See also Carrie R. Leana, "Downsizing Personnel at the Slovakia Steel Company," in Daniel Fogel, ed., _Managing in Emerging Market Economies: Cases from the Czech and Slovak Republics_ (Boulder: Westview Press, 1992), pp. 103–118.

---

account for more than 60 percent of Czech foreign trade, with the Russian share dipping to 8 percent. As the capacity to export to Western Europe surged ahead in the Czech Republic, Slovakia initially lagged behind, still dependent on the former CMEA bloc to sell nearly two-thirds of its exports;[39] by 1995, however, the Slovak export pattern had inverted, with Western markets dominant. The new pattern looks more Central European than Eastern or Western, however. In 1995, the major recipients of Slovak exports, in order of volume, were the Czech Republic, Germany, Italy, Austria, and Hungary. Slovakia imported primarily from the Czech Republic, Germany, and Austria.[40] The chief trading partners for the Czechs were Germany, Slovakia, Russia, and Austria. In the Czech Republic, exports have not kept pace with imports for the consumption-hungry Czech population; however, booming annual tourism revenues have neatly covered the resulting trade deficit.

Foreign investment might seem to be a simple issue for the governments: the more, the better. This was less simple than it appeared, however, and bred several important conflicts. The first was the disproportionate Czech share of the investment dollar, or, more accurately, the deutsche mark. Of the $8.8 billion worth of foreign investment committed to the four Visegrad countries from the inception of the economic transformation process through 1994, only some $366 million came to Slovakia—about 4 percent.[41] The Czech Republic was attracting almost nine dollars of foreign investment for every dollar that came to Slovakia.[42] As of 1994 the Czech Republic ranked second in direct foreign investment per capita among seventeen states in Eastern Europe and the European successor states of the former Soviet Union. Slovakia, with half of the Czech level of per capita investment, was fifth. In total volume of investment, the Czech Republic had garnered almost $3 billion, ranking third after Hungary and Russia; Slovakia was a rather distant fifth, with $390 million in total investment.[43] As the influx of foreign capital flooding the Czech Republic surged to over $3 billion in 1995, a top banking official actually bemoaned an excess of riches; the tidal wave of investment, he said, was too large for the Czech economy to absorb and was generating inflationary pressures.[44]

Although much of the disparity between capital flows to the Czech and Slovak Republics can be explained in terms of the greater attractiveness of the Czech investment environment, Slovak leaders early came to feel that more funds could have been diverted their way, and that no one in Prague was sending investors further East. Slovaks hoped for an expansion of investment after independence, when Bratislava could deal more directly with foreign investors. Thus far, Slovakia's greater political instability and weaker civilian industrial base have apparently dampened that hope. Whereas the largest investments in the Czech Republic have been from automotive firms, Slovakia's largest single foreign investor is not a high-tech Western firm, but rather the K-Mart retail chain, which moved heavily into the region in the wake of advertising appeals to visit their German stores to see what a K-Mart had to offer. Slovakia's most important investment barriers thus far have been political. The uncertain commitment to thoroughgoing economic transformation and the problematic political climate have brought the domestic politics of the triple transition into the arena of international economic decisionmaking.

A second investment issue, common to both Slovakia and the Czech Republic, was how to attract investment without sacrificing economic independence. Officially, Klaus and his CDP were not conflicted by this issue; nor had the preceding federal government been. Capital is capital, they argued; there is really no such thing as "German" or "British" capital. Václav Klaus recalled being asked by a journalist whether he would approve selling off a money-losing Slovak enterprise to a foreign concern. He laughingly responded: "Do you know what you are saying? A money-losing run-down plant and a foreigner wants to buy it? We should be lucky if we find a fool in the West who wants to buy it and try to make it profitable. Everyone will benefit from that, except perhaps the Western investor!"[45]

But not all parties agreed, particularly in light of the fact that more than three-quarters of early investment in Czechoslovakia came from Germany. As other investors moved into the Czech market, this German dominance has steadily eroded, to little more than one-third by the end of 1994.[46]

However, sensitivity to the prospect of being swamped by foreign investment remains. Each major foreign investment decision has continued to reopen the delicate question of foreign influence. It surfaced in the Czech hesitation over whether to reorganize its oil refineries "the Czech way," or to accept the participation of foreign investment consortia, and in debates over the troubled Czech agreement with Volkswagen. Trade Minister Vladimír Dlouhý, one of the most durable Czech cabinet ministers, even experimented with a "Buy Czech" campaign to stress the importance of consumer sensitivity to local economic concerns.

There is also a certain paranoia regarding the intentions of foreign investors. Is their true purpose to gain control over Czech enterprises that might compete with a corporation's Western subsidiaries? Volkswagen's massive investment in the Czech Skoda autoworks had been an early coup in the economic transition; when Volkswagen subsequently scaled down this commitment, some regarded the official explanation—that the cutback stemmed from German economic stagnation after the impact of its reunification—as insufficient, and drew a darker lesson from the experience—that Germany was manipulating its Czech subsidiary to protect the main industry at home. For this reason, the Czech government held out for residual veto power over key decisions when negotiating for Volkswagen to gain a majority stake in Skoda in late 1994.

After independence, right-wing parties in both Slovakia and the Czech Republic made the issue of dependence on foreign investment a particular rallying point. Official policymakers had to watch their step to avoid making deals that would leave the government vulnerable to such criticism. In Slovakia the government itself oscillated between the embrace of foreign investment and warnings about dependence on foreign power. Slovaks have been more protective of core industries such as those related to energy. Its key investors, however, have been similar to those in the Czech Republic, with Germany and Austria in the lead. Slovakia's third largest source of foreign investment is now the Czech Republic.

In the long run, neither the Czech nor the Slovak Republic can avoid substantial dependence on foreign markets and foreign investment. Their domestic markets are too small to produce efficiently without exporting their most competitive products and importing what they cannot efficiently produce. Their supplies of domestic investment capital are too limited to spurn foreign investment. Self-sufficiency makes a good campaign slogan, but bad public policy. It is one of the attractions of membership in the European Union that the two republics would be joining a vast continental market that would help to compensate for the smaller size of the domestic economies.

It might seem logical for such small economies to band together in regional co-operation agreements while they waited in line for the EU—and the potential benefits transcend the merely economic. Indeed, Western European states ardently encouraged regional cooperation efforts, not least because effective regional efforts might simultaneously enhance economic development and reduce the pressure for the fastest possible admission to the EU. The Czech Republic and Slovakia have engaged in a number of regional cooperation efforts, including the Central European Initiative (CEI). But the most important of these efforts has centered on interaction with the other two promising transitional states—Poland and Hungary. Policy coordination began among the four (originally three) countries as early as 1991 in the form of the Visegrad Triangle—a coordinating mechanism for foreign and economic policy; in 1993, the Visegrad group, now the Visegrad Four after the breakup of Czechoslovakia, agreed on the launching of a Central European Free Trade Area (CEFTA).

Progress has been uneven, however; from the beginning, no country wanted to tie itself to any agreement that might delay acceptance by the EU. Czech Deputy Foreign Minister Pavel Bratinka finds the EU supportive, "but we must be wary of [EU] lobbyists who don't like the idea of early membership and might use Visegrad as a pretext to say we must integrate here first." Václav Klaus even dismissed Visegrad, despite his own government's participation in it, as "an artificial creation of the West."[47]

The Czech government's hesitation is very obvious, and the reason for it is also obvious; in 1989, Czechoslovakia lagged behind Poland and Hungary in economic reform and could not expect to gain EU admission before the others. The progress made since then has changed the game: As long as the Czech economy continues to outperform neighboring economies, the Czech Republic might be able to hope for earlier admission to the EU than the others, and Czech leaders do not want to see Visegrad become a "package deal." Klaus has consistently argued that neighborly cooperation should focus on trade rather than any project that might appear as a regional alternative to the EU. This attitude is similar to Czech reservations about a concerted regional approach to security issues or to joining NATO.

Slovakia, of course, with considerably dimmer prospects for early EU admission on its own, has been much more vocal in its enthusiasm for regional cooperation, which not only promises direct benefit but which also identifies Slovakia more clearly with the Visegrad in-group that can be most hopeful of integration into the West European economic sphere. Even Visegrad, however, may not return Slovakia to the first tier if Slovakia's domestic strife fails to abate.

In addition to the dramatic turn to the West, the new states showed considerable pragmatism in reordering their foreign policy focus in areas beyond the European continent. Cuba and the remaining communist states in Asia were no longer the target of fraternal socialist assistance; they were now targets of human rights criticism instead. Asian guest workers were sent home. In January 1991 Czechoslovakia relinquished its intermediary role in representing unrecognized

Cuba's interests in the United States. In short, the dissolution of socialist ideological bonds left Czechoslovakia with little practical economic interest in sustaining elsewhere the kind of regime from which Czechoslovakia had so recently
liberated itself at home.[48]

The new focus for international interaction in the Third World was the group
of states with something to offer a transitional economy. Czechoslovakia, like the
Soviet Union and other former communist states, courted conservative Gulf oil
states that had previously been ideologically offensive and distanced themselves
from pariah Iraq and radical Syria, erstwhile allies. Additional new relationships
were forged with newly industrializing countries (NICs) in Latin America and
Asia, ties that enhanced the prospect of trade, aid, and investment from foreign
economies with appropriate middle-level technology—technology that was competitive in world markets.

Public Opinion and Foreign Policy

In most countries, the public has less impact and influence on foreign policy than
on domestic policy, and less urgent interest in it as well. The governing leaders
generally have considerable latitude to design and implement foreign policy. The
Czech and Slovak Republics are no exception. Like the citizens of other postcommunist states, Czech and Slovak citizens list domestic policies as their major
political concerns in poll after poll.

Nevertheless, the stakes in the "return to Europe" are obvious to everyone, and
exposure to the world has radically expanded since 1989. Citizens can travel
abroad freely if their finances permit. After the abolition of mandatory Russian
language study requirements in school, students flocked to study German and
English instead—both of them are now valuable for business and recreational
purposes. Moreover, the world has come to Slovakia and, especially, the Czech
Republic. Peace Corps volunteers and participants in other international programs have descended on the two countries to teach English and business skills.
Tourism has exploded. In 1994 there were more than 850,000 foreign visitors in
the Czech Republic each day (some 150 million foreigners crossed into the
Republic in 1993, twenty times as many as the entire Czech population!).[49]
Prague was the particular magnet, even for young Americans; there are thousands
of Americans resident in Prague. In general, this means that the citizens of larger
Czech cities are gaining a big dose of regular face-to-face exposure with the outside world in addition to the increased import of foreign goods and foreign culture as well as expanded local coverage of international events.

In general, this exposure has only reinforced popular sensitivity to the relevance of external influences to the domestic transition. As we have seen, there
have been ambivalences—fears of foreign economic and cultural dominance and
of possible spillover effects of regional instability. However, the general pattern
of public opinion supports the elite consensus in favor of integration into
European institutions. Interestingly, this convergence between leadership and

public attitudes was visible earlier in economic policy than in security policy. There was strong public support for membership in the European Union almost from the beginning. In that same early period, the public was very resistant to NATO membership and much more sympathetic to the idea of neutralism than its leaders were. Much of the public saw no security threat sufficient to activate concern about defense.

This attitude shifted over time, largely in response to the impact of upheaval in the nearby Soviet Union and Yugoslavia. Growing public concern was expressed in growing support for membership in Western military alliances. Even so, however, the support expressed for NATO membership was usually only a bit more than half the proportion of the Czech public that favored EU membership, whereas popular enthusiasm for NATO in Slovakia lagged twenty-two percentage points behind that for the EU, with 43 percent favoring NATO entry and 65 percent for the EU.[50] This could mean that the public remains focused on the bread-and-butter issues of foreign economic policy. But it may also indicate public doubts about NATO as the best security guarantor. The true reckoning will come when the two states have a clear opportunity to join NATO and the budgetary implications of that move sink in. Joining NATO will mean a very expensive restructuring and reequipping of the Czech and Slovak defense establishments to ensure compatibility with alliance operations. This may in fact be less expensive than joining the EU, but the payoffs are less self-evident. Therefore the popular acceptance of foreign policy directions since 1989 could erode in the future, when the quest for Western integration looms as a more concrete possibility.

The most resonant foreign policy issues, however—the ones that strike the strongest emotional cord—are those that ignite national identity. The Czech government is genuinely constrained in its dealings with Germany on the Sudeten German question by the intense public sentiment against concessions. Even the popular Havel created a firestorm of protest when he criticized the deportations of Germans following World War II, despite the fact that most Czech citizens had not yet been born when the deportations occurred. In Slovakia, relations with neighboring Hungary touch a similar nerve; in this case, however, the leadership itself has frequently raised the emotional temperature of the issue. Leaders who do not play the "national card" remain vulnerable to popular resentment at the polls. This pattern is not unique to the Czech and Slovak Republics, of course. Ethnic affinities and antagonisms influence the foreign policies of many states, but particularly the postcommunist regimes because of the multiple cross-boundary ethnonational connections between states. The mission of the CSCE High Commissioner on Minorities is therefore crucial on a volatile issue that not only engages the governments of the region but their publics as well.

In the final analysis, the relationship between public and government in foreign policy will not fall into a less emotionally charged pattern until a stable, inclusive economic and security architecture evolves in Europe. The multiple domestic postcommunist transitions have generated the need for a transition in the transnational continental structures. Until the Eastern states solidify relations with the EU and NATO—or find an alternative to them as guarantors of European economic and security—the attractions of the outside world will be balanced by its threats.

Conclusion

This chapter has emphasized the fact that the Czech and Slovak economic transitions are deeply embedded in the broader European context, shaped particularly by the ultimate goal of admission to the European Union. It is difficult to write a balance sheet on the economic impact of Czech and Slovak ties with global markets and international economic organizations. Adding up a running total of financial support of all kinds would be a tedious process that only tells us what the governments already know: External engagement has been woefully inadequate to the size of the transformation process under way.

However, we can say that the sheer monetary value of foreign economic transactions is a very imperfect measure of the growing Czech and Slovak engagement in the global and continental economic matrix. What is probably more important is the way in which this engagement has generally tended to reinforce the case for domestic economic reform. This is true for two reasons. In the first place, all forms of external support tend to gravitate toward postcommunist economies that have significantly reformed. Expanded foreign trade, for example, is clearly conditional on the ability of Czech and Slovak economies to produce goods that are competitive on world markets; greater competitiveness comes from the restructuring of enterprises to produce higher quality goods more cheaply and efficiently than the communist economy did. Foreign investment flows to postcommunist states that create a favorable capitalist investment environment; this puts a premium on removing communist-era restrictions on foreign ownership, introducing economic adjustment measures to stabilize prices and currency, and legislating a secure regulatory and commercial framework. Finally, aid comes to those who demonstrate sustained, across-the-board commitment to marketization and to political reform. The differential progress of Czech and Slovak governments in meeting these expectations is reflected in the Czech Republic's greater success in attracting foreign support.

The second, and broader, conclusion we can draw from the Czech and Slovak engagement in the global economy since the Velvet Revolution, however, lies in the recognition that the whole web of international economic relations is an incentive structure for pursuing the triple transition in a framework defined by the West. Western economic models exerted a powerful attraction before 1989, but that attraction has now in effect been "institutionalized" in a code of appropriate behavior, measured by the standards of the European Union in particular and international economic agencies in general. The Czech and Slovak Republics must comply with these standards or else risk forfeiting external support and particularly their chances for incorporation into the European Union. The Czech and Slovak Republics cannot flout international expectations without paying the penalty of economic and political isolation. Slovakia in particular faces this compelling reality.

We could regard this kind of external pressure as a form of benevolent blackmail, a way of pushing East European economies into making tough choices that will be good for them in the long run. The governments of the region have actually used this outside pressure to justify socially painful economic reforms that are otherwise quite unpopular at home; this is particularly true of economic adjustment measures like anti-inflationary and wage-control policies, budget balancing, and currency stabilization. In a sense, external pressures can function as a substitute for domestic business interests that are still too weak and disorganized to press for economic reform policies themselves.

There is a risk in this situation, however. The association of foreign influence with loss of sovereignty can be drawn back into domestic politics and create a backlash effect against foreign interference. Domestic opponents of economic reform (or indeed any politician who wishes to rally electoral support) can run for office on a populist nationalist program that links economic reform to subservience to alien interests and that labels reformers as tools of the IMF. Despite fears of excessive German influence, this dynamic has not been a central problem in Czech politics so far. Only the right-wing Republican Party has adopted this electoral strategy, and its parliamentary strength is limited, even more so after its split into competing factions. In Slovakia, however, governing parties like Mečiar's MDS have adopted the "foreign influence" rhetoric in electoral politics and have angrily rejected outside criticism. Even if the intent was merely to win votes with a simple message of Slovak self-assertion, the effect has surely been to undercut public confidence in reform. The influence of foreign actors on the economic agenda therefore can play back into the domestic politics of triple transition in both positive and negative feedback cycles that can either encourage or undermine reform, depending on the way political leaders interpret the external environment to their publics.

A final, even tougher question is whether the IMF or the EU really know and want what is best for transitional postcommunist states like the Czech Republic and Slovakia. After all, these external actors have their own interests to pursue, which may not always coincide with those of the transitional states. This is obvious, for example, in the case of EU trade barriers to East European agricultural and metallurgical products. More generally, it is also true that, for better or worse, Western expectations and Eastern eagerness to join Europe narrows the range for domestic economic policy experimentation. The search for a third way—an economic alternative to the current form of European capitalism—could mean disqualification from EU membership down the road. The economic performance of these states in coming years will to some extent be a test of whether that narrowing effect impeded East European stability and prosperity.

As this protracted discussion of the international context of Czech and Slovak transformation efforts has made clear, the foreign policy strategies of the two new states must be measured against a larger, more encompassing conception of security than any narrow, conventionally defined, military conception. Like their postcommunist neighbors, their search for security has led to a strategy of engagement in Europe that, as Vladimír Handl has put it, can serve as both a security and a modernization anchor.[51] The domestic components of the triple transition have the goal of a prosperous capitalist economy imbedded in a stable, consolidated democracy in which all national groups are adequately represented. Only such a state can be truly secure. The attempt to get to that point without outside assistance would impose additional burdens on an already burdensome process of change—hence the move to join Europe.

Yet outreach for foreign support imposes its own restrictions and in so doing also interweaves the multiple transition efforts still further. What we have been analyzing, in effect, is a broad, although fairly general, Western consensus on the need for good interethnic relations, democratic procedure, and rapid marketization and privatization. All three of these desiderata figure in Western calculations in making the important decisions about aid, trade, and investment, or inclusion in Western multilateral organizations.

The norms that the West seeks to enforce in postcommunist Europe are policed by a web of institutions (NATO, the European Union, the Council of Europe), each with a different focus but with overlapping agendas. The EU expects democracy and harmonious ethnic relations as much as it demands conformity to EU economic standards. NATO also expects its members to meet the standards of democratic capitalist practice. Although NATO and the EU are the key institutions that the Czech and Slovak governments aspire to join, other organizations in the Western web have crucial gatekeeping functions in assuring progress to that goal. Gaining membership in the Council of Europe, for example, reinforced Czech and Slovak democratic credentials but also imposed behavioral requirements—requirements that are embodied in the Council of Europe conventions and agreements that members are expected to observe. Good citizenship in the Council of Europe is therefore far from cost-free, but the incentive to join has been intimately related to the understanding that such membership would enhance prospects for EU membership. Negotiating this web of interlocking Western institutions has become the core of foreign policy for all the East Central European regimes. This broad complex of Western institutions collectively frame the larger questions of political, economic, and military security for the smaller neighboring states.

Notes

1. Poll results cited in *Prague Post*, September 20, 1994, p. 5.
2. Statistics cited in *The Economist*, August 13, 1994, p. 94.

3. *RFE/RL Daily Press Digest,* December 13, 1994.

4. Bratislava Radio, October 1, 1993, transcribed in *Foreign Broadcast Information Service–East Europe* FBIS-EEU-93-191, October 4, 1993, p. 16. The single largest group of Slovak citizens in 1993 (about one-third) emphasized the need for self-reliance rather than orientation toward East or West, but nearly a quarter favored a Western orientation, and only a handful (about 4 percent) looked East. "Ako by sa mala orientatovat' zahraničná politika SR?" *Národná obroda,* April 19, 1993.

5. *New York Times,* March 17, 1994.

6. *RFE/RL Daily Digest,* December 1, 1994.

7. *OMRI Daily Digest,* no. 203, October 18, 1995, and no. 225, November 17, 1995.

8. Alfred Stepan, "Paths Toward Redemocratization," in Guillermo O'Donnell et al., *Transitions from Authoritarian Rule: Comparative Perspectives* (Baltimore: Johns Hopkins University Press, 1986), pp. 71–72. See also Juan Linz, "Transitions to Democracy," *Washington Quarterly* 13:3 (Summer 1990):143–163.

9. *New York Times,* July 6, 1990.

10. See for example: Adrian G. V. Hyde-Price, "Democratization in Eastern Europe: The External Dimension," in Geoffrey Pridham and Tatu Vanhanen, eds., *Democratization in Eastern Europe: Domestic and International Perspectives* (London: Routledge, 1994), pp. 191–219; Joern G. Stegen, "The Parliamentary Assembly of the Council of Europe and its Relations with Central and Eastern Europe," in Lawrence D. Longley, ed., *Working Papers on Comparative Legislative Studies* (Appleton, Wis.: Research Committee of Legislative Specialists, IPSA, 1994), pp. 407–409; and William H. Robinson and Francis Miko, "Parliamentary Development Assistance in Central Europe and the Former Soviet Union: Some Lessons from Experience," in Longley, *Working Papers on Comparative Legislative Studies,* pp. 409–430.

11. There have been Western objections to the rules and conduct of some Balkan state elections, however, including those in Bulgaria, Romania, and the former Yugoslav states.

12. *OMRI Daily Digest,* no. 203, October 18, 1995, and no. 209, October 26, 1995.

13. *OMRI Daily Digest,* no. 225, November 17, 1995.

14. Budapest MTI, July 19, 1991, transcribed in FBIS-EEU-91-162, August 21, 1991, p. 15.

15. *Slovenská republika,* October 2, 1994, p. 6, reprinted in FBIS-EEU-94-198, October 13, 1994, p. 8.

16. Mečiar speech to the Slovak cultural organization Matica Slovenska, reprinted in *Smena,* August 25, 1990, p. 13.

17. Public opinion, however, appeared to favor the ratification of the treaty, according to polls taken in May 1995 by the Slovak Statistical Office. *OMRI Daily Digest,* June 29, 95.

18. Cited in FBIS-EEU-94-212, November 4, 1993, p. 8.

19. The fact that the Russian pipeline runs through Slovakia is also sensitive, since on at least one occasion the Mečiar government issued a veiled warning about Slovak control of Czech energy supplies. An alternative delivery route, the Adria pipeline, was shut down for three years until 1995 because of the Yugoslav war.

20. Poll results cited in Simon Duke, *The New European Security Disorder* (New York: St. Martin's Press, 1994), p. 81.

21. "Stěhování národů," *Český deník,* March 22, 1993.

22. In 1989 Czechoslovakia had as many as 37,000 Vietnamese "guest workers." Facing the rigors of economic transformation and popular hostility to these foreign residents, the

government failed to renew Vietnamese labor contracts, and the workers have gradually been returned home, willingly or not. See, for example, D. Joly and R. Poulton, *Refugees: Asylum in Europe?* (London: Minority Rights Group, 1992), p. 80. The problem since then has centered on new, postcommunist immigration.

23. OMRI reports that the largest groups were Poles and Slovaks, with significant additional contingents of Ukrainians, Vietnamese, Chinese, Germans, Americans, and citizens of former Yugoslav states. *OMRI Daily Digest,* April 5, 1995.

24. *RFE/RL Daily Report,* December 16, 1994.

25. See Michael Mihalka, "German and Western Response to Immigration from the East," *RFE/RL Research Report* 3:23 (June 10, 1994):36–48.

26. Poll results cited in Duke, *The New European Security Disorder,* p. 334.

27. There is broad but not unanimous partisan support for holding a popular referendum on the issue. The motivations for supporting a referendum vary, however. Some parties wish to validate the official government stance on full membership by popular approval, whereas others (a much smaller group) with reservations about EU membership want the chance to appeal to the public over the heads of the leadership. In January 1995 Klaus's Civic Democratic Party went on record as supporting such a move.

28. Norway's voters subsequently rejected the admission offer in November 1994. The accession of the remaining new members may actually help the postcommunist applicants. The new members are actually richer than many of the existing EU members; their admission raises the average per capita income and the average GNP of the EU member countries, thereby providing a cushion that could make it more feasible to incorporate lower-income postcommunist states without diverting subsidies from poorer EU members such as Portugal or Greece.

29. Alexis Galinos, "Central Europe and the EU: Prospects for Closer Integration," *RFE/RL Research Report* 3:29 (July 22, 1994):20–21.

30. *RFE/RL Daily Digest,* November 22, 1994.

31. *Hospodářské noviny,* September 14, 1994, p. 5, reprinted in FBIS-EEU-94-190, September 30, 1994, p. 8.

32. "Creating a Capitalist Czechoslovakia: An Interview with Václav Klaus," in Tim D. Whipple, ed., *After the Velvet Revolution: Václav Havel and the New Leaders of Czechoslovakia Speak Out* (Lanham, Md.: Freedom House, 1991), p. 151.

33. Janine Wedel, "U.S. Aid to Central and Eastern Europe: Results and Recommendations," *Problems of Post-Communism,* 43:2 (May-June 1995):46.

34. Václav Klaus remarked: "As for classical foreign aid, this is the last thing on our agenda. I know what it has done to other countries." See "Creating a Capitalist Czechoslovakia," in Whipple, *After the Velvet Revolution,* p. 151.

35. Stanley J. Kabala, "EC Helps Czechoslovakia Pay 'Debt to the Environment,'" *RFE/RL Research Report* 1:20 (May 15, 1992):54–58.

36. Mark Sommer, *Living in Freedom* (San Francisco: Mercury House, 1992), p. 55.

37. Robinson and Miko, "Parliamentary Development Assistance in Central Europe and the Former Soviet Union," in Longley, *Working Papers on Comparative Legislative Studies,* p. 421.

38. Wedel, "U.S. Aid to Central and Eastern Europe," p. 47.

39. Galinos, "Central Europe and the EU," pp. 19–25.

40. *OMRI Daily Digest,* August 8, 1995.

41. Sharon Fisher, "The Slovak Economy: Signs of Recovery," *RFE/RL Research Report*, 33:3 (August 26, 1994):62.

42. By the end of 1994 direct foreign investment in the Czech Republic had reached $3.1 billion.

43. UN Economic Commission for Europe data, cited in Anne Henderson, "The Politics of Foreign Investment in Eastern Europe," *Problems of Post-Communism* 42:3 (May-June 1995):53.

44. *OMRI Daily Digest,* June 23, 1995.

45. "Creating a Capitalist Czechoslovakia," in Whipple, *After the Velvet Revolution*, p. 152.

46. "Německý kapitál jasne v čele," *Hospodářské noviny*, March 26, 1992. Germany remains the single largest source of outside capital.

47. *Prague Post*, March 17–23, 1993, p. 3.

48. See Yang Zhong, "The Fallen Wall and Its Aftermath: Impact of Regime Change upon Foreign Policy Behavior in Six East European Countries," *East European Quarterly* 28:2 (Summer 1994):235–257.

49. *RFE/RL Daily Report*, December 16, 1994.

50. ČTK News from Slovakia, February 29, 1996.

51. Vladimír Handl, "The Czech Republic in Search of a Home," *Foreign Policy Research Institute Wire* 3:2 (June 1995), p. 1.

9

CONCLUSION

Although this study has often highlighted the Czech advantages over the Slovaks, in most respects the Czech and Slovak Republics have both been among the more fortunate of the postcommunist states. They have weathered the transition thus far without the searing violence of the former Yugoslavian states and some parts of the former Soviet Union and without the degree of economic chaos that seems to plague Russia. Economic growth rebounded in both states in 1994. Immediate security threats fall below the level of overt military conflict in the future as well. Until recently the two republics have been included on all the best guest lists for early admission to West European organizations. In politics, the Slovak government, increasingly embroiled in internationally damaging domestic controversy, has fared less well than the Czech coalition. In neither case, however, have politicians yet abandoned parliamentary and electoral strategies of democracy in order to gain their ends.

Nevertheless, the preceding chapters demonstrate that the multiple transitions have been problematic in important respects. Political institutions are still insecurely linked to a popular base. Parties have been almost as vulnerable to internal disintegration as to electoral defeat. In Slovakia, where the first prime minister, Vladimír Mečiar, alternated in power with two successive coalitions that failed subsequent electoral tests, there seems to have been a radical disconnection between the political groups prepared to govern and those capable of gaining popular support. Mečiar's third reincarnation as prime minister in the five years since the Velvet Revolution merely extended the pattern of governmental crisis. The greater stability and popularity of the Czech government have thus far spared it these roller-coaster political adventures. However, neither state has escaped the sometimes disorienting impact of the economic transformation, and the social costs of the transition represent a bill that may yet come due even in the Czech Republic, where the impact of privatization on employment has yet to be felt.

Most of these problems are common to their neighbors in transition as well. In fact, one of the most important difficulties of transition is that so many individual state transformation projects have been occurring simultaneously. Imagine, for a moment, Czechoslovakia's advantages had it undergone this form of transition alone. The West would have been much more capable of rewarding the effort with investment, trade, and aid if the European economic agenda had not been knee deep in alternative postcommunist claimants for attention and assistance. Another economic drawback of simultaneous regional transition was the negative impact of the collapsing bloc trade that accompanied the transitional effort.

Alone, Czechoslovakia might have been able to retain its existing Eastern markets while reorienting to Western ones. The security structures of cold-war Europe would also have been more stable; the grooming of a single NATO applicant is quite different from devising an entirely new security architecture for the continent. Of course this scenario would have hardly been likely; it is difficult to envisage the capacity of a single country to break from the bloc unscathed in the absence of the turmoil in the Soviet Union that allowed *all* countries to exit independently. This thought experiment is mainly valuable in pointing out the extra complexity that the disruption of an entire international subsystem—the communist bloc—imposed upon the individual countries.

The interaction of the triple transition at home was equally a complicating factor. The best illustration is the impact of the deteriorating Czech-Slovak relationship in delaying or impeding political and economic transformation. The hardships of the economic transition hardened Slovak demands on the state, even while Slovak reluctance to embrace full-speed reform alienated key Czech leaders. In this case, it was the economic transition that helped to complicate the resolution of the national question. And, of course, no permanent constitution to lend stability and legitimacy to the political order was possible until the national question was resolved. In addition to the specific impact of the national question in Czechoslovakia, however, the interaction of the three transitions has imposed additional burdens on all postcommunist societies. Though none faced a national question configured like Czechoslovakia's, each country, even the relatively homogeneous ones like Poland, faced the task of national redefinition after communism.

These domestic transitional interactions alone were complex, but the international context added a still broader complexity. One of the most striking differences between the postcommunist transitions and those of earlier democratizing states, in Latin America, for example, was the prominent role of the international community in the individual domestic transitions. Catalyzed by Gorbachev's revisions of traditional Soviet policy, the collapse of communism in Eastern Europe was itself a product both of internal performance failures and of international conditions.

Even more striking has been the subsequent impact of the European institutional framework to which the postcommunist states of East and Central Europe aspired to belong. The desire to "return to Europe" by joining institutions like the European Union and NATO interacted with every aspect of the internal triple transition. The need to demonstrate the ability to accommodate Western expectations of democracy and capitalism affected the economic program by putting a premium on fiscal responsibility, serious privatization efforts, and a host of smaller technical adjustments to the market. The penalty for failure to adhere to the policy prescriptions of a range of foreign institutions included delays in economic assistance, lower levels of investment and trade, and uncomfortable moments in negotiating membership and association agreements with GATT, the IMF, the European Union, NATO, the Council of Europe, and many additional specialized organizations. Moreover, Europe does not reward ethnonational tension. Its scrutiny of minority policy through the CSCE is only one of the ways in which the West has used its leverage to encourage the moderation of ethnic tensions in the region. In the absence of military defeat and occupation, it is hard to imagine another internal reform effort that has been so closely monitored from outside.

These external constraints are not always decisive. The MDS in Slovakia won its impressive share of the popular vote in 1994 on a platform that emphasized "priority to *domestic* resources, *domestic* development opportunities, on support for the creation of a *domestic* business stratum and *not selling out to foreigners, not kowtowing to the west* . . . [emphasis added]."[1] Yet even the MDS, when in power, must at least pay lip service to the goals of marketization and democracy sanctioned by the West. The fact that the Czech and Slovak Republics are embedded in a European context was a source of considerable suffering at times in the past, particularly in the two world wars. In the present, the character of this continental influence is rather more benign. Yet it is nonetheless very powerful and has done much to shape the politics and economics of the Czech and Slovak transition from authoritarian rule.

For students of comparative politics, Czechoslovakia's postcommunist experience is above all an object lesson in the complexities of defining what democracy means. Scholars in postcommunist Europe studied both Western institutions and Western democratic philosophy avidly during the period of constitutional reconstruction.[2] They sorted through the dozens of arcane mathematical methods developed to allocate votes proportionally as well as the classics of democratic theory. By the end of my first year of contact with these busy constitutionalists, I had given away all my copies of *The Federalist Papers*. Despite the familiar landmarks of the political landscape—parties, elections, legislatures, and executive agencies—the European-style parliamentary systems designed in the Czech and Slovak Republics are clearly distant cousins of the U.S. system. Moreover, despite the ease with which one can trace and identify certain components of the system—the use of the German electoral threshold concept, for example, or the technicalities of Slovakia's adoption of the Hare system of proportional representation—postcommunist politics still do not work in quite the same way as they do in the West. Institutions are not democratic until they have been used for a while, become familiar, and can be modified to fit the kinds of problems a given country faces. This experimentation process is sometimes called consolidation, but it may defy formal definition.

Even more important, perhaps, is what the experience of Czechoslovakia tells us about the limits of some of the standard definitions of democracy when applied to multinational states. If citizens in such states are to accept the rules of the democratic game, the decisionmaking process cannot rely on a straightforward application of majority rule. In the United States, many Americans with cherished immigrant backgrounds are content to preserve their roots in a private family setting. Where ethnonational identity takes on a political meaning, however, the welfare and survival of one's national group become a reference point for the distribution of society's resources. At that point, majority rule is insufficiently democratic for the smaller nationalities in the state. After all, being in a minority because of national identity is very different from being in the minority on a policy issue. A citizen whose policy views are in the minority can hope to become part of a majority in the future if the balance of elite and public opinion shifts. But a national minority is a permanent one by definition. It can only hope to join the majority by renouncing its own distinctive identity (an unacceptable solution) or by outgrowing the majority demographically (an unlikely solution). In this context, majority rule is seen as *antidemocratic,* because the majority can always outvote and subordinate the interests of the minority.

A political system with one or more permanent historically and territorially rooted minorities, therefore, must face the fact that a workable definition of democracy must safeguard minority rights in some institutionally acceptable way; Arend Lijphart has termed states that achieve these multinational bargains "consociational democracies" and described their very complex balancing acts.[3] The alternative, however, is an unconsolidated, quasi democracy that is viewed as illegitimate by a substantial segment of the population. In multinational Europe, this is not a trivial problem. Slovakia has yet to resolve this question with its own Hungarian minority, and the state of Czechoslovakia broke up over it. In a multinational state, quarrels about the national question are really quarrels about the meaning of democracy.

Political scientists hate being asked to predict the future, especially in print. The unpredictability of specific events plays havoc with any projections concrete enough to satisfy the questioner. A constructive compromise is to identify the most important things to watch for, and that is how I will conclude this study. If this checklist really corresponds to the important issues facing the Czech and Slovak states, it should help in making sense of subsequent developments.

In domestic politics, the two new states share certain problems and face their own particular challenges. The problems they share are common to other transitional East European states: completing economic restructuring, for example, and deepening the linkages between the public and the governing institutions so as to increase political responsiveness. In the Czech Republic, some of the key things to watch for include the capacity of the current government to resist the temptations of their solid grip on power—the temptations of corruption in dividing the spoils, and the temptations of retaining strong centralist control. The spate of recent scandals has strained cooperation within the coalition, tarnished its public image, revived the left, and even begun to diminish Klaus's striking popularity. All democratizing political systems must confront the need to regulate political behavior; corruption erodes government accountability to the public by undermining the integrity of its formal program, the program that it was elected to implement. This will be important because, as Andrew Green has argued, Czech democracy is still rather shallowly rooted in the public sphere, and there is still pervasive popular uncertainty about government responsiveness to social needs.[4]

The temptation to maintain power at the center by delaying the constitutionally mandated establishment of regional government also undermines accountability; regionally important issues like northern Bohemia's environmental pollution or Moravia's claims for a measure of autonomy need a political outlet. The center has not been particularly responsive to such regional concerns, which could be addressed more effectively by intermediary levels of government between Prague and the localities. The alternative is a festering discontent that is now destabilizing politics, as popular doubt about the responsiveness of the Klaus government to these issues and to the popular concerns about social security appeared to have a significant impact in the strong opposition showing of the Social Democrats in the 1996 elections. On the other hand, the popular malaise may have moved the Czech Republic closer to a political system with a viable opposition that poses a coherent alternative to the governing coalition parties, now governing as a minority and vulnerable to defeat.

In economic terms, the most important thing to watch for may well be Czech unemployment statistics. Because the strikingly low Czech levels of unemployment may result in part from continued padding of the payrolls and subsidies to state-owned firms, the recently completed privatization process could push the percentage of unemployed sharply upward as firms become more efficient in using labor. Only a rapidly growing private sector could absorb the released workers, and it is too soon to know whether Czech economic growth is sufficient to absorb them quickly. This is important because rising unemployment levels have been a key culprit in undermining political stability and support for reforms in other postcommunist states. We do not yet know the ending of the apparent Czech success story.

In Slovakia, the most important things to watch for in domestic policy touch on all aspects of the triple transition. The cycle of Slovak political instability could only be broken if the Mečiar government comes to terms with the constraints of democracy; the best indices of this would be the subsiding of the media wars between his government and a free press, and the political wars between the MDS coalition and its parliamentary and presidential opposition. The way in which the current controversies are resolved will leave a pronounced imprint, for better or worse, on future political stability. In economic policy, Slovakia's incomplete privatization program bears close monitoring. The pace and character of privatization has been subject to intense controversy; the outcome of this dispute will tell a great deal about the currently murky Slovak economic program and ultimately about Slovakia's eligibility to join Western institutions.

Continuing tension between the Slovak and Hungarian national groups is a third area to monitor; such tensions are unlikely to evaporate, but one sign that they are intensifying would be evidence that the Hungarian minority has become committed to pursuing a program of regional political autonomy for itself rather than accepting less formal political guarantees and cultural freedoms and the recourse to external organizations for relief unobtainable at home through the normal political process. Evidence that tensions have begun to abate would come from the willingness of Slovak-based parties to accept the idea of formal inclusion of the Hungarians in a government coalition. At present, every ethnically Slovak party rejects out of hand the idea of formal governmental cooperation with the Hungarian parliamentary delegation.

Because the fate of the domestic transformations in the Czech and Slovak Republics is so closely tied to their international standing, it is equally important to identify significant indicators of change in the European context. At this level, the most important day of reckoning has yet to come. East European states have become increasingly resentful of delays in defining their future status in Europe. Both NATO and the European Union pledged in late 1994 to develop clearer guidelines about qualifications for membership.

The publication of these guidelines in 1995 has clarified to some extent the political and economic costs of joining Europe, but the prospects for inclusion of any given postcommunist state remain difficult to calculate. The critical moment for each state will come with the clarification of these prospects. States with hope of early accession to membership are likely to work to bind themselves ever more closely to the European framework, a commitment that is likely to accelerate economic change and increase the inclination to mend fences with neighbors and with domestic national groups. States who despair of joining in the foreseeable future, because they lag in meeting significant entrance requirements or find the political price of those requirements too great to pay, face a different situation. With the rewards of complying with European standards receding into a more distant future, the incentive to comply with Western expectations on a range of issues—including sustained market reform, observance of human rights norms, and tolerance of national diversity—will weaken considerably. At present, all East European states are partially constrained in their domestic and foreign policy behavior by the hope of joining Europe. Those who lose hope may become increasingly unpredictable and more nationalist in their policies.

As far as the Czech Republic and Slovakia are concerned, the important thing to watch for is Slovakia's longer term response to external pressures for fuller democratization and marketization. Until recently, the hope of joining Europe has clearly moderated the expression of national antagonisms and given economic reformers an argument for persisting in marketization and privatization. After 1994, however, diminishing Western confidence in Slovakia's democratization efforts has led to intensified external criticism and generated a confrontational response from the Slovak government. A Slovakia that has relinquished its expectations of steady progress into Europe could certainly become more volatile and politically polarized. In fact, Slovakia—with its minority problems and political volatility—is a test case for European capacity to influence the course of postcommunist transitions.

A number of scholars have been critical of the ambiguities and complexities of the Western institutional response to the postcommunist states, and with good reason; Western engagement in the East has been underfunded, protective of its own economic interests, ambiguous in defining a timetable for admission to Western organizations, and even at times counterproductive in its interventions. However, in one sense the ambiguities of Western policy have been useful, because evasiveness in offering a schedule for joining Europe has postponed the day when a new line would be drawn across the continent, defining who is "European" and who is not—who will sit down at the table of Western institutions and who must struggle along in a "gray zone." Waiting in line to join Europe has generated impatience, but it was also often a force for moderation, certainly in the Czech and Slovak Republics. The single most important future development to watch for, then, is where the two states are positioned in relation to the boundary line of the new Europe.

In examining this international context, one final and centrally important point worthy of emphasis is the logic underpinning the dynamics of East-West interaction. In the wake of the traumatic experience of World War II, West European political leaders in a sense anticipated the later findings of political scientists that democracies do not fight each other[5] by postulating that peace and stability was not merely a function of conventional defense; the Hitler threat was the threat of an authoritarian government. The new order would therefore be founded on the norms of democratic capitalism, on the assumption that prosperity, political legitimacy, and popular control would anchor peaceful international relations. Further, the postwar leaders read the Hitler threat as the threat of a state seeking dominance for its own sovereign ends. Such an image made cooperative multilateral approaches to problem-solving all the more attractive. Thus, postwar Western Europe moved toward the construction of multilateral institutions that would reinforce mutual cooperation on the basis of the "democratic capitalist peace." It was this network of institutions that Eastern Europe has sought to join, as we have seen. At the same time, Western encouragement to the East to emulate Western practices has been based on the assumption that democratic capitalist norms would produce stability in the East as well. This may well be true in the long run; postcommunist countries that successfully surmount the challenges of the triple transition may indeed fulfill the expectation that the new states will prove viable partners in the project of the democratic capitalist peace.

However, political scientists are beginning to formalize an understanding of the relationship between stability and democracy that is more complex. *Democratic* states may not fight each other, but the record shows that *democratizing* regimes (or indeed any regime undergoing profound change) do indeed experience serious and destabilizing growing pains that can lead to tensions and war.[6] Thus, all of Europe is engaged in calculating the odds on a gamble—the gamble that postcommunist states are moving toward the Western model and will survive the interim instability. The endpoint of successful triple transitions may well contribute to a more stable international environment, but the process of getting there is another matter. The tribulations of the Czech and Slovak experiments in transformation are a good indication that there is a delicate balancing act to perform even in states that have traversed the minefield of transition without exploding into violence. The shape of the new Europe is far from determined.

Notes

1. Vladimír Mečiar, in the fourth roundtable election debate, Bratislava STV 1 Television, September 18, 1994, transcribed in *Foreign Broadcast Information Service–East Europe* FBIS-EEU-91-181, September 19, 1994, p. 9.

2. See A. E. Dick Howard, "How Ideas Travel: Rights at Home and Abroad," in A. E. Dick Howard, ed., *Constitution Making in Eastern Europe* (Washington, D.C.: Woodrow Wilson Center Press, 1993), pp. 9–21.

3. For a brief definition, see Arend Lijphart, *Democracies: Patterns of Majoritarian and Consensus Government in Twenty-one Countries* (New Haven: Yale University Press, 1984), p. xiv.

4. Andrew Green, letter to author, April 25, 1996.

5. See especially Bruce Russett, *Grasping the Democratic Peace: Principles for a Post–Cold War World* (Princeton: Princeton University Press, 1993).

6. See Edward Mansfield and Jack Snyder, "Democratization and War," *Foreign Affairs* 74:3 (May-June 1995):79–97.

Selected Bibliography

Dubček, Alexander. *Hope Dies Last: The Autobiography of Alexander Dubček* (New York: Kodanska, 1993).

Fogel, Daniel S., ed. *Managing in Emerging Market Economies: Cases from the Czech and Slovak Republics* (Boulder: Westview Press, 1993).

Havel, Václav. *Disturbing the Peace: A Conversation with Karel Hvížd'ala* (New York: Alfred A. Knopf, 1990).

Johnson, Owen V. *Slovakia, 1918–1938: Education and the Making of a Nation* (New York: Columbia University Press, 1985).

Leff, Carol Skalnik. *National Conflict in Czechoslovakia: The Making and Remaking of a State, 1918–1987* (Princeton: Princeton University Press, 1988).

Mamatey, Victor S., and Radomír Luža, eds. *A History of the Czechoslovak Republic, 1918–1948* (Princeton: Princeton University Press, 1973).

Mathernova, Katarina. "Czecho?Slovakia: Constitutional Disappointments," in A. E. Dick Howard, ed., *Constitution Making in Eastern Europe* (Baltimore: Woodrow Wilson Center Press, distributed by The Johns Hopkins University Press, 1993).

Remington, Robin, ed. *Winter in Prague: Documents on Czechoslovak Communism in Crisis* (Cambridge, Mass.: MIT Press, 1969).

Rice, Condoleeza. *The Soviet Union and the Czechoslovak Army, 1948–1983* (Princeton: Princeton University Press, 1984).

Skilling, H. Gordon. *Czechoslovakia's Interrupted Revolution* (Princeton: Princeton University Press, 1976).

Stone, Norman, and Eduard Strouhal, eds. *Czechoslovakia: Crossroads and Crises, 1918–1988* (New York: St. Martin's Press, 1989).

Wheaton, Bernard, and Zdeněk Kavan. *The Velvet Revolution: Czechoslovakia, 1988–1991* (Boulder: Westview Press, 1992).

Whipple, Tim D. *After the Velvet Revolution: Václav Havel and the New Leaders of Czechoslovakia Speak Out* (Lanham, Md.: Freedom House, 1991).

Wolchik, Sharon, *Czechoslovakia in Transition* (London: Pinter, 1991).

Students interested in current developments in the Czech and Slovak Republics as well as Eastern Europe generally can gain a great deal of valuable information on the World Wide Web, much of it in English. Each country has a home page that brings together various information from official and scholarly sources—everything from business and weather reports, tourist dictionaries, and country emblems to election results and news services. On a daily basis, several English-language bulletins summarize events of the day. For example, *OMRI Daily Digest* covers the whole postcommunist region. The Czech News Agency (ČTK) publishes daily English-language news summaries for both the Czech Republic and Slovakia as well as a press survey and background information published from the ČTK archives. The Slovak Home Page and the Slovak Document Store provide compilations of government reports and Slovak newspapers as well as general information for travelers and investors. The U.S. State Department makes available on-line its annual Human Rights Reports for all postcommunist countries. New resources and current news appear on the internet on a daily basis.

About the Book and Author

This clear, objective introduction to the politics of Czechoslovakia and the successor Czech and Slovak Republics provides a comprehensive analysis of Czechoslovakia in the postcommunist period. Carol Leff builds a framework for understanding the dynamics of the "triple transition": democratization, marketization, and a national transformation that has reconfigured the dynamic between state and nation. She shows how the interaction of these three transformational agendas has shaped Czechoslovakia's development, ultimately culminating in the paradoxical disintegration of a state that most of its citizens wished to preserve.

The book offers a valuable case study of a country coming back to Europe, but it also provides an opportunity for analyzing the influence of communism on what had been a significant interwar European state. The book's strong comparative element will make it invaluable as well for those seeking to understand contemporary Central and Eastern Europe.

Carol Skalnik Leff is assistant professor of political science at the University of Illinois at Urbana-Champaign.

Index